## Yuto Tsukuda

...ve the song "Red ...nbourine" by Blankey Jet ...y. The lyrics really resonate with me.

## Shun Saeki

I saw this bird at Tokyo Disneyland. I would be grateful if someone could tell me what kind of bird it is.

### About the authors

Yuto Tsukuda won the 34th Jump Juniketsu Newcomers' Manga Award for his one-shot story *Kiba ni Naru*. He made his *Weekly Shonen Jump* debut in 2010 with the series *Shonen Shikku*. His follow-up series, *Food Wars!: Shokugeki no Soma*, is his first English-language release.

Shun Saeki made his *Jump NEXT!* debut in 2011 with the one-shot story *Kimi to Watashi no Renai Soudan*. *Food Wars!: Shokugeki no Soma* is his first *Shonen Jump* series.

# Food Wars!
## SHOKUGEKI NO SOMA

Volume 7
Shonen Jump Manga Edition
Story by Yuto Tsukuda, Art by Shun Saeki
Contributor Yuki Morisaki

Translation: Adrienne Beck
Touch-Up Art & Lettering: NRP Studios
Design: Izumi Evers
Editor: Jennifer LeBlanc



Printed in the U.S.A.

Published by VIZ Media, LLC
P.O. Box 77010
San Francisco, CA 94107

10 9 8 7 6 5 4 3 2 1
First printing, August 2015

www.viz.com

THE WORLD'S MOST CUTTING-EDGE MANGA
SHONEN JUMP ADVANCED
www.shonenjump.com

RATED T+ FOR OLDER TEEN

**PARENTAL ADVISORY**
FOOD WARS! is rated T+ for Older Teen and is recommended for ages 16 and up. This volume contains sexual situations/humor.

ratings.viz.com

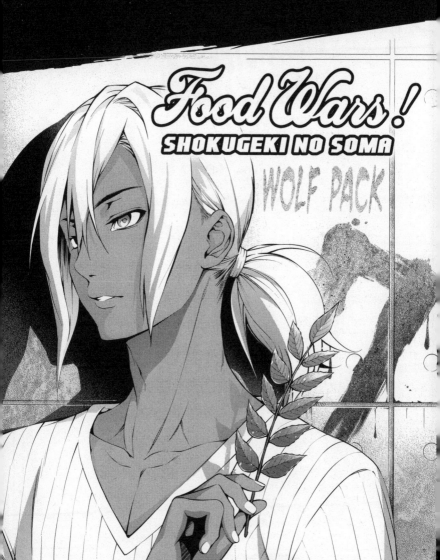

# Food Wars!
## SHOKUGEKI NO SOMA

WOLF PACK

| ORIGINAL CREATOR: | ARTIST: | CONTRIBUTOR: |
|---|---|---|
| YUTO TSUKUDA | SHUN SAEKI | YUKI MORISAKI |

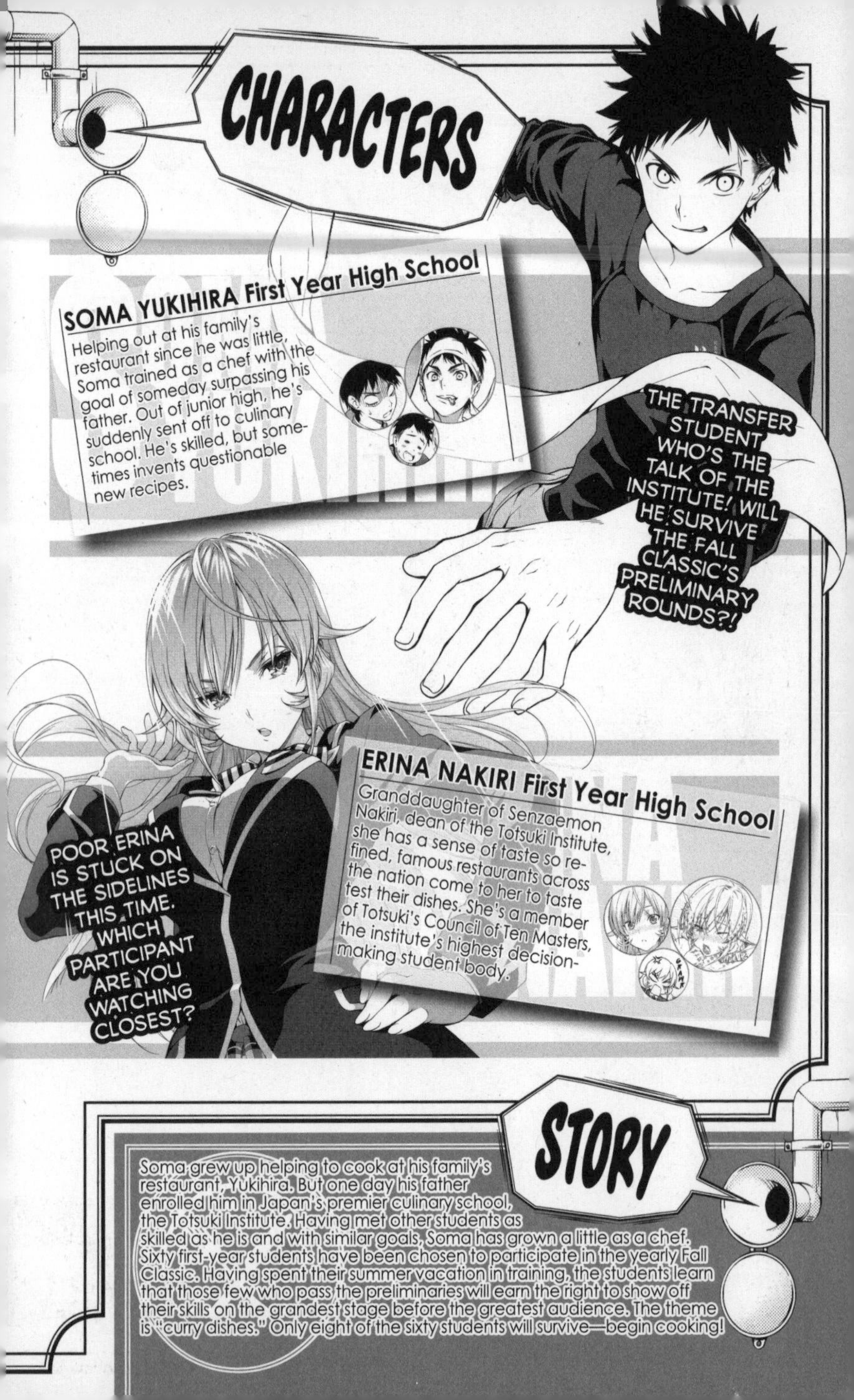
CHARACTERS
SOMA YUKIHIRA First Year High School
Helping out at his family's restaurant since he was little, Soma trained as a chef with the goal of someday surpassing his father. Out of junior high, he's suddenly sent off to culinary school. He's skilled, but sometimes invents questionable new recipes.
THE TRANSFER STUDENT WHO'S THE TALK OF THE INSTITUTE! WILL HE SURVIVE THE FALL CLASSIC'S PRELIMINARY ROUNDS?!
ERINA NAKIRI First Year High School
Granddaughter of Senzaemon Nakiri, dean of the Totsuki Institute, she has a sense of taste so refined, famous restaurants across the nation come to her to taste test their dishes. She's a member of Totsuki's Council of Ten Masters, the institute's highest decision-making student body.
POOR ERINA IS STUCK ON THE SIDELINES THIS TIME. WHICH PARTICIPANT ARE YOU WATCHING CLOSEST?

## STORY

Soma grew up helping to cook at his family's restaurant, Yukihira. But one day his father enrolled him in Japan's premier culinary school, the Totsuki Institute. Having met other students as skilled as he is and with similar goals, Soma has grown a little as a chef. Sixty first-year students have been chosen to participate in the yearly Fall Classic. Having spent their summer vacation in training, the students learn that those few who pass the preliminaries will earn the right to show off their skills on the grandest stage before the greatest audience. The theme is "curry dishes." Only eight of the sixty students will survive—begin cooking!

**A** In Preliminary Block A
**B** In Preliminary Block B

*Shokugeki no SOMA*

### SHUN IBUSAKI
The strong scent of his smoked cooking grabs the judges' attention!
**A**

### RYOKO SAKAKI

Can she successfully meld the strong flavors of her koji with the equally strong flavors of curry?
**A**

### ZENJI MARUI

A strong will hides behind those glasses. How good is he really?
**A**

### AKIRA HAYAMA

A master of spices and the current favorite to win the preliminaries!
**A**

### IKUMI MITO

What can beat the smell of sizzling meat? Will the biggest dark horse be from the Bowl Club?!
**A**

### ALICE'S AIDE

He acts quiet, but how great is his skill, which even Alice herself values?
**A**

### MEGUMI TADOKORO

Once last in the class, does she have a miracle in her to make the finals?
**B**

### YUKI YOSHINO
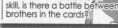
Game (animal) girl power to the max!
**B**

### TAKUMI ALDINI
The prince of Italian cooking, will he get his wish to face off against Soma?
**B**

### ISAMI ALDINI
A match for his brother in skill, is there a battle between brothers in the cards?!
**B**

### ALICE NAKIRI

A master of food science and a pioneer of new cooking!
**B**

### MIYOKO HOJO
What delicacies can this strong-armed master of the iron wok create?
**B**

### ERINA'S AIDE

Will we finally get to see her skills—and maybe even learn her name?!
**B**

HERE ARE SOME OF THE FALL CLASSIC PARTICIPANTS!♪

### NAO SADATSUKA
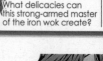
Is that creepy gaze fixed on the finals? Or on one of its participants?
**B**

# Food Wars! Shokugeki no Soma 7

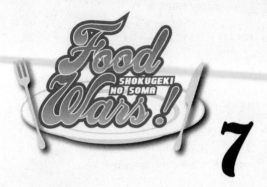

# Table of Contents

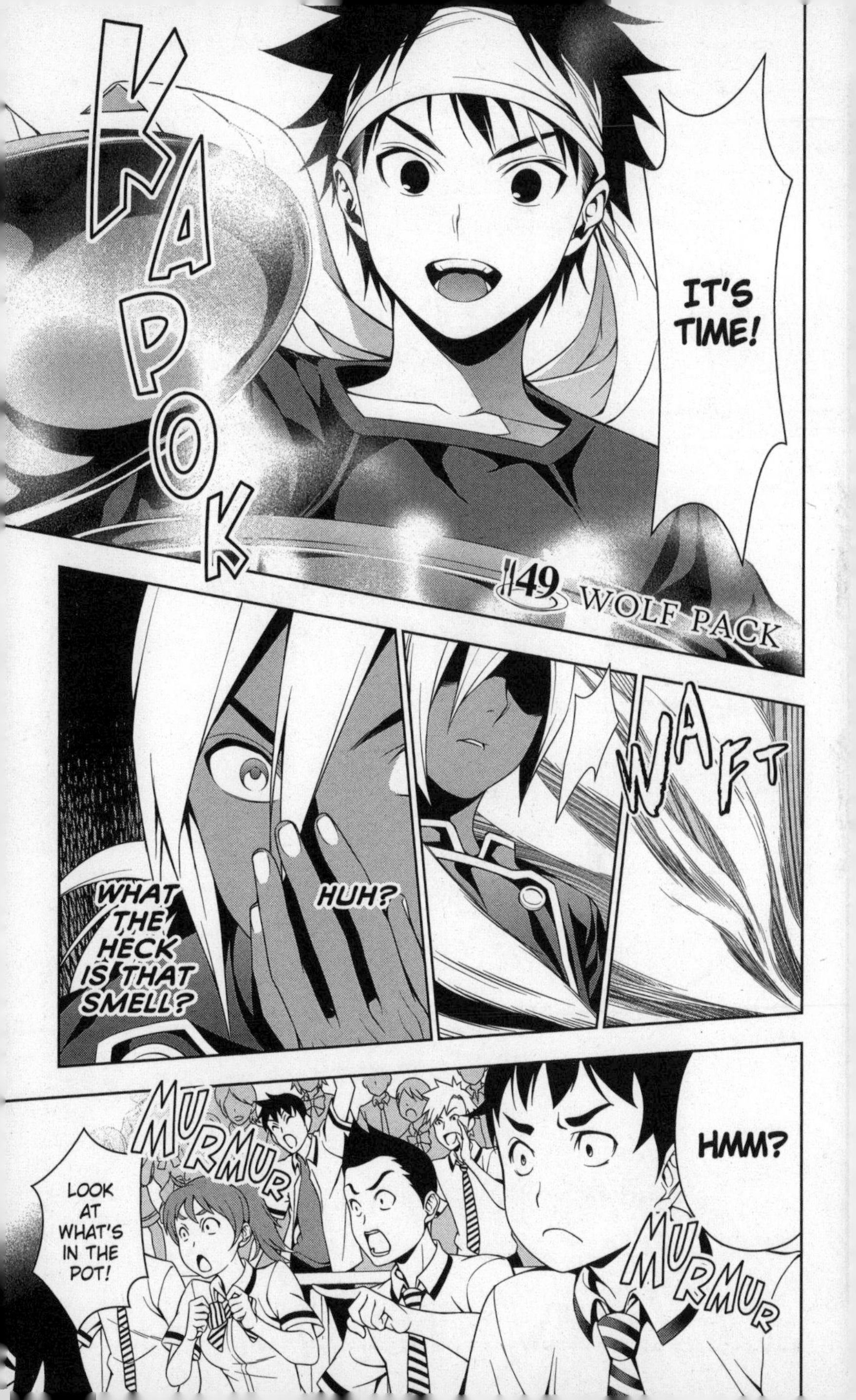
IT'S TIME!
KAPOK
49 WOLF PACK
WAFT
HUH?
WHAT THE HECK IS THAT SMELL?
HMM?
MURMUR
MURMUR
LOOK AT WHAT'S IN THE POT!

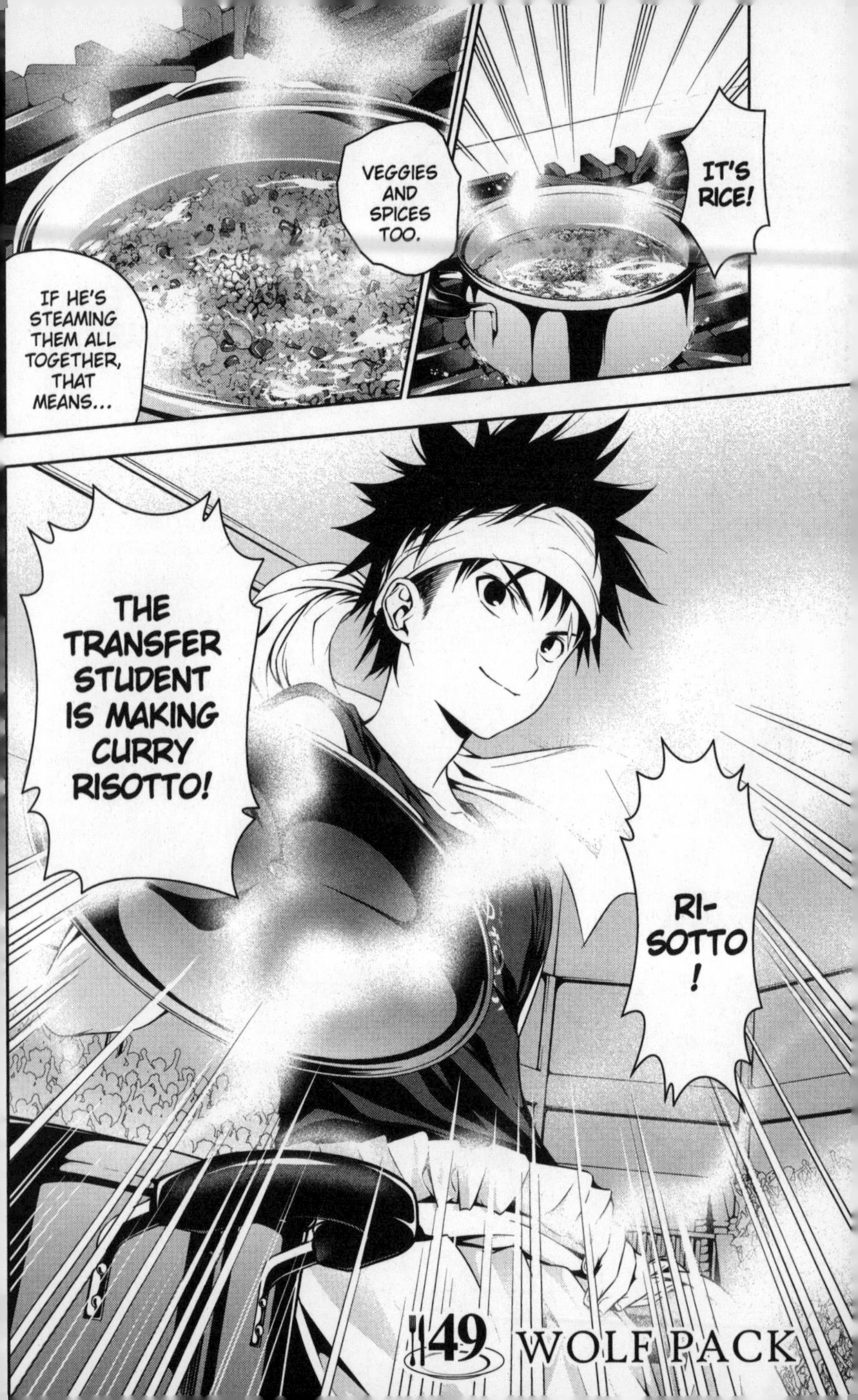
IT'S RICE!
VEGGIES AND SPICES TOO.
IF HE'S STEAMING THEM ALL TOGETHER, THAT MEANS...
THE TRANSFER STUDENT IS MAKING CURRY RISOTTO!
RI-SOTTO!
49 WOLF PACK

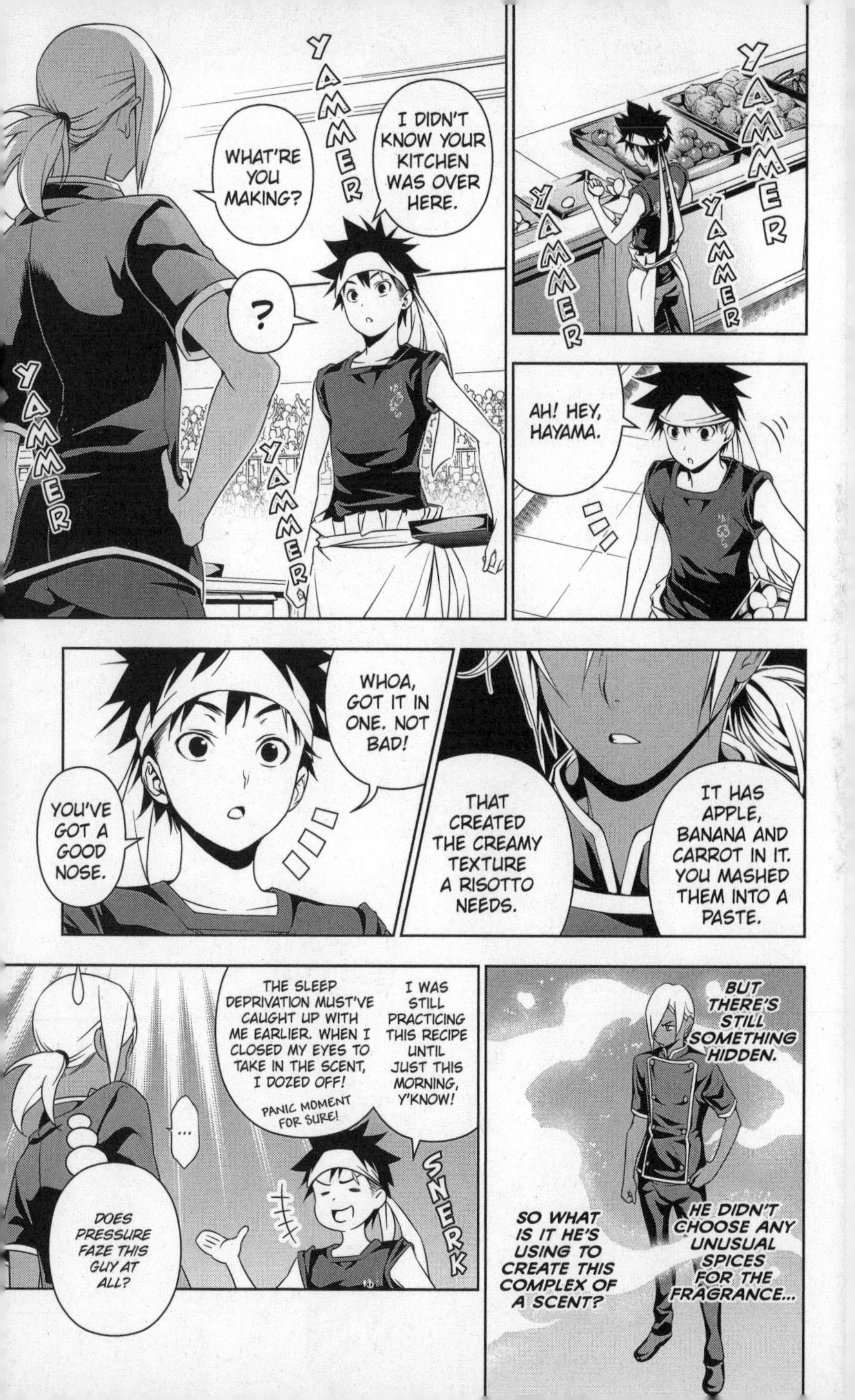
YAMMER
YAMMER
YAMMER
AH! HEY, HAYAMA.
...
YAMMER
I DIDN'T KNOW YOUR KITCHEN WAS OVER HERE.
WHAT'RE YOU MAKING?
?
YAMMER
YAMMER
IT HAS APPLE, BANANA AND CARROT IN IT. YOU MASHED THEM INTO A PASTE.
THAT CREATED THE CREAMY TEXTURE A RISOTTO NEEDS.
WHOA, GOT IT IN ONE. NOT BAD!
...
YOU'VE GOT A GOOD NOSE.
BUT THERE'S STILL SOMETHING HIDDEN.
HE DIDN'T CHOOSE ANY UNUSUAL SPICES FOR THE FRAGRANCE...
SO WHAT IS IT HE'S USING TO CREATE THIS COMPLEX OF A SCENT?
I WAS STILL PRACTICING THIS RECIPE UNTIL JUST THIS MORNING, Y'KNOW!
THE SLEEP DEPRIVATION MUST'VE CAUGHT UP WITH ME EARLIER. WHEN I CLOSED MY EYES TO TAKE IN THE SCENT, I DOZED OFF!
PANIC MOMENT FOR SURE!
SNERK
...
DOES PRESSURE FAZE THIS GUY AT ALL?

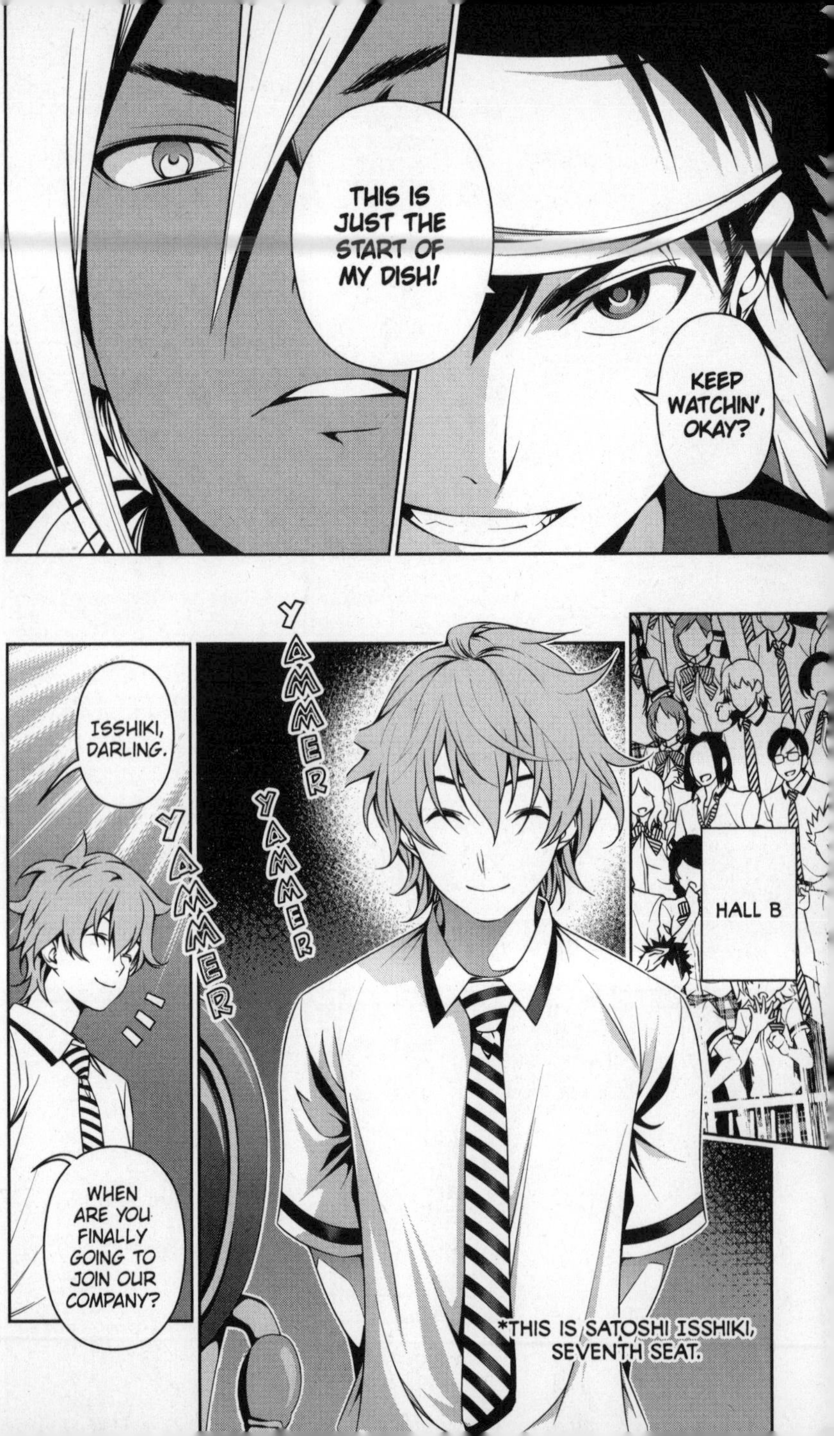
THIS IS JUST THE START OF MY DISH!
KEEP WATCHIN', OKAY?
HALL B
YAMMER
YAMMER
YAMMER
*THIS IS SATOSHI ISSHIKI, SEVENTH SEAT.
ISSHIKI, DARLING.
...
WHEN ARE YOU FINALLY GOING TO JOIN OUR COMPANY?

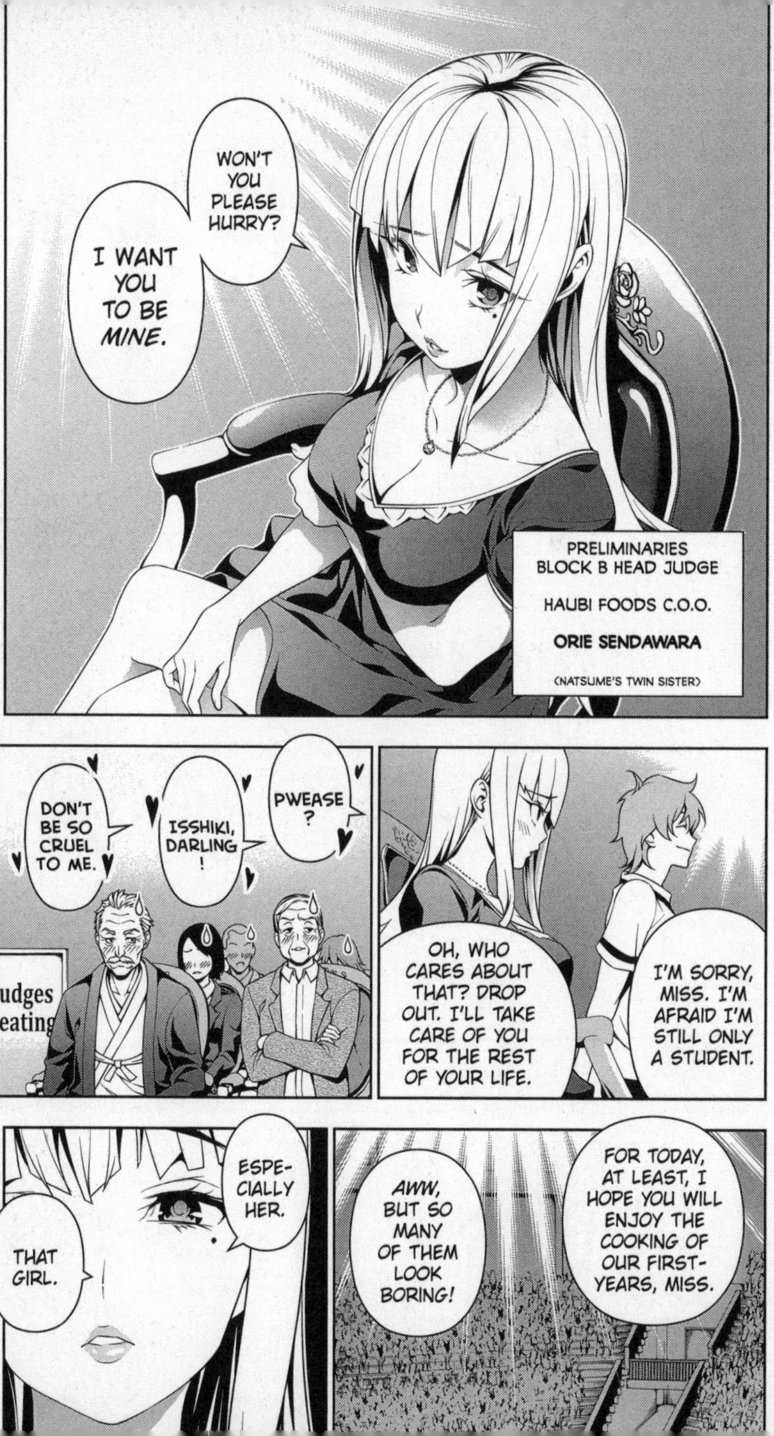
WON'T YOU PLEASE HURRY?
I WANT YOU TO BE *MINE.*
PRELIMINARIES BLOCK B HEAD JUDGE
HAUBI FOODS C.O.O.
**ORIE SENDAWARA**
(NATSUME'S TWIN SISTER)
I'M SORRY, MISS. I'M AFRAID I'M STILL ONLY A STUDENT.
OH, WHO CARES ABOUT THAT? DROP OUT. I'LL TAKE CARE OF YOU FOR THE REST OF YOUR LIFE.
PWEASE?
ISSHIKI, DARLING!
DON'T BE SO CRUEL TO ME.
Judges Seating
FOR TODAY, AT LEAST, I HOPE YOU WILL ENJOY THE COOKING OF OUR FIRST-YEARS, MISS.
*AWW,* BUT SO MANY OF THEM LOOK BORING!
ESPE-CIALLY HER.
THAT GIRL.

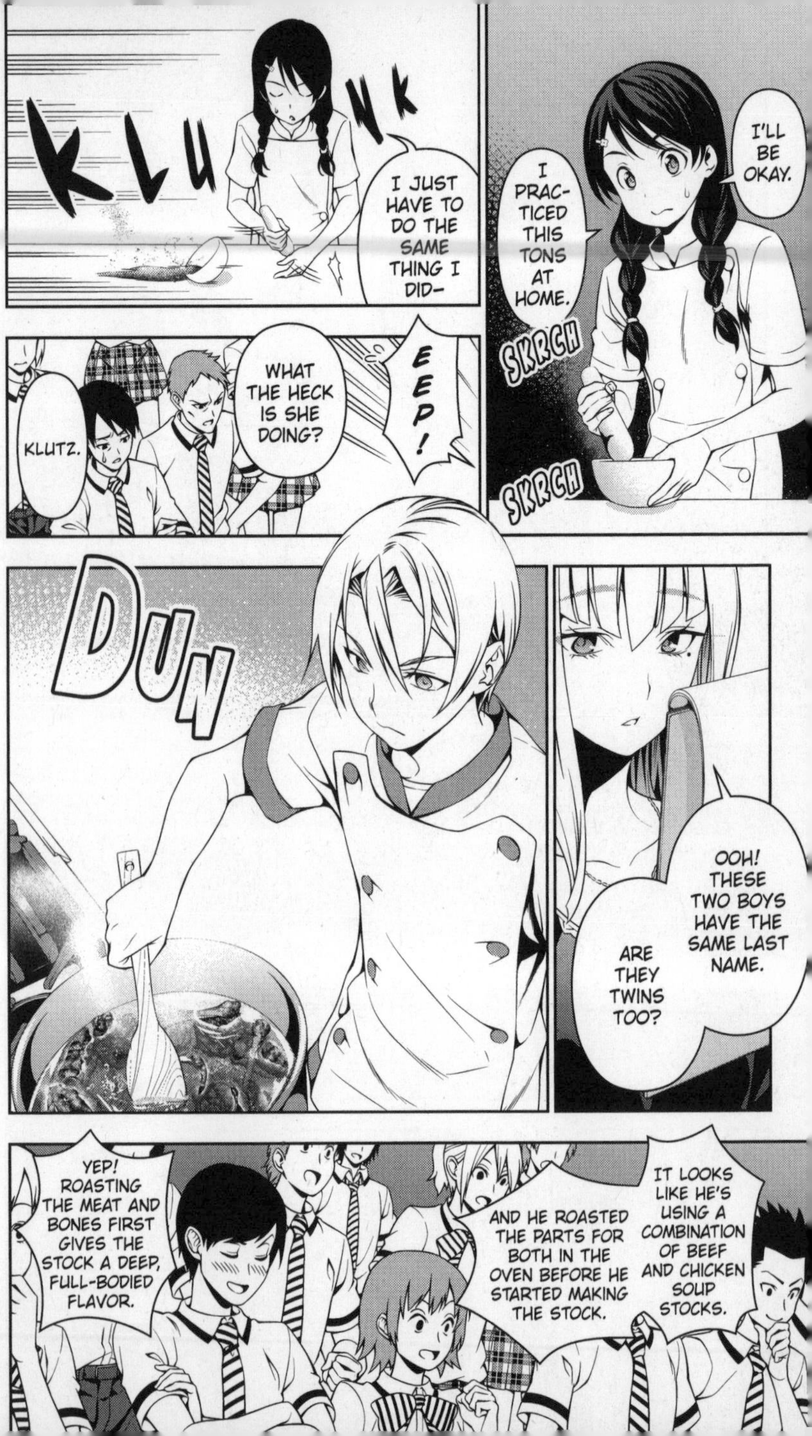
I'LL BE OKAY.
I PRACTICED THIS TONS AT HOME.
SKRCH
SKRCH
KLUNK
I JUST HAVE TO DO THE SAME THING I DID—
EEP!
WHAT THE HECK IS SHE DOING?
KLUTZ.
OOH! THESE TWO BOYS HAVE THE SAME LAST NAME.
ARE THEY TWINS TOO?
DUN
IT LOOKS LIKE HE'S USING A COMBINATION OF BEEF AND CHICKEN SOUP STOCKS.
AND HE ROASTED THE PARTS FOR BOTH IN THE OVEN BEFORE HE STARTED MAKING THE STOCK.
YEP! ROASTING THE MEAT AND BONES FIRST GIVES THE STOCK A DEEP, FULL-BODIED FLAVOR.

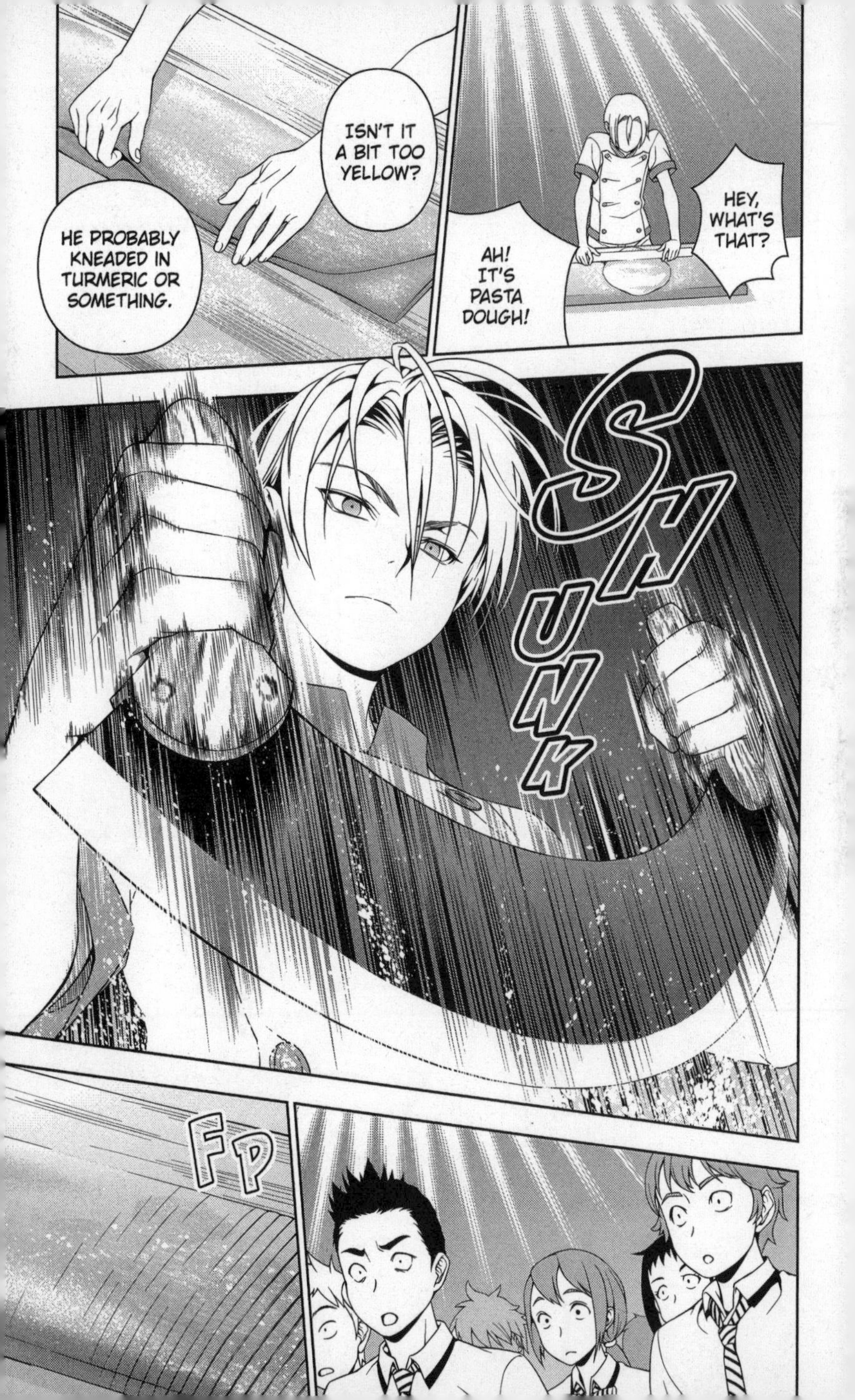
HEY, WHAT'S THAT?
AH! IT'S PASTA DOUGH!
ISN'T IT A BIT TOO YELLOW?
HE PROBABLY KNEADED IN TURMERIC OR SOMETHING.
SHUNK
FP

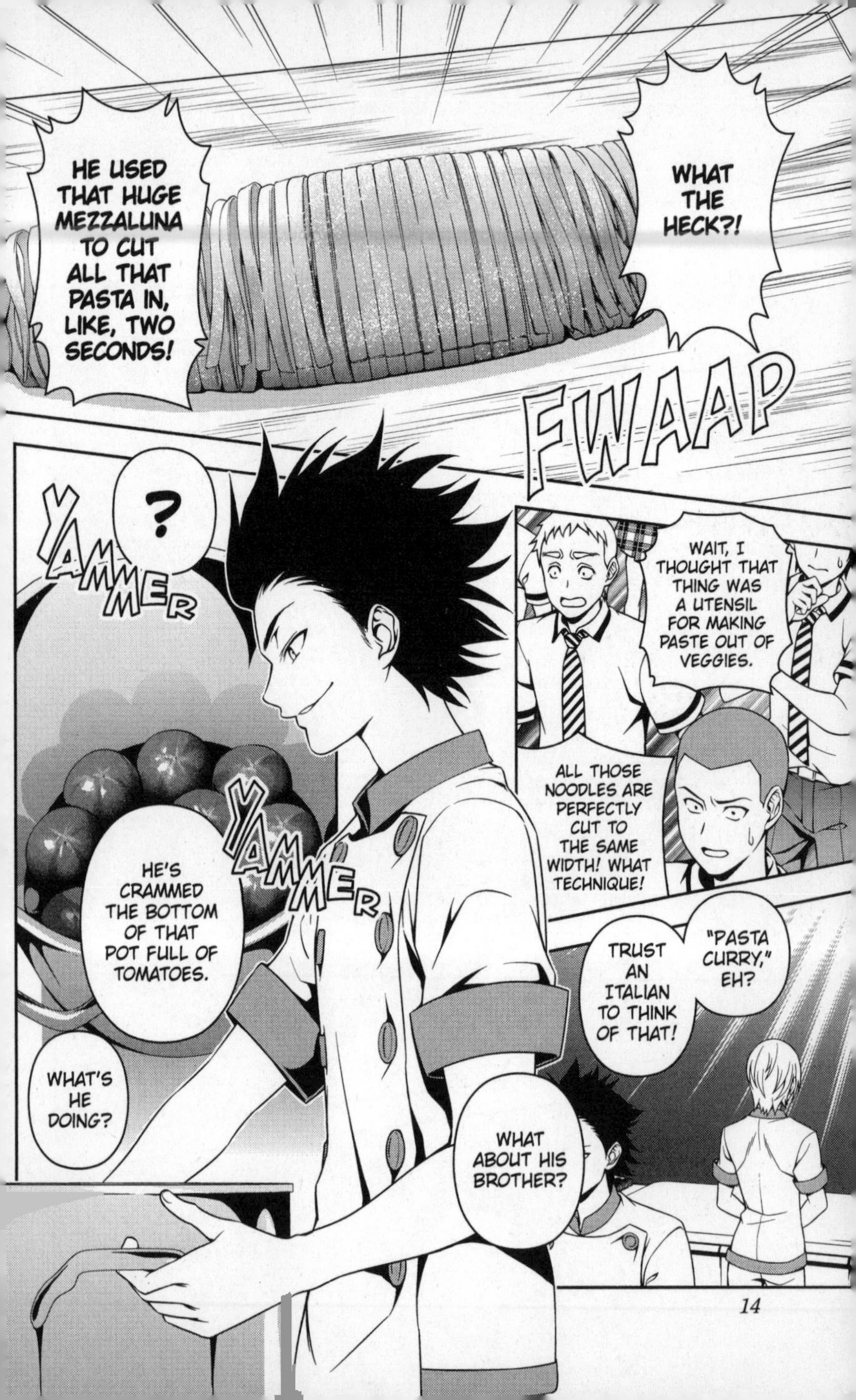
WHAT THE HECK?!
HE USED THAT HUGE MEZZALUNA TO CUT ALL THAT PASTA IN, LIKE, TWO SECONDS!
FWAAP
WAIT, I THOUGHT THAT THING WAS A UTENSIL FOR MAKING PASTE OUT OF VEGGIES.
ALL THOSE NOODLES ARE PERFECTLY CUT TO THE SAME WIDTH! WHAT TECHNIQUE!
"PASTA CURRY," EH?
TRUST AN ITALIAN TO THINK OF THAT!
WHAT ABOUT HIS BROTHER?
?
YAMMER
YAMMER
HE'S CRAMMED THE BOTTOM OF THAT POT FULL OF TOMATOES.
WHAT'S HE DOING?

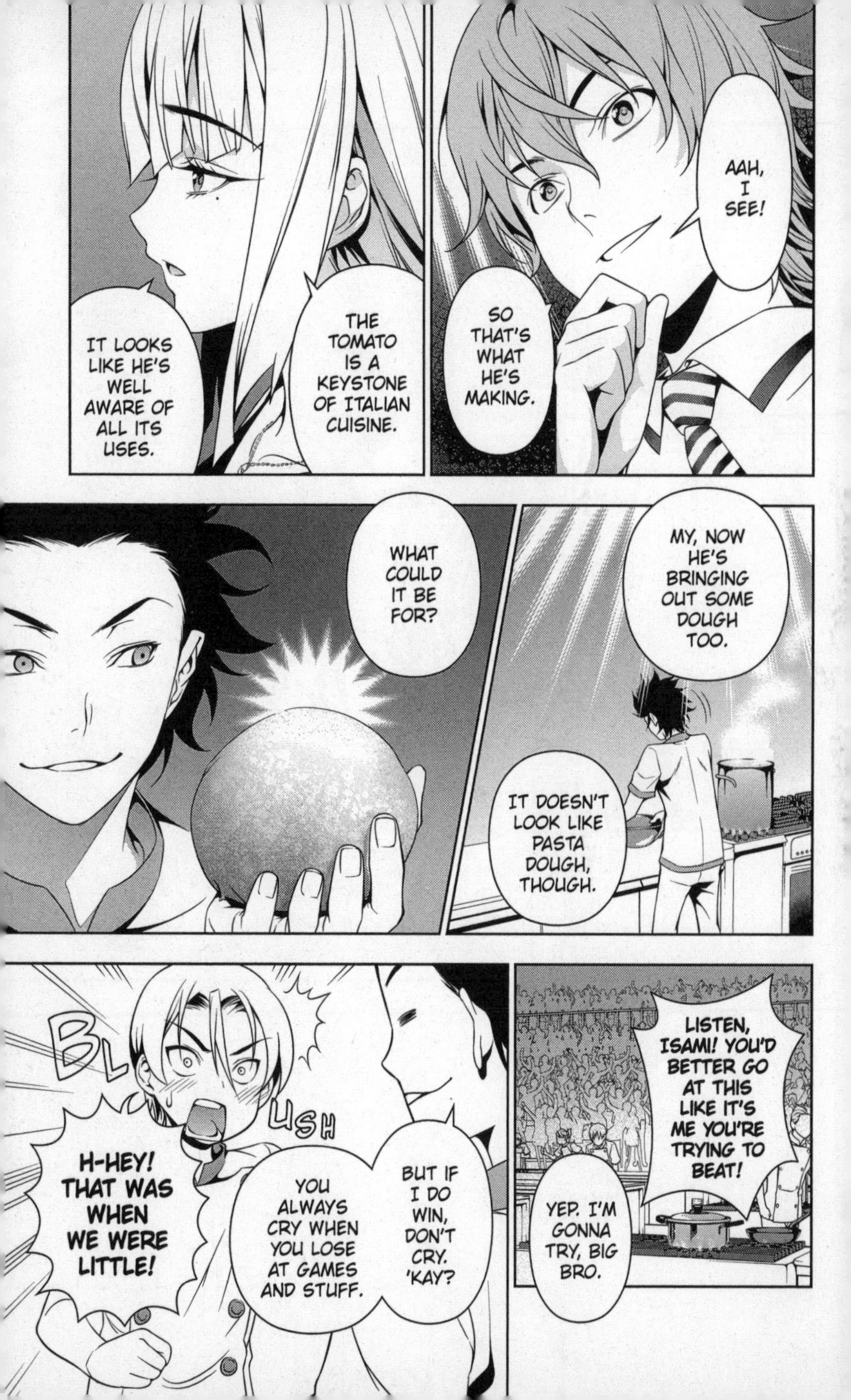
AAH, I SEE!
SO THAT'S WHAT HE'S MAKING.
THE TOMATO IS A KEYSTONE OF ITALIAN CUISINE.
IT LOOKS LIKE HE'S WELL AWARE OF ALL ITS USES.
MY, NOW HE'S BRINGING OUT SOME DOUGH TOO.
IT DOESN'T LOOK LIKE PASTA DOUGH, THOUGH.
WHAT COULD IT BE FOR?
LISTEN, ISAMI! YOU'D BETTER GO AT THIS LIKE IT'S ME YOU'RE TRYING TO BEAT!
YEP. I'M GONNA TRY, BIG BRO.
BUT IF I DO WIN, DON'T CRY. 'KAY?
YOU ALWAYS CRY WHEN YOU LOSE AT GAMES AND STUFF.
BLUSH
H-HEY! THAT WAS WHEN WE WERE LITTLE!

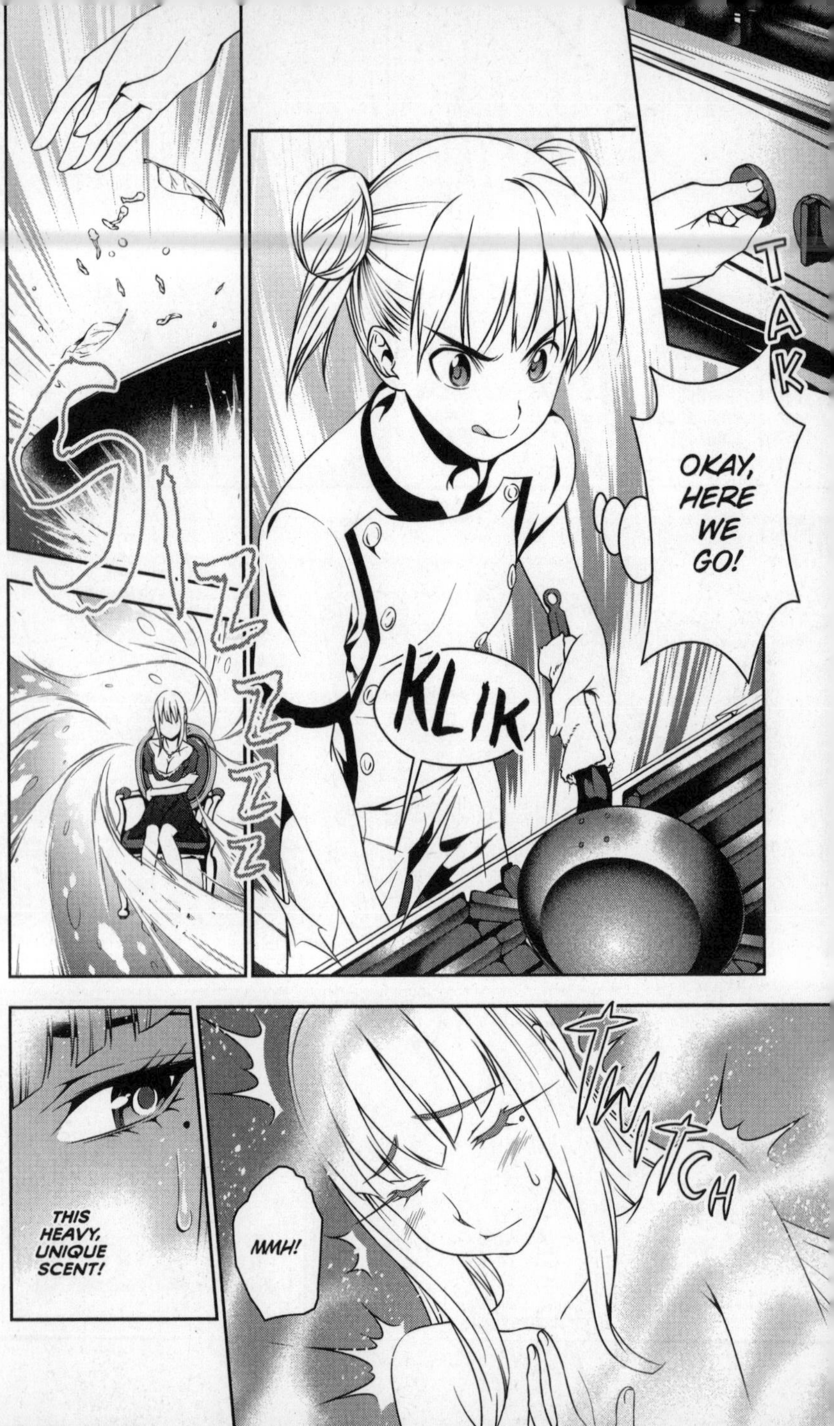
TAK
OKAY, HERE WE GO!
KLIK
SIZZZZZ
TWITCH
MMH!
THIS HEAVY, UNIQUE SCENT!

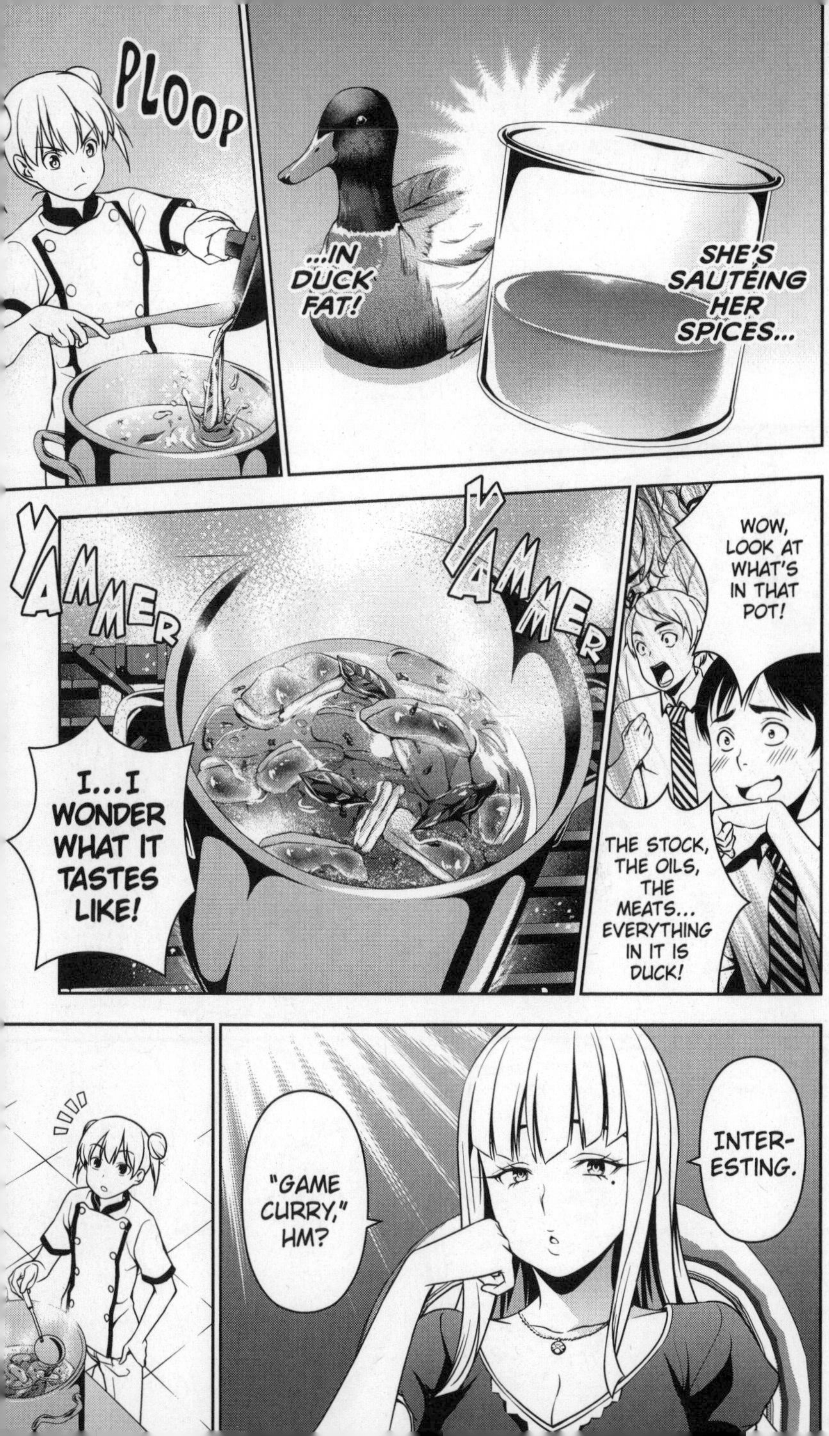
SHE'S SAUTÉING HER SPICES...
...IN DUCK FAT!
PLOOP
WOW, LOOK AT WHAT'S IN THAT POT!
THE STOCK, THE OILS, THE MEATS... EVERYTHING IN IT IS DUCK!
YAMMER
YAMMER
I...I WONDER WHAT IT TASTES LIKE!
INTER-ESTING.
"GAME CURRY," HM?

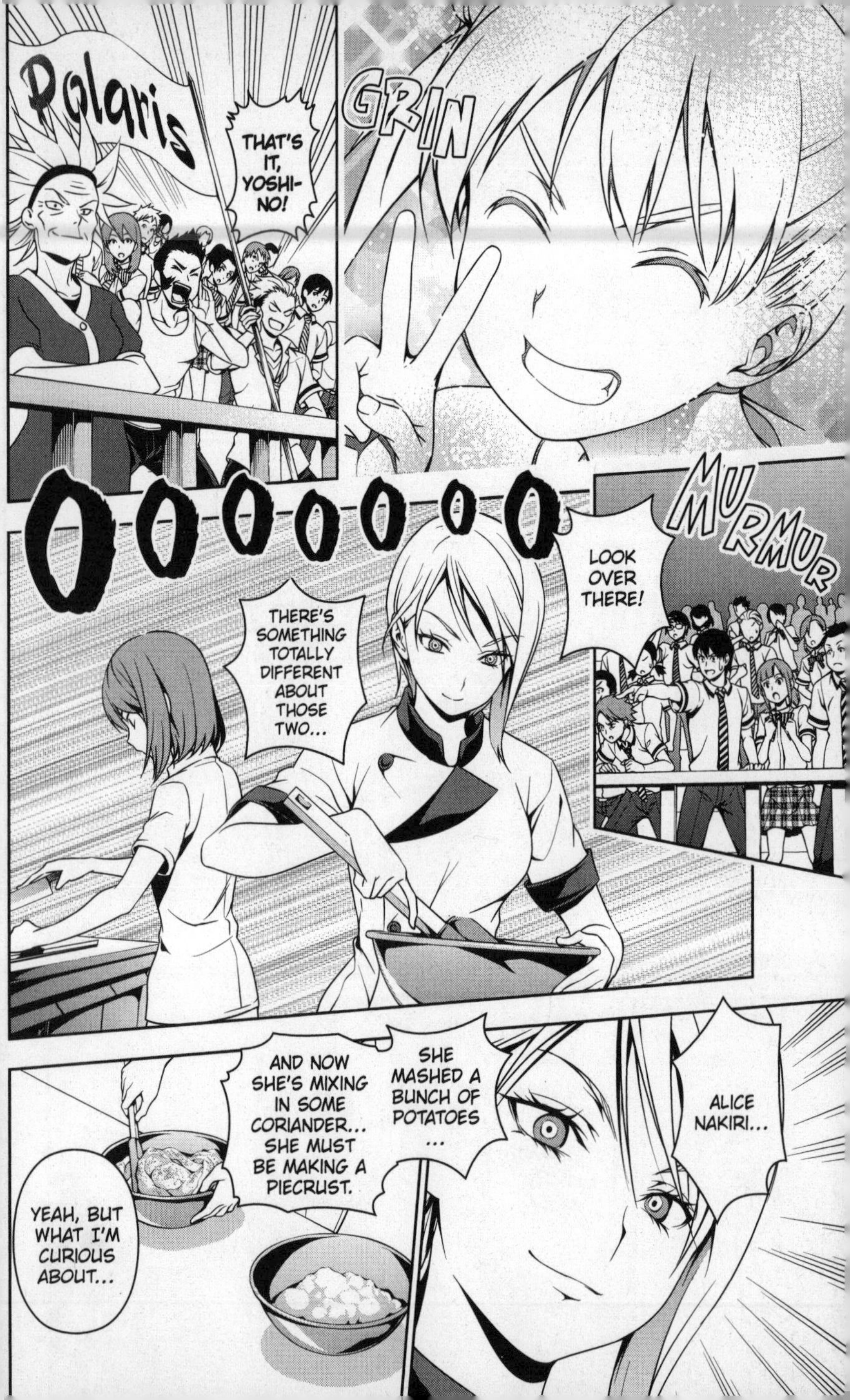
GRIN
Polaris
THAT'S IT, YOSHINO!
MURMUR
OOOOOOO
LOOK OVER THERE!
THERE'S SOMETHING TOTALLY DIFFERENT ABOUT THOSE TWO...
ALICE NAKIRI...
SHE MASHED A BUNCH OF POTATOES...
AND NOW SHE'S MIXING IN SOME CORIANDER... SHE MUST BE MAKING A PIECRUST.
YEAH, BUT WHAT I'M CURIOUS ABOUT...

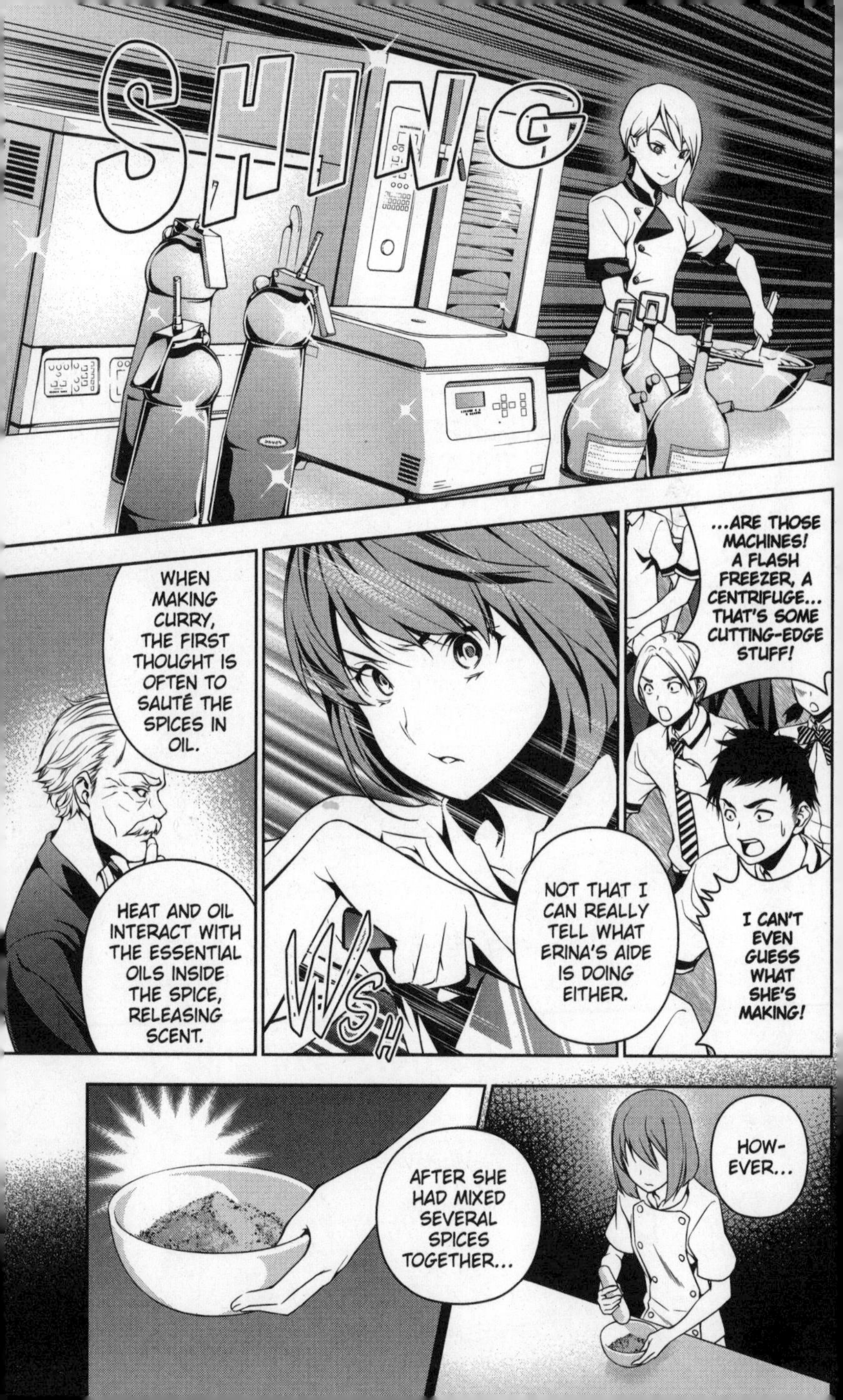
SHING
...ARE THOSE MACHINES! A FLASH FREEZER, A CENTRIFUGE... THAT'S SOME CUTTING-EDGE STUFF!
I CAN'T EVEN GUESS WHAT SHE'S MAKING!
NOT THAT I CAN REALLY TELL WHAT ERINA'S AIDE IS DOING EITHER.
WSH
WHEN MAKING CURRY, THE FIRST THOUGHT IS OFTEN TO SAUTÉ THE SPICES IN OIL.
HEAT AND OIL INTERACT WITH THE ESSENTIAL OILS INSIDE THE SPICE, RELEASING SCENT.
HOW-EVER...
AFTER SHE HAD MIXED SEVERAL SPICES TOGETHER...

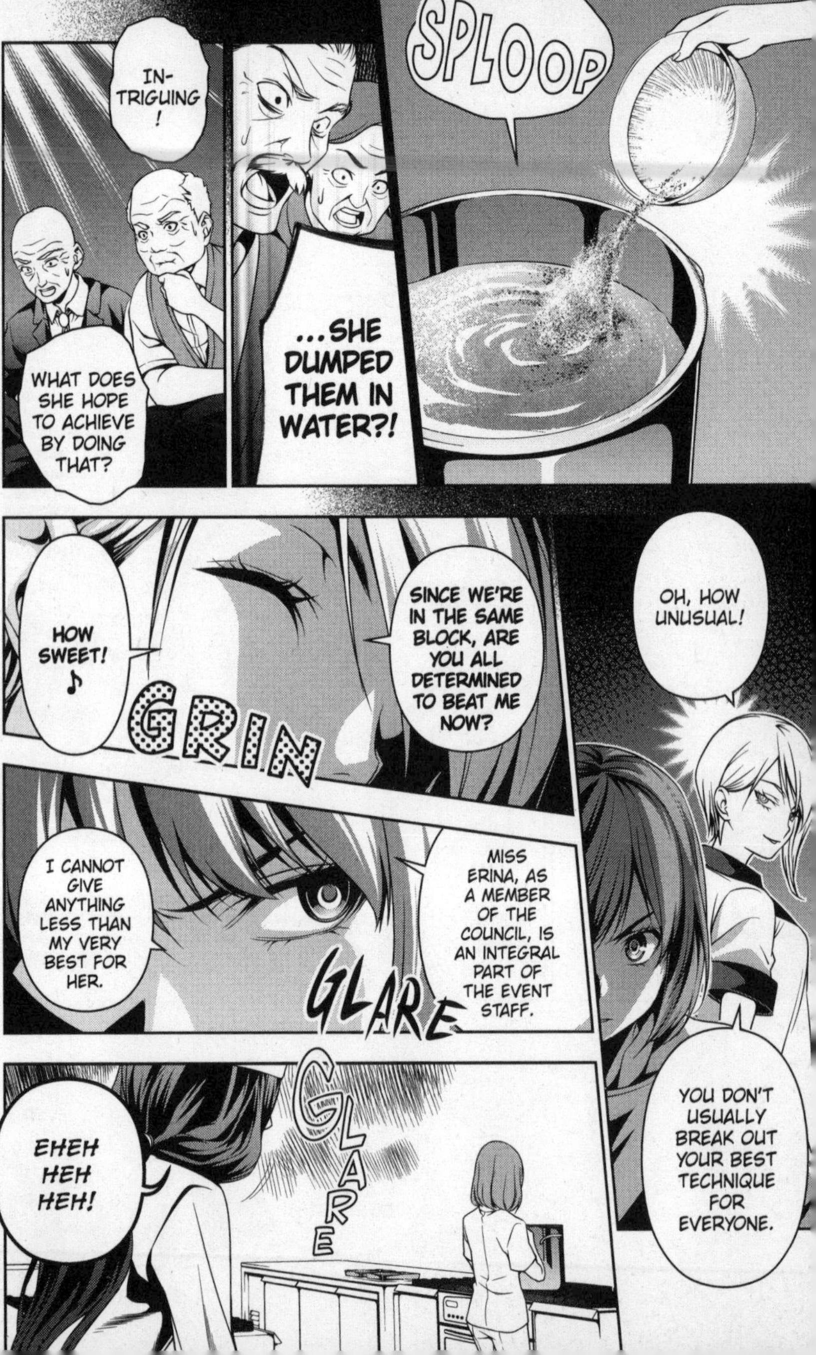
SPLOOP
...SHE DUMPED THEM IN WATER?!
IN-TRIGUING!
WHAT DOES SHE HOPE TO ACHIEVE BY DOING THAT?
OH, HOW UNUSUAL!
YOU DON'T USUALLY BREAK OUT YOUR BEST TECHNIQUE FOR EVERYONE.
SINCE WE'RE IN THE SAME BLOCK, ARE YOU ALL DETERMINED TO BEAT ME NOW?
HOW SWEET! ♪
GRIN
MISS ERINA, AS A MEMBER OF THE COUNCIL, IS AN INTEGRAL PART OF THE EVENT STAFF.
I CANNOT GIVE ANYTHING LESS THAN MY VERY BEST FOR HER.
GLARE
GLARE
EHEH HEH HEH!

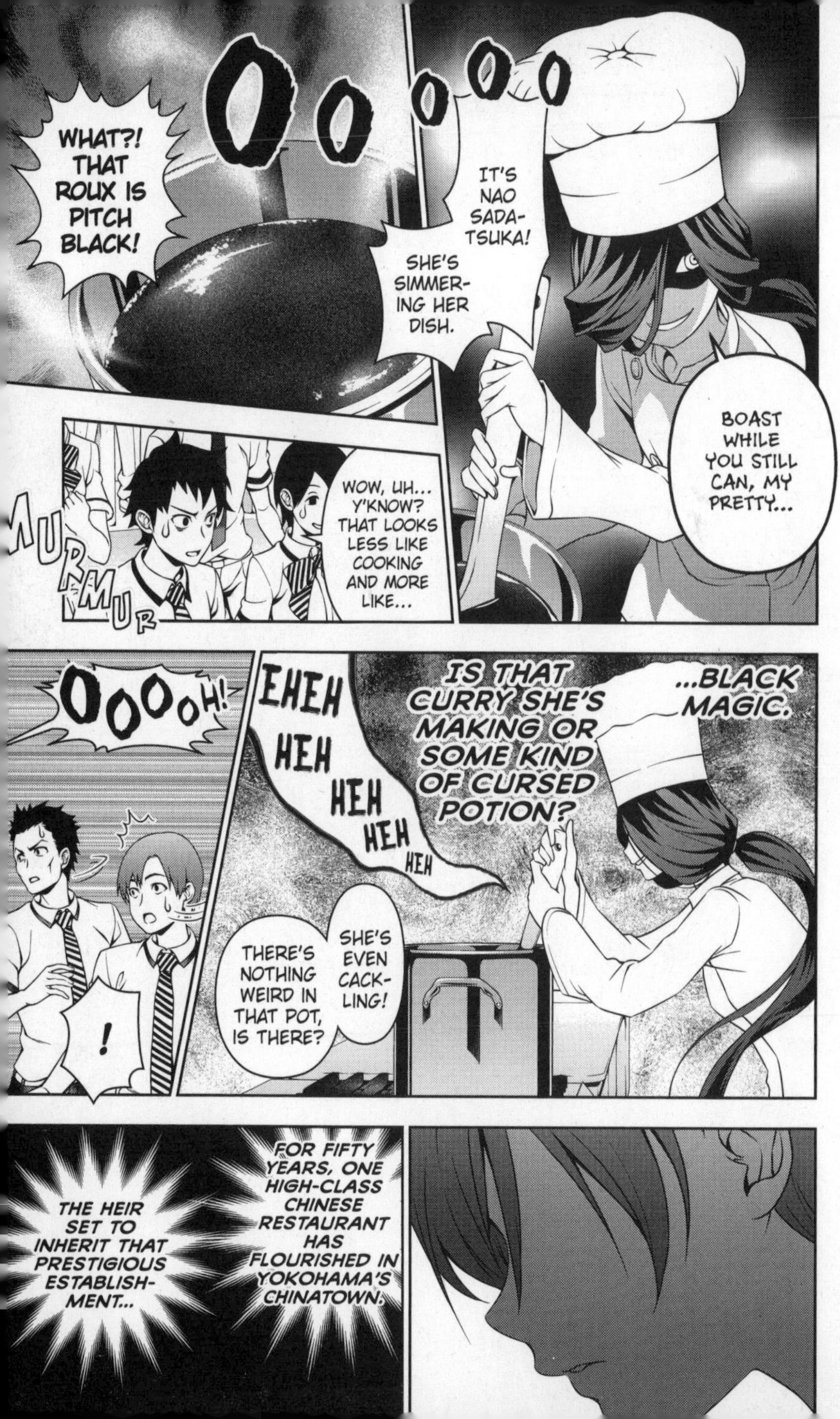
OOOOO
IT'S NAO SADA-TSUKA!
SHE'S SIMMER-ING HER DISH.
BOAST WHILE YOU STILL CAN, MY PRETTY...
WHAT?! THAT ROUX IS PITCH BLACK!
WOW, UH... Y'KNOW? THAT LOOKS LESS LIKE COOKING AND MORE LIKE...
MURMUR MURMUR
...BLACK MAGIC.
IS THAT CURRY SHE'S MAKING OR SOME KIND OF CURSED POTION?
EHEH HEH HEH HEH HEH
SHE'S EVEN CACK-LING!
THERE'S NOTHING WEIRD IN THAT POT, IS THERE?
OOOOH!
!
FOR FIFTY YEARS, ONE HIGH-CLASS CHINESE RESTAURANT HAS FLOURISHED IN YOKOHAMA'S CHINATOWN.
THE HEIR SET TO INHERIT THAT PRESTIGIOUS ESTABLISH-MENT...

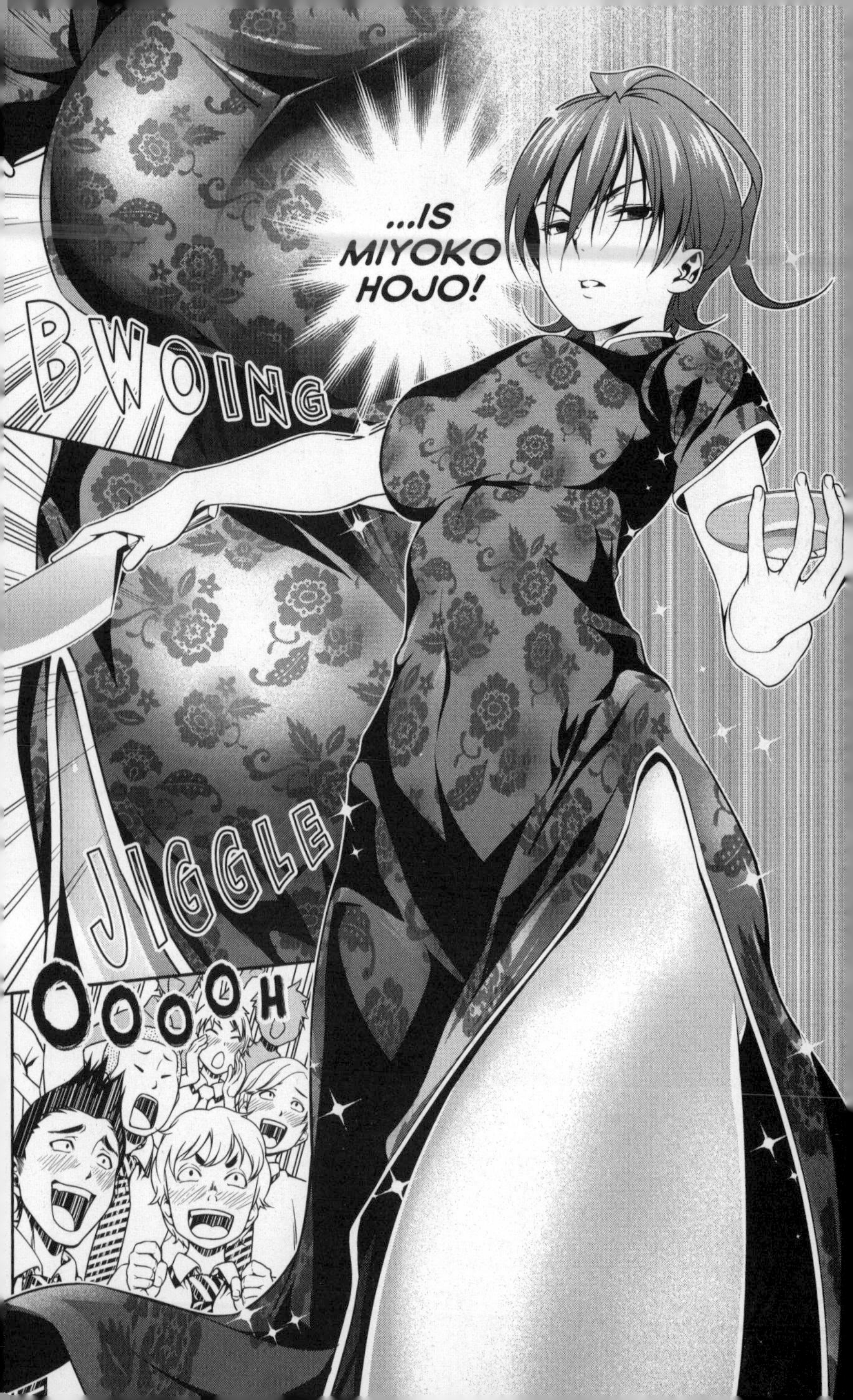
...IS MIYOKO HOJO!
BWOING
JIGGLE
OOOOH

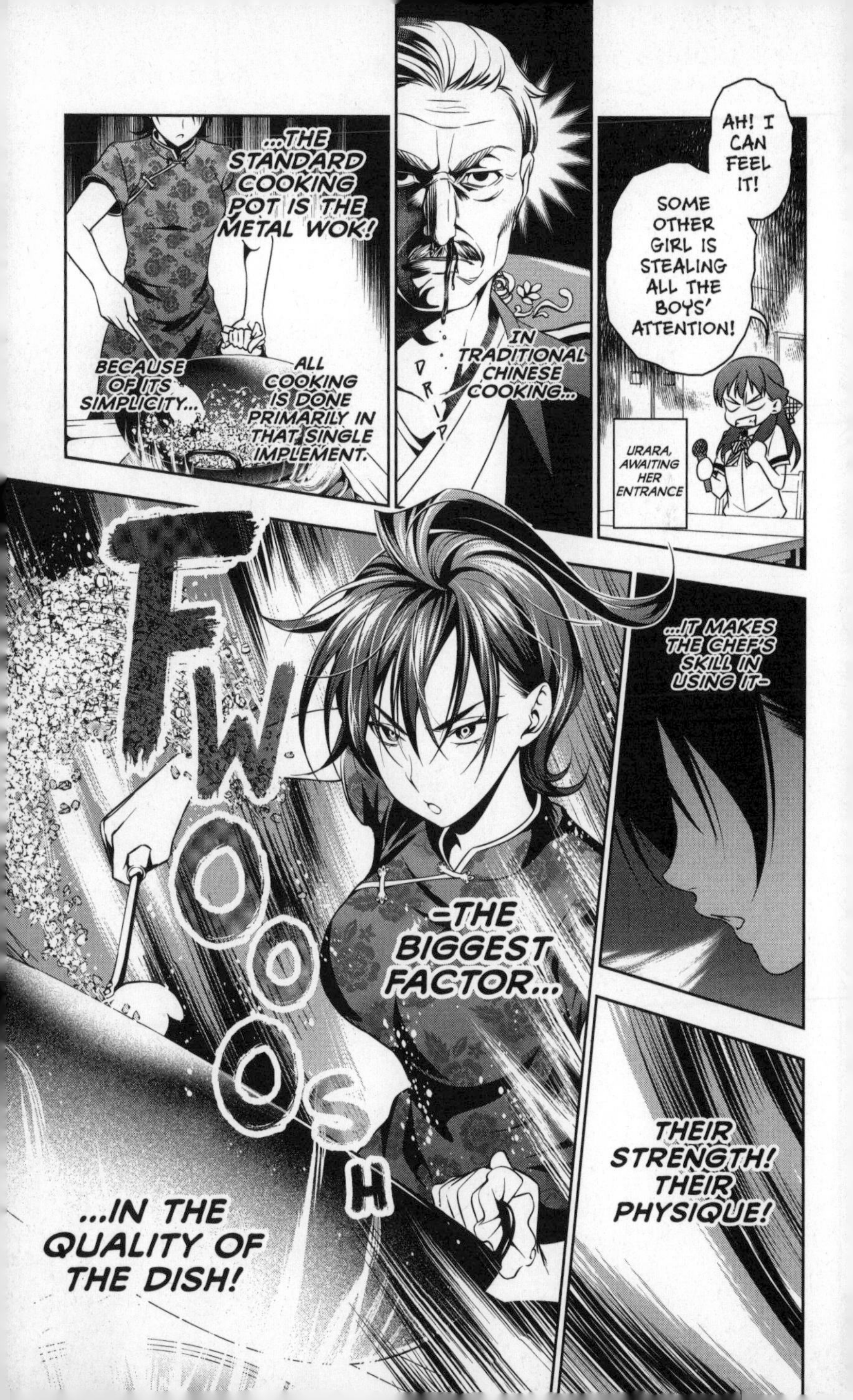
AH! I CAN FEEL IT!
SOME OTHER GIRL IS STEALING ALL THE BOYS' ATTENTION!
URARA, AWAITING HER ENTRANCE
IN TRADITIONAL CHINESE COOKING...
DRIP
...THE STANDARD COOKING POT IS THE METAL WOK!
BECAUSE OF ITS SIMPLICITY...
ALL COOKING IS DONE PRIMARILY IN THAT SINGLE IMPLEMENT.
...IT MAKES THE CHEF'S SKILL IN USING IT-
THEIR STRENGTH! THEIR PHYSIQUE!
-THE BIGGEST FACTOR...
FWOOOOSH
...IN THE QUALITY OF THE DISH!

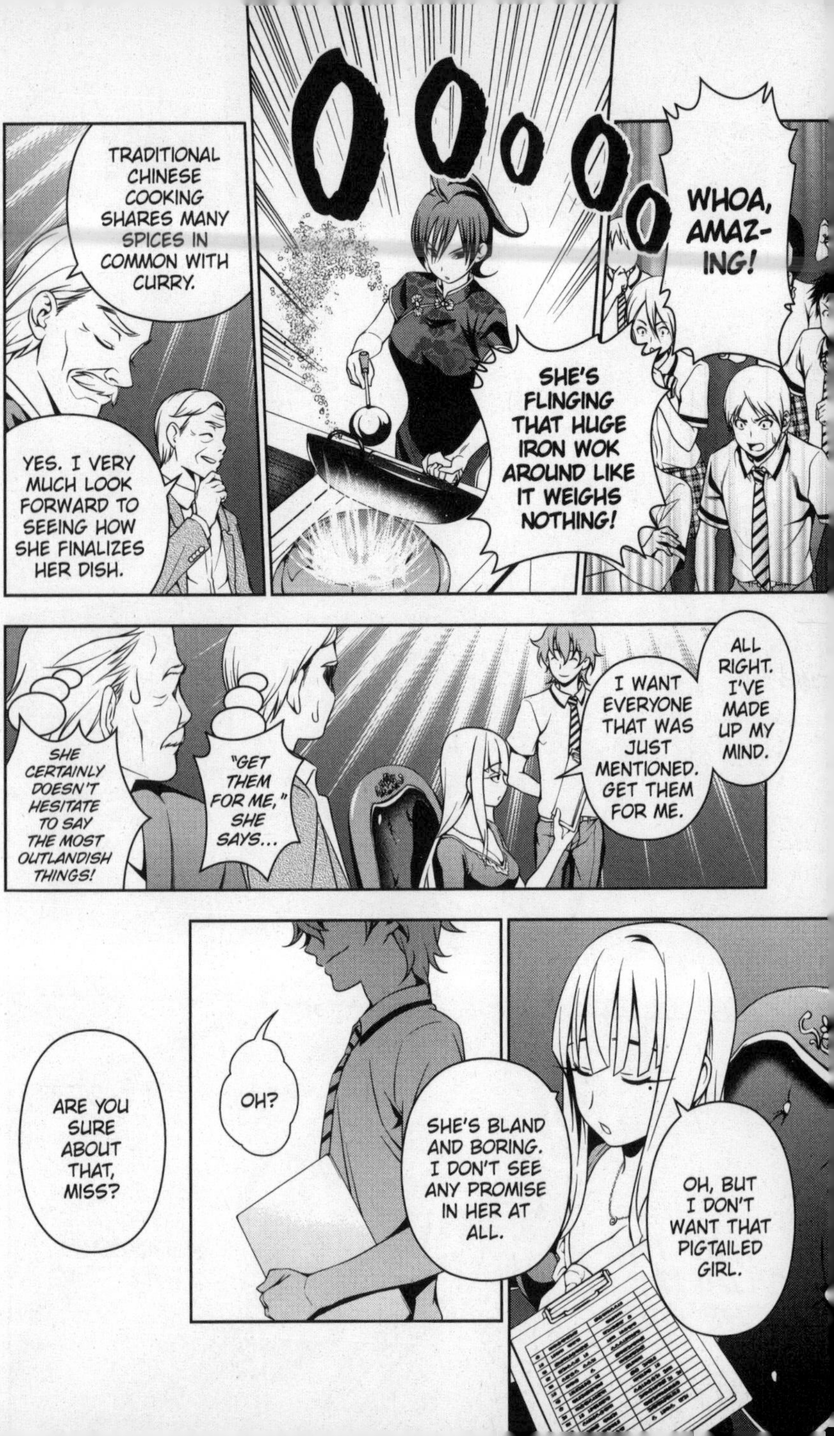
WHOA, AMAZ-ING!
SHE'S FLINGING THAT HUGE IRON WOK AROUND LIKE IT WEIGHS NOTHING!
TRADITIONAL CHINESE COOKING SHARES MANY SPICES IN COMMON WITH CURRY.
YES. I VERY MUCH LOOK FORWARD TO SEEING HOW SHE FINALIZES HER DISH.
ALL RIGHT. I'VE MADE UP MY MIND.
I WANT EVERYONE THAT WAS JUST MENTIONED. GET THEM FOR ME.
"GET THEM FOR ME," SHE SAYS...
SHE CERTAINLY DOESN'T HESITATE TO SAY THE MOST OUTLANDISH THINGS!
OH, BUT I DON'T WANT THAT PIGTAILED GIRL.
SHE'S BLAND AND BORING. I DON'T SEE ANY PROMISE IN HER AT ALL.
OH?
ARE YOU SURE ABOUT THAT, MISS?

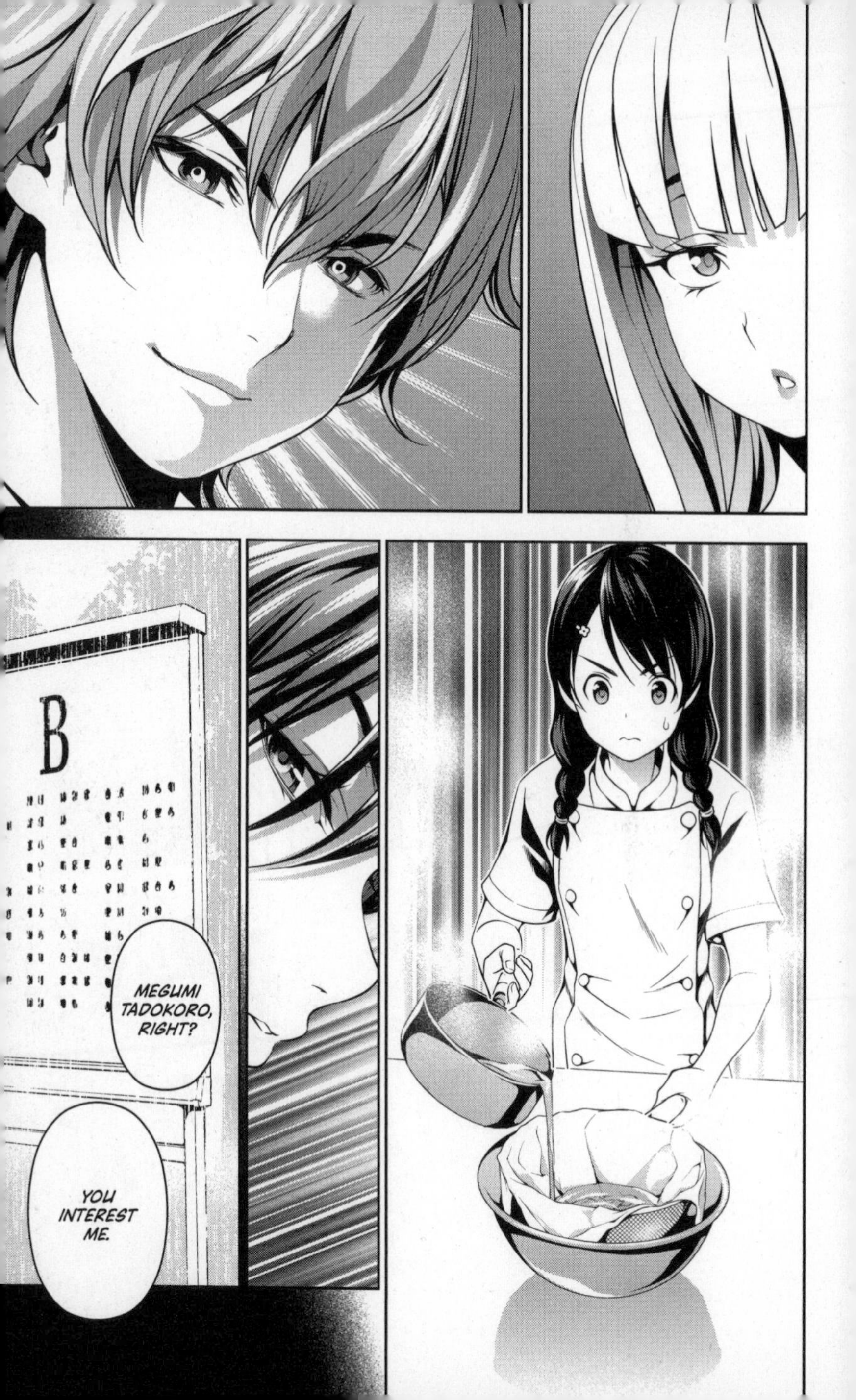
MEGUMI TADOKORO, RIGHT?
YOU INTEREST ME.

# WOLF PACK

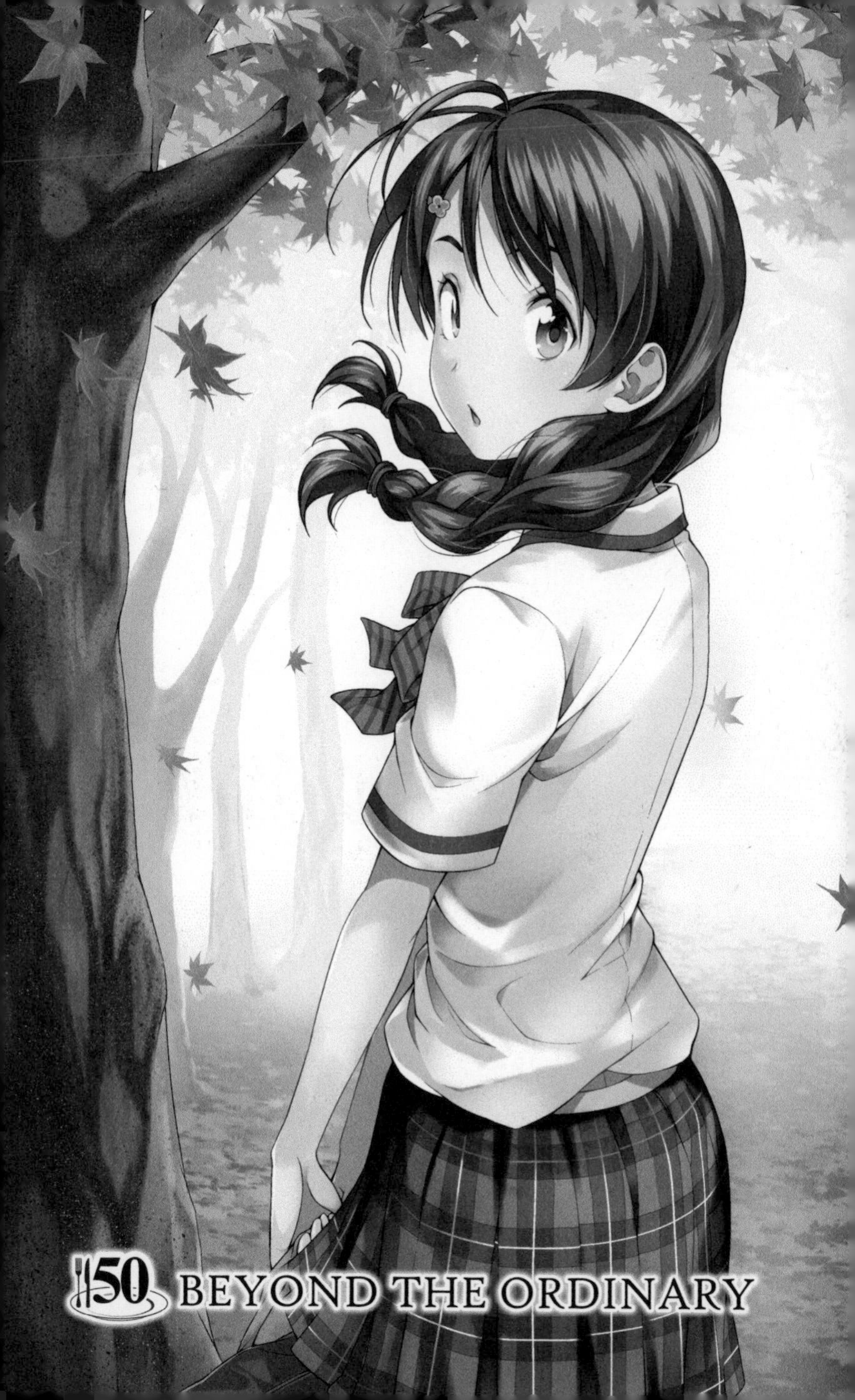
50 BEYOND THE ORDINARY

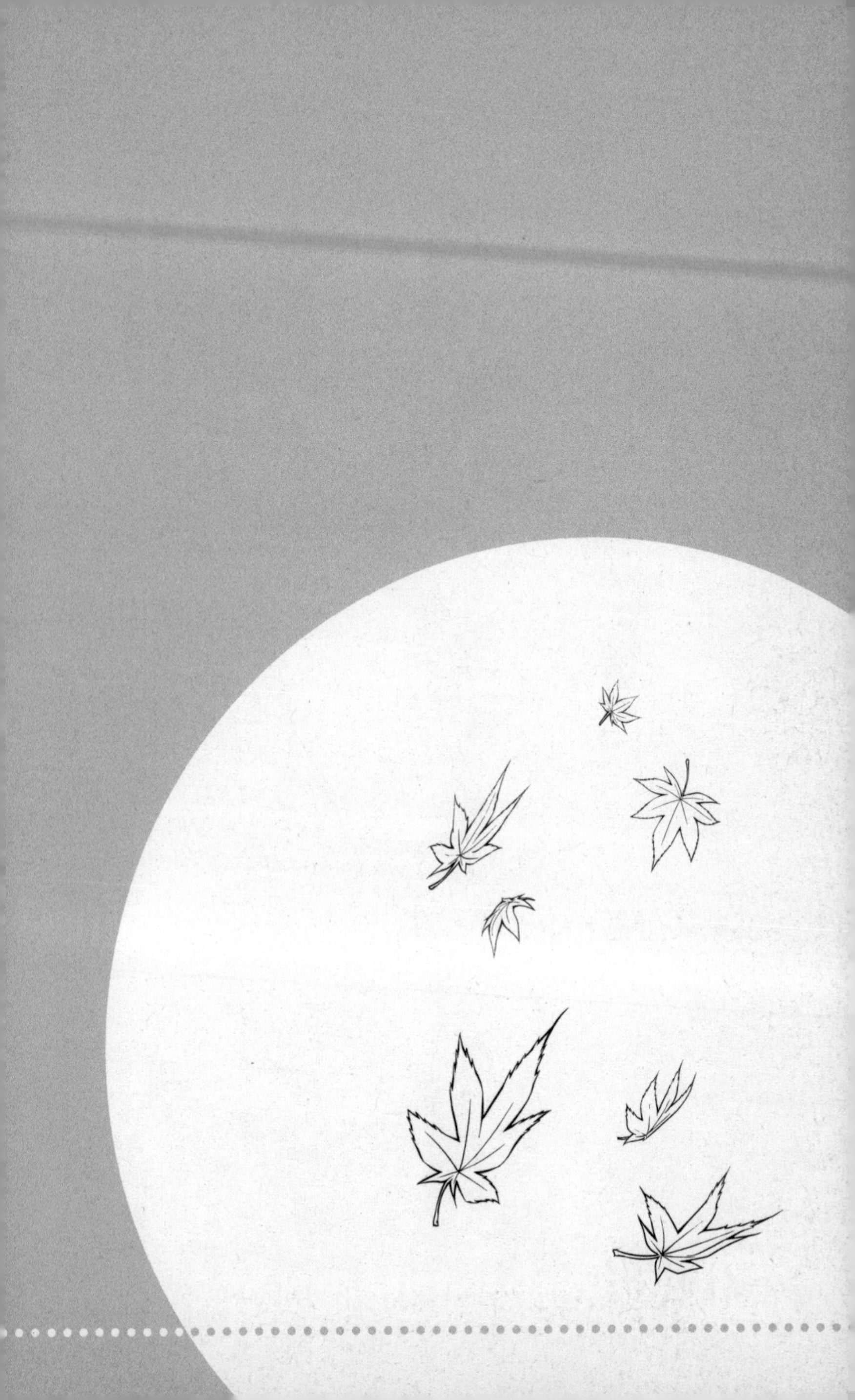

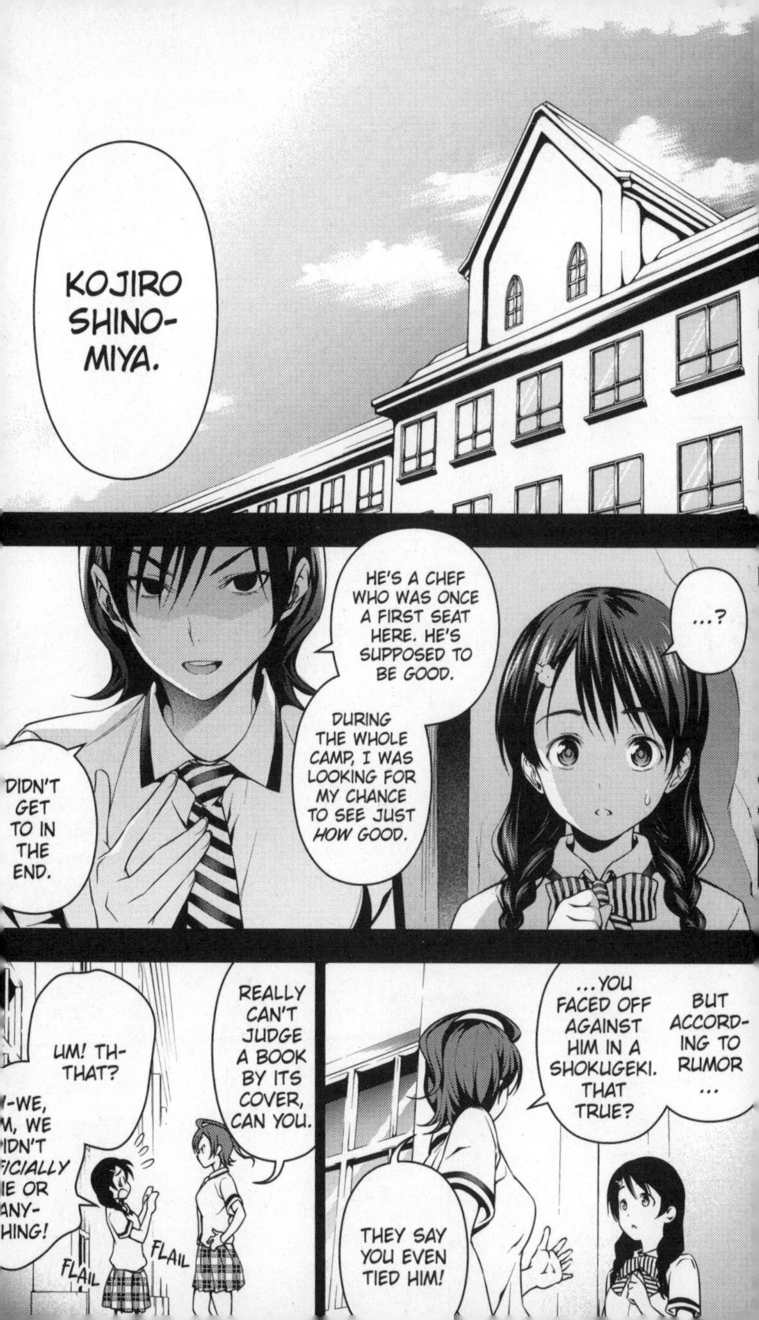
KOJIRO SHINO-MIYA.
...?
HE'S A CHEF WHO WAS ONCE A FIRST SEAT HERE. HE'S SUPPOSED TO BE GOOD.
DURING THE WHOLE CAMP, I WAS LOOKING FOR MY CHANCE TO SEE JUST *HOW* GOOD.
DIDN'T GET TO IN THE END.
BUT ACCORD-ING TO RUMOR...
...YOU FACED OFF AGAINST HIM IN A SHOKUGEKI. THAT TRUE?
THEY SAY YOU EVEN TIED HIM!
REALLY CAN'T JUDGE A BOOK BY ITS COVER, CAN YOU.
UM! TH-THAT?
-WE, M, WE IDN'T FICIALLY IE OR ANY-HING!
FLAIL
FLAIL

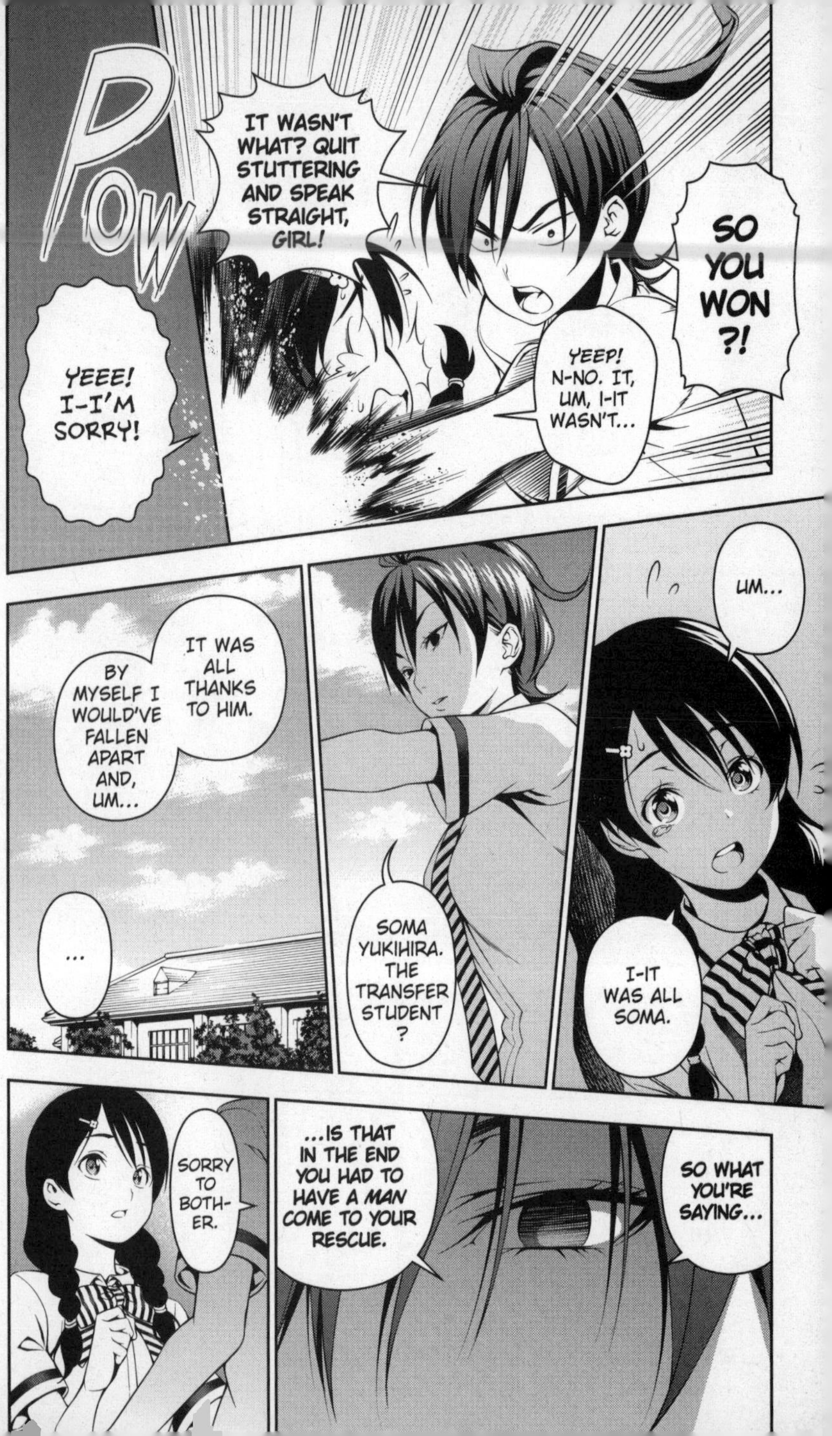
SO YOU WON?!
YEEP! N-NO. IT, UM, I-IT WASN'T...
IT WASN'T WHAT? QUIT STUTTERING AND SPEAK STRAIGHT, GIRL!
POW
YEEE! I-I'M SORRY!
UM...
I-IT WAS ALL SOMA.
SOMA YUKIHIRA. THE TRANSFER STUDENT?
IT WAS ALL THANKS TO HIM.
BY MYSELF I WOULD'VE FALLEN APART AND, UM...
...
SO WHAT YOU'RE SAYING...
...IS THAT IN THE END YOU HAD TO HAVE A *MAN* COME TO YOUR RESCUE.
SORRY TO BOTHER.

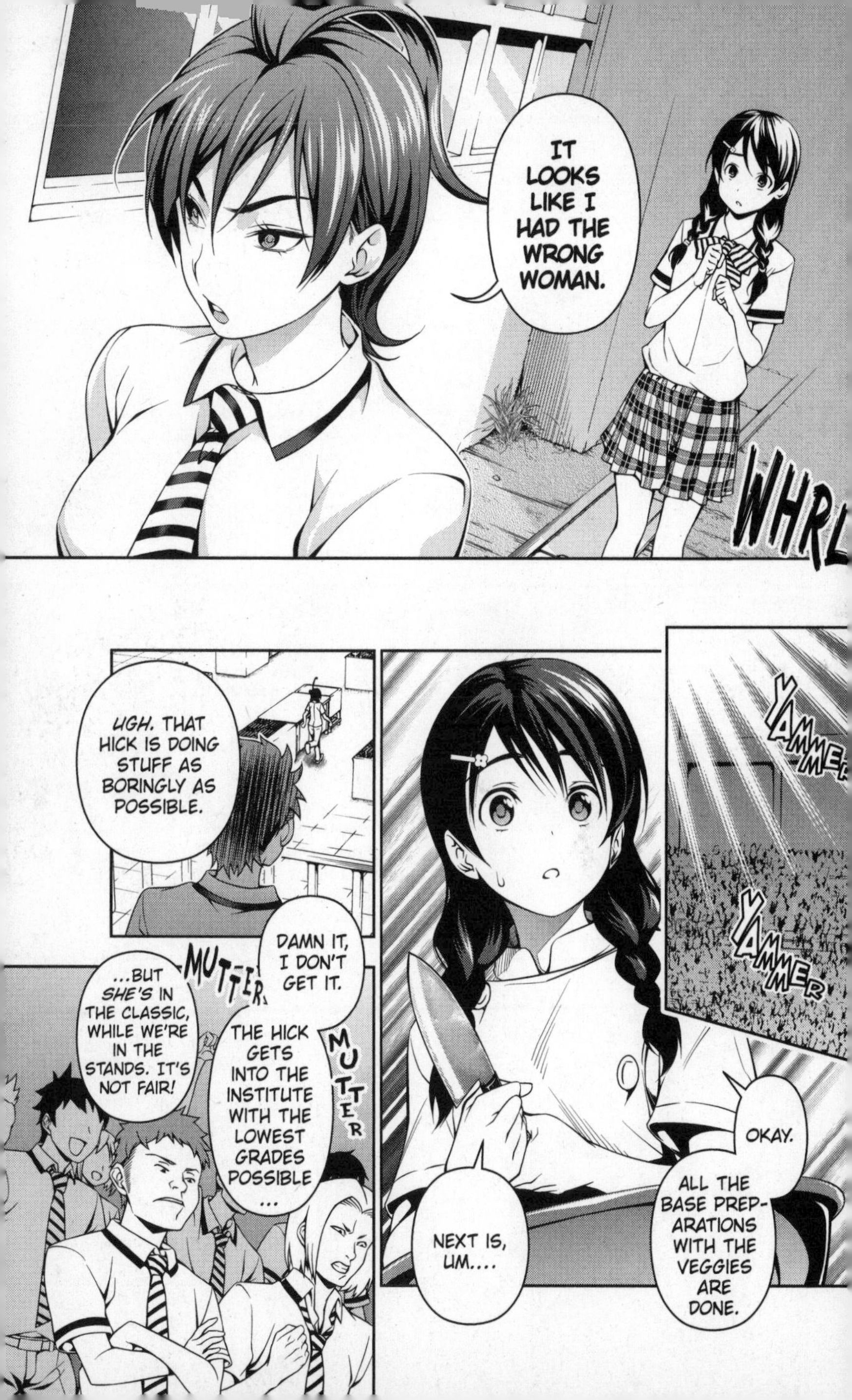
IT LOOKS LIKE I HAD THE WRONG WOMAN.
WHRL
YAMMER
YAMMER
OKAY.
ALL THE BASE PREP-ARATIONS WITH THE VEGGIES ARE DONE.
NEXT IS, UM....
*UGH*. THAT HICK IS DOING STUFF AS BORINGLY AS POSSIBLE.
DAMN IT, I DON'T GET IT.
THE HICK GETS INTO THE INSTITUTE WITH THE LOWEST GRADES POSSIBLE...
MUTTER
MUTTER
...BUT *SHE'S* IN THE CLASSIC, WHILE WE'RE IN THE STANDS. IT'S NOT FAIR!

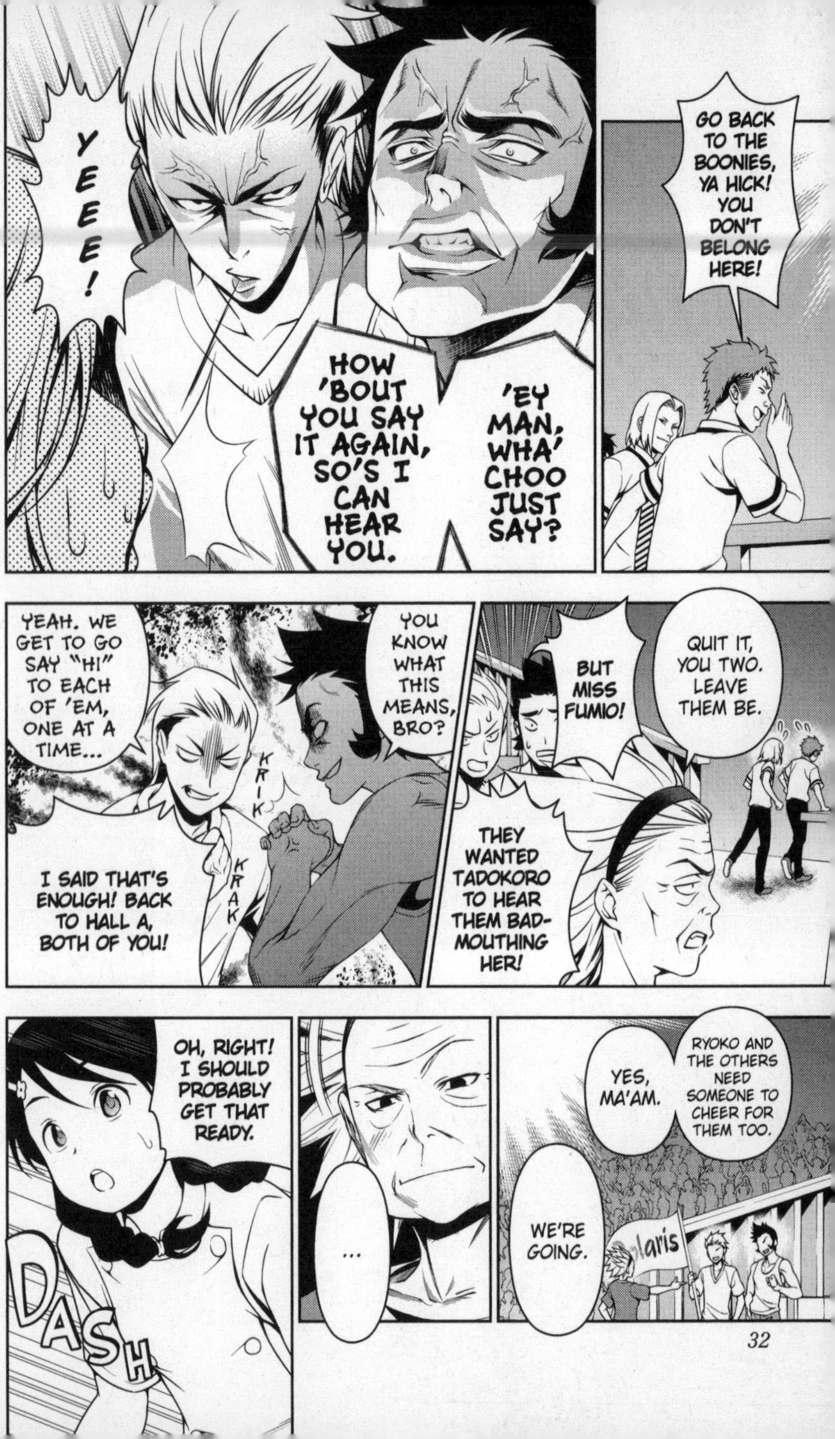
GO BACK TO THE BOONIES, YA HICK! YOU DON'T BELONG HERE!
YEEEE!
'EY MAN, WHA' CHOO JUST SAY?
HOW 'BOUT YOU SAY IT AGAIN, SO'S I CAN HEAR YOU.
QUIT IT, YOU TWO. LEAVE THEM BE.
BUT MISS FUMIO!
THEY WANTED TADOKORO TO HEAR THEM BAD-MOUTHING HER!
YOU KNOW WHAT THIS MEANS, BRO?
YEAH. WE GET TO GO SAY "HI" TO EACH OF 'EM, ONE AT A TIME...
KRIK
KRAK
I SAID THAT'S ENOUGH! BACK TO HALL A, BOTH OF YOU!
RYOKO AND THE OTHERS NEED SOMEONE TO CHEER FOR THEM TOO.
YES, MA'AM.
WE'RE GOING.
...
OH, RIGHT! I SHOULD PROBABLY GET THAT READY.
DASH

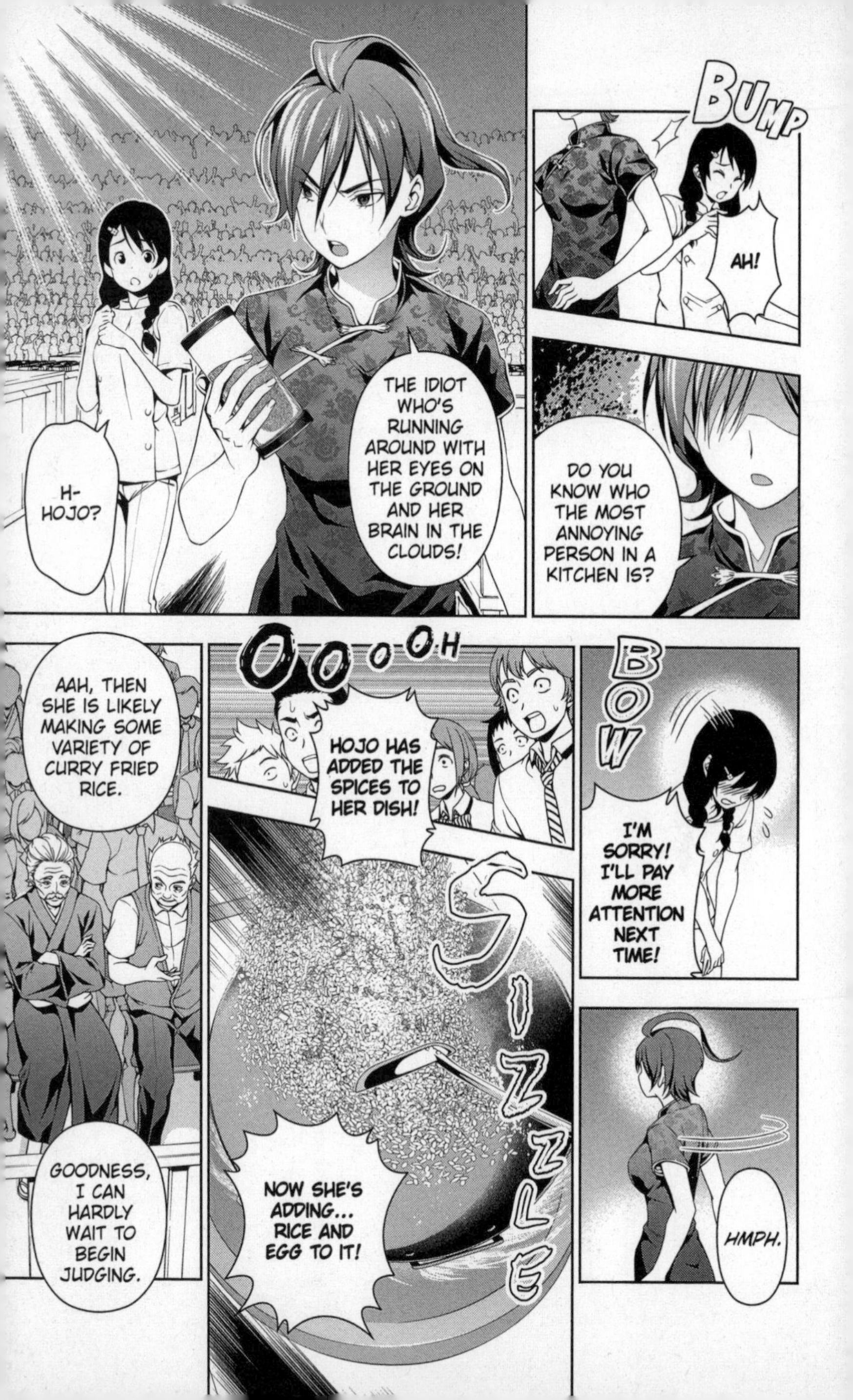
BUMP
AH!
DO YOU KNOW WHO THE MOST ANNOYING PERSON IN A KITCHEN IS?
THE IDIOT WHO'S RUNNING AROUND WITH HER EYES ON THE GROUND AND HER BRAIN IN THE CLOUDS!
H-HOJO?
BOW
I'M SORRY! I'LL PAY MORE ATTENTION NEXT TIME!
HMPH.
OOOOH
HOJO HAS ADDED THE SPICES TO HER DISH!
SIZZLE
NOW SHE'S ADDING... RICE AND EGG TO IT!
AAH, THEN SHE IS LIKELY MAKING SOME VARIETY OF CURRY FRIED RICE.
GOODNESS, I CAN HARDLY WAIT TO BEGIN JUDGING.

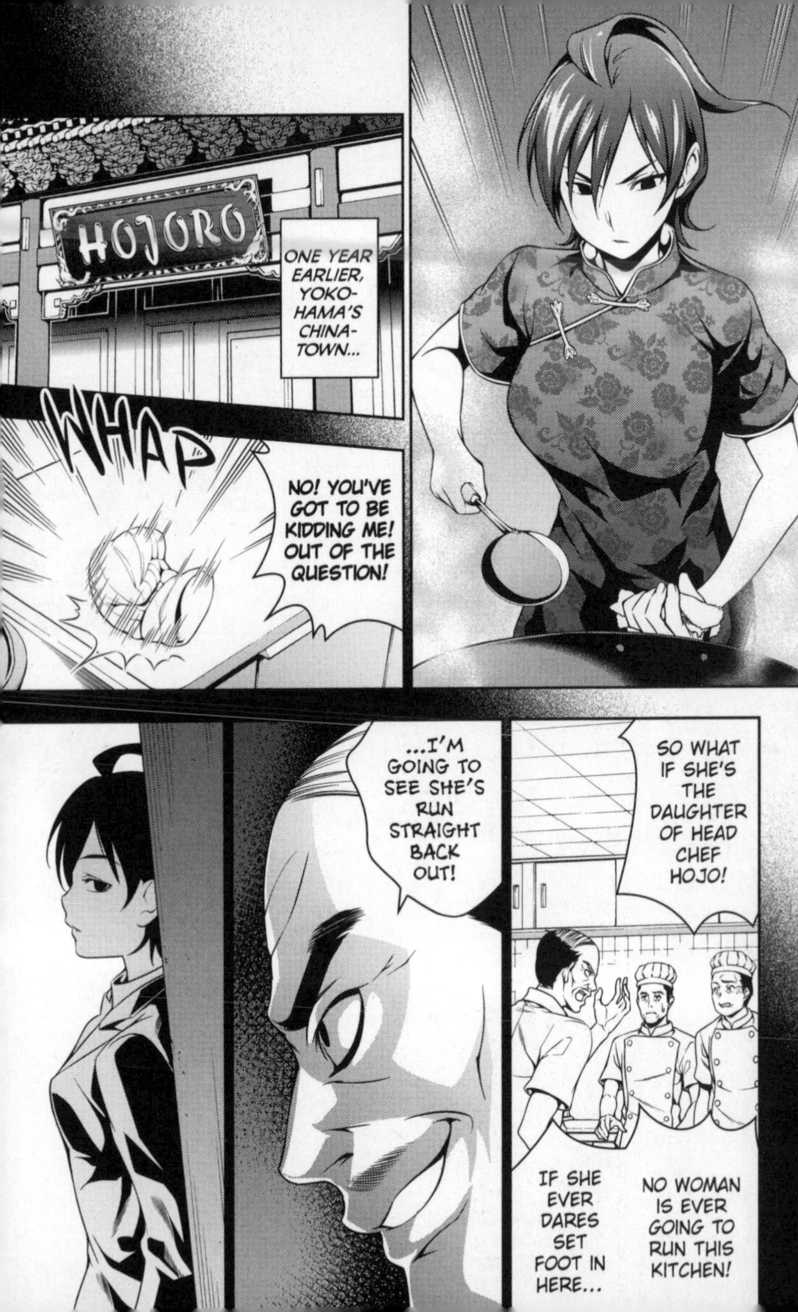
HOJORO
ONE YEAR EARLIER, YOKOHAMA'S CHINATOWN...
WHAP
NO! YOU'VE GOT TO BE KIDDING ME! OUT OF THE QUESTION!
SO WHAT IF SHE'S THE DAUGHTER OF HEAD CHEF HOJO!
NO WOMAN IS EVER GOING TO RUN THIS KITCHEN!
IF SHE EVER DARES SET FOOT IN HERE...
...I'M GOING TO SEE SHE'S RUN STRAIGHT BACK OUT!

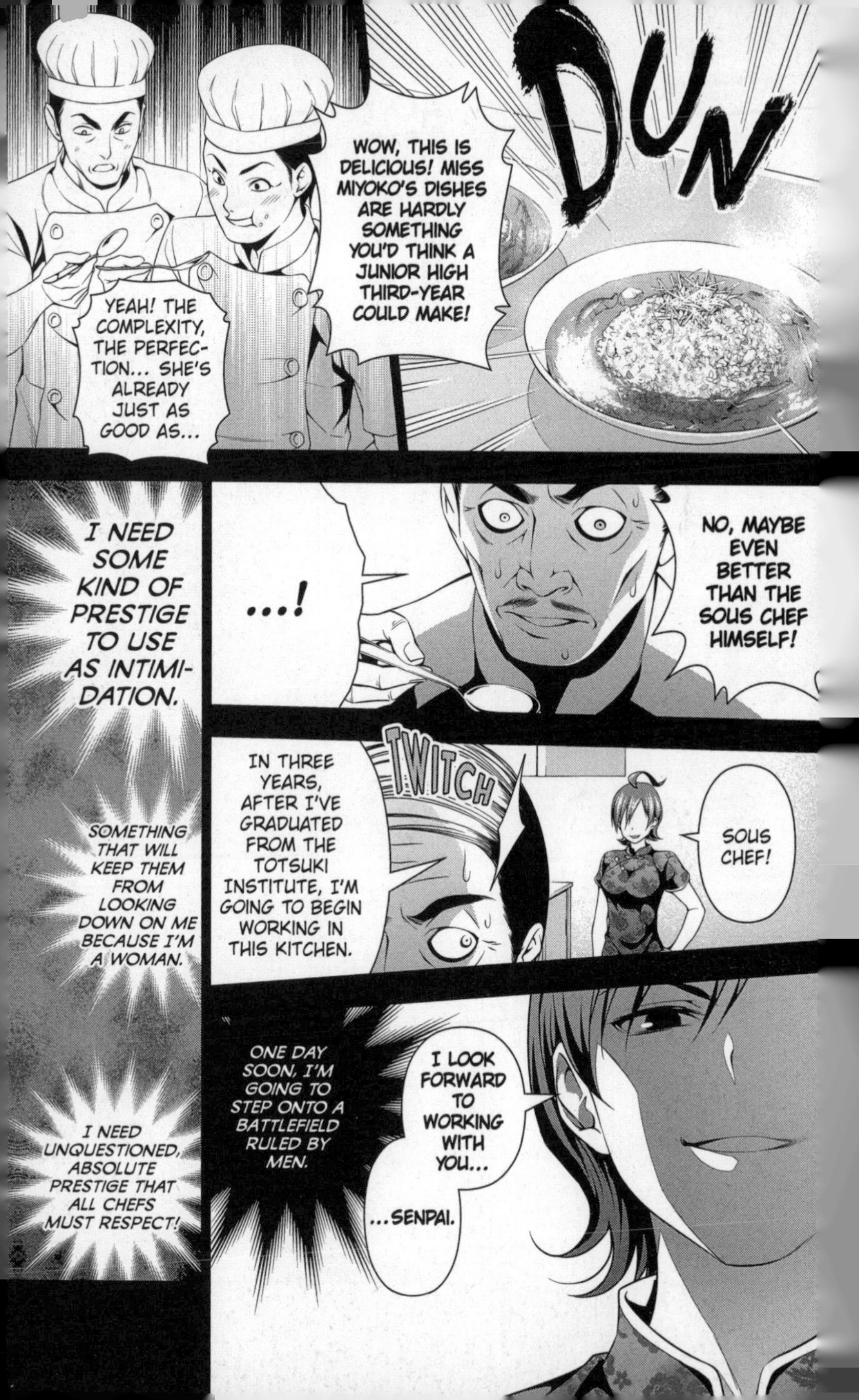
DUN
WOW, THIS IS DELICIOUS! MISS MIYOKO'S DISHES ARE HARDLY SOMETHING YOU'D THINK A JUNIOR HIGH THIRD-YEAR COULD MAKE!
YEAH! THE COMPLEXITY, THE PERFEC-TION... SHE'S ALREADY JUST AS GOOD AS...
NO, MAYBE EVEN BETTER THAN THE SOUS CHEF HIMSELF!
...!
SOUS CHEF!
TWITCH
IN THREE YEARS, AFTER I'VE GRADUATED FROM THE TOTSUKI INSTITUTE, I'M GOING TO BEGIN WORKING IN THIS KITCHEN.
I LOOK FORWARD TO WORKING WITH YOU...
...SENPAI.
ONE DAY SOON, I'M GOING TO STEP ONTO A BATTLEFIELD RULED BY MEN.
I NEED SOME KIND OF PRESTIGE TO USE AS INTIMI-DATION.
SOMETHING THAT WILL KEEP THEM FROM LOOKING DOWN ON ME BECAUSE I'M A WOMAN.
I NEED UNQUESTIONED, ABSOLUTE PRESTIGE THAT ALL CHEFS MUST RESPECT!

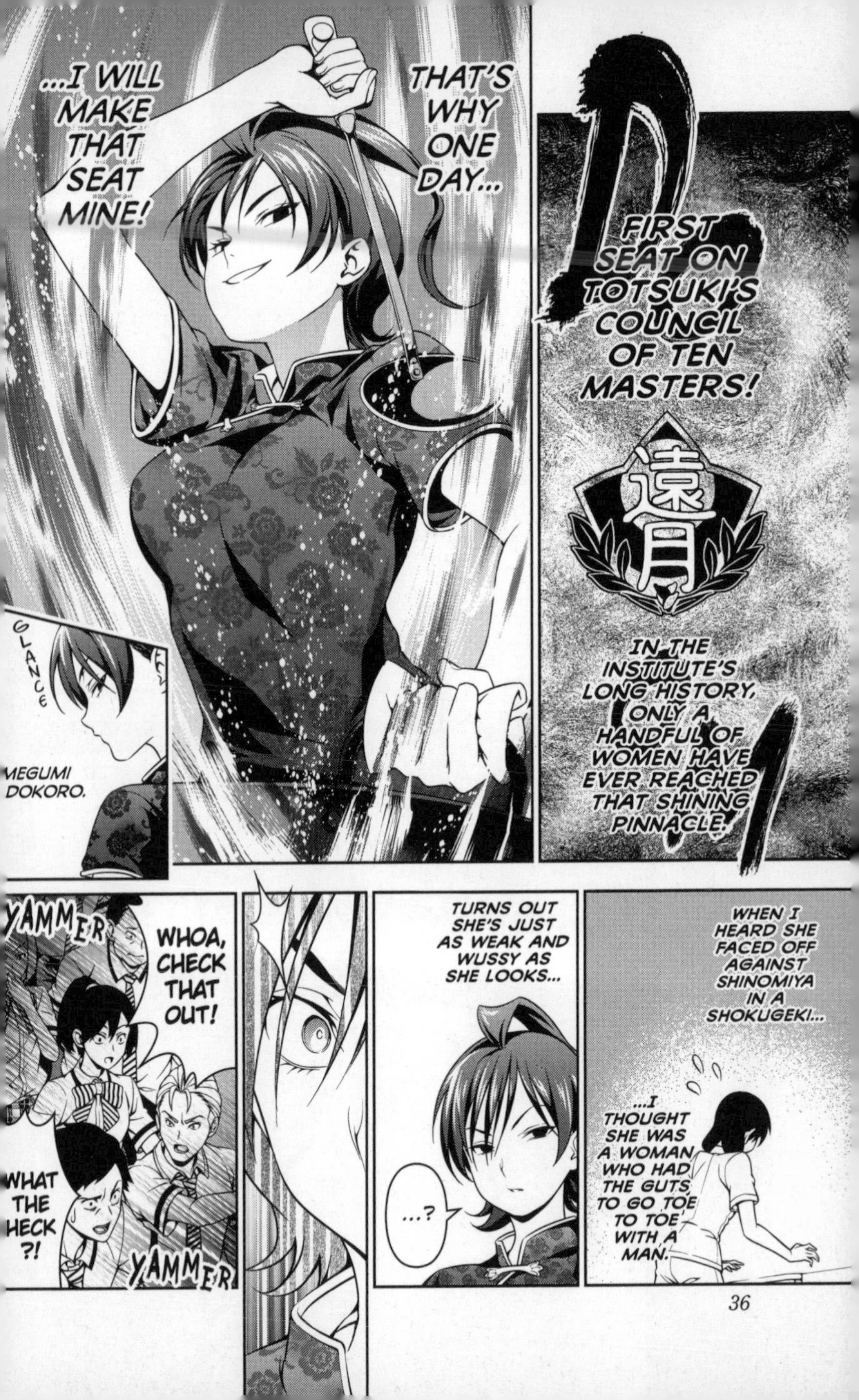
FIRST SEAT ON TOTSUKI'S COUNCIL OF TEN MASTERS!
IN THE INSTITUTE'S LONG HISTORY, ONLY A HANDFUL OF WOMEN HAVE EVER REACHED THAT SHINING PINNACLE.
THAT'S WHY ONE DAY...
...I WILL MAKE THAT SEAT MINE!
GLANCE
MEGUMI DOKORO.
WHEN I HEARD SHE FACED OFF AGAINST SHINOMIYA IN A SHOKUGEKI...
...I THOUGHT SHE WAS A WOMAN WHO HAD THE GUTS TO GO TOE TO TOE WITH A MAN.
TURNS OUT SHE'S JUST AS WEAK AND WUSSY AS SHE LOOKS...
...?
YAMMER
WHOA, CHECK THAT OUT!
WHAT THE HECK ?!
YAMMER

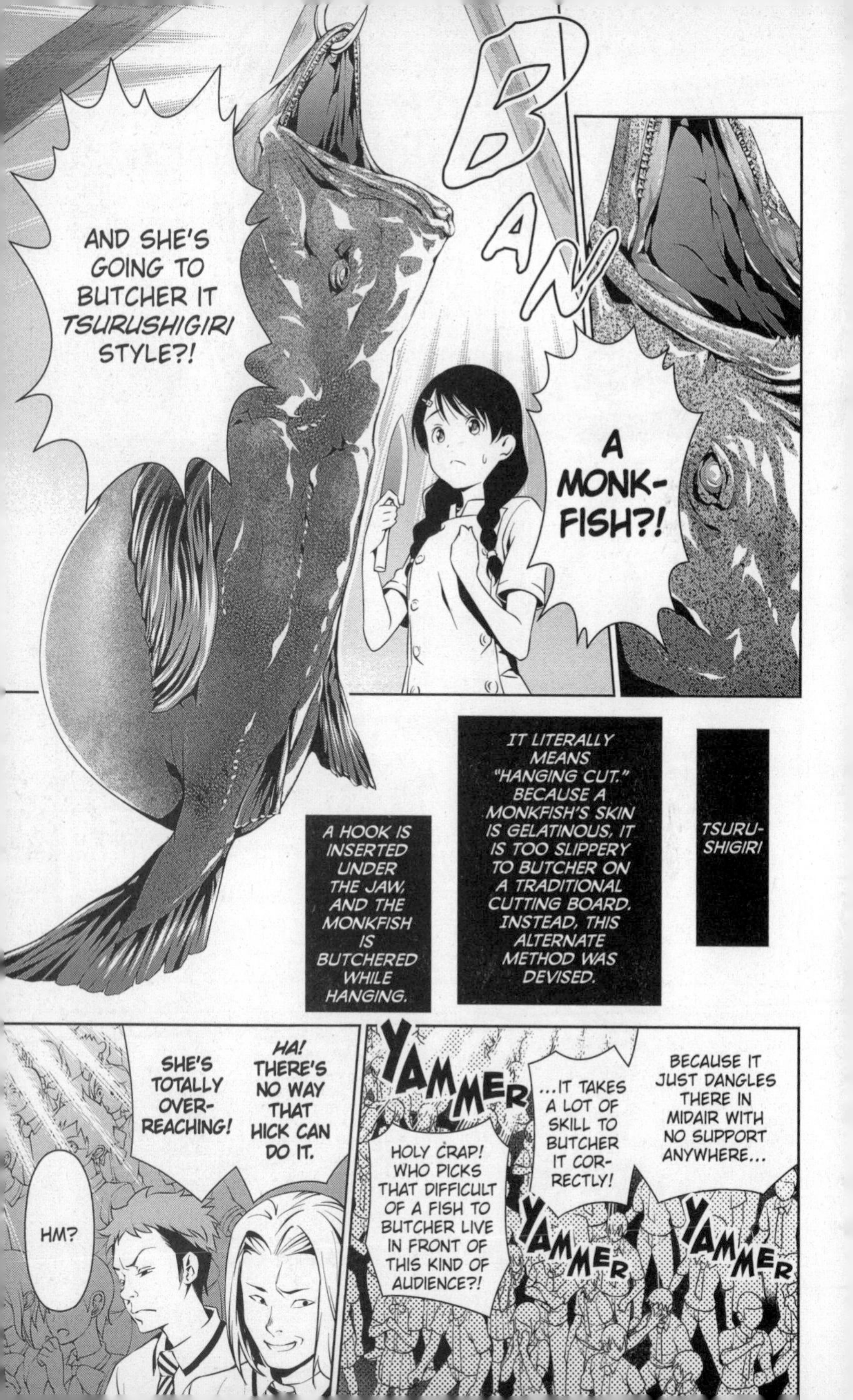
A MONK-FISH?!
BAN
AND SHE'S GOING TO BUTCHER IT TSURUSHIGIRI STYLE?!
TSURU-SHIGIRI
IT LITERALLY MEANS "HANGING CUT." BECAUSE A MONKFISH'S SKIN IS GELATINOUS, IT IS TOO SLIPPERY TO BUTCHER ON A TRADITIONAL CUTTING BOARD. INSTEAD, THIS ALTERNATE METHOD WAS DEVISED.
A HOOK IS INSERTED UNDER THE JAW, AND THE MONKFISH IS BUTCHERED WHILE HANGING.
YAMMER
BECAUSE IT JUST DANGLES THERE IN MIDAIR WITH NO SUPPORT ANYWHERE...
...IT TAKES A LOT OF SKILL TO BUTCHER IT COR-RECTLY!
HOLY CRAP! WHO PICKS THAT DIFFICULT OF A FISH TO BUTCHER LIVE IN FRONT OF THIS KIND OF AUDIENCE?!
YAMMER
YAMMER
HA! THERE'S NO WAY THAT HICK CAN DO IT.
SHE'S TOTALLY OVER-REACHING!
HM?

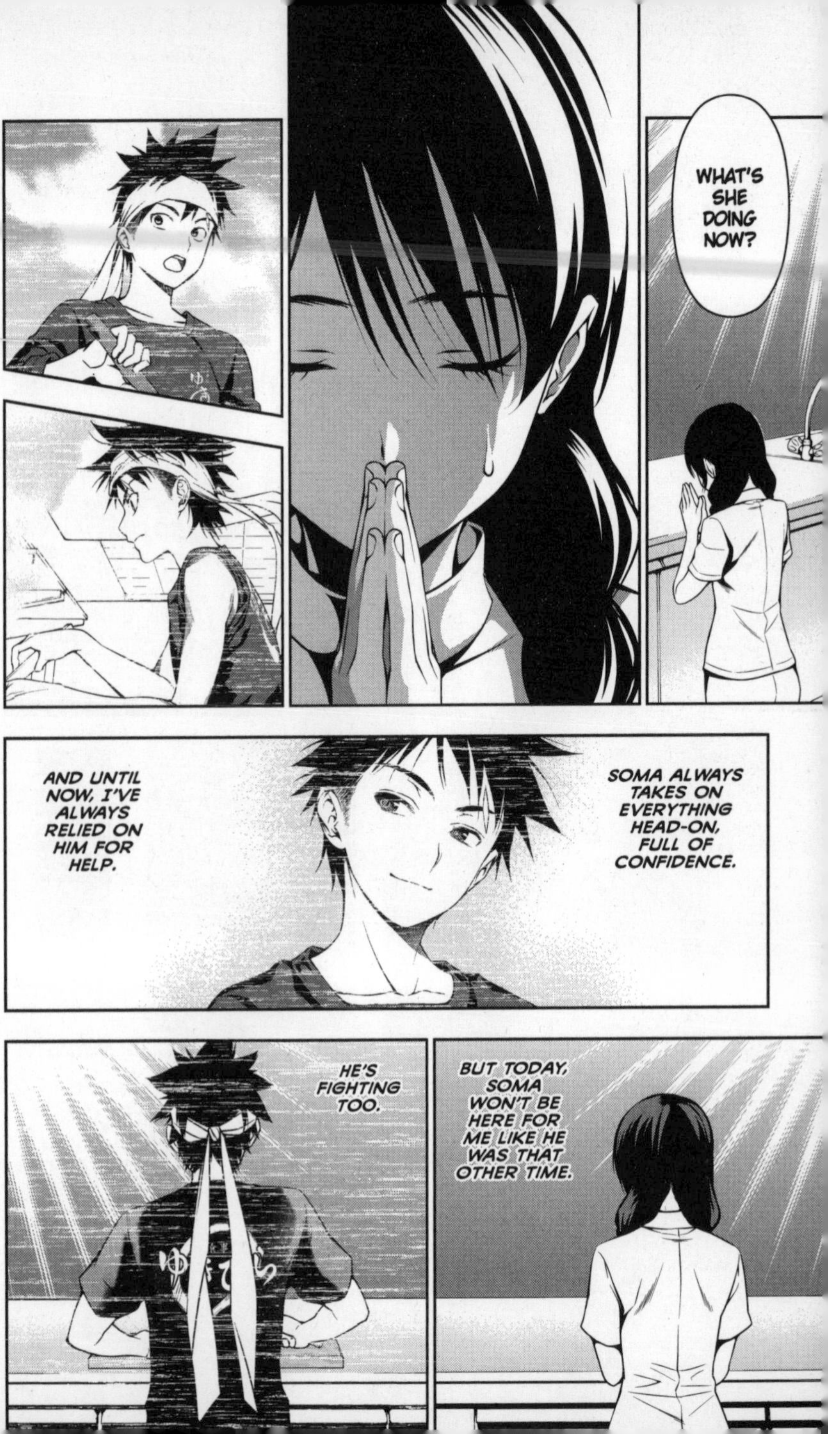
WHAT'S SHE DOING NOW?
SOMA ALWAYS TAKES ON EVERYTHING HEAD-ON, FULL OF CONFIDENCE.
AND UNTIL NOW, I'VE ALWAYS RELIED ON HIM FOR HELP.
BUT TODAY, SOMA WON'T BE HERE FOR ME LIKE HE WAS THAT OTHER TIME.
HE'S FIGHTING TOO.

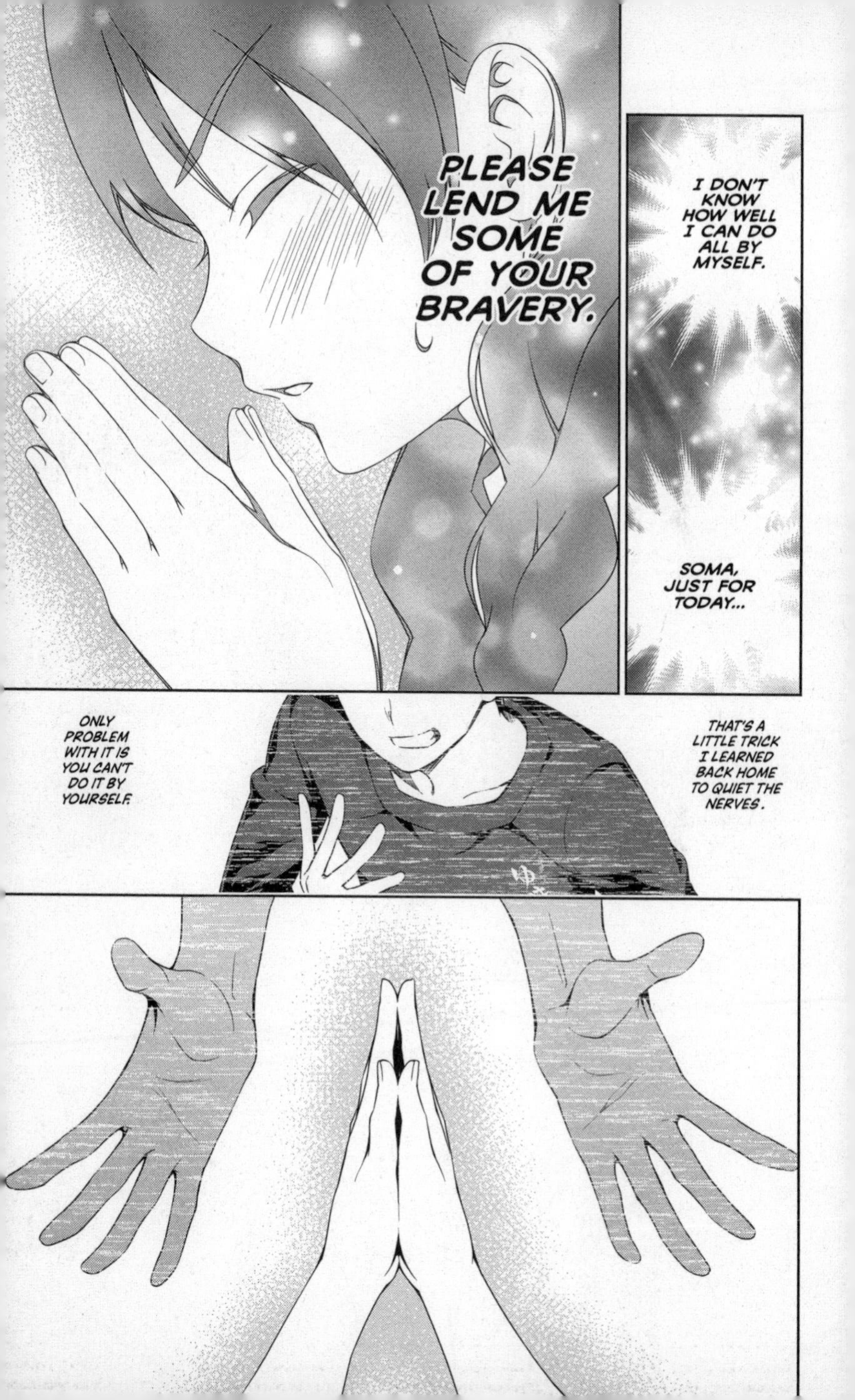
I DON'T KNOW HOW WELL I CAN DO ALL BY MYSELF.
SOMA, JUST FOR TODAY...
PLEASE LEND ME SOME OF YOUR BRAVERY.
THAT'S A LITTLE TRICK I LEARNED BACK HOME TO QUIET THE NERVES.
ONLY PROBLEM WITH IT IS YOU CAN'T DO IT BY YOURSELF.

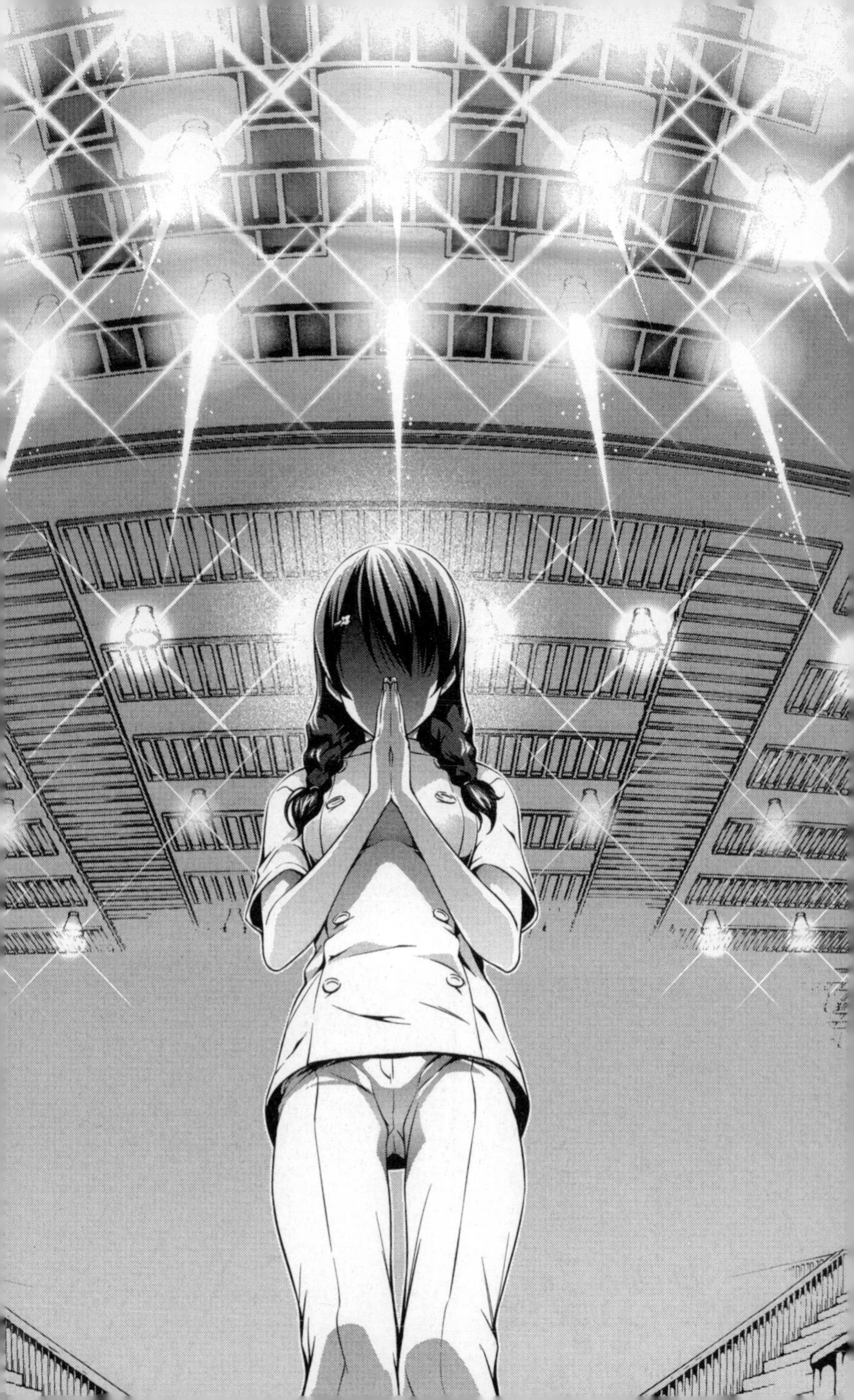

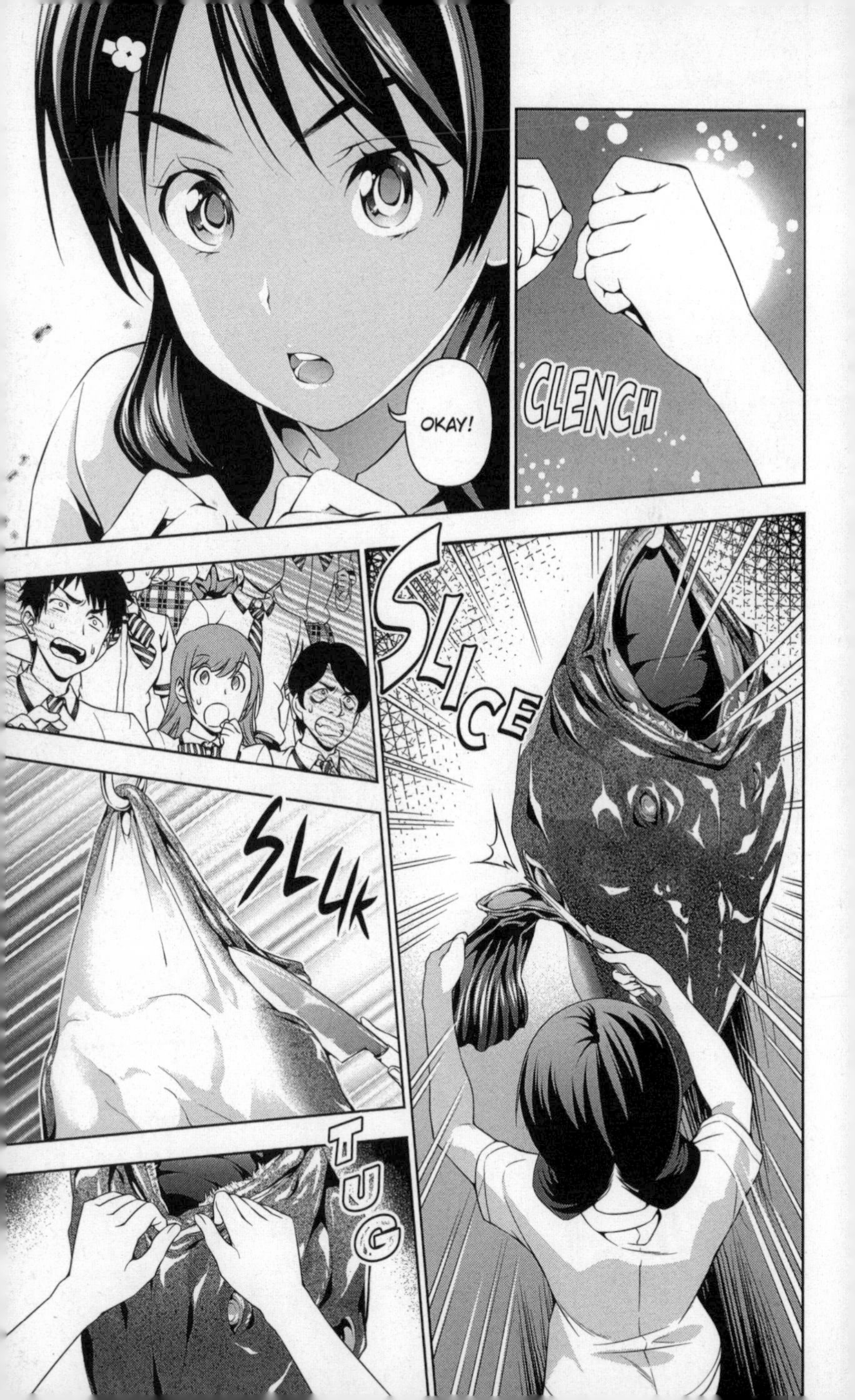
CLENCH
OKAY!
SLICE
SLUK
TUG

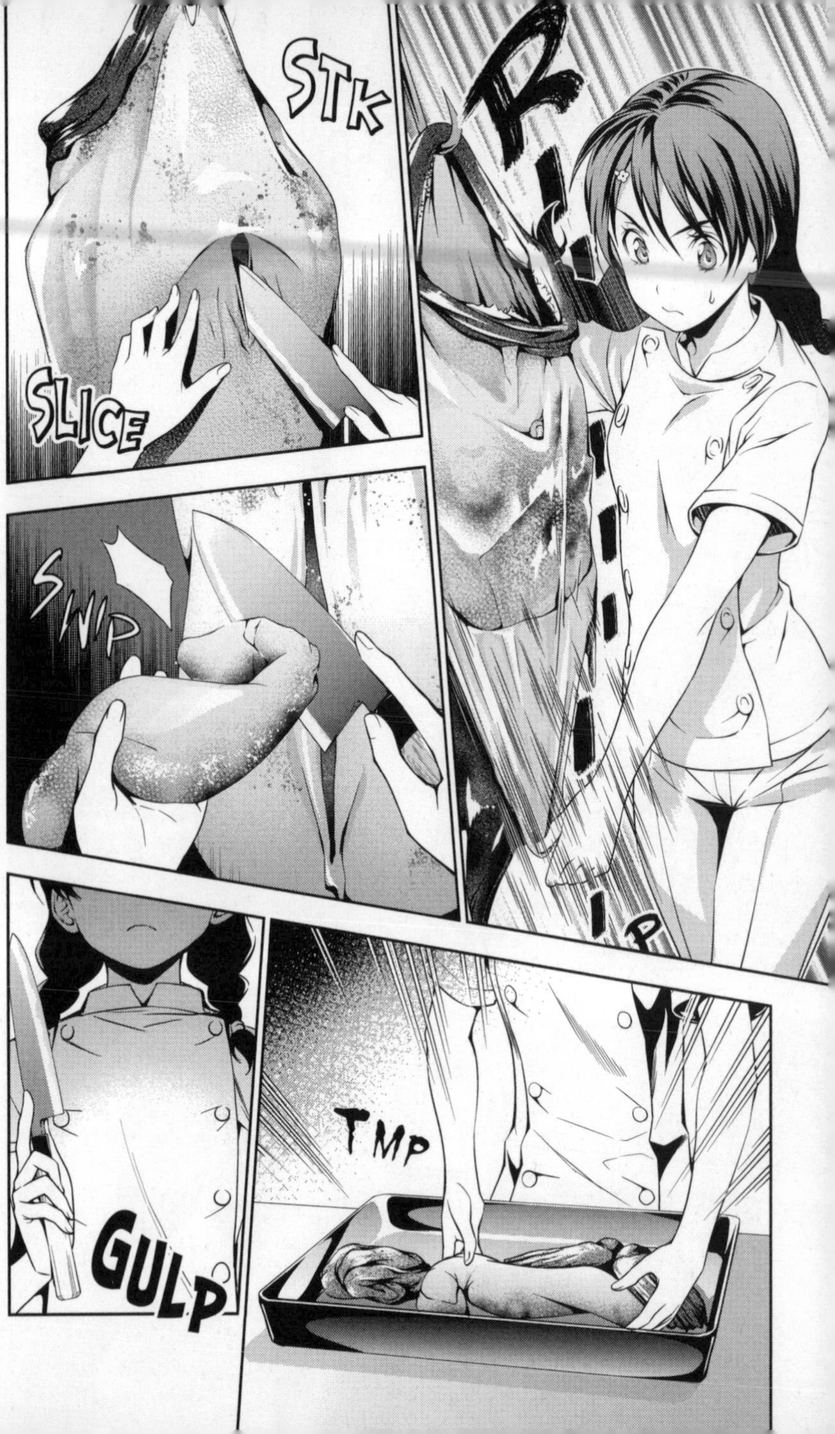
RIIIIP
STK
SLICE
SWIP
TMP
GULP

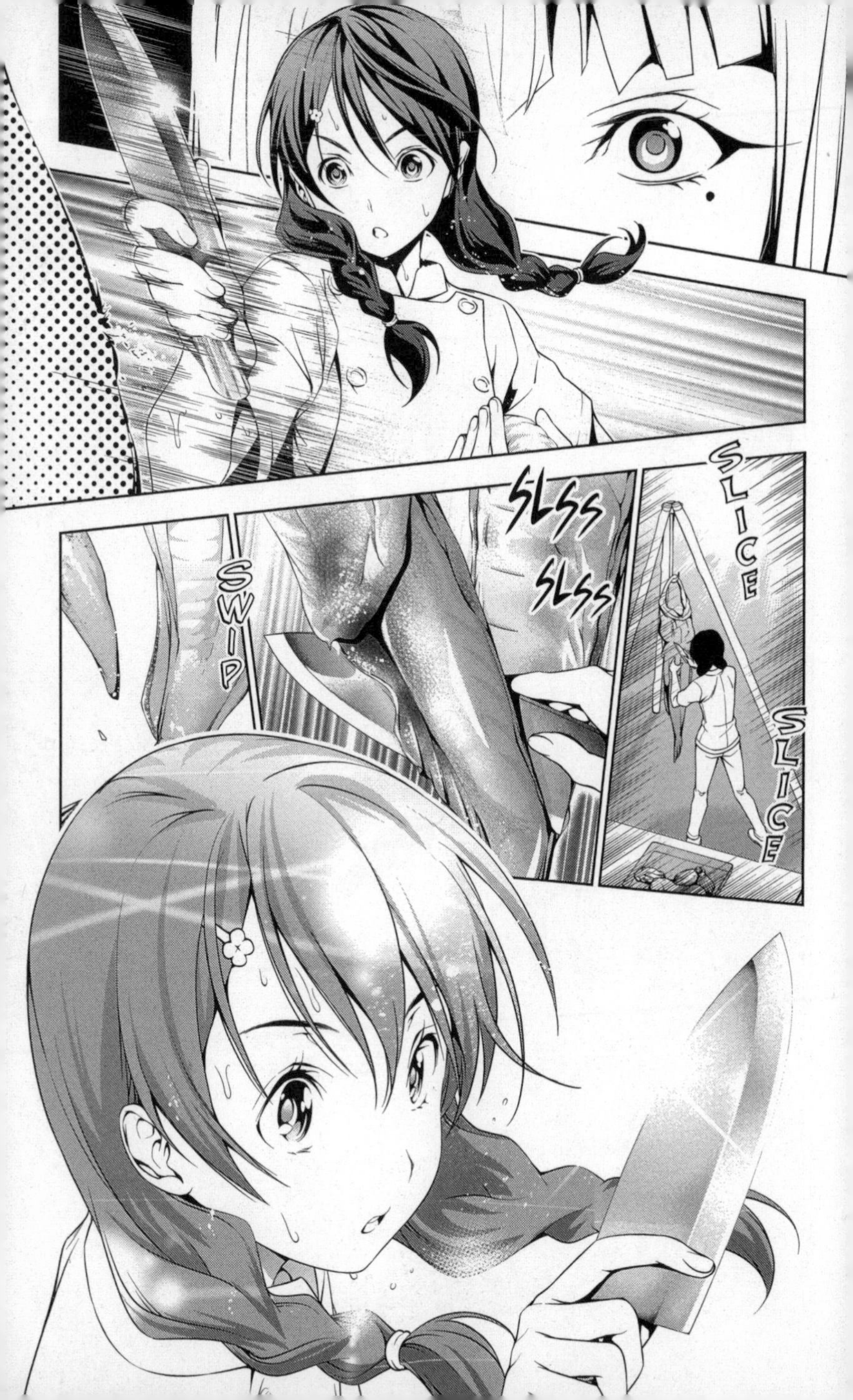
SLICE
SLICE
SLSS
SLSS
SWIP

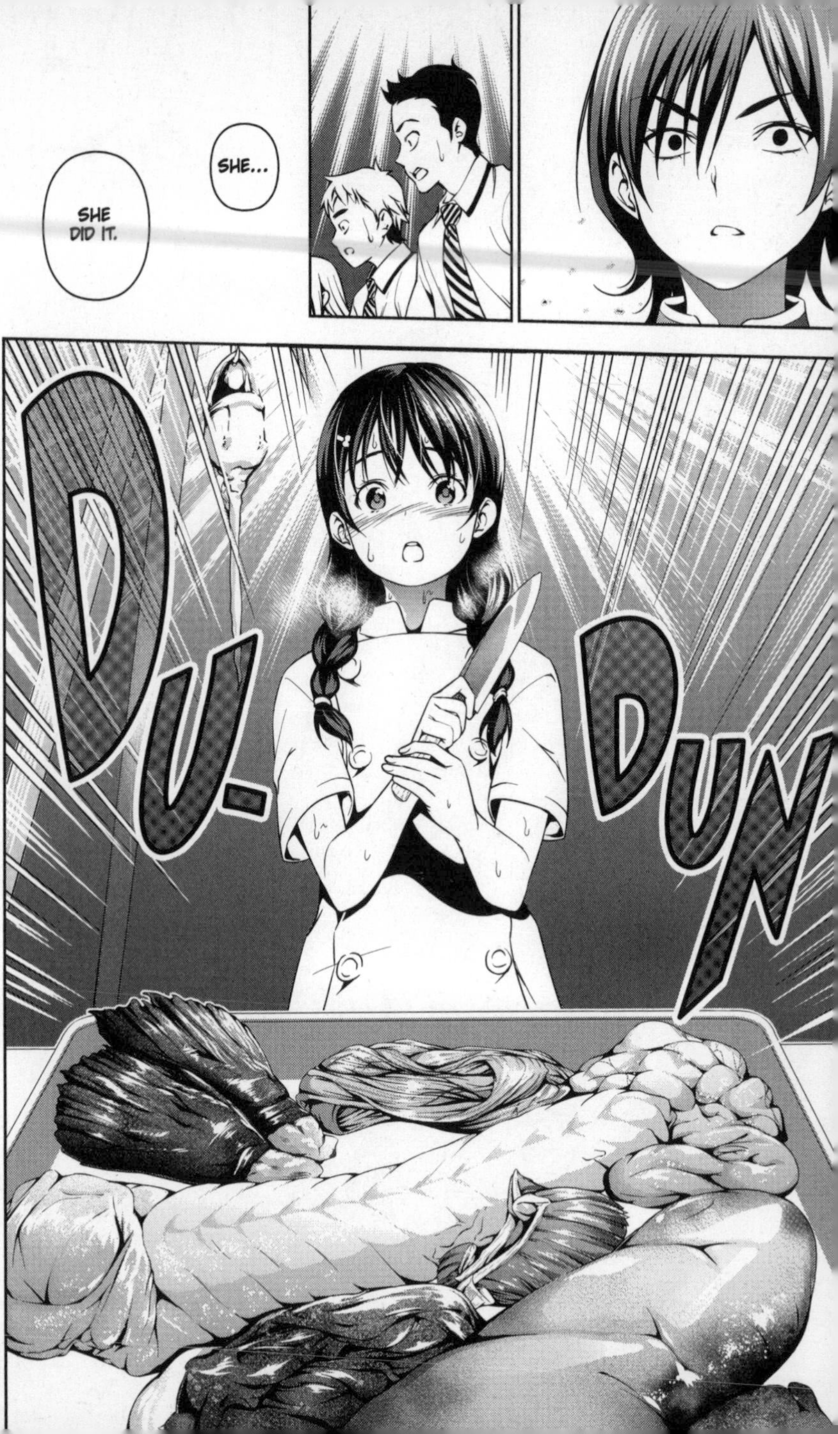
SHE...
SHE DID IT.
DU-DUN

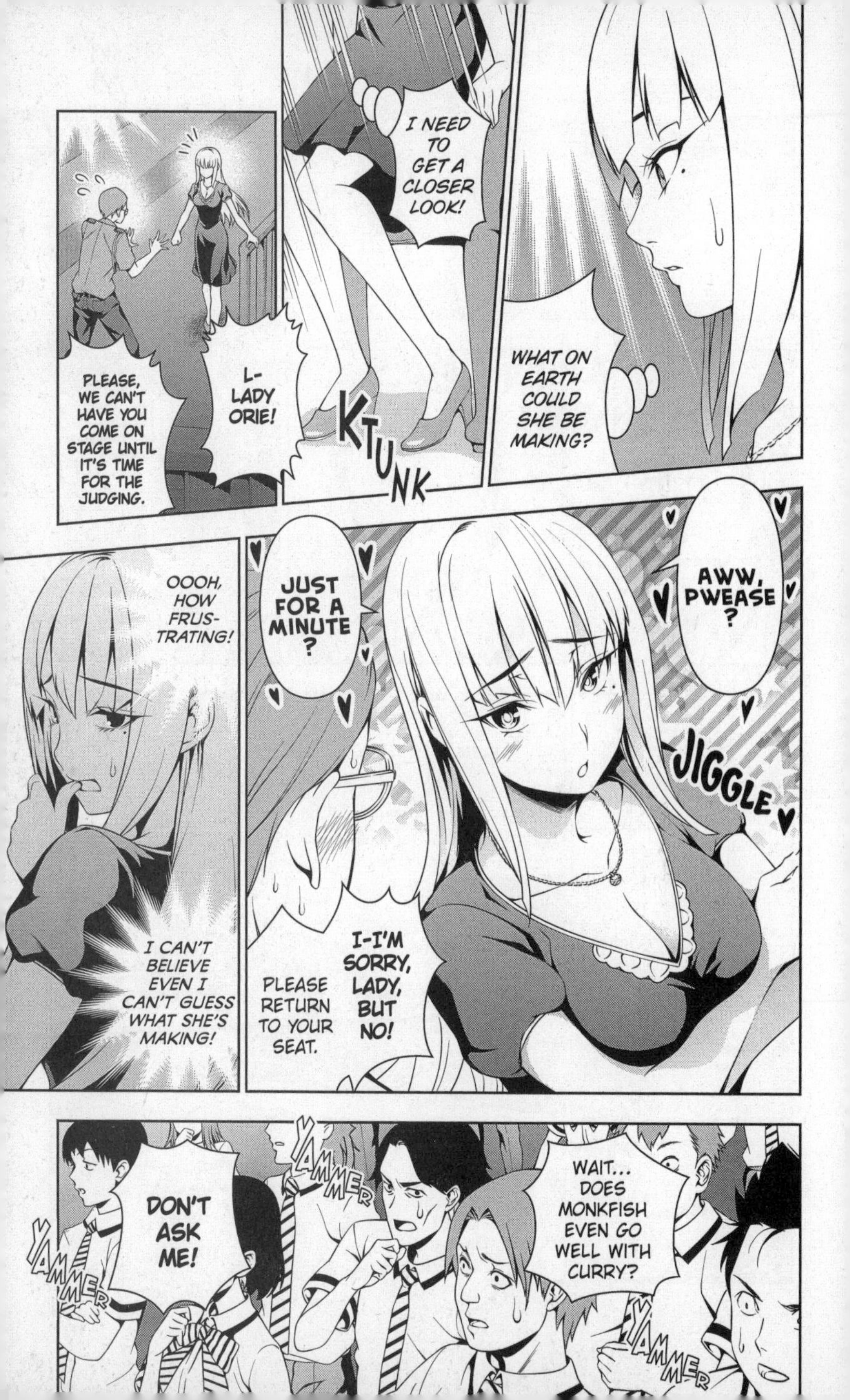
WHAT ON EARTH COULD SHE BE MAKING?
I NEED TO GET A CLOSER LOOK!
KTUNK
L- LADY ORIE!
PLEASE, WE CAN'T HAVE YOU COME ON STAGE UNTIL IT'S TIME FOR THE JUDGING.
AWW, PWEASE?
JIGGLE
JUST FOR A MINUTE?
I-I'M SORRY, LADY, BUT NO!
PLEASE RETURN TO YOUR SEAT.
OOOH, HOW FRUS-TRATING!
I CAN'T BELIEVE EVEN I CAN'T GUESS WHAT SHE'S MAKING!
WAIT... DOES MONKFISH EVEN GO WELL WITH CURRY?
YAMMER
YAMMER
DON'T ASK ME!
YAMMER

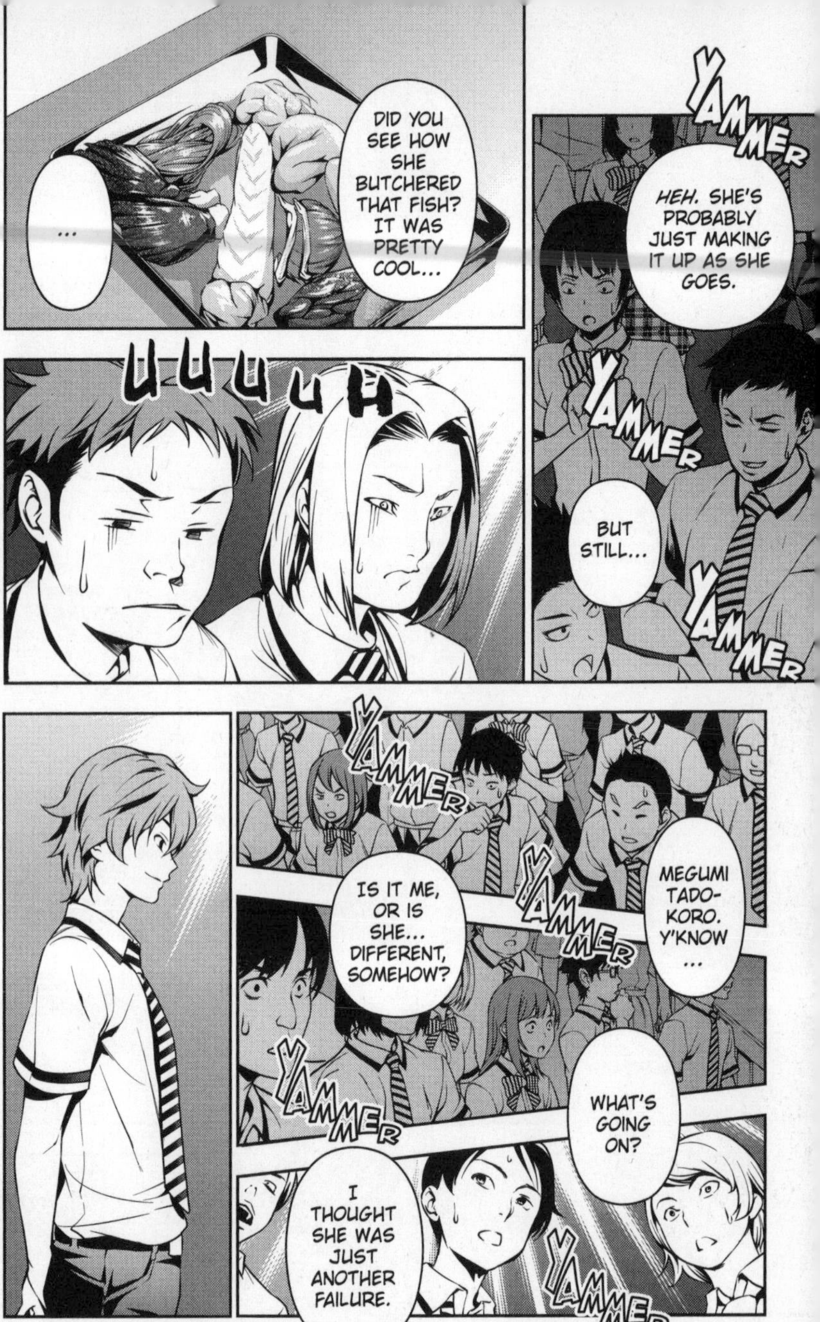
YAMMER
HEH. SHE'S PROBABLY JUST MAKING IT UP AS SHE GOES.
YAMMER
BUT STILL...
YAMMER
DID YOU SEE HOW SHE BUTCHERED THAT FISH? IT WAS PRETTY COOL...
...
UUUUUH
YAMMER
MEGUMI TADOKORO. Y'KNOW...
YAMMER
IS IT ME, OR IS SHE... DIFFERENT, SOMEHOW?
YAMMER
WHAT'S GOING ON?
YAMMER
I THOUGHT SHE WAS JUST ANOTHER FAILURE.

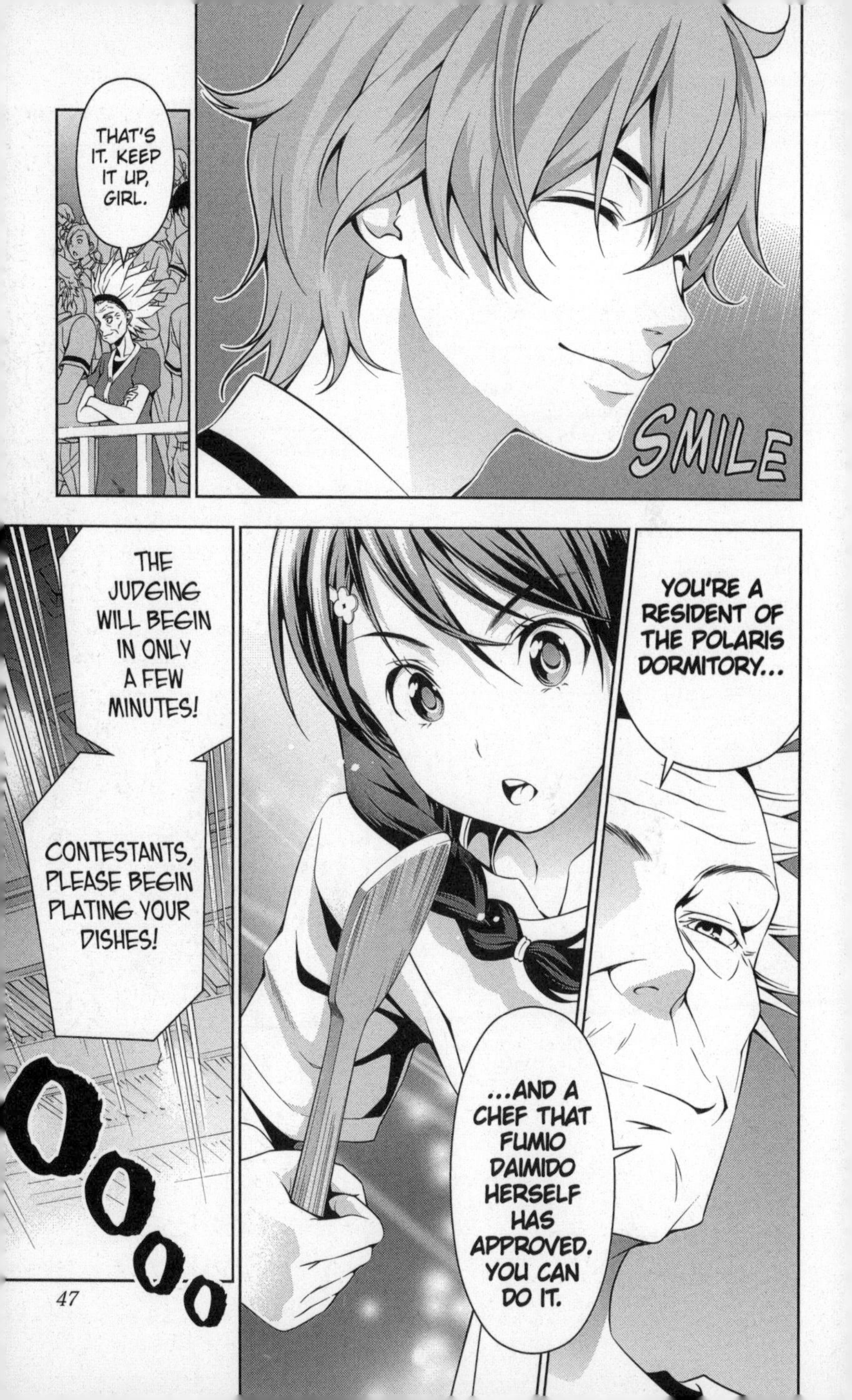
SMILE
THAT'S IT. KEEP IT UP, GIRL.
YOU'RE A RESIDENT OF THE POLARIS DORMITORY...
...AND A CHEF THAT FUMIO DAIMIDO HERSELF HAS APPROVED. YOU CAN DO IT.
THE JUDGING WILL BEGIN IN ONLY A FEW MINUTES!
CONTESTANTS, PLEASE BEGIN PLATING YOUR DISHES!
Oooo

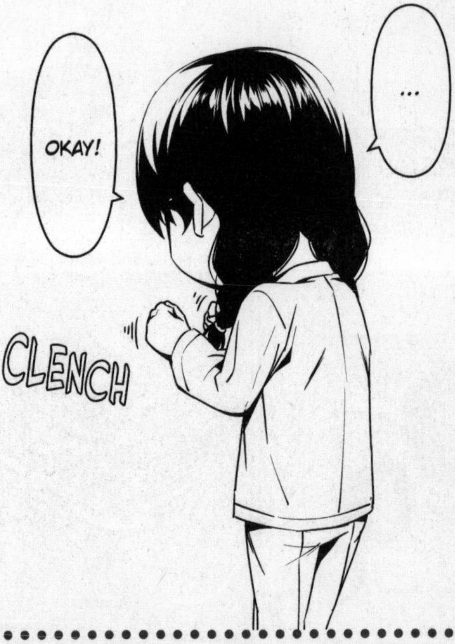
...
OKAY!
CLENCH

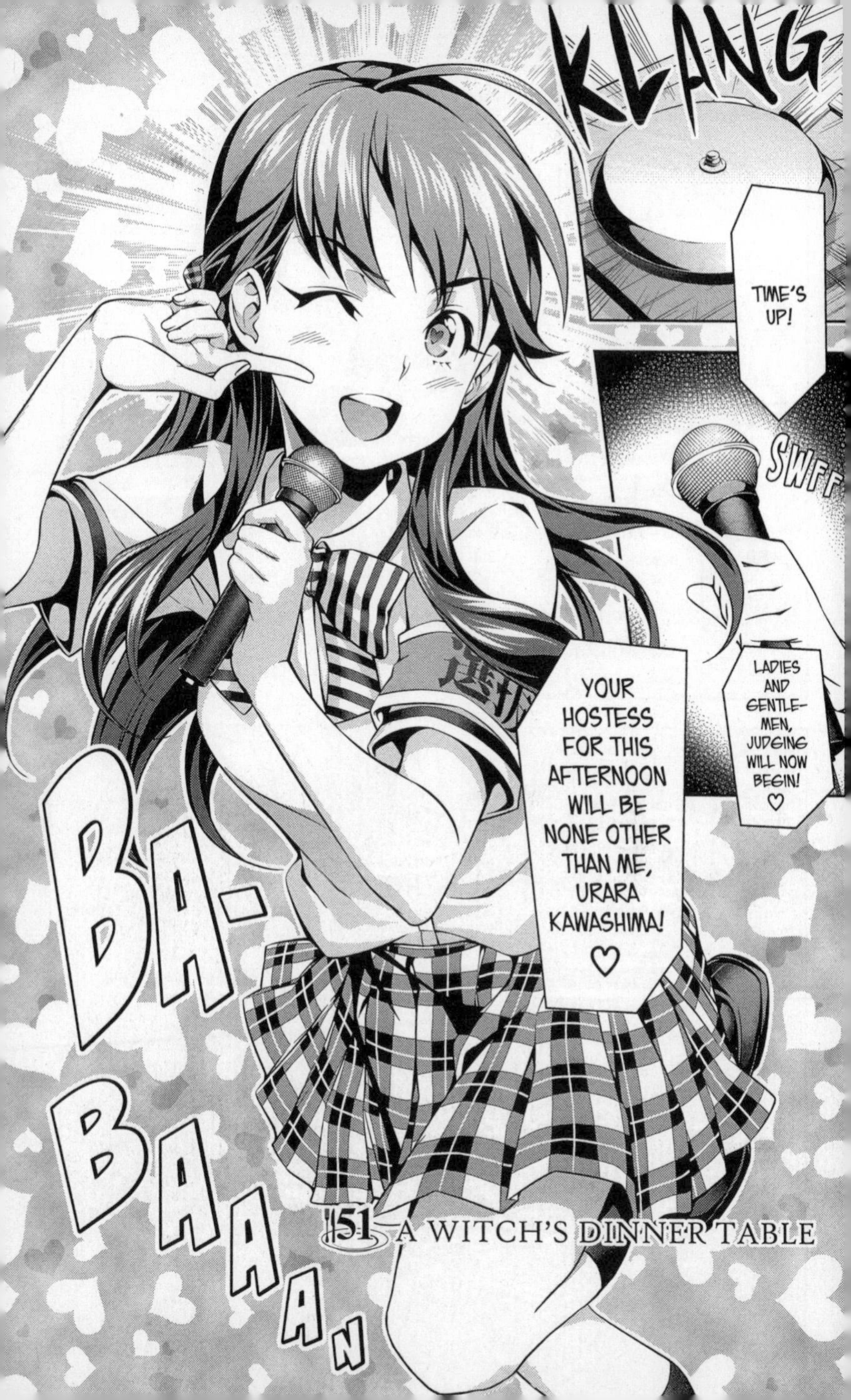
KLANG
TIME'S UP!
SWFF
LADIES AND GENTLE-MEN, JUDGING WILL NOW BEGIN! ♡
YOUR HOSTESS FOR THIS AFTERNOON WILL BE NONE OTHER THAN ME, URARA KAWASHIMA! ♡
BA-BAAAAN

## 51 A WITCH'S DINNER TABLE

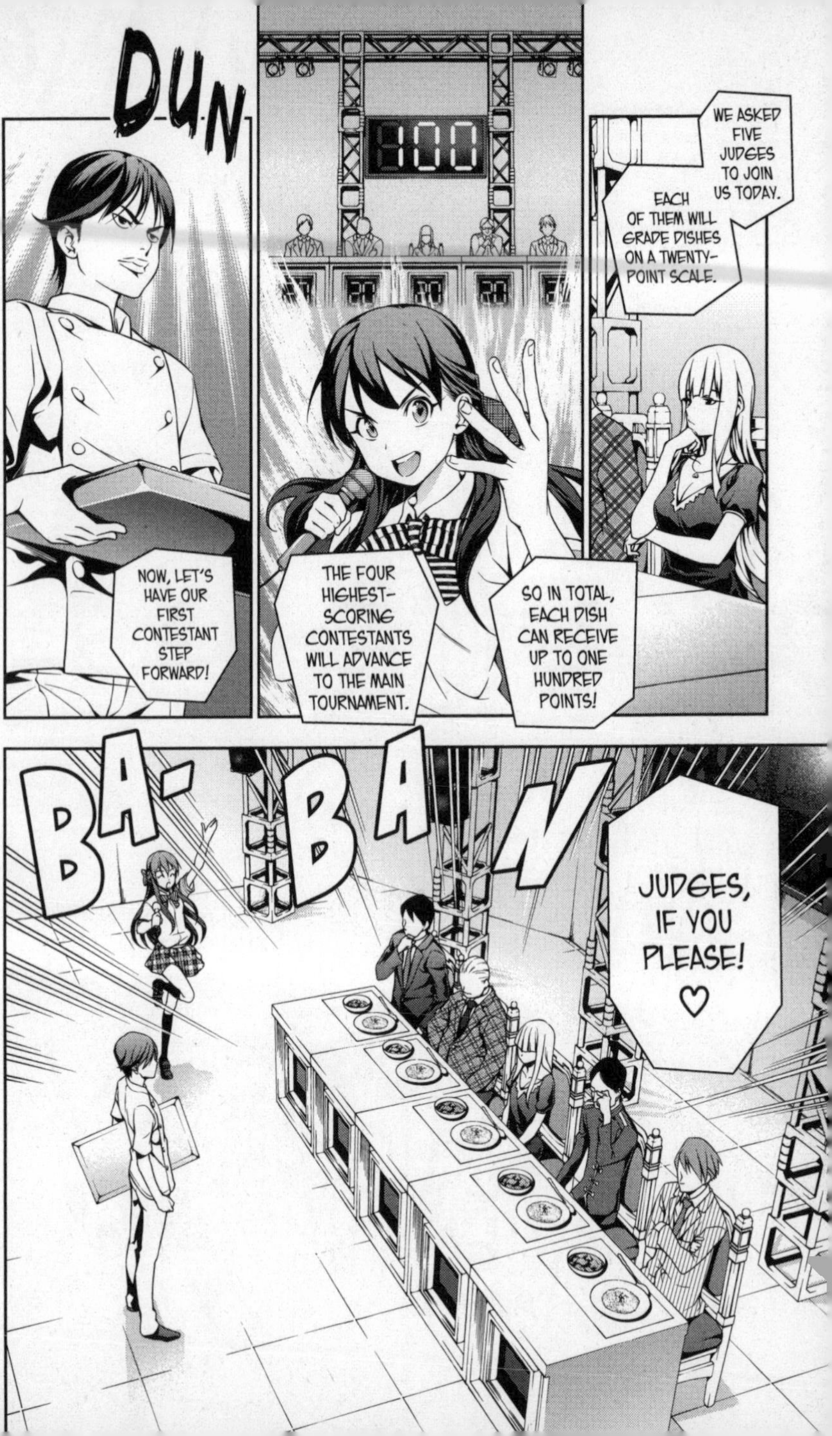
WE ASKED FIVE JUDGES TO JOIN US TODAY.
EACH OF THEM WILL GRADE DISHES ON A TWENTY-POINT SCALE.
100
SO IN TOTAL, EACH DISH CAN RECEIVE UP TO ONE HUNDRED POINTS!
THE FOUR HIGHEST-SCORING CONTESTANTS WILL ADVANCE TO THE MAIN TOURNAMENT.
DUN
NOW, LET'S HAVE OUR FIRST CONTESTANT STEP FORWARD!
JUDGES, IF YOU PLEASE! ♡
BA-BAN

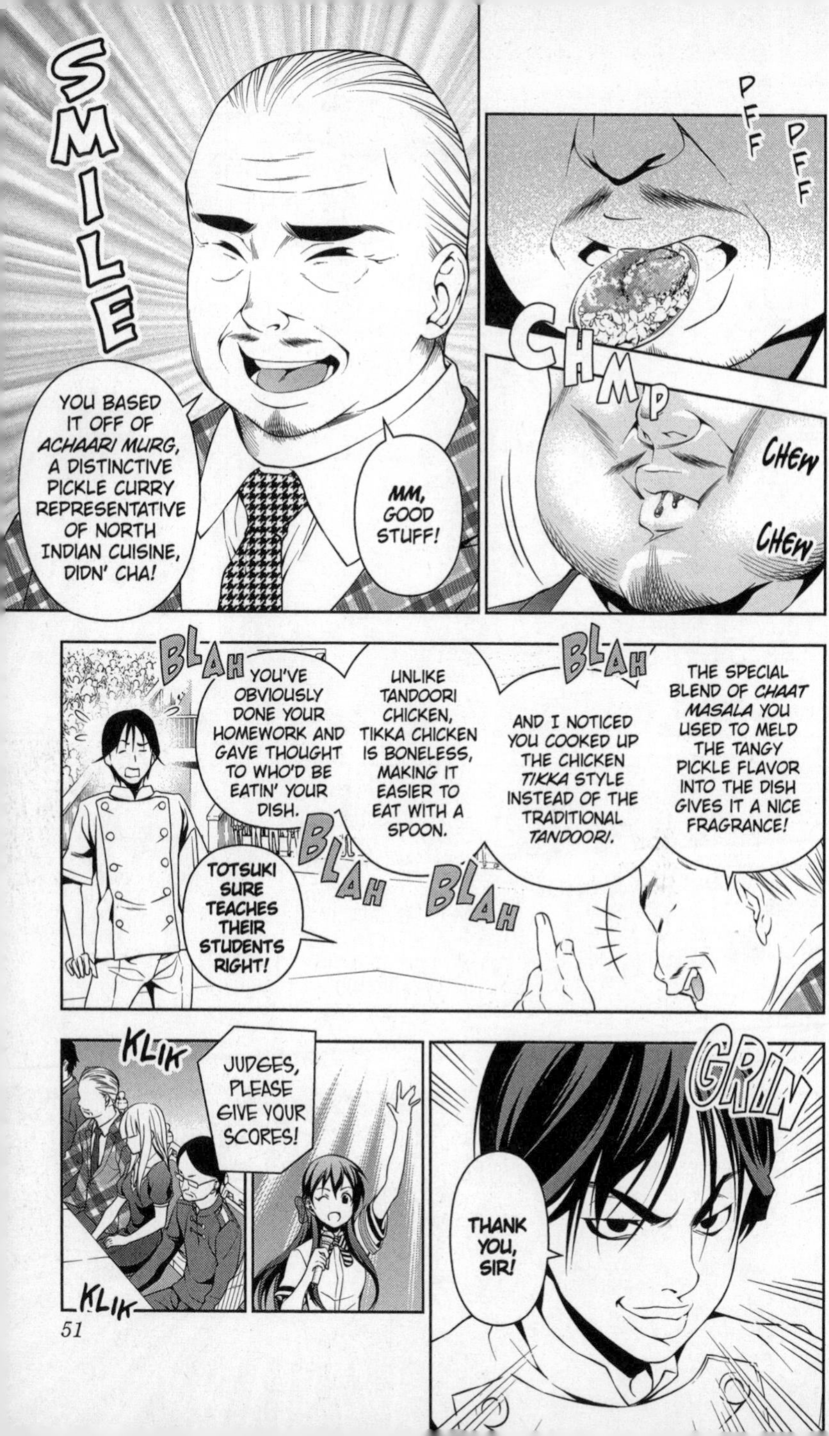

PFF PFF
PFF PFF
CHMP
CHEW
CHEW
SMILE
MM, GOOD STUFF!
YOU BASED IT OFF OF *ACHAARI MURG*, A DISTINCTIVE PICKLE CURRY REPRESENTATIVE OF NORTH INDIAN CUISINE, DIDN' CHA!
BLAH
THE SPECIAL BLEND OF *CHAAT MASALA* YOU USED TO MELD THE TANGY PICKLE FLAVOR INTO THE DISH GIVES IT A NICE FRAGRANCE!
AND I NOTICED YOU COOKED UP THE CHICKEN *TIKKA* STYLE INSTEAD OF THE TRADITIONAL *TANDOORI*.
UNLIKE TANDOORI CHICKEN, TIKKA CHICKEN IS BONELESS, MAKING IT EASIER TO EAT WITH A SPOON.
BLAH
YOU'VE OBVIOUSLY DONE YOUR HOMEWORK AND GAVE THOUGHT TO WHO'D BE EATIN' YOUR DISH.
BLAH
BLAH
TOTSUKI SURE TEACHES THEIR STUDENTS RIGHT!
GRIN
THANK YOU, SIR!
KLIK
JUDGES, PLEASE GIVE YOUR SCORES!
KLIK

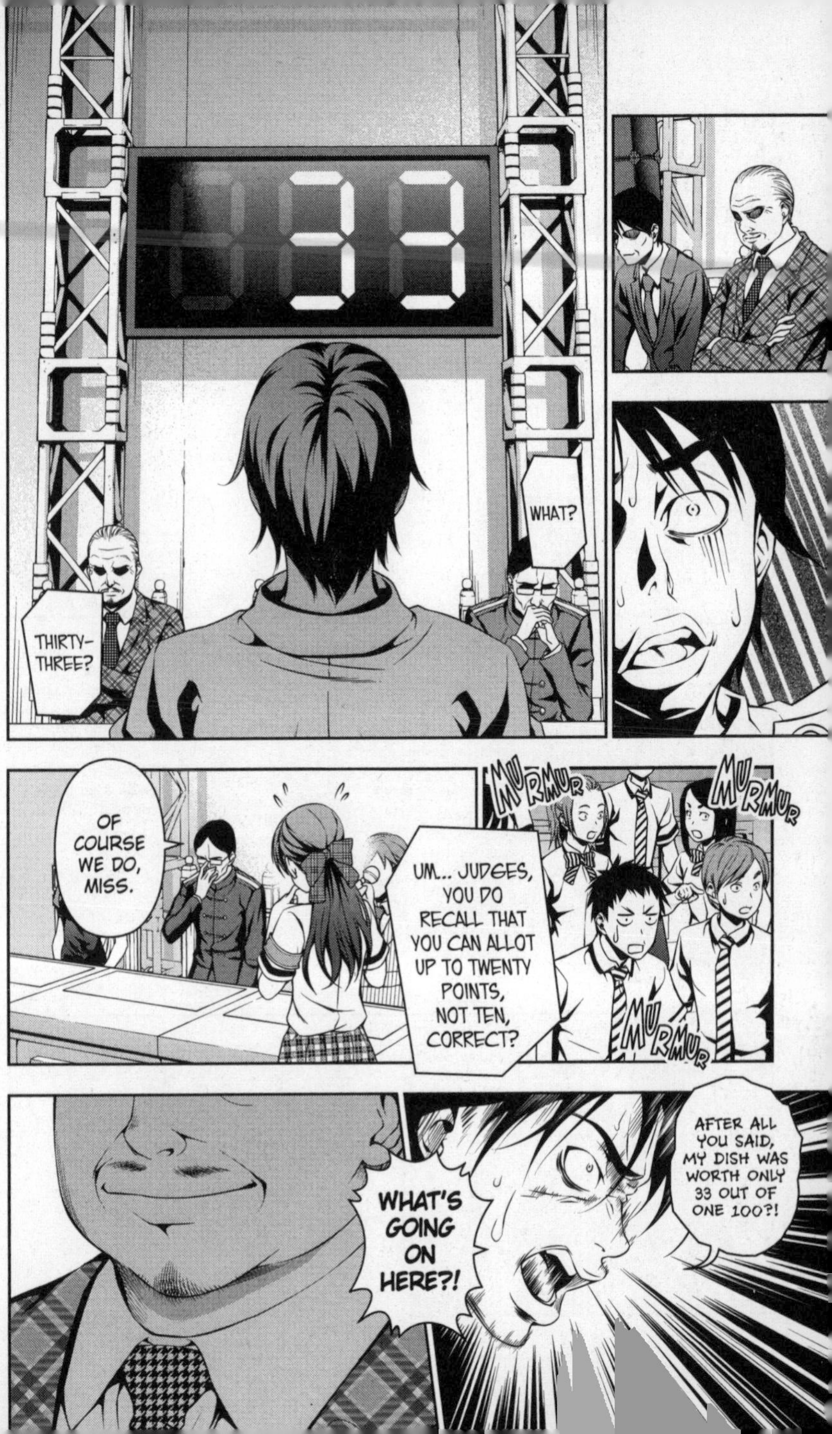

WHAT?
THIRTY-THREE?
MURMUR
MURMUR
MURMUR
UM... JUDGES, YOU DO RECALL THAT YOU CAN ALLOT UP TO TWENTY POINTS, NOT TEN, CORRECT?
OF COURSE WE DO, MISS.
AFTER ALL YOU SAID, MY DISH WAS WORTH ONLY 33 OUT OF ONE 100?!
WHAT'S GOING ON HERE?!

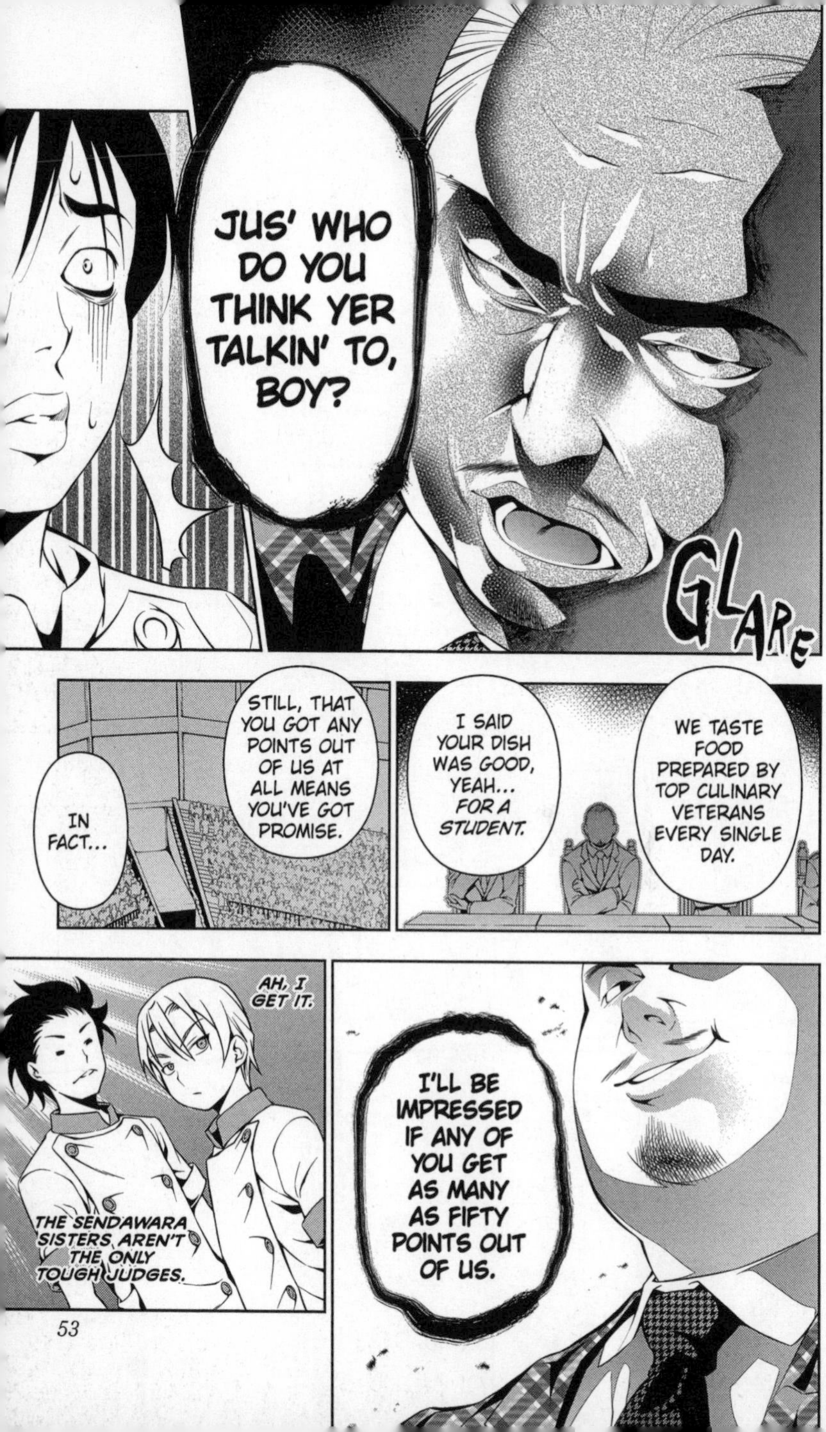
JUS' WHO DO YOU THINK YER TALKIN' TO, BOY?
GLARE
WE TASTE FOOD PREPARED BY TOP CULINARY VETERANS EVERY SINGLE DAY.
I SAID YOUR DISH WAS GOOD, YEAH... FOR A STUDENT.
STILL, THAT YOU GOT ANY POINTS OUT OF US AT ALL MEANS YOU'VE GOT PROMISE.
IN FACT...
I'LL BE IMPRESSED IF ANY OF YOU GET AS MANY AS FIFTY POINTS OUT OF US.
AH, I GET IT.
THE SENDAWARA SISTERS AREN'T THE ONLY TOUGH JUDGES.

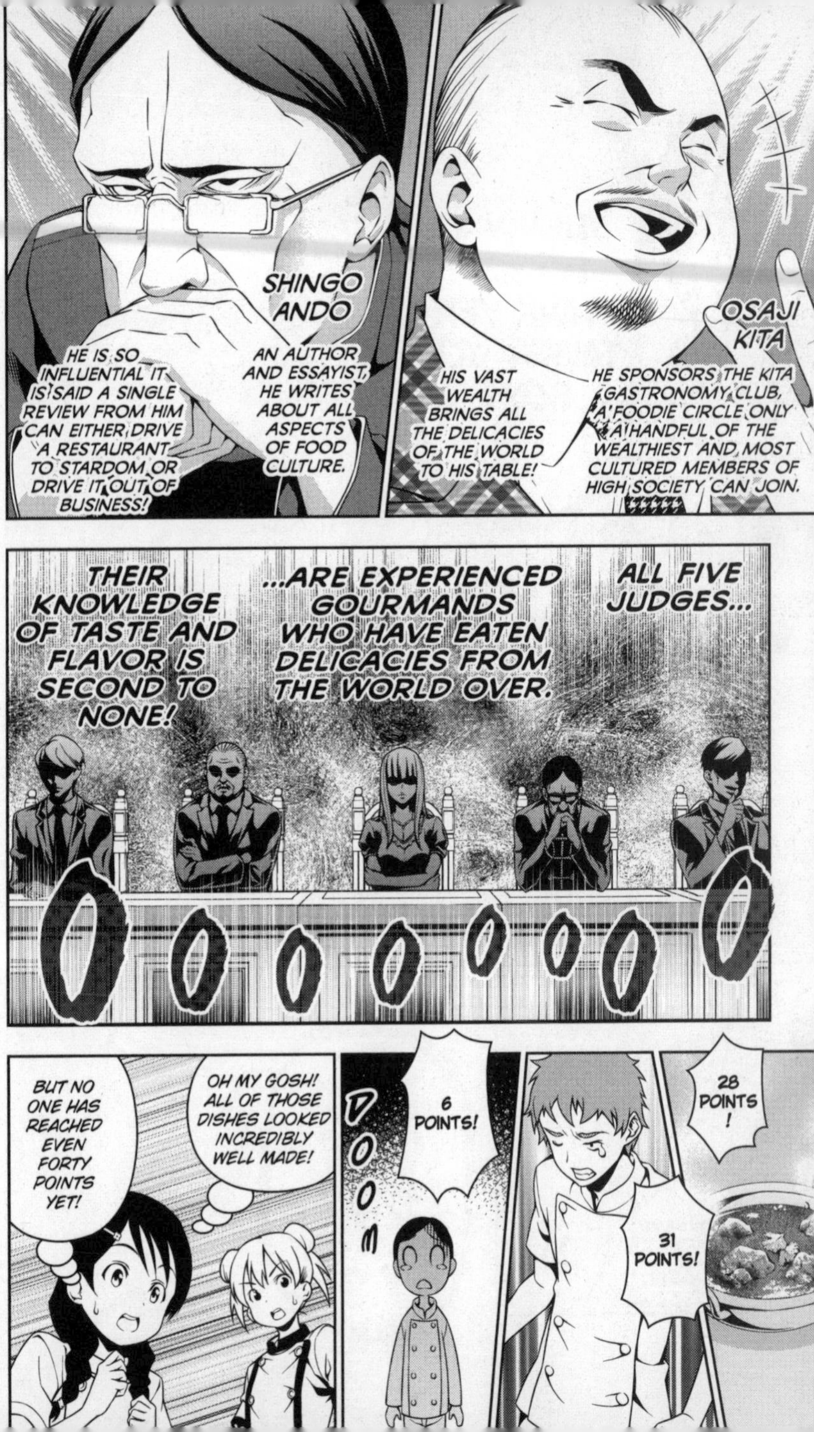
OSAJI KITA
HE SPONSORS THE KITA GASTRONOMY CLUB, A FOODIE CIRCLE ONLY A HANDFUL OF THE WEALTHIEST AND MOST CULTURED MEMBERS OF HIGH SOCIETY CAN JOIN.
HIS VAST WEALTH BRINGS ALL THE DELICACIES OF THE WORLD TO HIS TABLE!
SHINGO ANDO
AN AUTHOR AND ESSAYIST, HE WRITES ABOUT ALL ASPECTS OF FOOD CULTURE.
HE IS SO INFLUENTIAL IT IS SAID A SINGLE REVIEW FROM HIM CAN EITHER DRIVE A RESTAURANT TO STARDOM OR DRIVE IT OUT OF BUSINESS!
ALL FIVE JUDGES...
...ARE EXPERIENCED GOURMANDS WHO HAVE EATEN DELICACIES FROM THE WORLD OVER.
THEIR KNOWLEDGE OF TASTE AND FLAVOR IS SECOND TO NONE!
28 POINTS!
31 POINTS!
6 POINTS!
DOOM
OH MY GOSH! ALL OF THOSE DISHES LOOKED INCREDIBLY WELL MADE!
BUT NO ONE HAS REACHED EVEN FORTY POINTS YET!

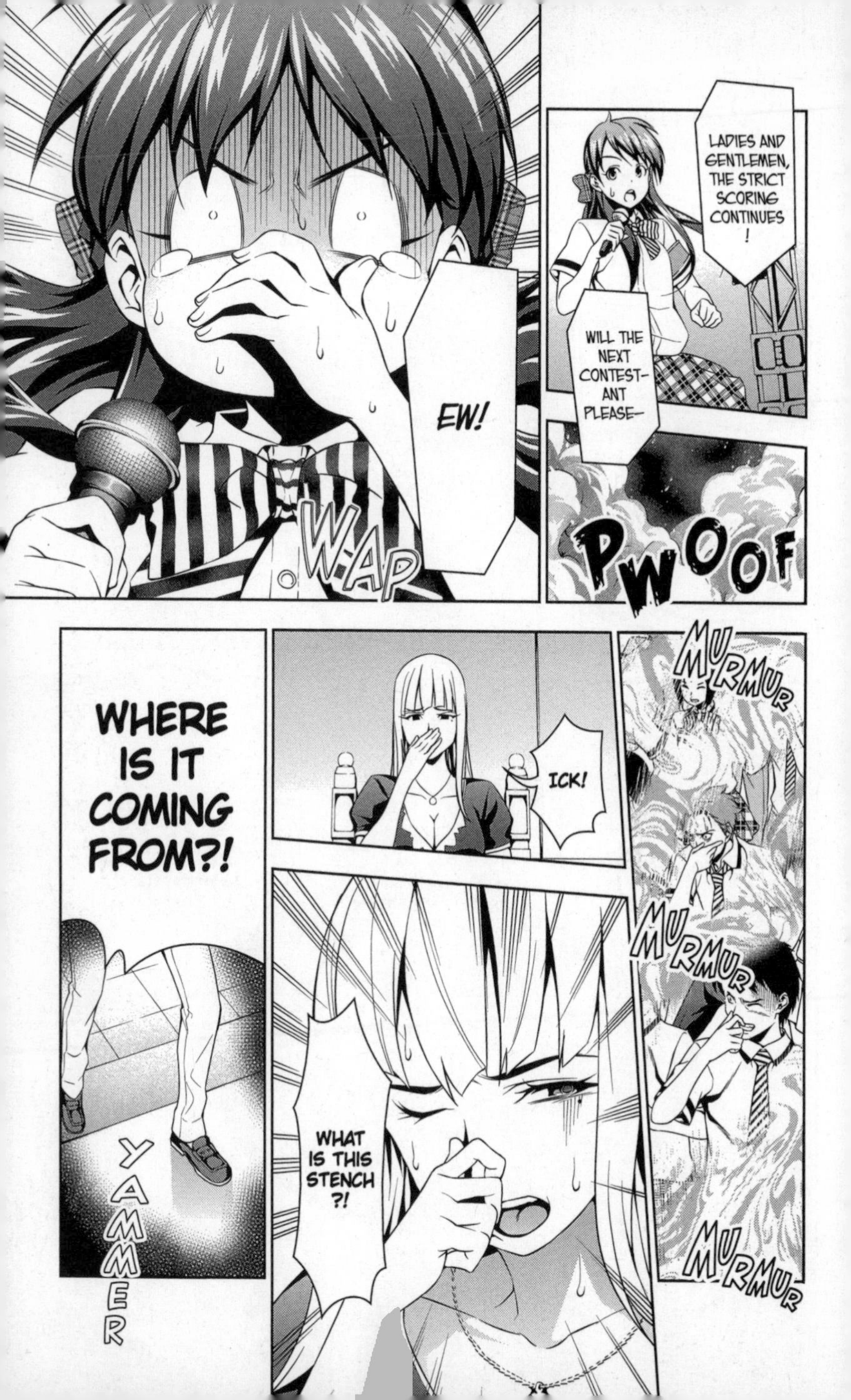
LADIES AND GENTLEMEN, THE STRICT SCORING CONTINUES!
WILL THE NEXT CONTEST-ANT PLEASE—
PWOOF
EW!
WAP
MURMUR
MURMUR
MURMUR
ICK!
WHAT IS THIS STENCH?!
WHERE IS IT COMING FROM?!
YAMMER

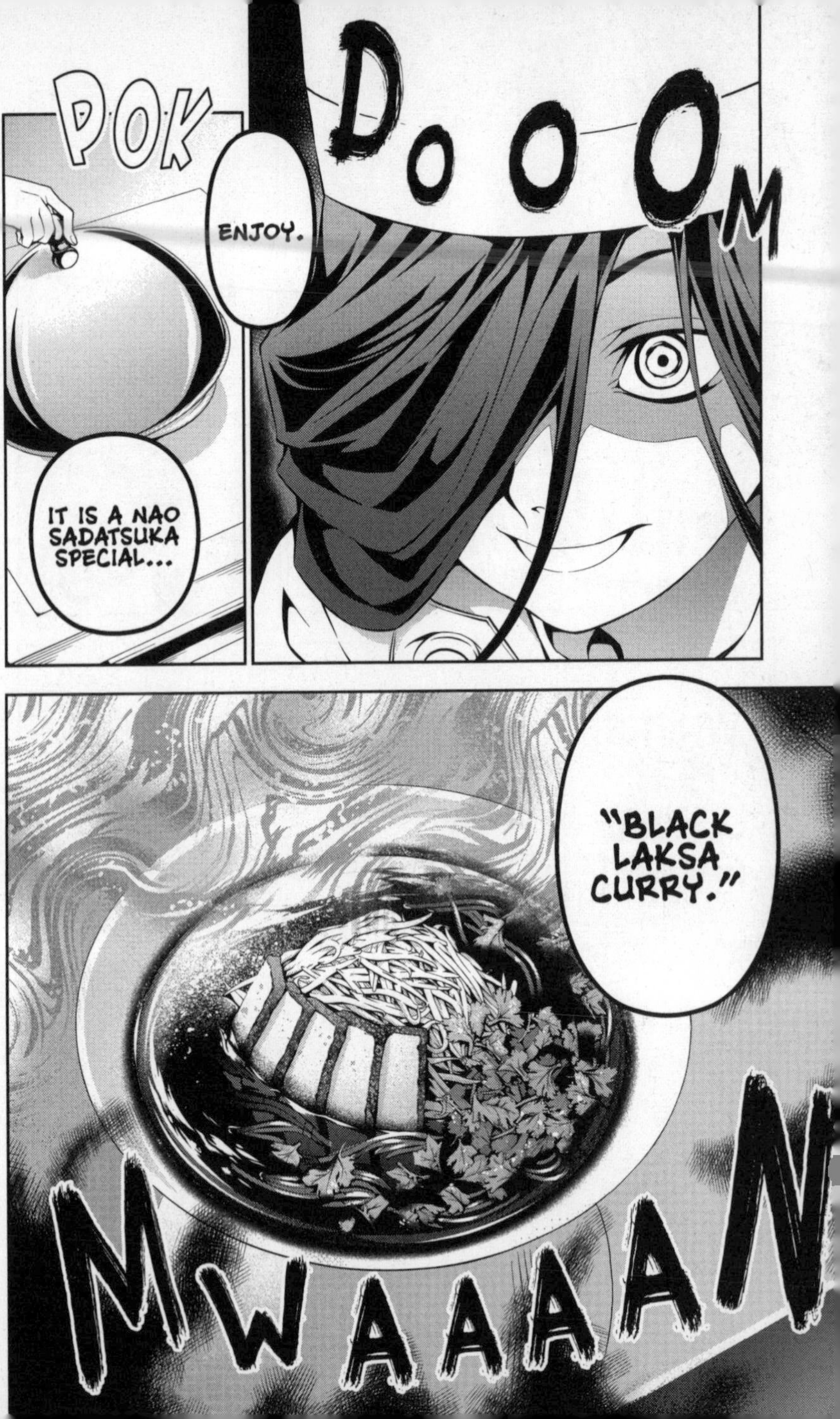
DOOOM
ENJOY.
POK
IT IS A NAO SADATSUKA SPECIAL...
"BLACK LAKSA CURRY."
MWAAAAN

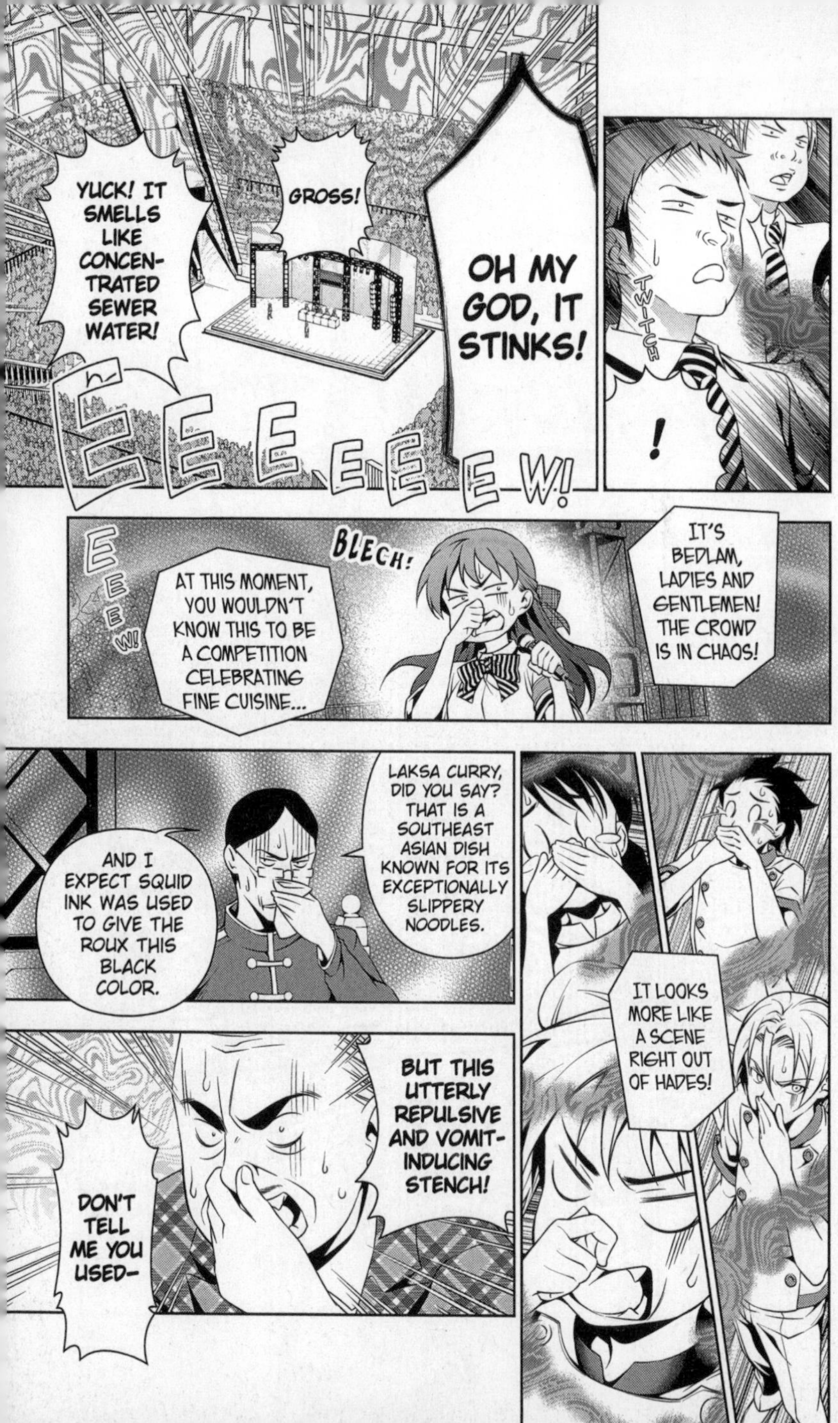
TWITCH
!
OH MY GOD, IT STINKS!
GROSS!
YUCK! IT SMELLS LIKE CONCEN-TRATED SEWER WATER!
EEEEEEEEW!
IT'S BEDLAM, LADIES AND GENTLEMEN! THE CROWD IS IN CHAOS!
BLECH!
AT THIS MOMENT, YOU WOULDN'T KNOW THIS TO BE A COMPETITION CELEBRATING FINE CUISINE...
EEEEW!
IT LOOKS MORE LIKE A SCENE RIGHT OUT OF HADES!
LAKSA CURRY, DID YOU SAY? THAT IS A SOUTHEAST ASIAN DISH KNOWN FOR ITS EXCEPTIONALLY SLIPPERY NOODLES.
AND I EXPECT SQUID INK WAS USED TO GIVE THE ROUX THIS BLACK COLOR.
BUT THIS UTTERLY REPULSIVE AND VOMIT-INDUCING STENCH!
DON'T TELL ME YOU USED—

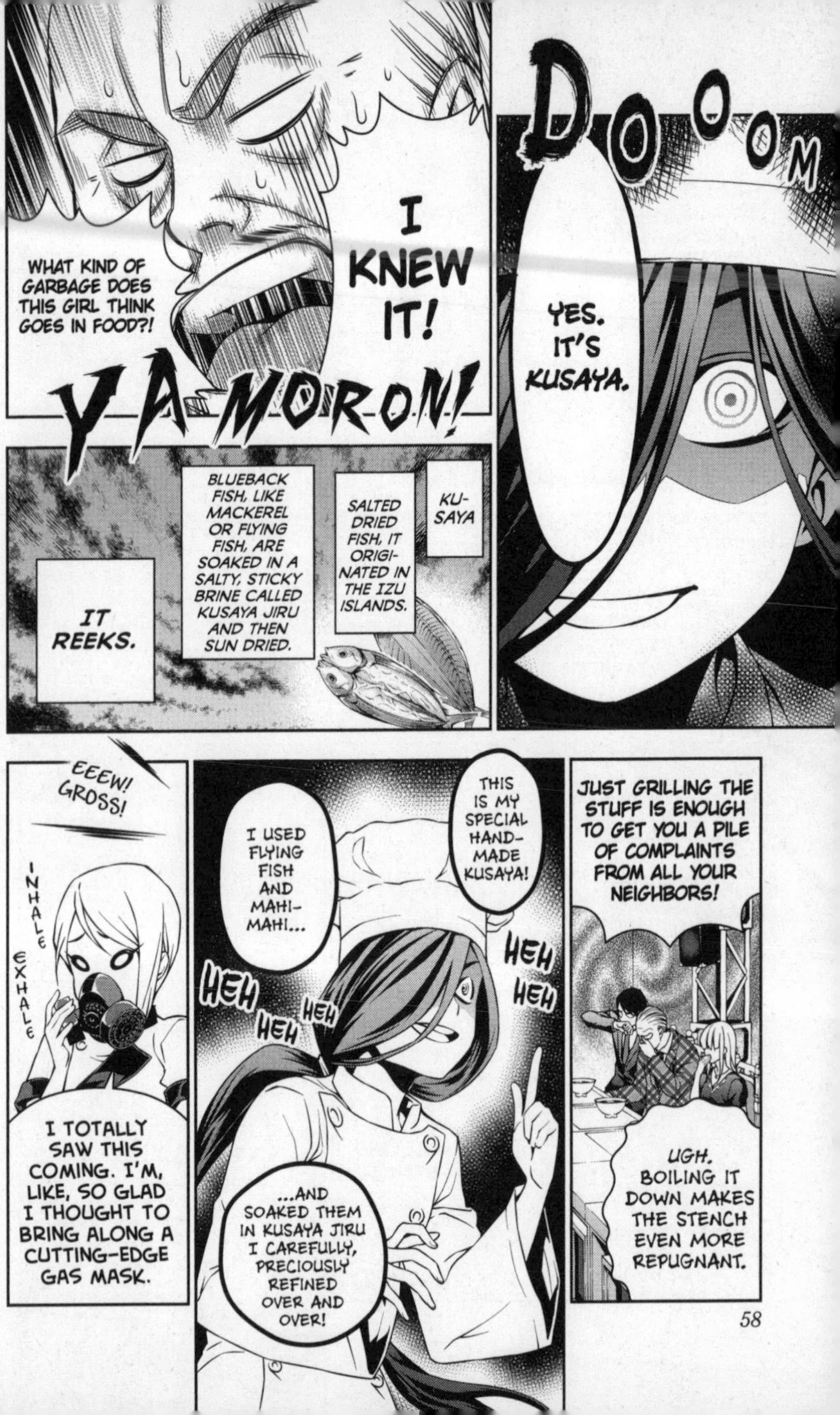
DOOOOM
YES. IT'S KUSAYA.
I KNEW IT!
WHAT KIND OF GARBAGE DOES THIS GIRL THINK GOES IN FOOD?!
YA MORON!
KU-SAYA
SALTED DRIED FISH, IT ORIGINATED IN THE IZU ISLANDS.
BLUEBACK FISH, LIKE MACKEREL OR FLYING FISH, ARE SOAKED IN A SALTY, STICKY BRINE CALLED KUSAYA JIRU AND THEN SUN DRIED.
IT REEKS.
JUST GRILLING THE STUFF IS ENOUGH TO GET YOU A PILE OF COMPLAINTS FROM ALL YOUR NEIGHBORS!
UGH. BOILING IT DOWN MAKES THE STENCH EVEN MORE REPUGNANT.
THIS IS MY SPECIAL HAND-MADE KUSAYA!
HEH HEH
I USED FLYING FISH AND MAHI-MAHI...
HEH HEH HEH
...AND SOAKED THEM IN KUSAYA JIRU I CAREFULLY, PRECIOUSLY REFINED OVER AND OVER!
EEEW! GROSS!
INHALE
EXHALE
I TOTALLY SAW THIS COMING. I'M, LIKE, SO GLAD I THOUGHT TO BRING ALONG A CUTTING-EDGE GAS MASK.

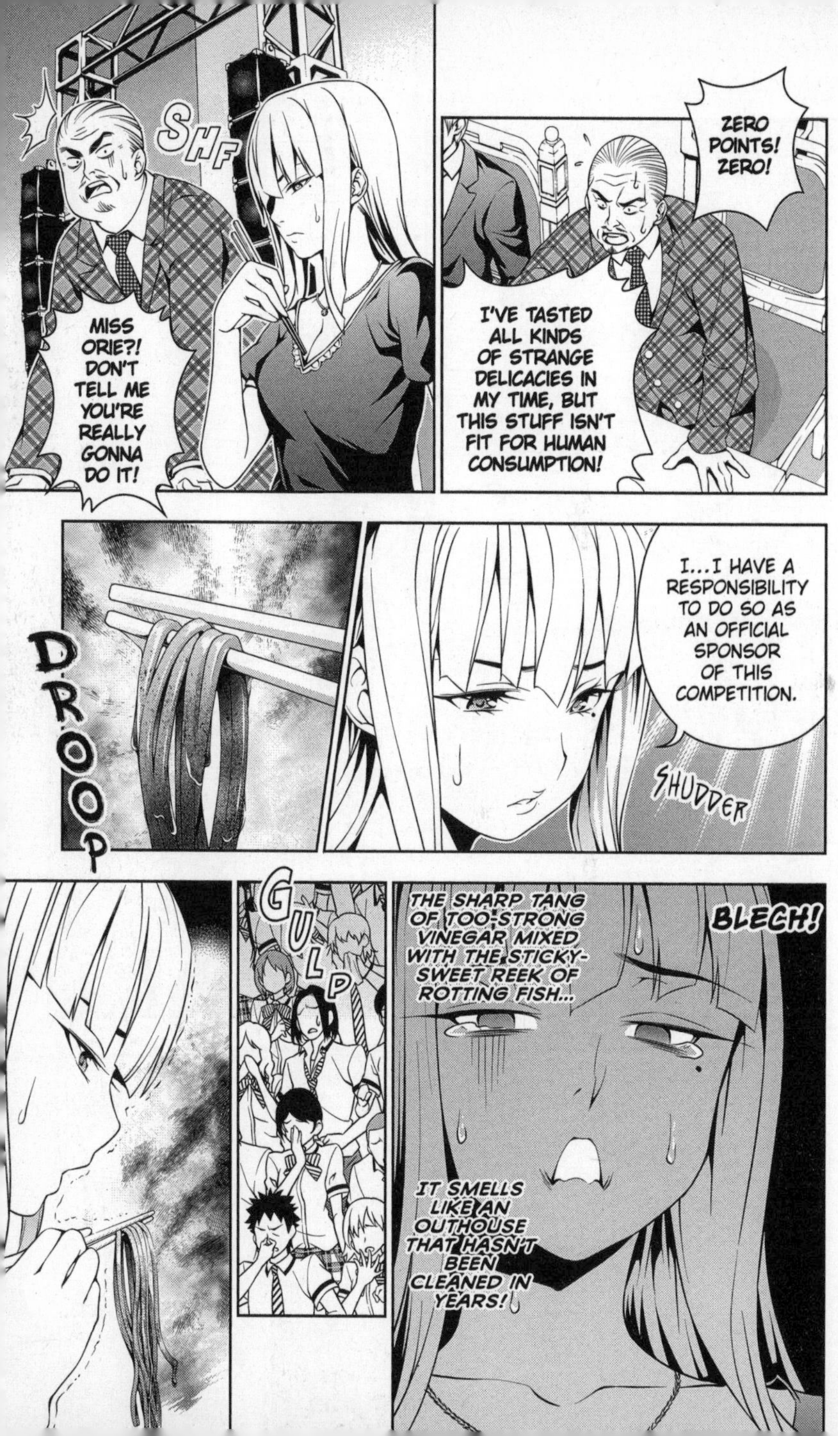
ZERO POINTS! ZERO!
I'VE TASTED ALL KINDS OF STRANGE DELICACIES IN MY TIME, BUT THIS STUFF ISN'T FIT FOR HUMAN CONSUMPTION!
SHF
MISS ORIE?! DON'T TELL ME YOU'RE REALLY GONNA DO IT!
I...I HAVE A RESPONSIBILITY TO DO SO AS AN OFFICIAL SPONSOR OF THIS COMPETITION.
SHUDDER
DROOP
BLECH!
THE SHARP TANG OF TOO-STRONG VINEGAR MIXED WITH THE STICKY-SWEET REEK OF ROTTING FISH...
IT SMELLS LIKE AN OUTHOUSE THAT HASN'T BEEN CLEANED IN YEARS!
GULP

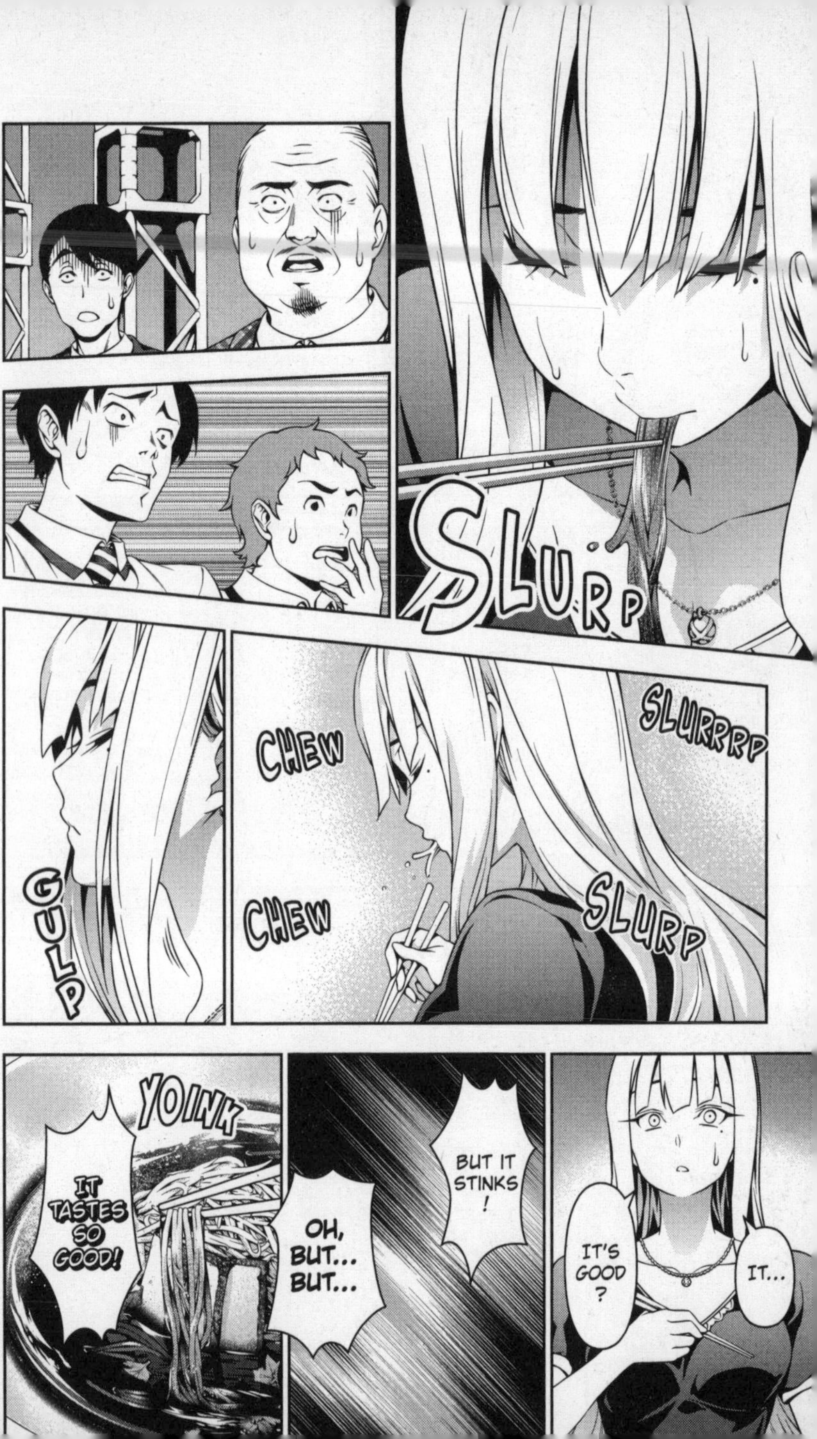
SLURP
SLURRRP
SLURP
CHEW
CHEW
GULP
IT...
IT'S GOOD?
BUT IT STINKS!
OH, BUT... BUT...
YOINK
IT TASTES SO GOOD!

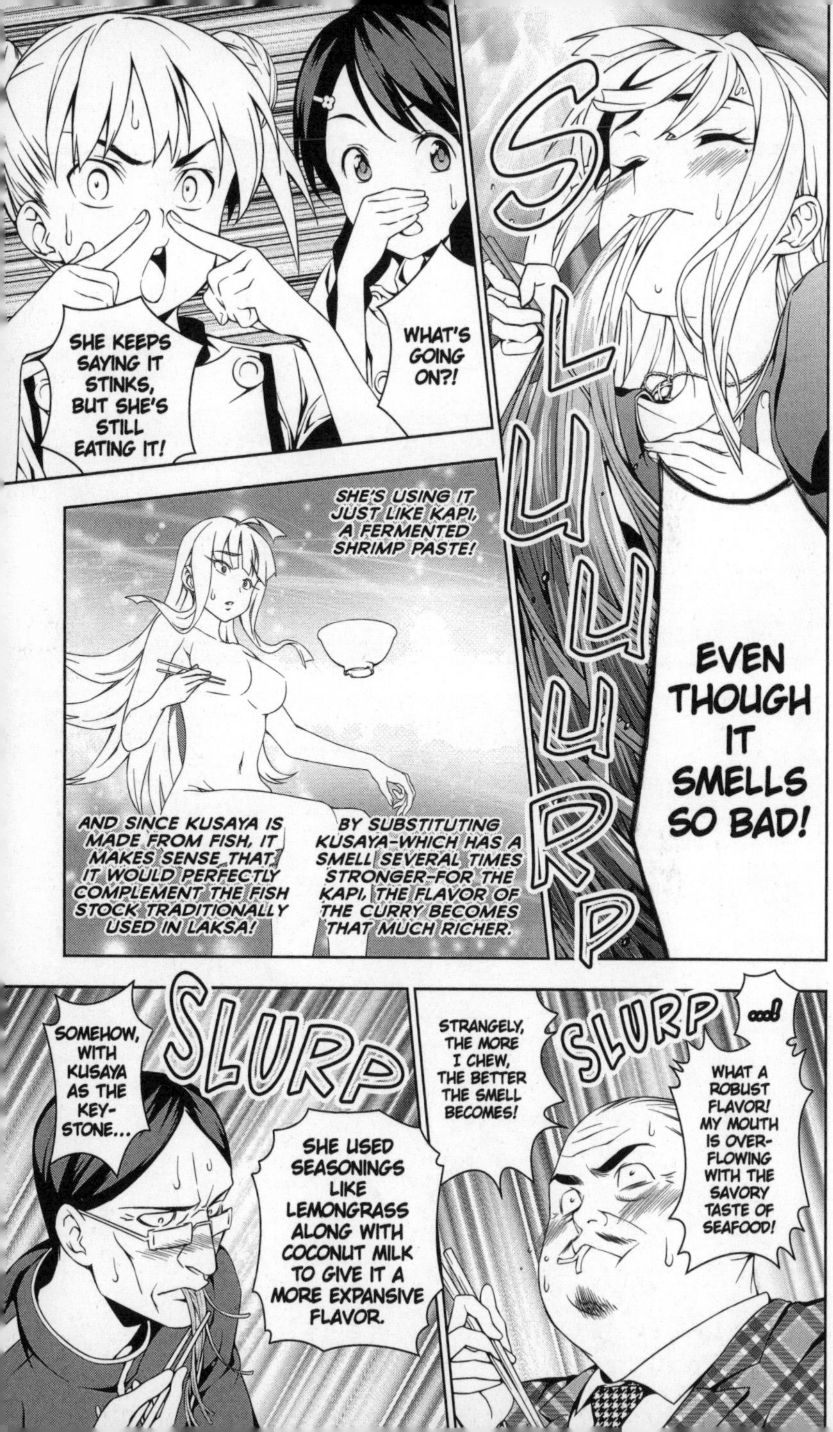
SLUUURP
EVEN THOUGH IT SMELLS SO BAD!
WHAT'S GOING ON?!
SHE KEEPS SAYING IT STINKS, BUT SHE'S STILL EATING IT!
SHE'S USING IT JUST LIKE KAPI, A FERMENTED SHRIMP PASTE!
BY SUBSTITUTING KUSAYA—WHICH HAS A SMELL SEVERAL TIMES STRONGER—FOR THE KAPI, THE FLAVOR OF THE CURRY BECOMES THAT MUCH RICHER.
AND SINCE KUSAYA IS MADE FROM FISH, IT MAKES SENSE THAT IT WOULD PERFECTLY COMPLEMENT THE FISH STOCK TRADITIONALLY USED IN LAKSA!
SLURP
...!
WHAT A ROBUST FLAVOR! MY MOUTH IS OVER-FLOWING WITH THE SAVORY TASTE OF SEAFOOD!
STRANGELY, THE MORE I CHEW, THE BETTER THE SMELL BECOMES!
SLURP
SOMEHOW, WITH KUSAYA AS THE KEY-STONE...
SHE USED SEASONINGS LIKE LEMONGRASS ALONG WITH COCONUT MILK TO GIVE IT A MORE EXPANSIVE FLAVOR.

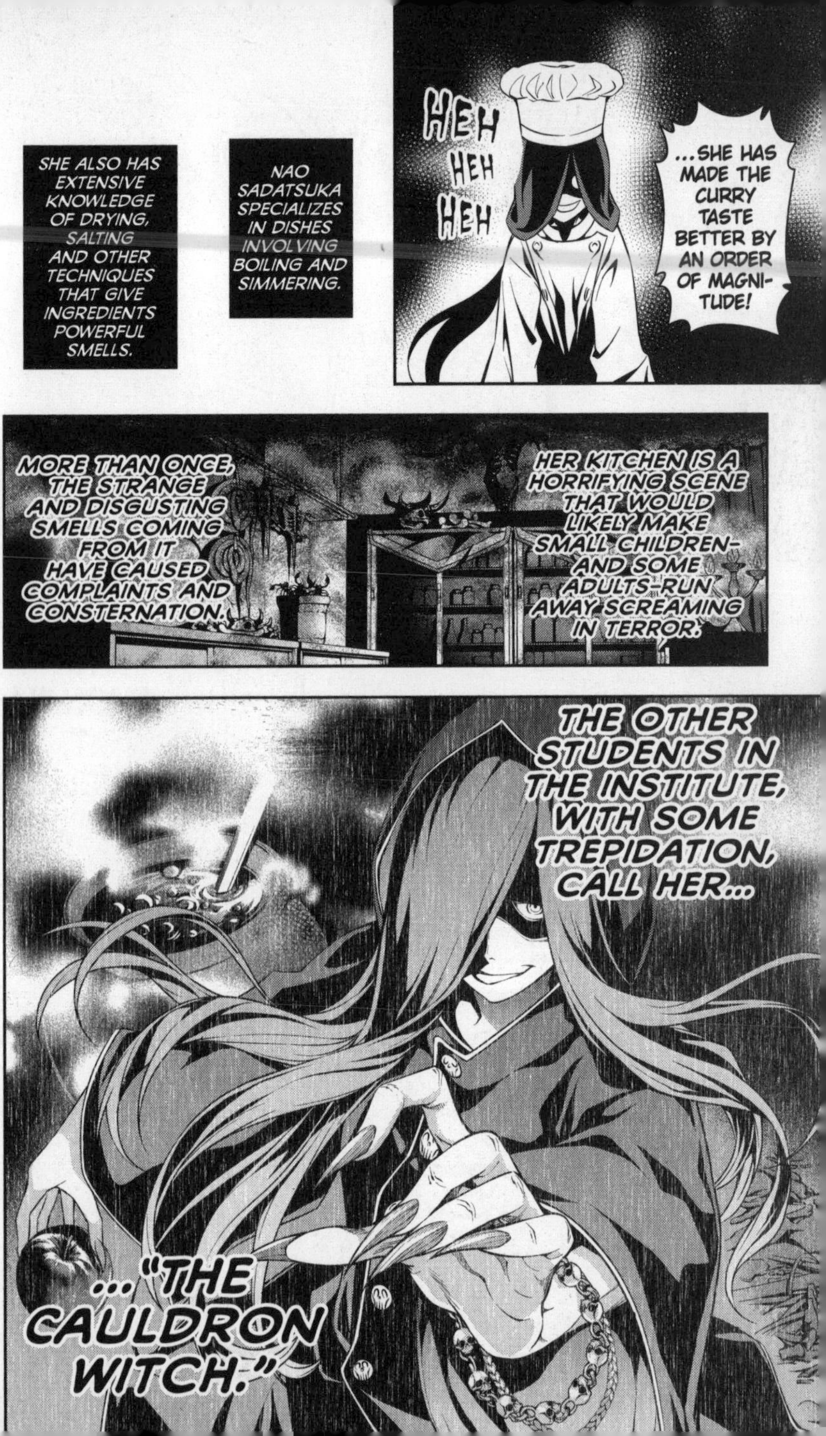
...SHE HAS MADE THE CURRY TASTE BETTER BY AN ORDER OF MAGNITUDE!
HEH HEH HEH
NAO SADATSUKA SPECIALIZES IN DISHES INVOLVING BOILING AND SIMMERING.
SHE ALSO HAS EXTENSIVE KNOWLEDGE OF DRYING, SALTING AND OTHER TECHNIQUES THAT GIVE INGREDIENTS POWERFUL SMELLS.
HER KITCHEN IS A HORRIFYING SCENE THAT WOULD LIKELY MAKE SMALL CHILDREN-AND SOME ADULTS-RUN AWAY SCREAMING IN TERROR.
MORE THAN ONCE, THE STRANGE AND DISGUSTING SMELLS COMING FROM IT HAVE CAUSED COMPLAINTS AND CONSTERNATION.
THE OTHER STUDENTS IN THE INSTITUTE, WITH SOME TREPIDATION, CALL HER...
..."THE CAULDRON WITCH."

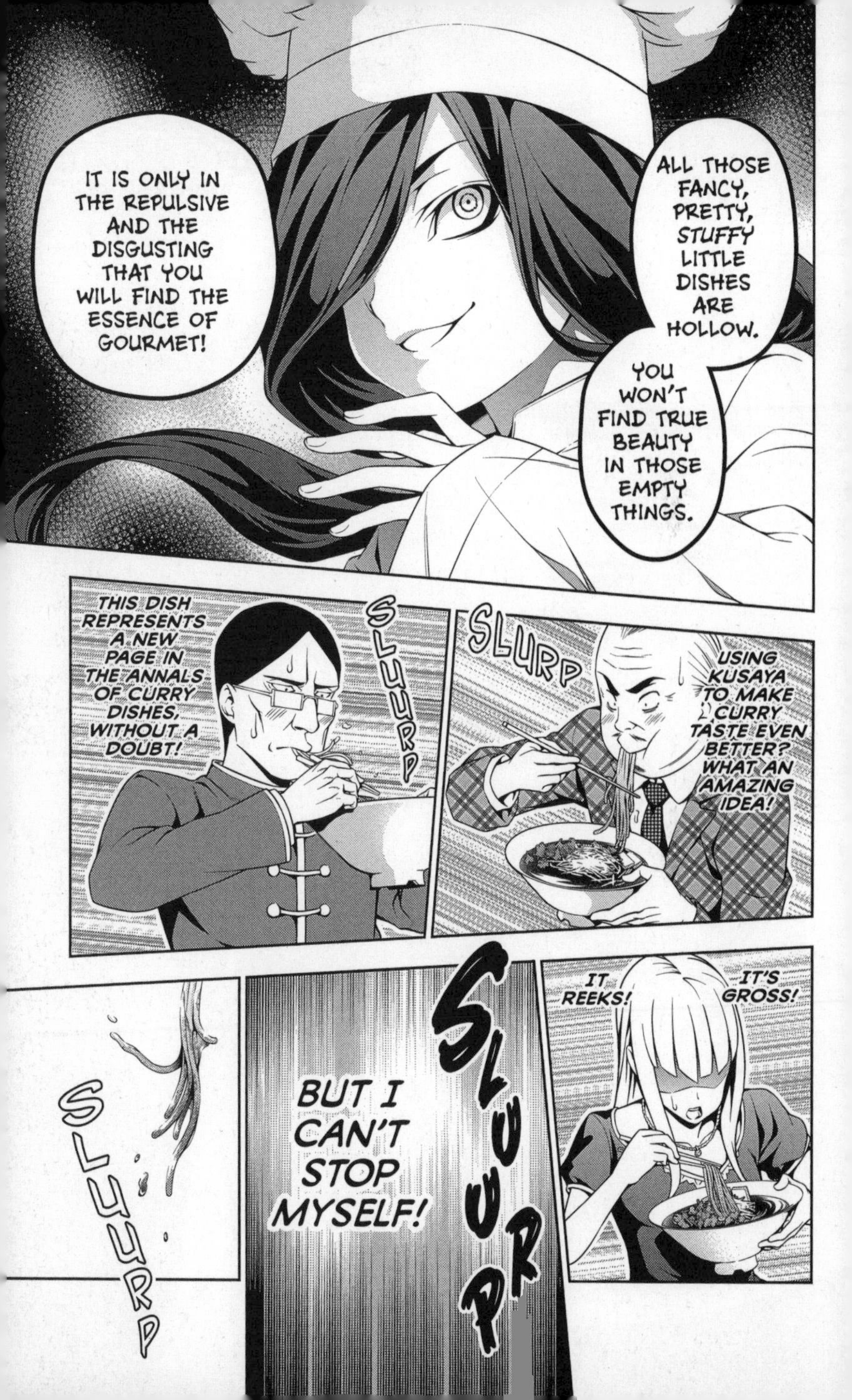
ALL THOSE FANCY, PRETTY, STUFFY LITTLE DISHES ARE HOLLOW.
YOU WON'T FIND TRUE BEAUTY IN THOSE EMPTY THINGS.
IT IS ONLY IN THE REPULSIVE AND THE DISGUSTING THAT YOU WILL FIND THE ESSENCE OF GOURMET!
SLURP
USING KUSAYA TO MAKE CURRY TASTE EVEN BETTER? WHAT AN AMAZING IDEA!
SLUURP
THIS DISH REPRESENTS A NEW PAGE IN THE ANNALS OF CURRY DISHES, WITHOUT A DOUBT!
IT'S GROSS!
IT REEKS!
SLUURP
BUT I CAN'T STOP MYSELF!
SLUURP

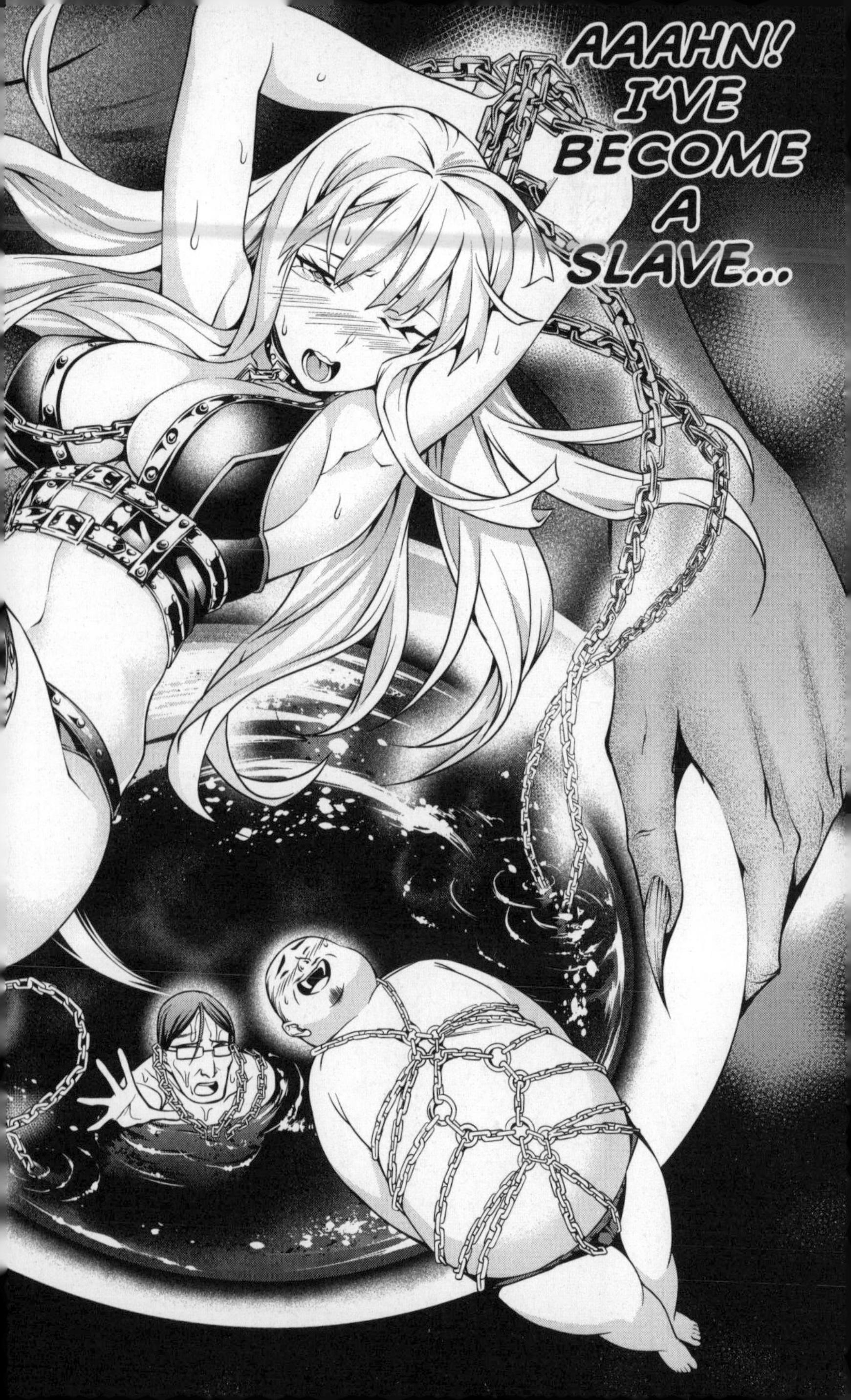
AAAHN! I'VE BECOME A SLAVE...

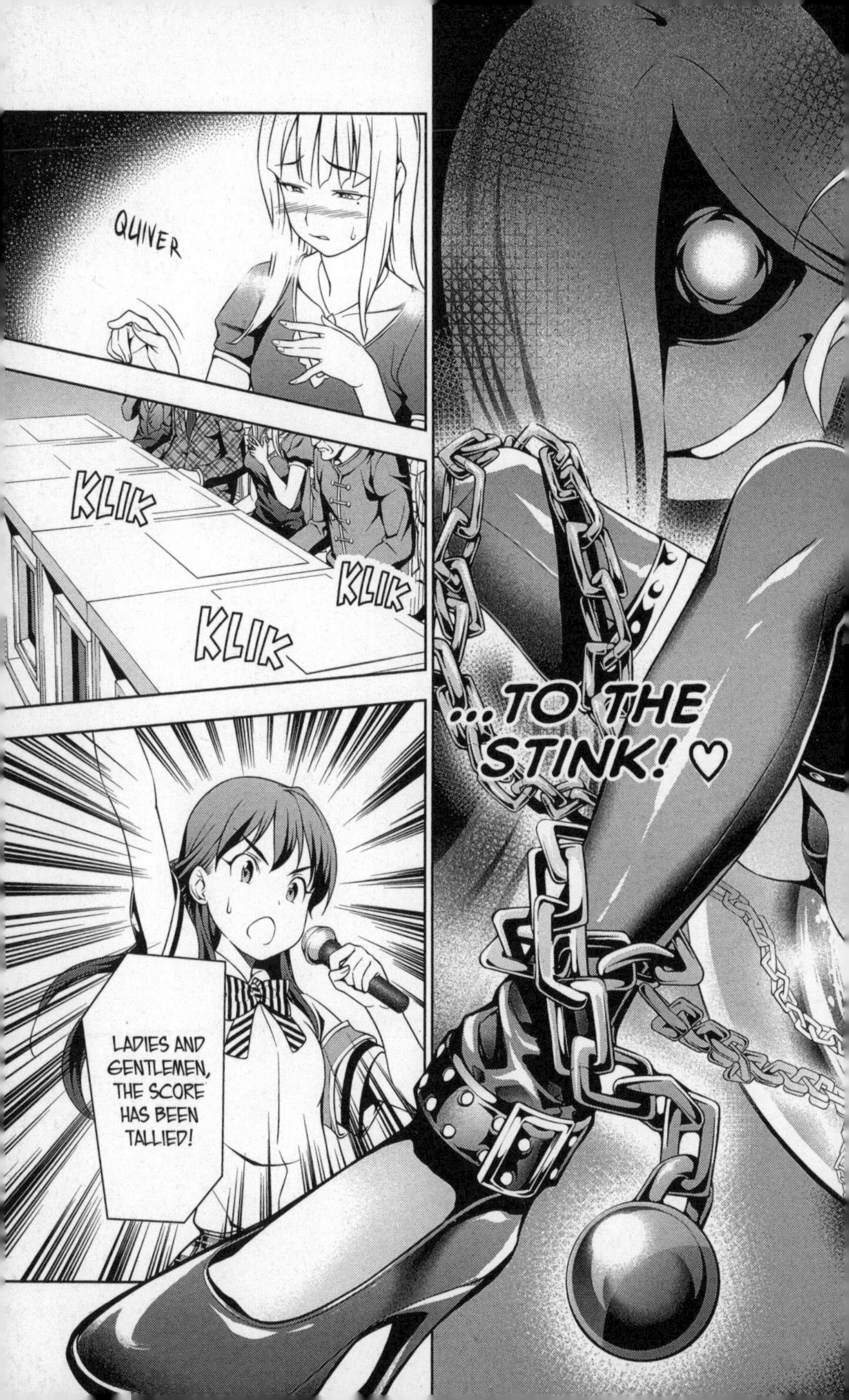
...TO THE STINK! ♥
QUIVER
KLIK
KLIK
KLIK
LADIES AND GENTLEMEN, THE SCORE HAS BEEN TALLIED!

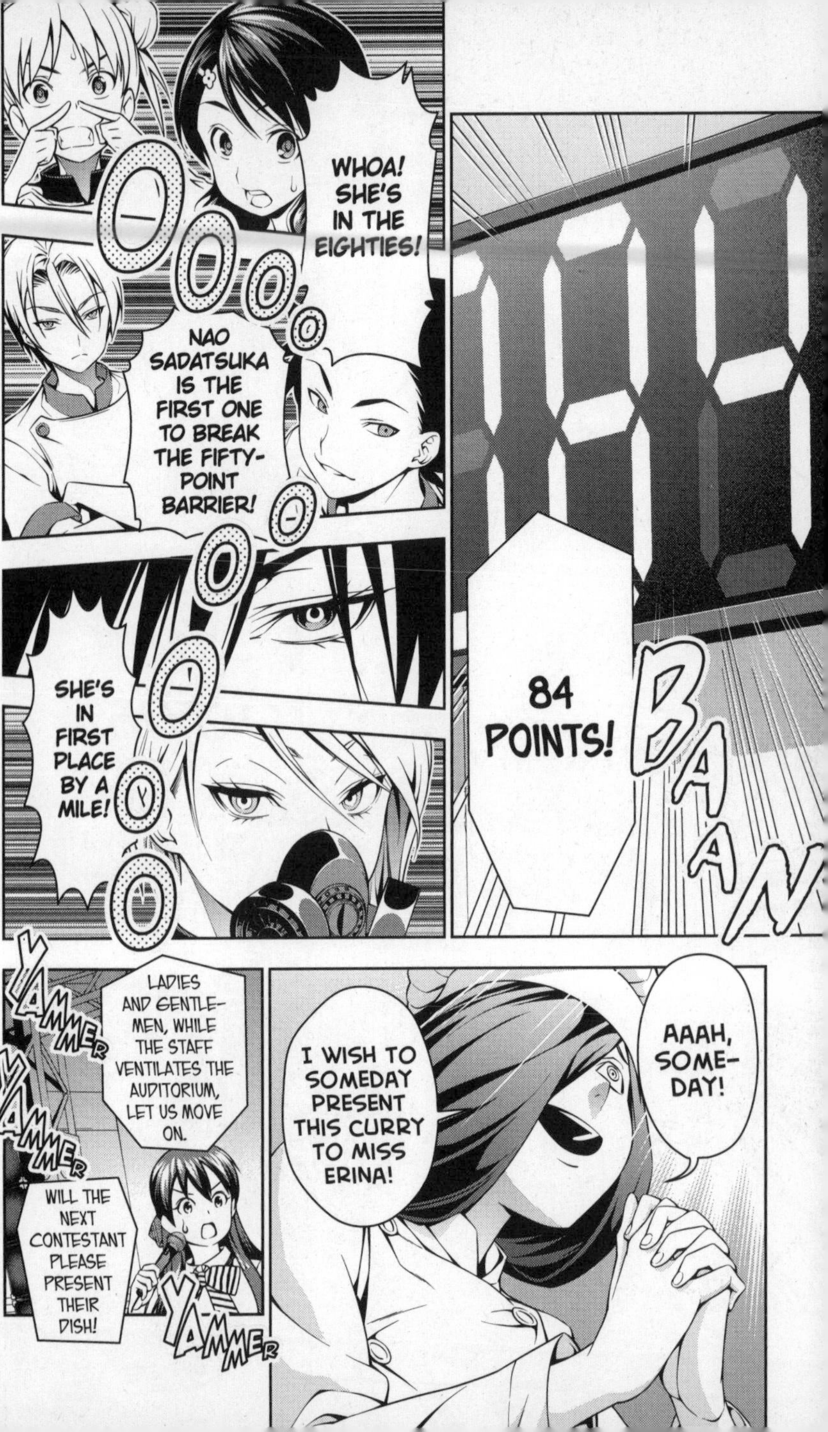
84 POINTS!
BAAAN
WHOA! SHE'S IN THE EIGHTIES!
NAO SADATSUKA IS THE FIRST ONE TO BREAK THE FIFTY-POINT BARRIER!
SHE'S IN FIRST PLACE BY A MILE!
AAAH, SOME-DAY!
I WISH TO SOMEDAY PRESENT THIS CURRY TO MISS ERINA!
YAMMER
YAMMER
LADIES AND GENTLE-MEN, WHILE THE STAFF VENTILATES THE AUDITORIUM, LET US MOVE ON.
WILL THE NEXT CONTESTANT PLEASE PRESENT THEIR DISH!
YAMMER

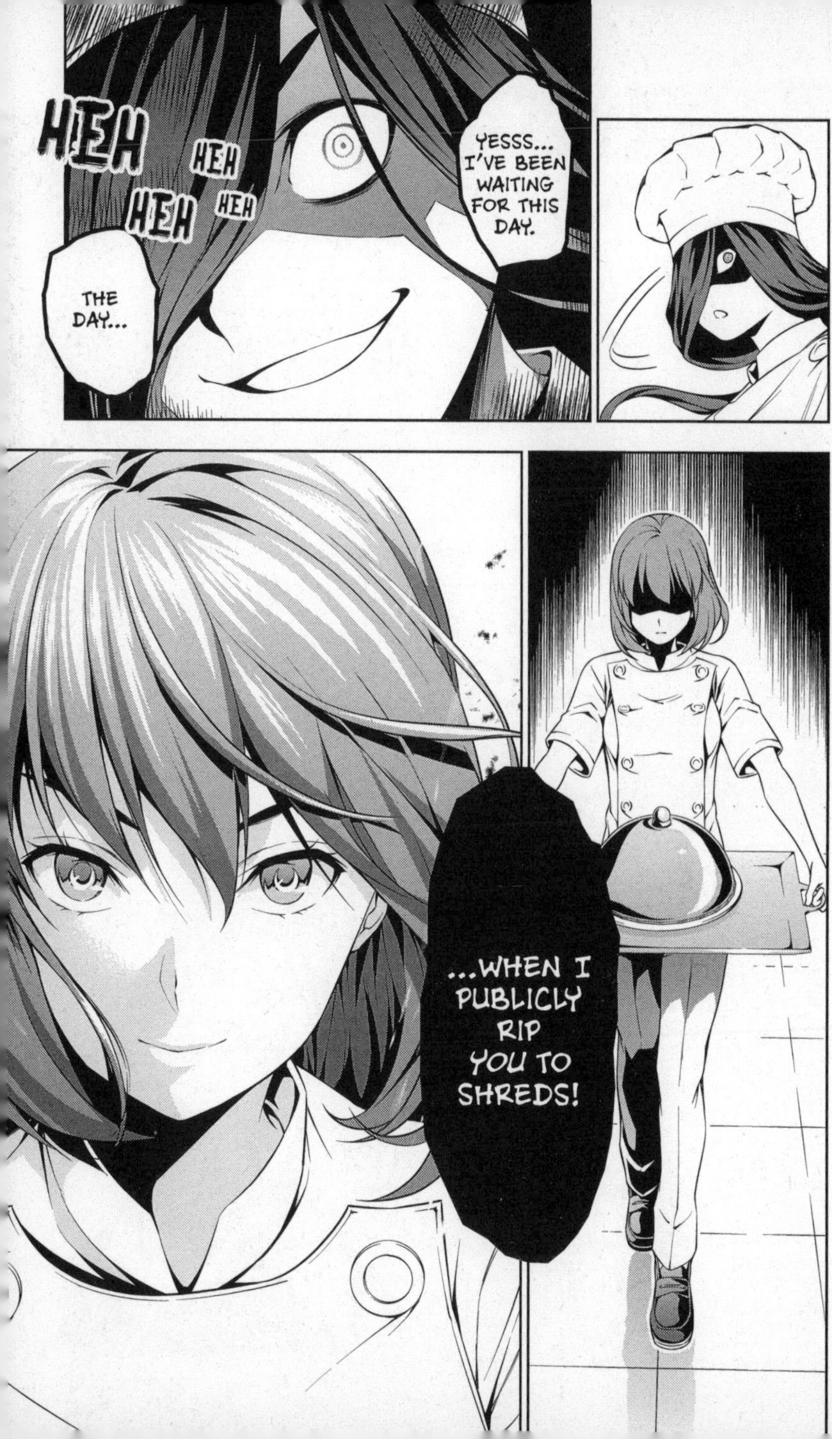
YESSS... I'VE BEEN WAITING FOR THIS DAY.
HEH HEH HEH HEH
THE DAY...
...WHEN I PUBLICLY RIP YOU TO SHREDS!

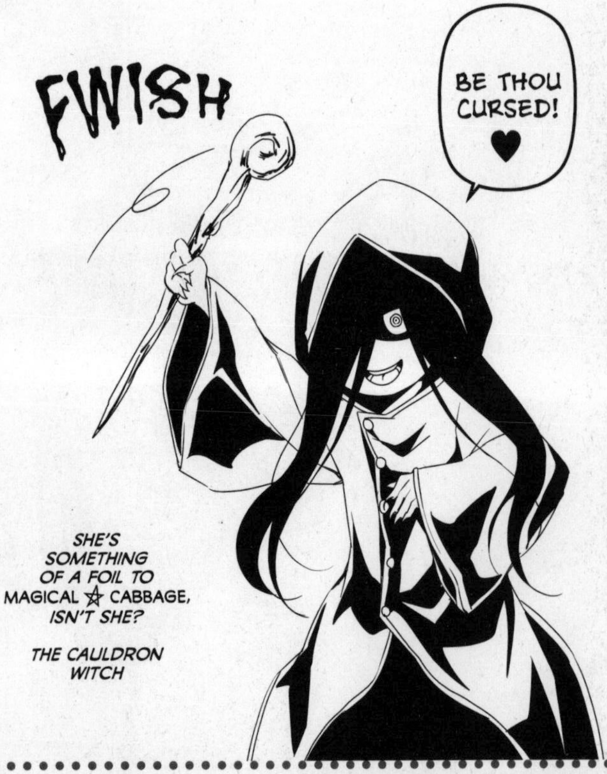
BE THOU CURSED! ♥
FWISH
SHE'S SOMETHING OF A FOIL TO MAGICAL ☆ CABBAGE, ISN'T SHE?
THE CAULDRON WITCH

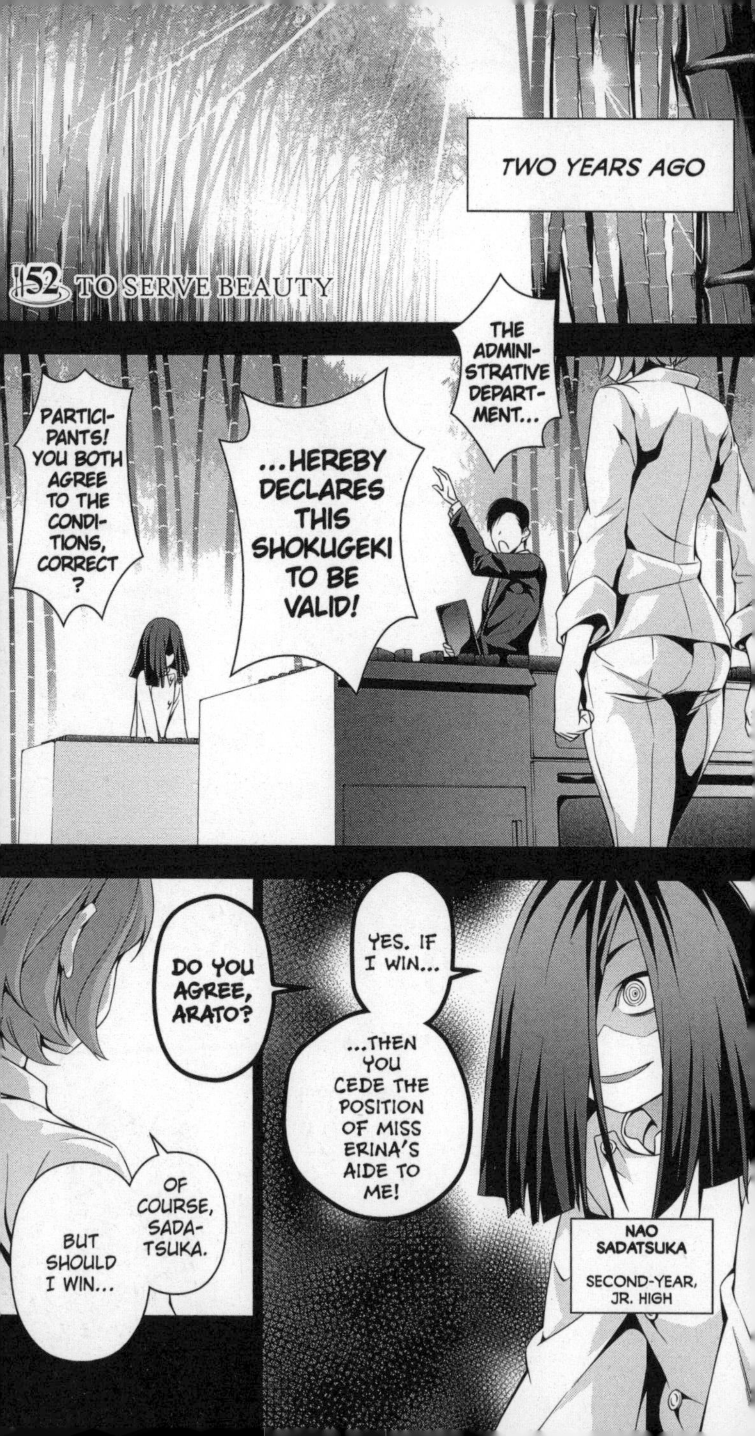
TWO YEARS AGO
152 TO SERVE BEAUTY
THE ADMINISTRATIVE DEPARTMENT...
...HEREBY DECLARES THIS SHOKUGEKI TO BE VALID!
PARTICIPANTS! YOU BOTH AGREE TO THE CONDITIONS, CORRECT?
YES. IF I WIN...
...THEN YOU CEDE THE POSITION OF MISS ERINA'S AIDE TO ME!
NAO SADATSUKA
SECOND-YEAR, JR. HIGH
DO YOU AGREE, ARATO?
OF COURSE, SADATSUKA.
BUT SHOULD I WIN...

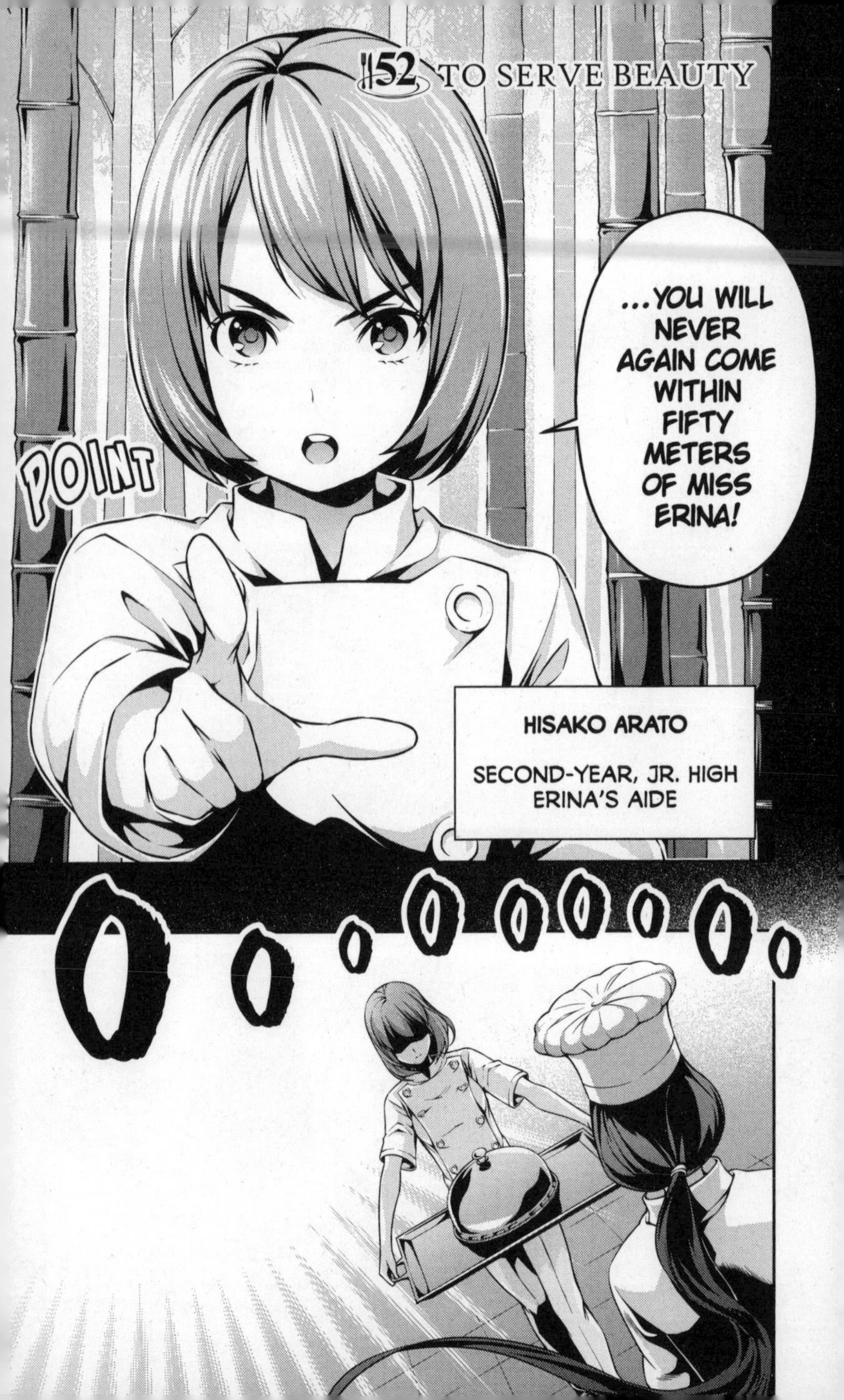
52 TO SERVE BEAUTY
...YOU WILL NEVER AGAIN COME WITHIN FIFTY METERS OF MISS ERINA!
HISAKO ARATO
SECOND-YEAR, JR. HIGH
ERINA'S AIDE
POINT
OO.O.OOOO.O.O

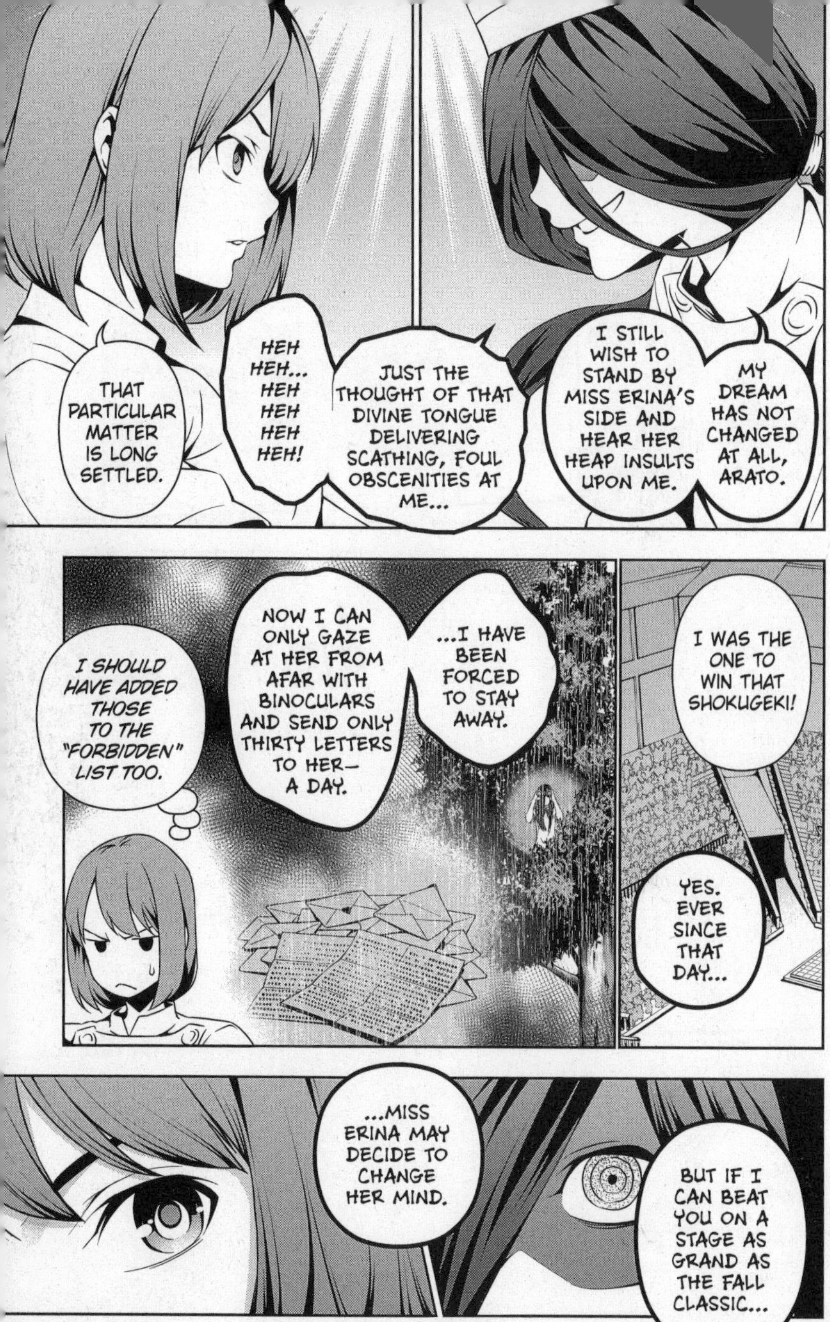
MY DREAM HAS NOT CHANGED AT ALL, ARATO.
I STILL WISH TO STAND BY MISS ERINA'S SIDE AND HEAR HER HEAP INSULTS UPON ME.
JUST THE THOUGHT OF THAT DIVINE TONGUE DELIVERING SCATHING, FOUL OBSCENITIES AT ME...
HEH HEH... HEH HEH HEH HEH!
THAT PARTICULAR MATTER IS LONG SETTLED.
I WAS THE ONE TO WIN THAT SHOKUGEKI!
YES. EVER SINCE THAT DAY...
...I HAVE BEEN FORCED TO STAY AWAY.
NOW I CAN ONLY GAZE AT HER FROM AFAR WITH BINOCULARS AND SEND ONLY THIRTY LETTERS TO HER— A DAY.
I SHOULD HAVE ADDED THOSE TO THE "FORBIDDEN" LIST TOO.
BUT IF I CAN BEAT YOU ON A STAGE AS GRAND AS THE FALL CLASSIC...
...MISS ERINA MAY DECIDE TO CHANGE HER MIND.

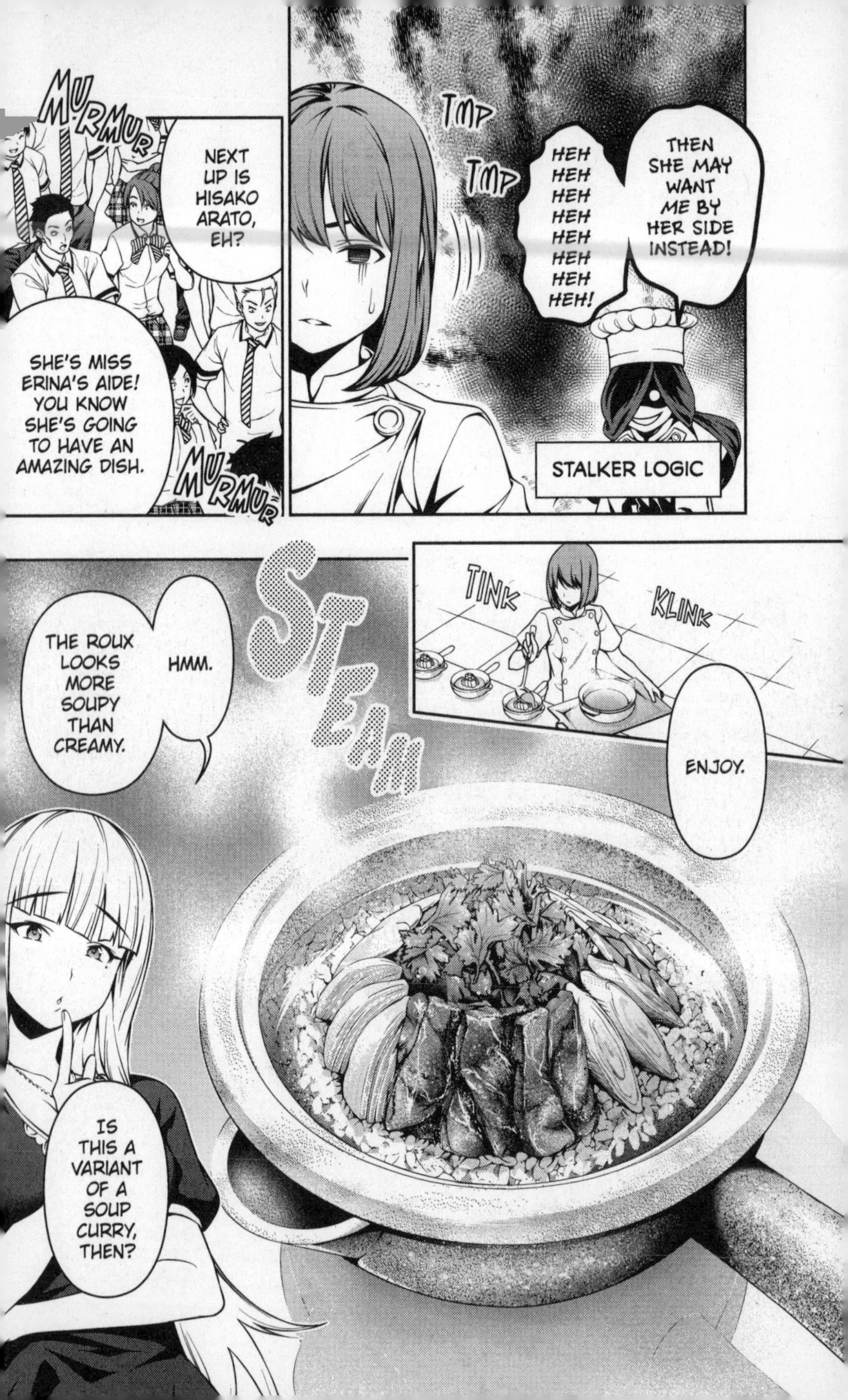
TMP
TMP
THEN SHE MAY WANT ME BY HER SIDE INSTEAD!
HEH HEH HEH HEH HEH HEH HEH HEH!
STALKER LOGIC
MURMUR
NEXT UP IS HISAKO ARATO, EH?
SHE'S MISS ERINA'S AIDE! YOU KNOW SHE'S GOING TO HAVE AN AMAZING DISH.
MURMUR
TINK
KLINK
STEAM
ENJOY.
HMM.
THE ROUX LOOKS MORE SOUPY THAN CREAMY.
IS THIS A VARIANT OF A SOUP CURRY, THEN?

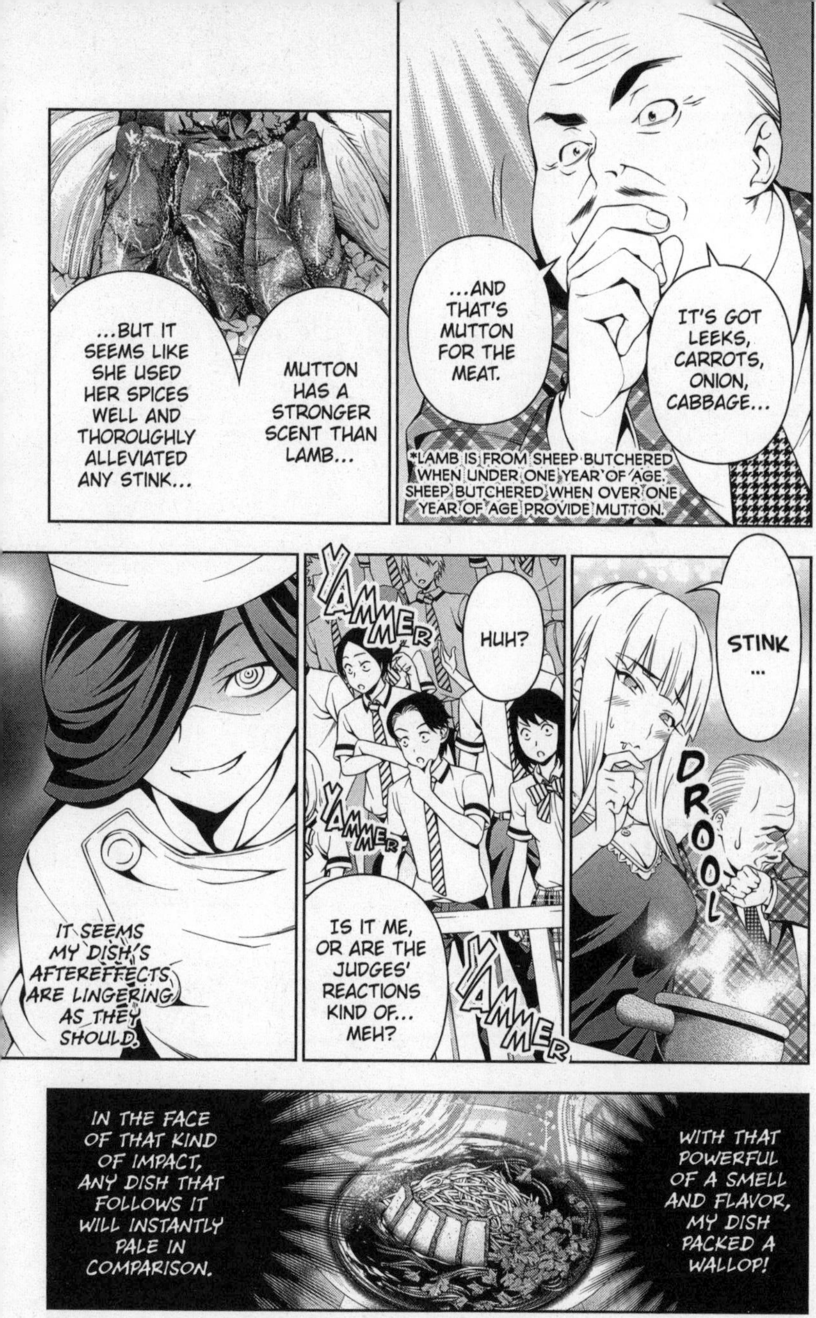
IT'S GOT LEEKS, CARROTS, ONION, CABBAGE...
...AND THAT'S MUTTON FOR THE MEAT.
*LAMB IS FROM SHEEP BUTCHERED WHEN UNDER ONE YEAR OF AGE. SHEEP BUTCHERED WHEN OVER ONE YEAR OF AGE PROVIDE MUTTON.
MUTTON HAS A STRONGER SCENT THAN LAMB...
...BUT IT SEEMS LIKE SHE USED HER SPICES WELL AND THOROUGHLY ALLEVIATED ANY STINK...
STINK ...
DROOL
YAMMER
HUH?
YAMMER
IS IT ME, OR ARE THE JUDGES' REACTIONS KIND OF... MEH?
YAMMER
IT SEEMS MY DISH'S AFTEREFFECTS ARE LINGERING AS THEY SHOULD.
WITH THAT POWERFUL OF A SMELL AND FLAVOR, MY DISH PACKED A WALLOP!
IN THE FACE OF THAT KIND OF IMPACT, ANY DISH THAT FOLLOWS IT WILL INSTANTLY PALE IN COMPARISON.

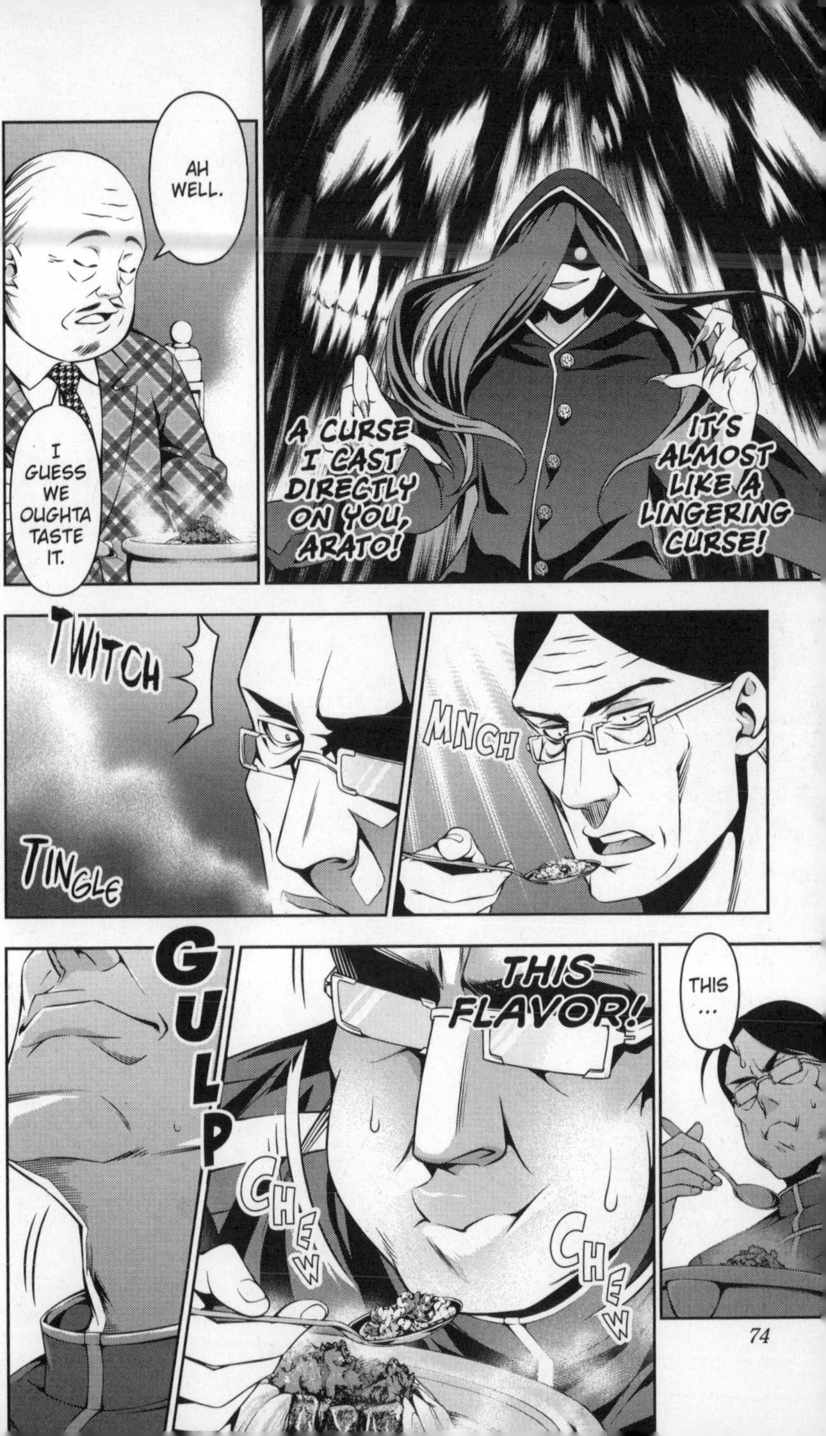
IT'S ALMOST LIKE A LINGERING CURSE!
A CURSE I CAST DIRECTLY ON YOU, ARATO!
AH WELL.
I GUESS WE OUGHTA TASTE IT.
MNCH
TWITCH
TINGLE
THIS ...
THIS FLAVOR!
GULP
CHEW
CHEW

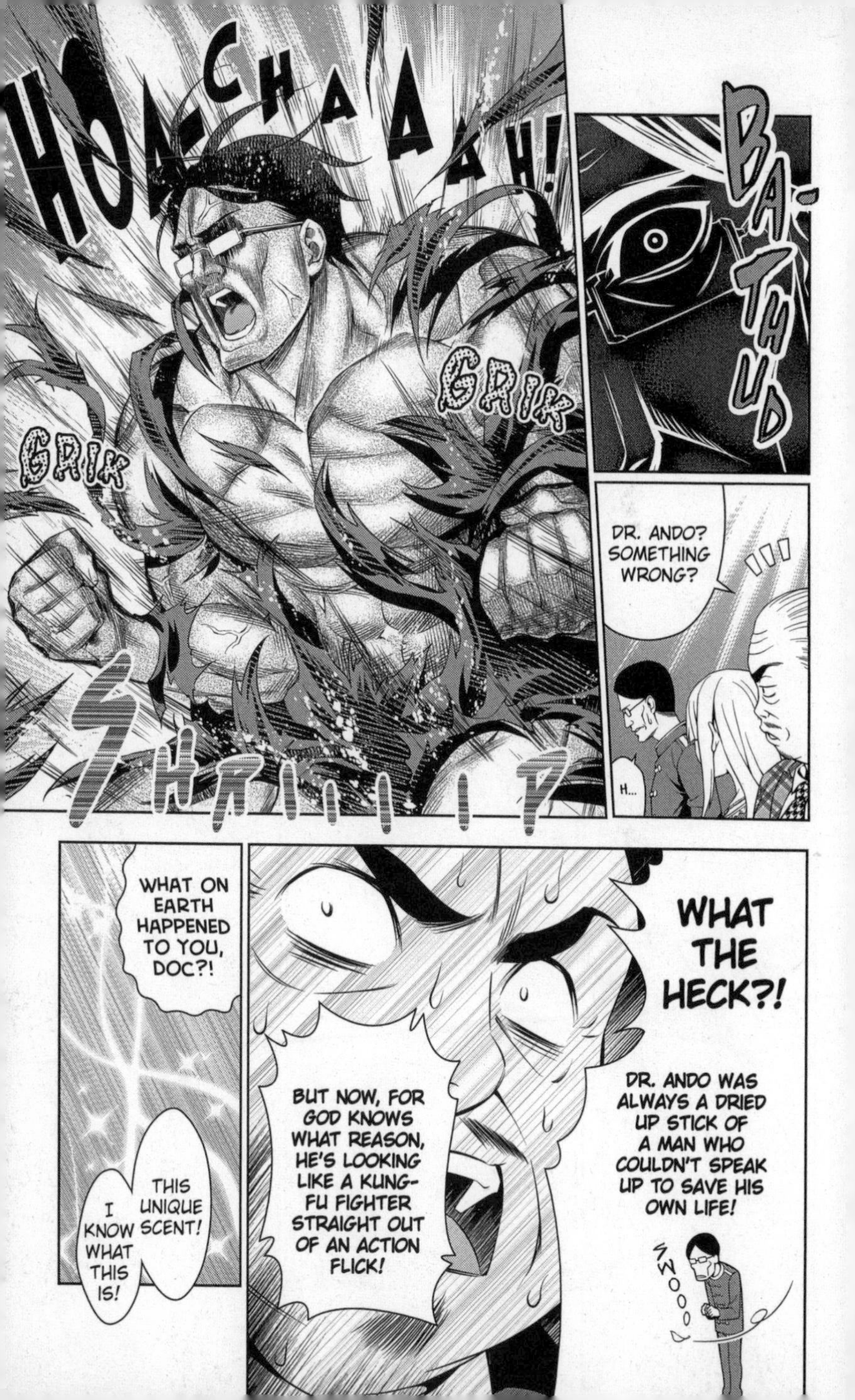
BA-THUD
DR. ANDO? SOMETHING WRONG?
!!!
H...
HOA-CHAAAAH!
GRIK
GRIK
SHRIIIIIP
WHAT THE HECK?!
DR. ANDO WAS ALWAYS A DRIED UP STICK OF A MAN WHO COULDN'T SPEAK UP TO SAVE HIS OWN LIFE!
SWOOOO
BUT NOW, FOR GOD KNOWS WHAT REASON, HE'S LOOKING LIKE A KUNG-FU FIGHTER STRAIGHT OUT OF AN ACTION FLICK!
WHAT ON EARTH HAPPENED TO YOU, DOC?!
THIS UNIQUE SCENT!
I KNOW WHAT THIS IS!

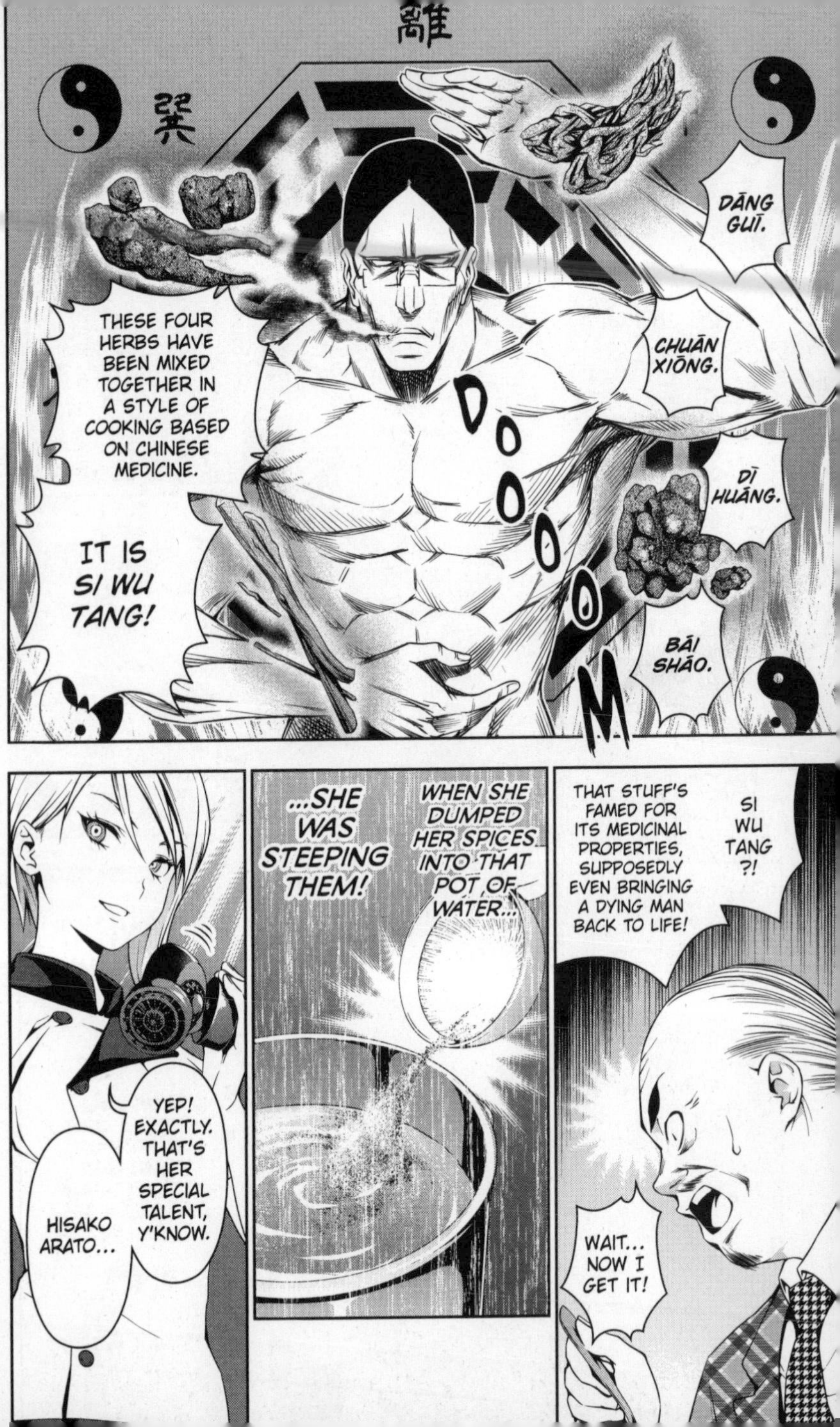
離
巽
DĀNG GUĪ.
CHUĀN XIŌNG.
DÌ HUÁNG.
BĀI SHĀO.
DOOOOOM
THESE FOUR HERBS HAVE BEEN MIXED TOGETHER IN A STYLE OF COOKING BASED ON CHINESE MEDICINE.
IT IS SI WU TANG!
SI WU TANG?!
THAT STUFF'S FAMED FOR ITS MEDICINAL PROPERTIES, SUPPOSEDLY EVEN BRINGING A DYING MAN BACK TO LIFE!
WAIT... NOW I GET IT!
WHEN SHE DUMPED HER SPICES INTO THAT POT OF WATER...
...SHE WAS STEEPING THEM!
YEP! EXACTLY. THAT'S HER SPECIAL TALENT, Y'KNOW.
HISAKO ARATO...

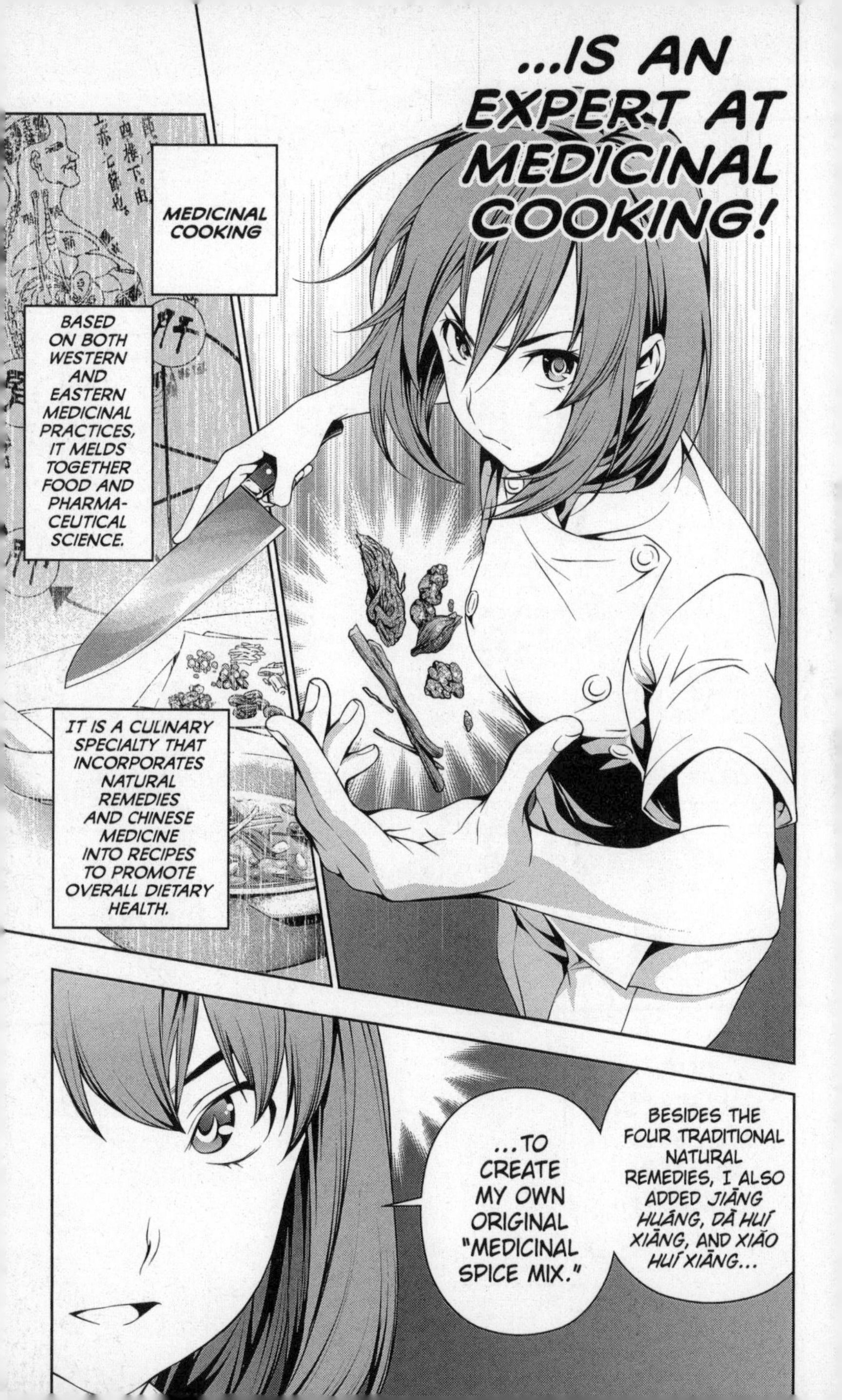
...IS AN EXPERT AT MEDICINAL COOKING!
MEDICINAL COOKING
BASED ON BOTH WESTERN AND EASTERN MEDICINAL PRACTICES, IT MELDS TOGETHER FOOD AND PHARMA-CEUTICAL SCIENCE.
IT IS A CULINARY SPECIALTY THAT INCORPORATES NATURAL REMEDIES AND CHINESE MEDICINE INTO RECIPES TO PROMOTE OVERALL DIETARY HEALTH.
BESIDES THE FOUR TRADITIONAL NATURAL REMEDIES, I ALSO ADDED JIĀNG HUÁNG, DÀ HUÍ XIĀNG, AND XIĀO HUÍ XIĀNG...
...TO CREATE MY OWN ORIGINAL "MEDICINAL SPICE MIX."

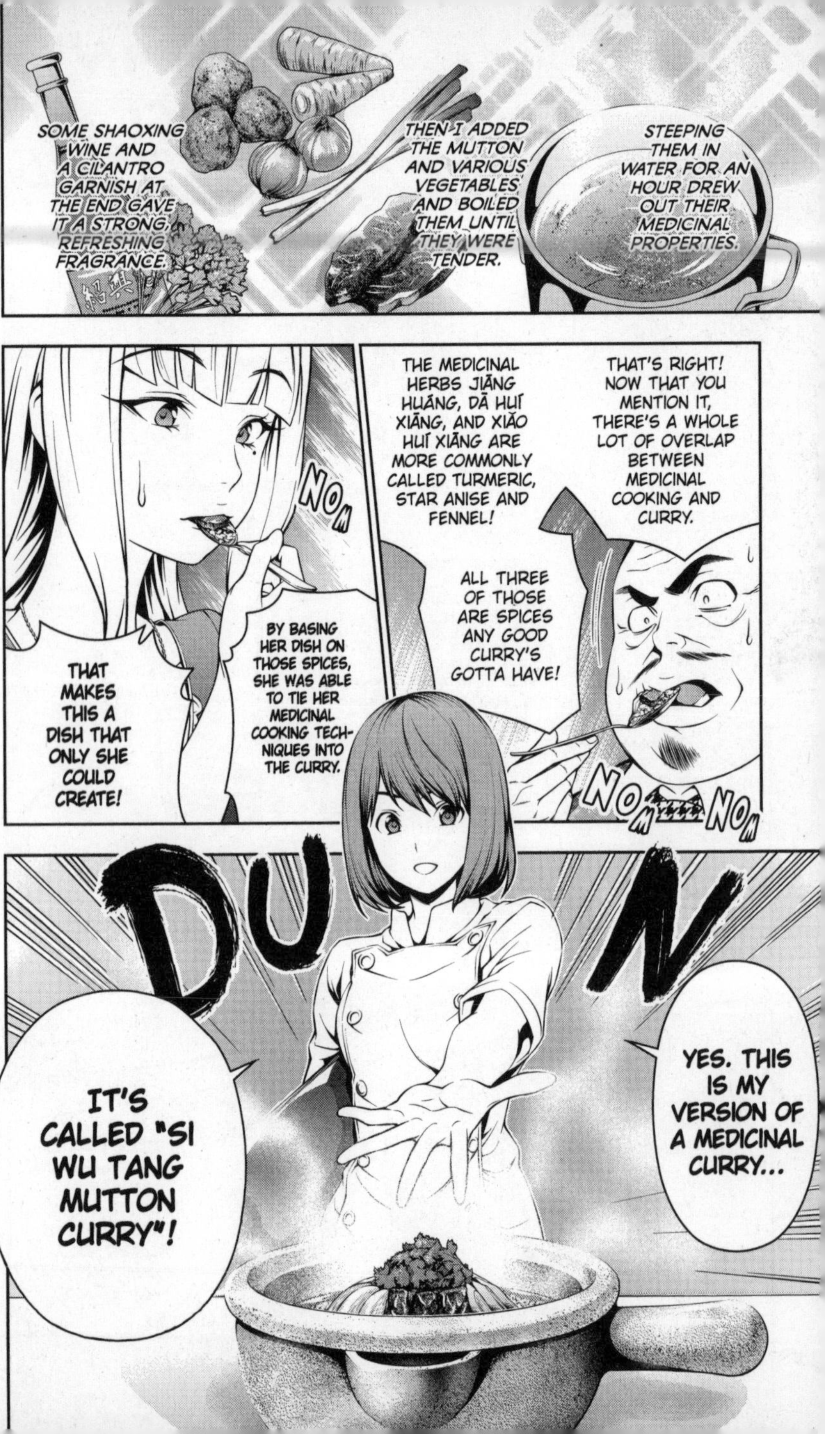
STEEPING THEM IN WATER FOR AN HOUR DREW OUT THEIR MEDICINAL PROPERTIES.
THEN I ADDED THE MUTTON AND VARIOUS VEGETABLES AND BOILED THEM UNTIL THEY WERE TENDER.
SOME SHAOXING WINE AND A CILANTRO GARNISH AT THE END GAVE IT A STRONG, REFRESHING FRAGRANCE.
THAT'S RIGHT! NOW THAT YOU MENTION IT, THERE'S A WHOLE LOT OF OVERLAP BETWEEN MEDICINAL COOKING AND CURRY.
THE MEDICINAL HERBS JIĀNG HUÁNG, DĀ HUÍ XIĀNG, AND XIǍO HUÍ XIĀNG ARE MORE COMMONLY CALLED TURMERIC, STAR ANISE AND FENNEL!
ALL THREE OF THOSE ARE SPICES ANY GOOD CURRY'S GOTTA HAVE!
NOM NOM
NOM
BY BASING HER DISH ON THOSE SPICES, SHE WAS ABLE TO TIE HER MEDICINAL COOKING TECHNIQUES INTO THE CURRY.
THAT MAKES THIS A DISH THAT ONLY SHE COULD CREATE!
DUN
YES. THIS IS MY VERSION OF A MEDICINAL CURRY...
IT'S CALLED "SI WU TANG MUTTON CURRY"!

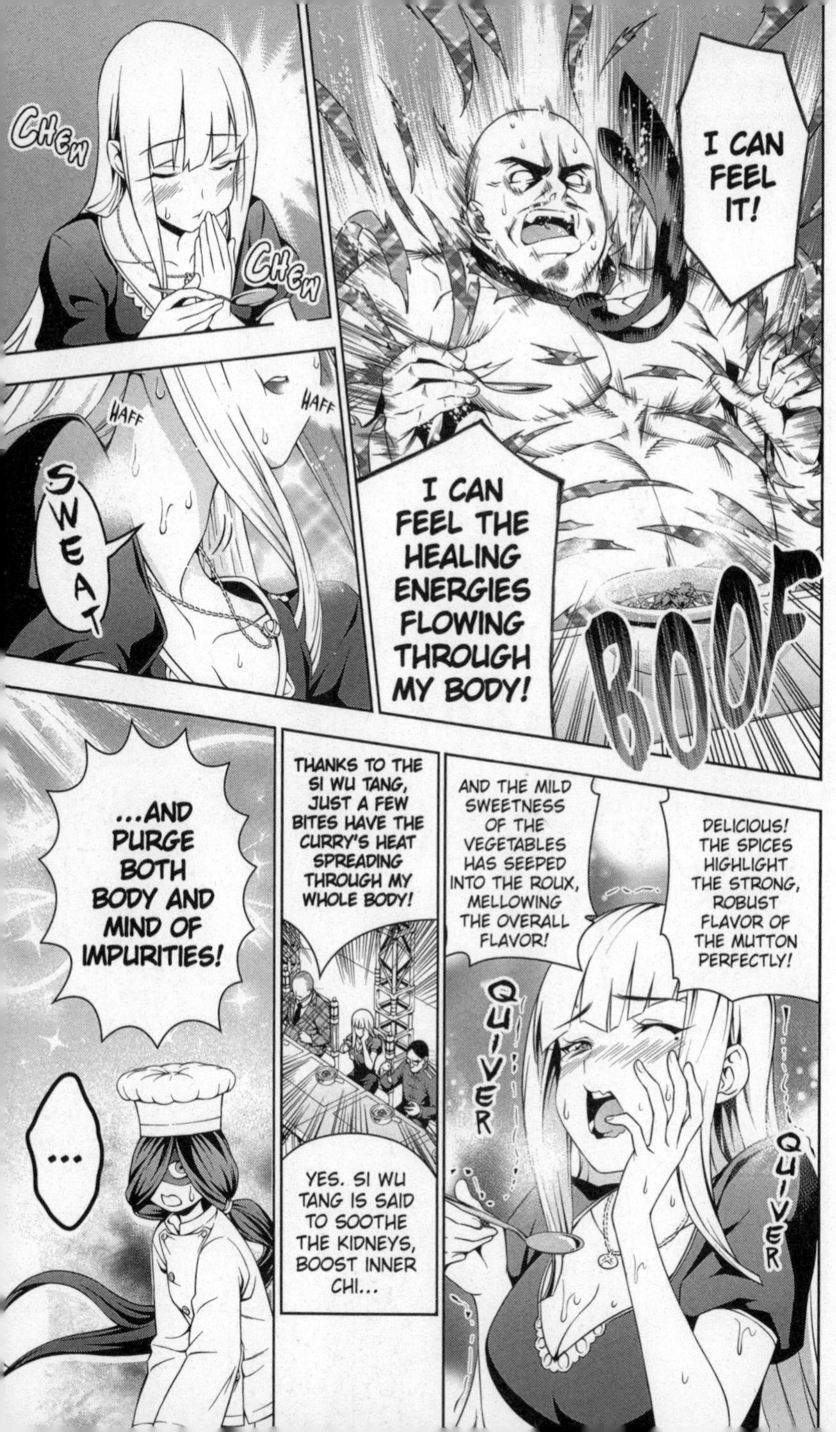
I CAN FEEL IT!
I CAN FEEL THE HEALING ENERGIES FLOWING THROUGH MY BODY!
BOOF
CHEW
CHEW
HAFF
HAFF
SWEAT
DELICIOUS! THE SPICES HIGHLIGHT THE STRONG, ROBUST FLAVOR OF THE MUTTON PERFECTLY!
AND THE MILD SWEETNESS OF THE VEGETABLES HAS SEEPED INTO THE ROUX, MELLOWING THE OVERALL FLAVOR!
QUIVER
QUIVER
THANKS TO THE SI WU TANG, JUST A FEW BITES HAVE THE CURRY'S HEAT SPREADING THROUGH MY WHOLE BODY!
YES. SI WU TANG IS SAID TO SOOTHE THE KIDNEYS, BOOST INNER CHI...
...AND PURGE BOTH BODY AND MIND OF IMPURITIES!
...

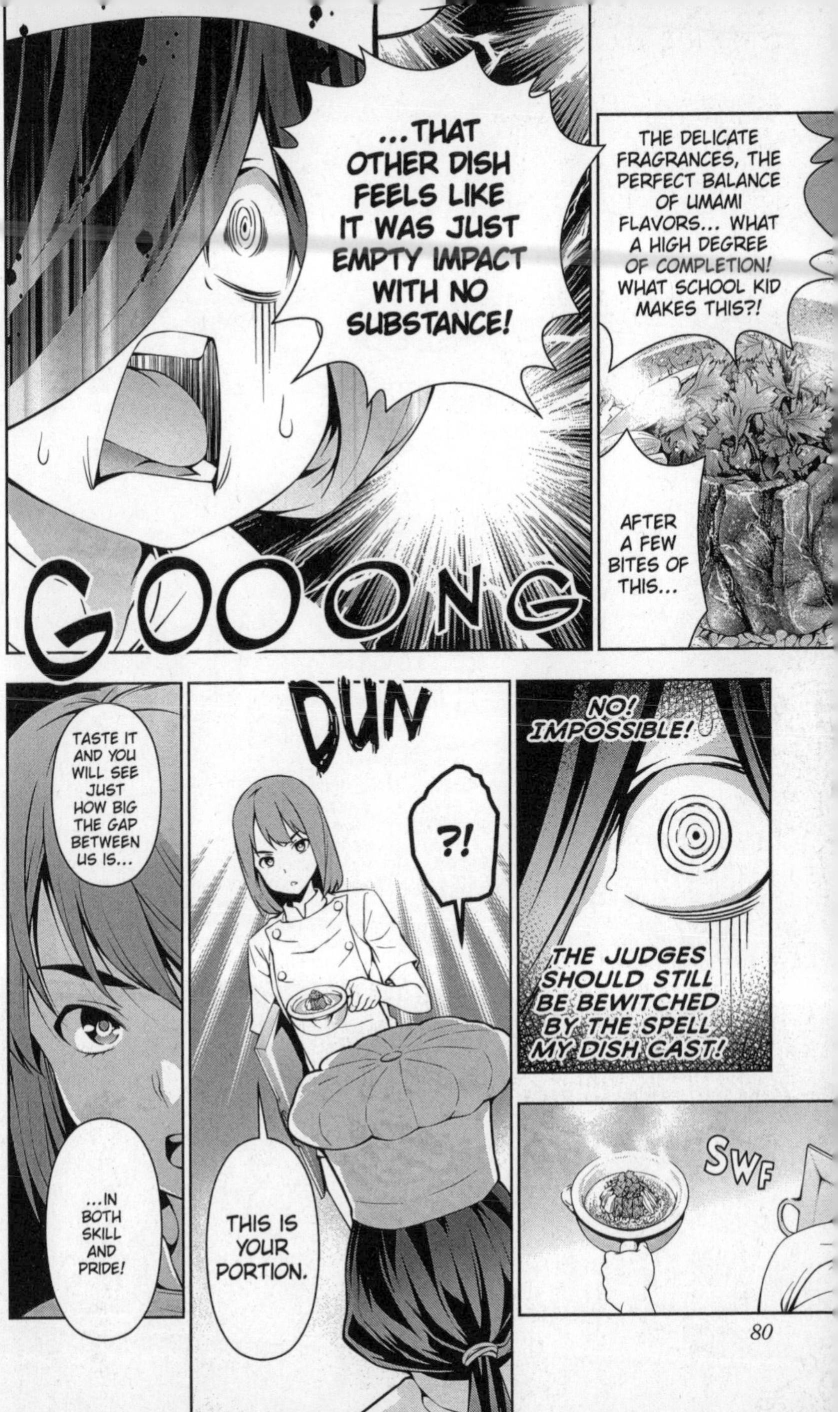
THE DELICATE FRAGRANCES, THE PERFECT BALANCE OF UMAMI FLAVORS... WHAT A HIGH DEGREE OF COMPLETION! WHAT SCHOOL KID MAKES THIS?!
AFTER A FEW BITES OF THIS...
...THAT OTHER DISH FEELS LIKE IT WAS JUST EMPTY IMPACT WITH NO SUBSTANCE!
GOOONG
NO! IMPOSSIBLE!
THE JUDGES SHOULD STILL BE BEWITCHED BY THE SPELL MY DISH CAST!
SWF
DUN
?!
THIS IS YOUR PORTION.
TASTE IT AND YOU WILL SEE JUST HOW BIG THE GAP BETWEEN US IS...
...IN BOTH SKILL AND PRIDE!

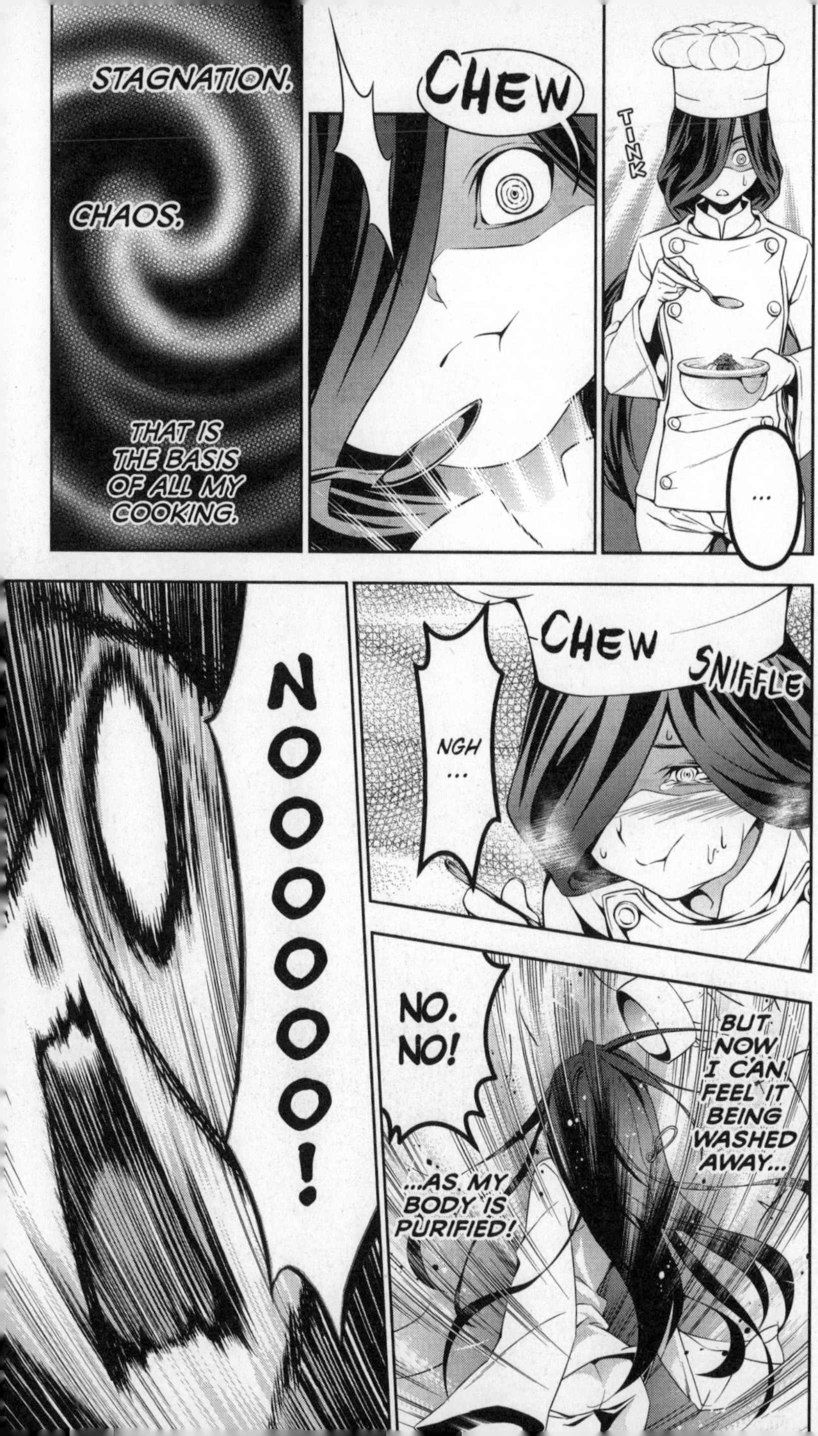
TINK
...
CHEW
STAGNATION.
CHAOS.
THAT IS THE BASIS OF ALL MY COOKING.
CHEW
SNIFFLE
NGH...
BUT NOW I CAN FEEL IT BEING WASHED AWAY...
NO. NO!
...AS MY BODY IS PURIFIED!
NOOOOOOO!

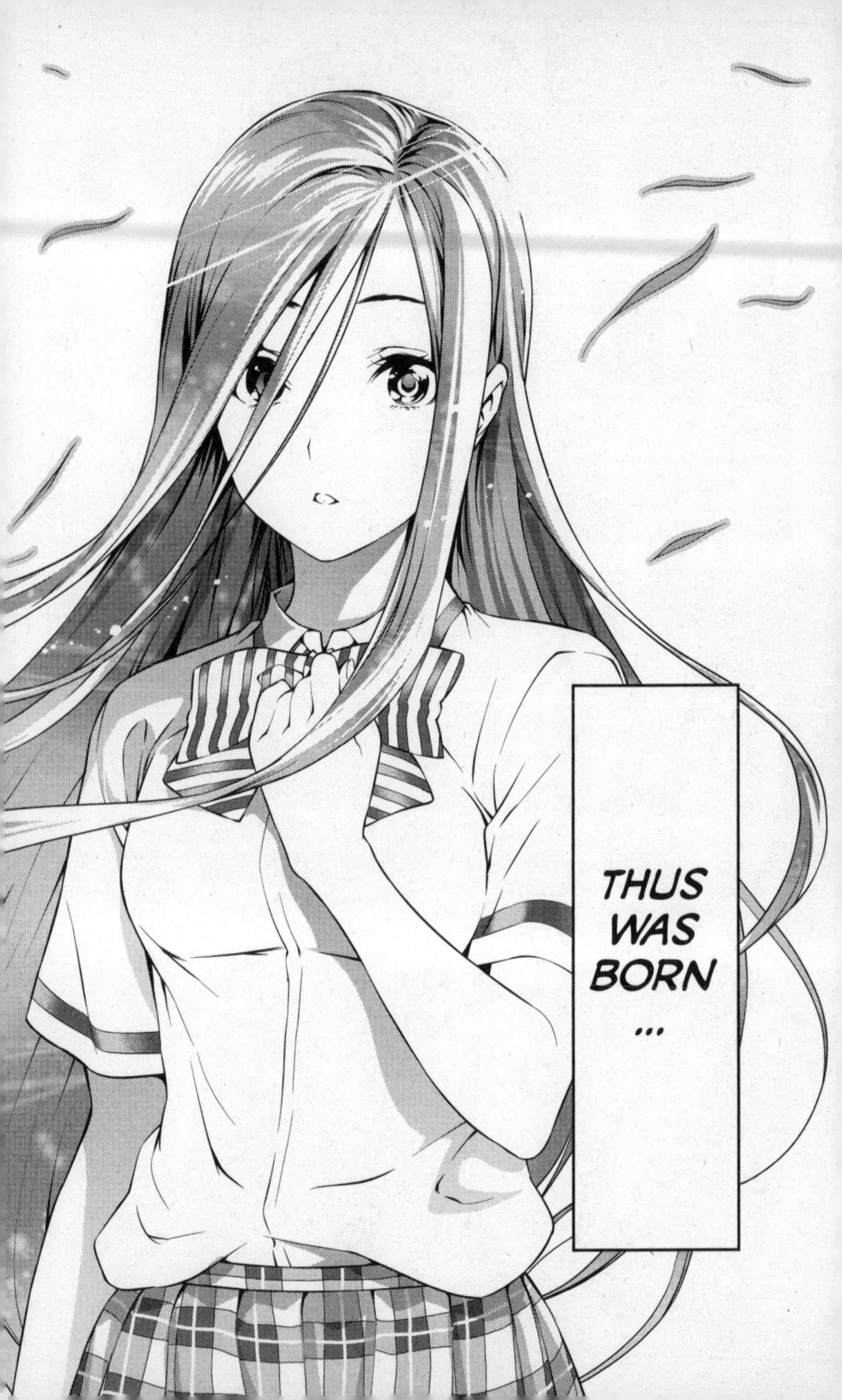
THUS WAS BORN ...

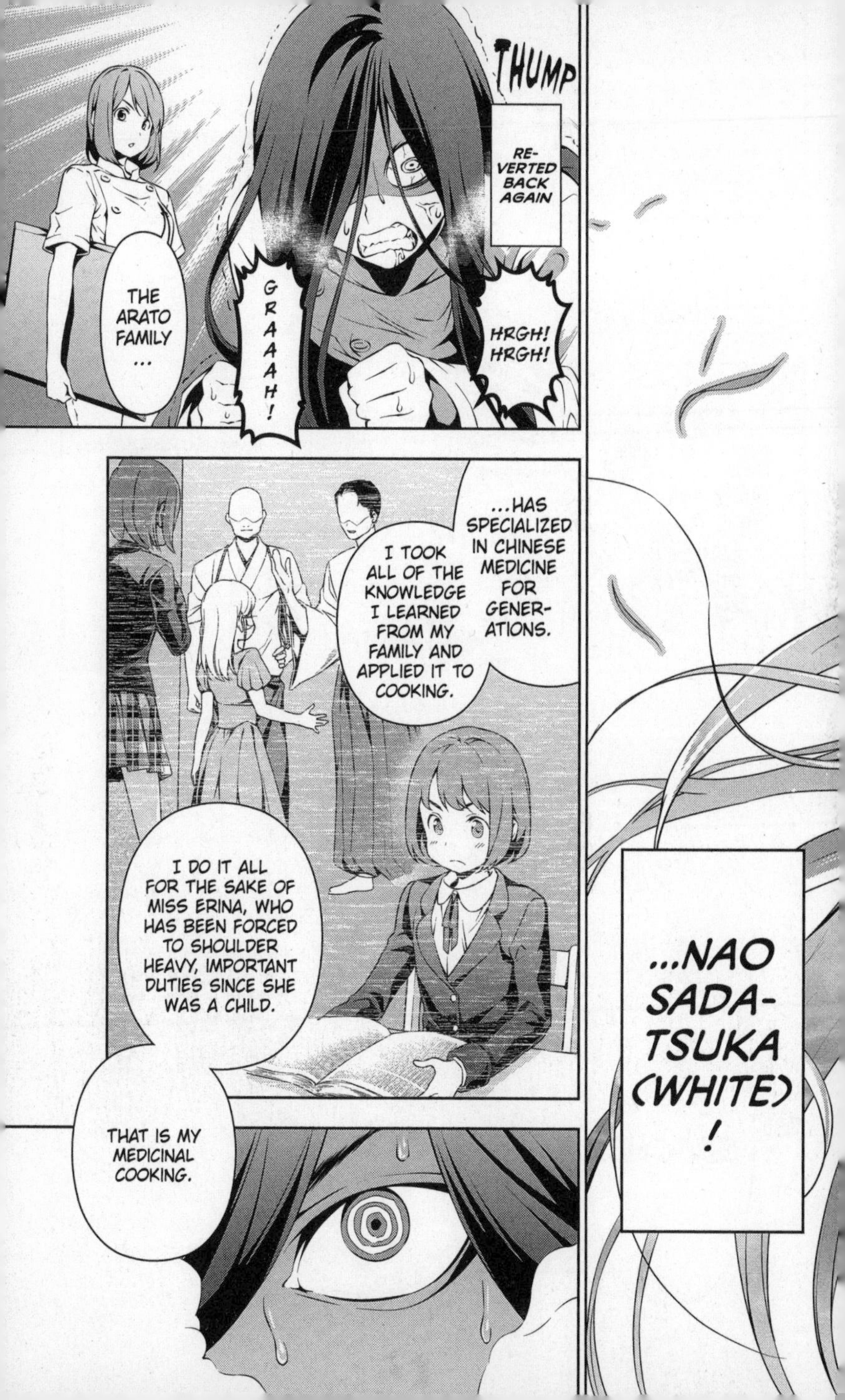
...NAO SADATSUKA (WHITE)!
THUMP
REVERTED BACK AGAIN
HRGH! HRGH!
GRAAAAH!
THE ARATO FAMILY...
...HAS SPECIALIZED IN CHINESE MEDICINE FOR GENERATIONS.
I TOOK ALL OF THE KNOWLEDGE I LEARNED FROM MY FAMILY AND APPLIED IT TO COOKING.
I DO IT ALL FOR THE SAKE OF MISS ERINA, WHO HAS BEEN FORCED TO SHOULDER HEAVY, IMPORTANT DUTIES SINCE SHE WAS A CHILD.
THAT IS MY MEDICINAL COOKING.

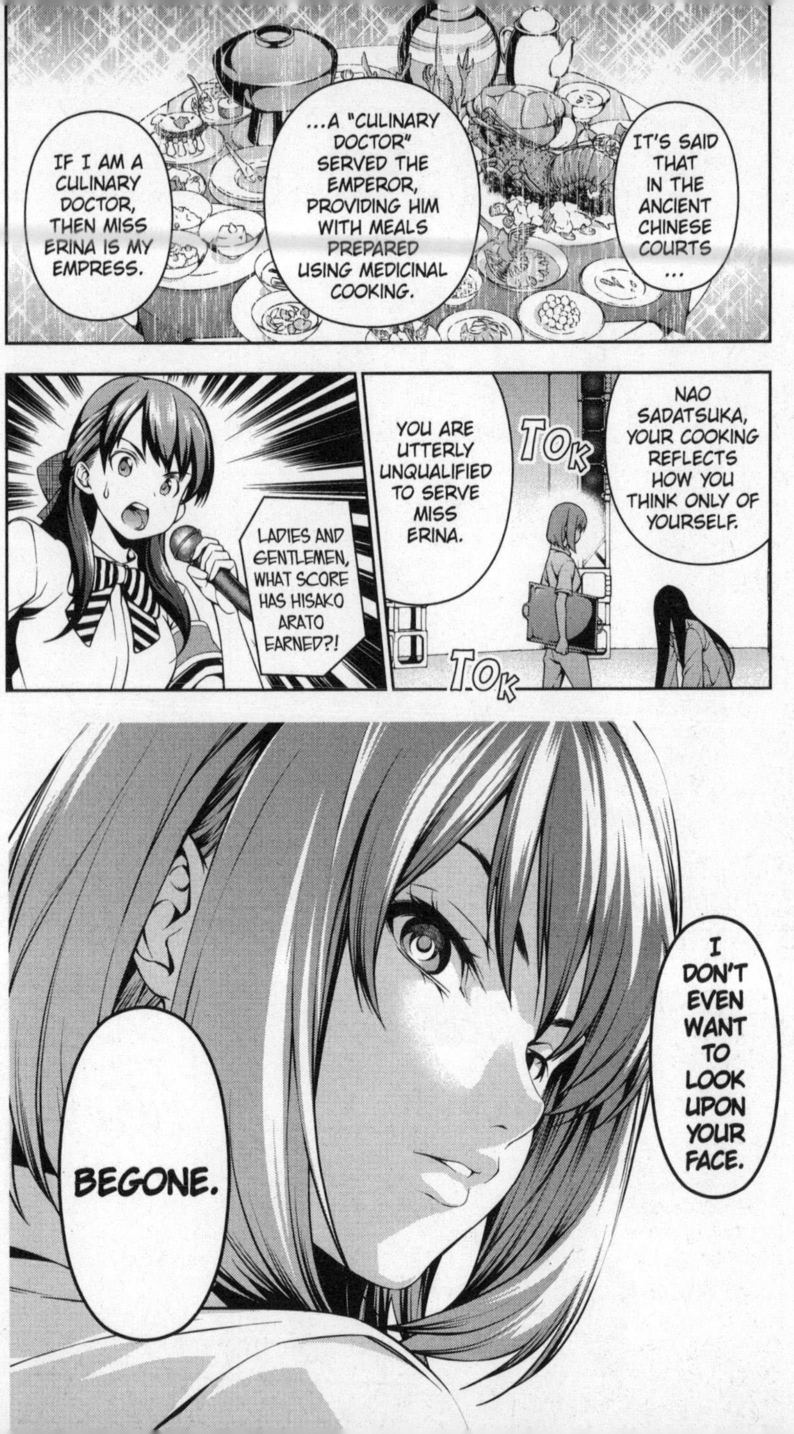
IT'S SAID THAT IN THE ANCIENT CHINESE COURTS ...
...A "CULINARY DOCTOR" SERVED THE EMPEROR, PROVIDING HIM WITH MEALS PREPARED USING MEDICINAL COOKING.
IF I AM A CULINARY DOCTOR, THEN MISS ERINA IS MY EMPRESS.
NAO SADATSUKA, YOUR COOKING REFLECTS HOW YOU THINK ONLY OF YOURSELF.
TOK
YOU ARE UTTERLY UNQUALIFIED TO SERVE MISS ERINA.
TOK
LADIES AND GENTLEMEN, WHAT SCORE HAS HISAKO ARATO EARNED?!
I DON'T EVEN WANT TO LOOK UPON YOUR FACE.
BEGONE.

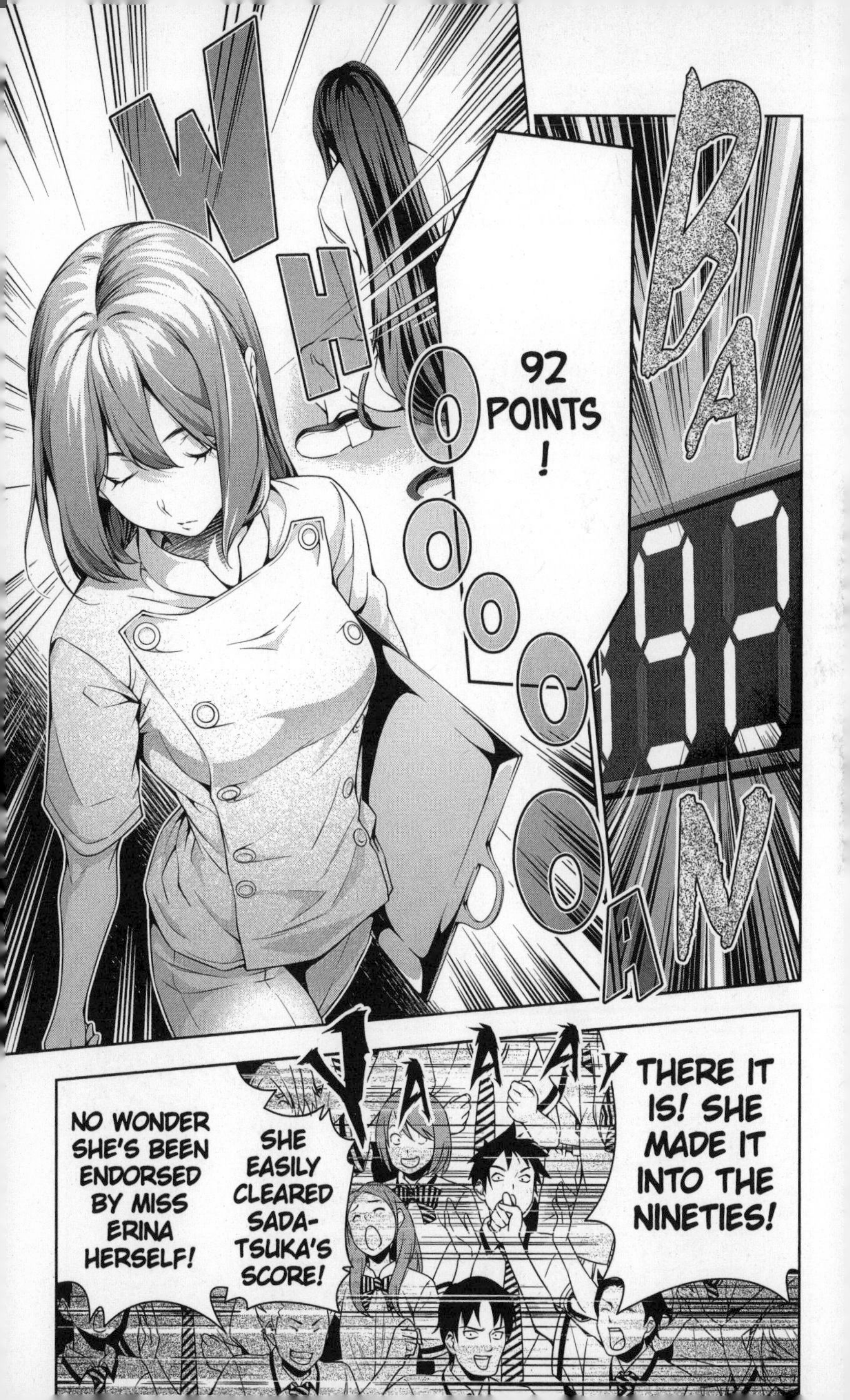
92 POINTS!
THERE IT IS! SHE MADE IT INTO THE NINETIES!
YAAAY
SHE EASILY CLEARED SADA-TSUKA'S SCORE!
NO WONDER SHE'S BEEN ENDORSED BY MISS ERINA HERSELF!

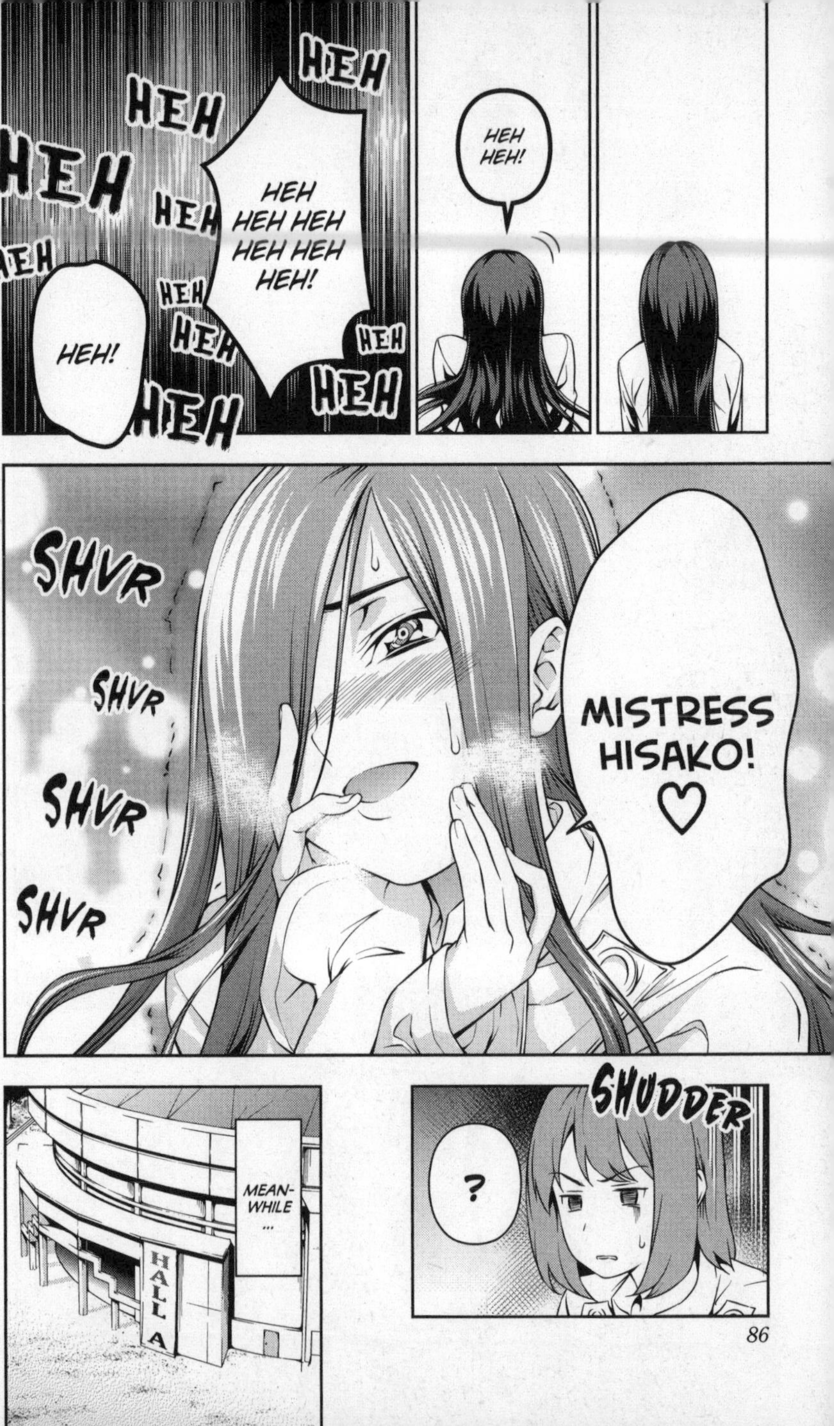
HEH HEH!
HEH HEH HEH HEH HEH HEH HEH HEH HEH HEH
HEH HEH HEH HEH HEH HEH!
HEH!
MISTRESS HISAKO! ♡
SHVR
SHVR
SHVR
SHVR
SHUDDER
?
MEAN-WHILE ...
HALL A

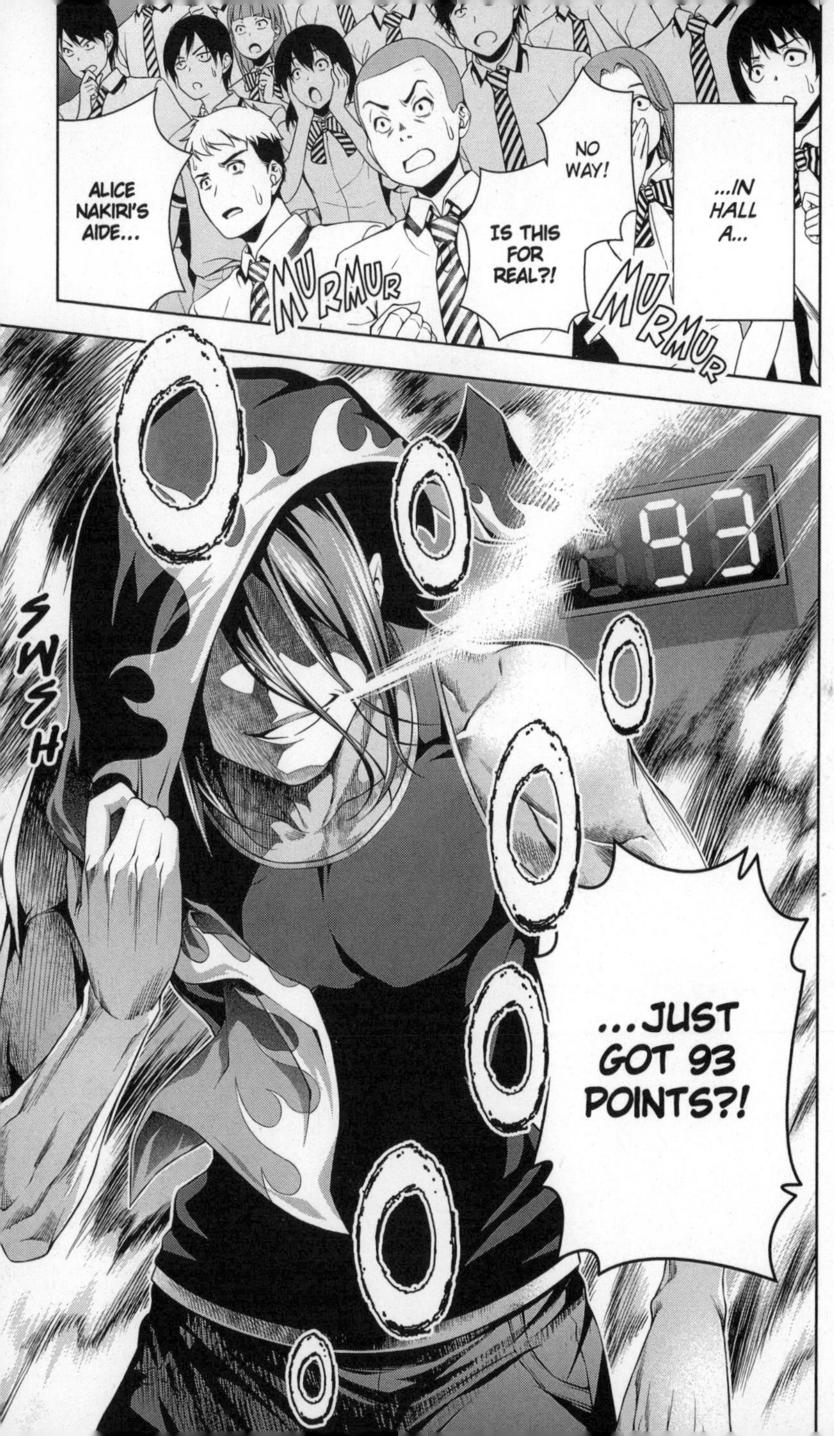
...IN HALL A...
NO WAY!
MURMUR
IS THIS FOR REAL?!
ALICE NAKIRI'S AIDE...
MURMUR
93
...JUST GOT 93 POINTS?!
SWSH

*ERINA'S AIDE...*
## HISAKO ARATO

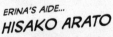

Let's all remember her name!

*APPARENTLY, JUDGING BY LOOKS ONLY, THE STORY'S WRITER THINKS SHE'S ONE OF THE PRETTIEST "TRADITIONAL BEAUTIES" IN THE ENTIRE SERIES.*

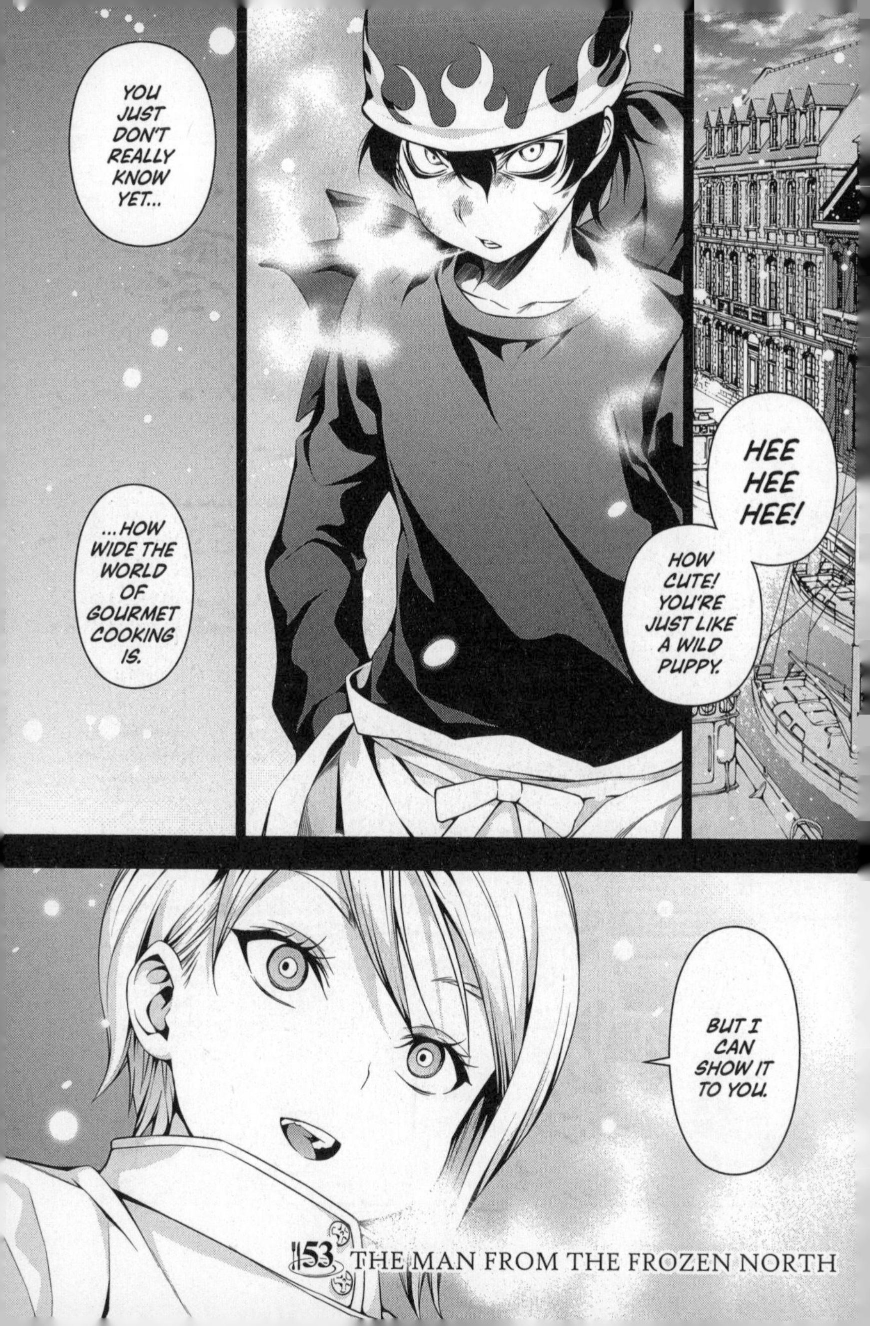
HEE HEE HEE!
HOW CUTE! YOU'RE JUST LIKE A WILD PUPPY.
YOU JUST DON'T REALLY KNOW YET...
...HOW WIDE THE WORLD OF GOURMET COOKING IS.
BUT I CAN SHOW IT TO YOU.

# 53 THE MAN FROM THE FROZEN NORTH

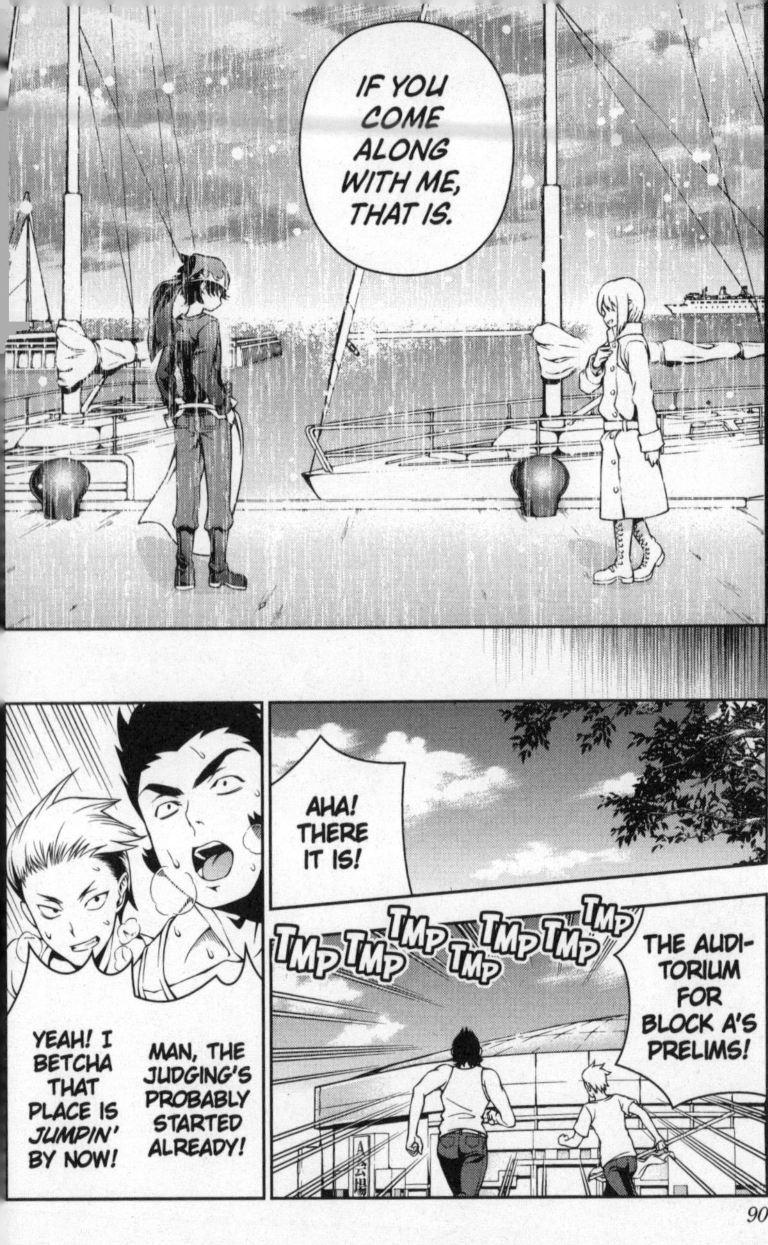
IF YOU COME ALONG WITH ME, THAT IS.
AHA! THERE IT IS!
TMP TMP TMP TMP TMP TMP TMP TMP
THE AUDITORIUM FOR BLOCK A'S PRELIMS!
MAN, THE JUDGING'S PROBABLY STARTED ALREADY!
YEAH! I BETCHA THAT PLACE IS JUMPIN' BY NOW!

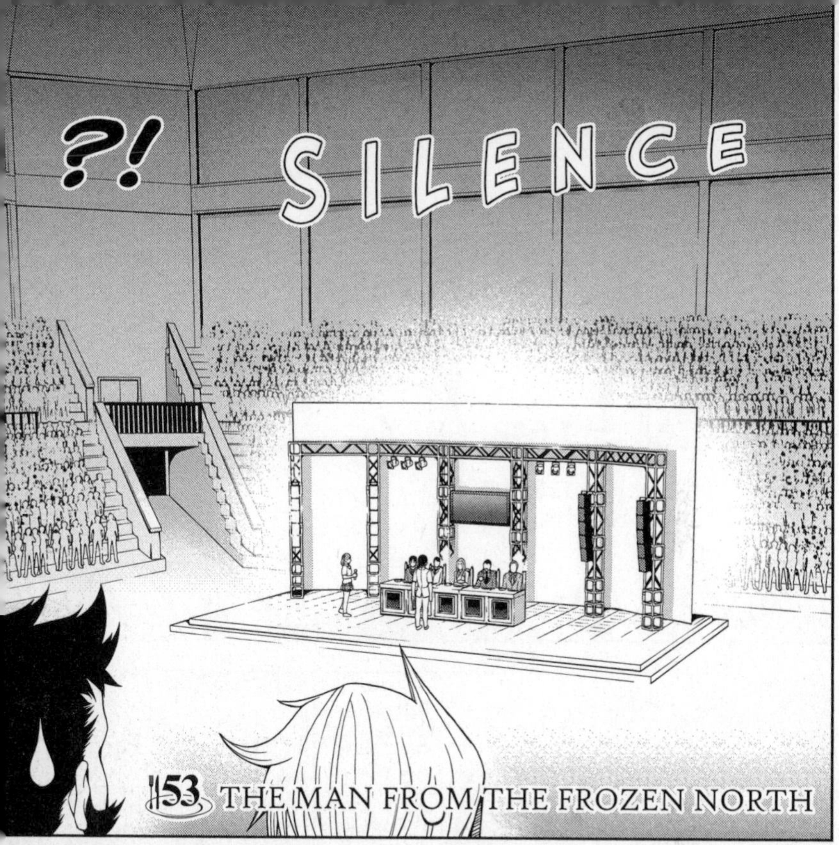
?!
SILENCE
53 THE MAN FROM THE FROZEN NORTH

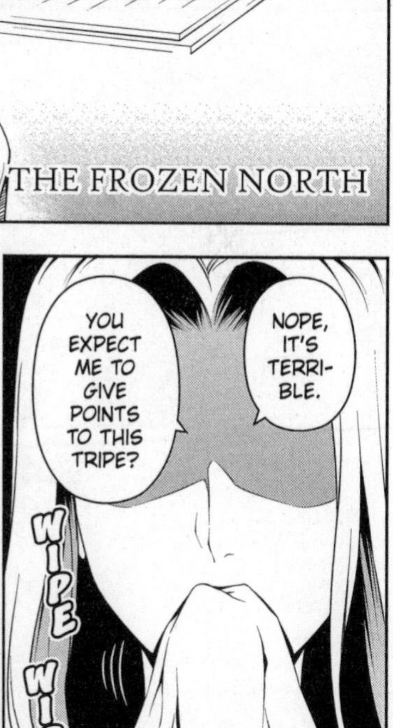
NOPE, IT'S TERRI-BLE.
YOU EXPECT ME TO GIVE POINTS TO THIS TRIPE?
WIPE WIPE

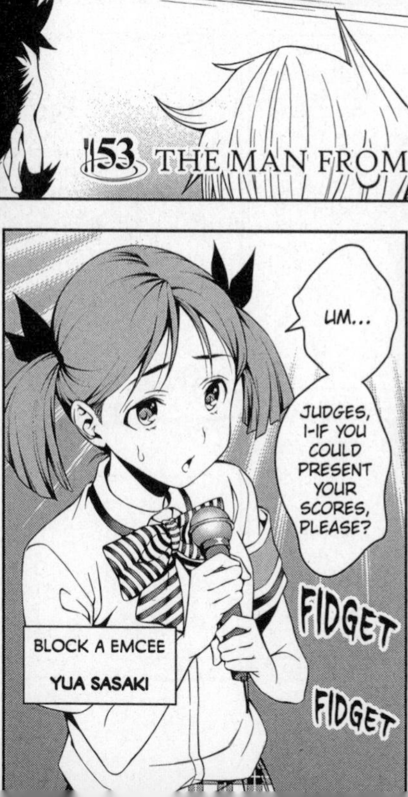
UM...
JUDGES, I-IF YOU COULD PRESENT YOUR SCORES, PLEASE?
FIDGET
FIDGET
BLOCK A EMCEE
YUA SASAKI

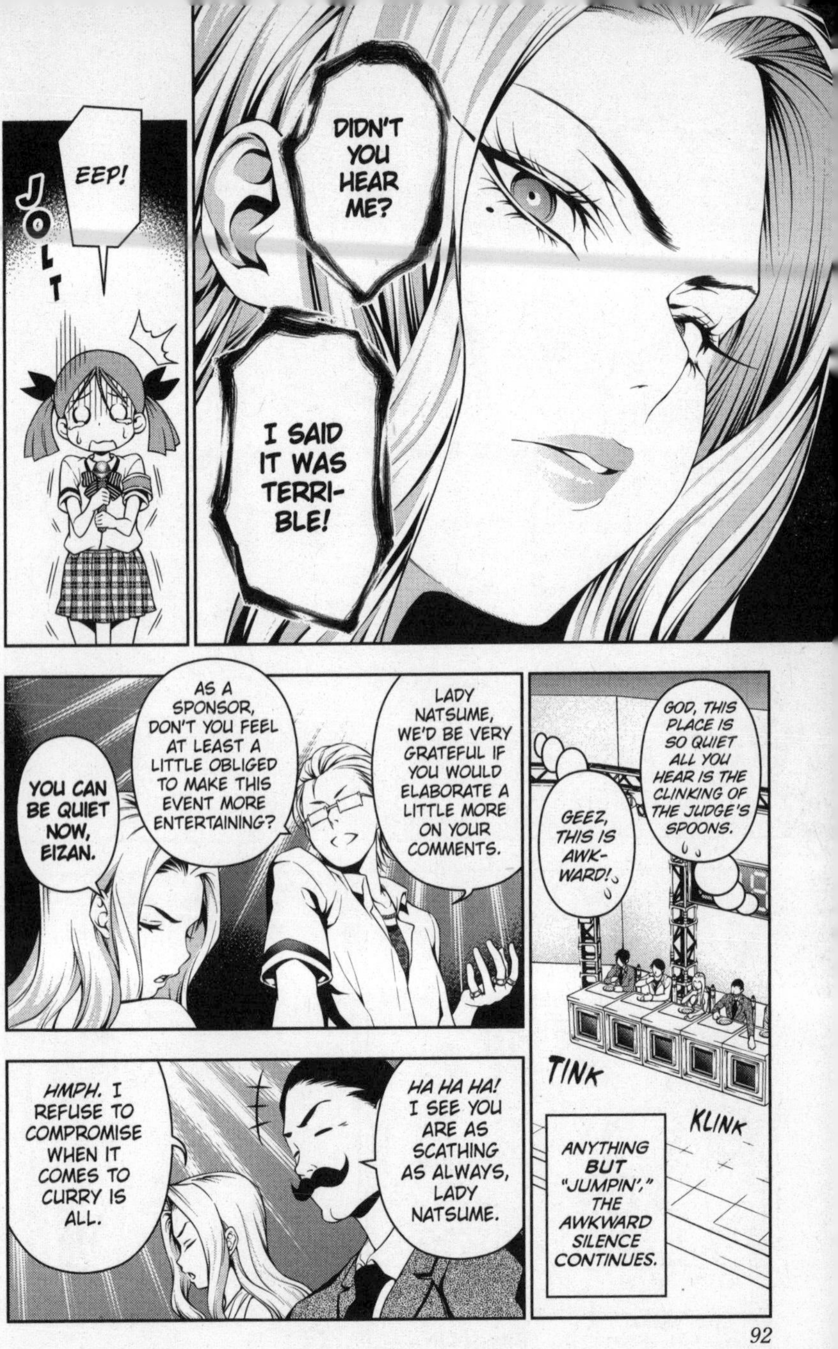
DIDN'T YOU HEAR ME?
I SAID IT WAS TERRI-BLE!
JOLT
EEP!
GOD, THIS PLACE IS SO QUIET ALL YOU HEAR IS THE CLINKING OF THE JUDGE'S SPOONS.
GEEZ, THIS IS AWK-WARD!
TINK
KLINK
ANYTHING BUT "JUMPIN'," THE AWKWARD SILENCE CONTINUES.
LADY NATSUME, WE'D BE VERY GRATEFUL IF YOU WOULD ELABORATE A LITTLE MORE ON YOUR COMMENTS.
AS A SPONSOR, DON'T YOU FEEL AT LEAST A LITTLE OBLIGED TO MAKE THIS EVENT MORE ENTERTAINING?
YOU CAN BE QUIET NOW, EIZAN.
HA HA HA! I SEE YOU ARE AS SCATHING AS ALWAYS, LADY NATSUME.
HMPH. I REFUSE TO COMPROMISE WHEN IT COMES TO CURRY IS ALL.

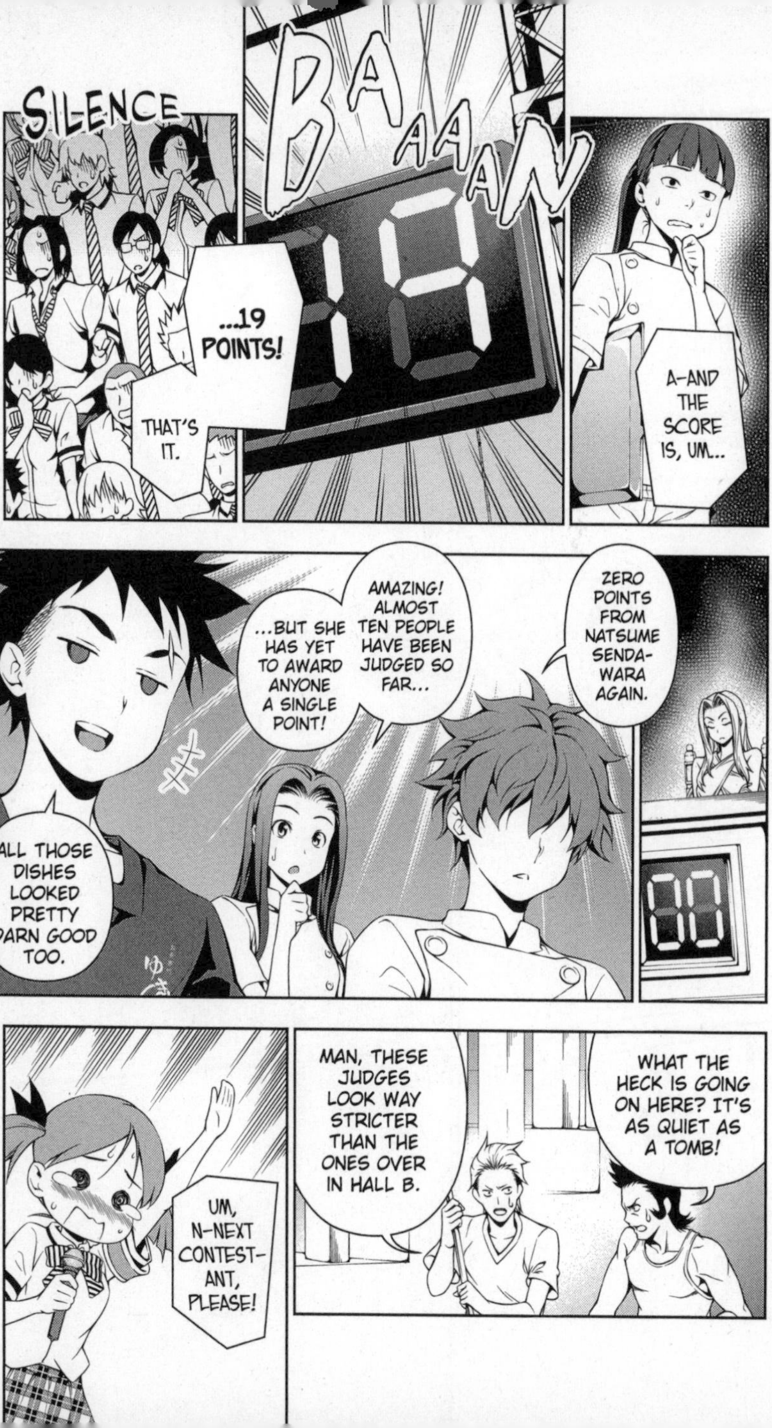
A-AND THE SCORE IS, UM...
BAAAAN
...19 POINTS!
SILENCE
THAT'S IT.
ZERO POINTS FROM NATSUME SENDAWARA AGAIN.
AMAZING! ALMOST TEN PEOPLE HAVE BEEN JUDGED SO FAR...
...BUT SHE HAS YET TO AWARD ANYONE A SINGLE POINT!
ALL THOSE DISHES LOOKED PRETTY DARN GOOD TOO.
WHAT THE HECK IS GOING ON HERE? IT'S AS QUIET AS A TOMB!
MAN, THESE JUDGES LOOK WAY STRICTER THAN THE ONES OVER IN HALL B.
UM, N-NEXT CONTESTANT, PLEASE!

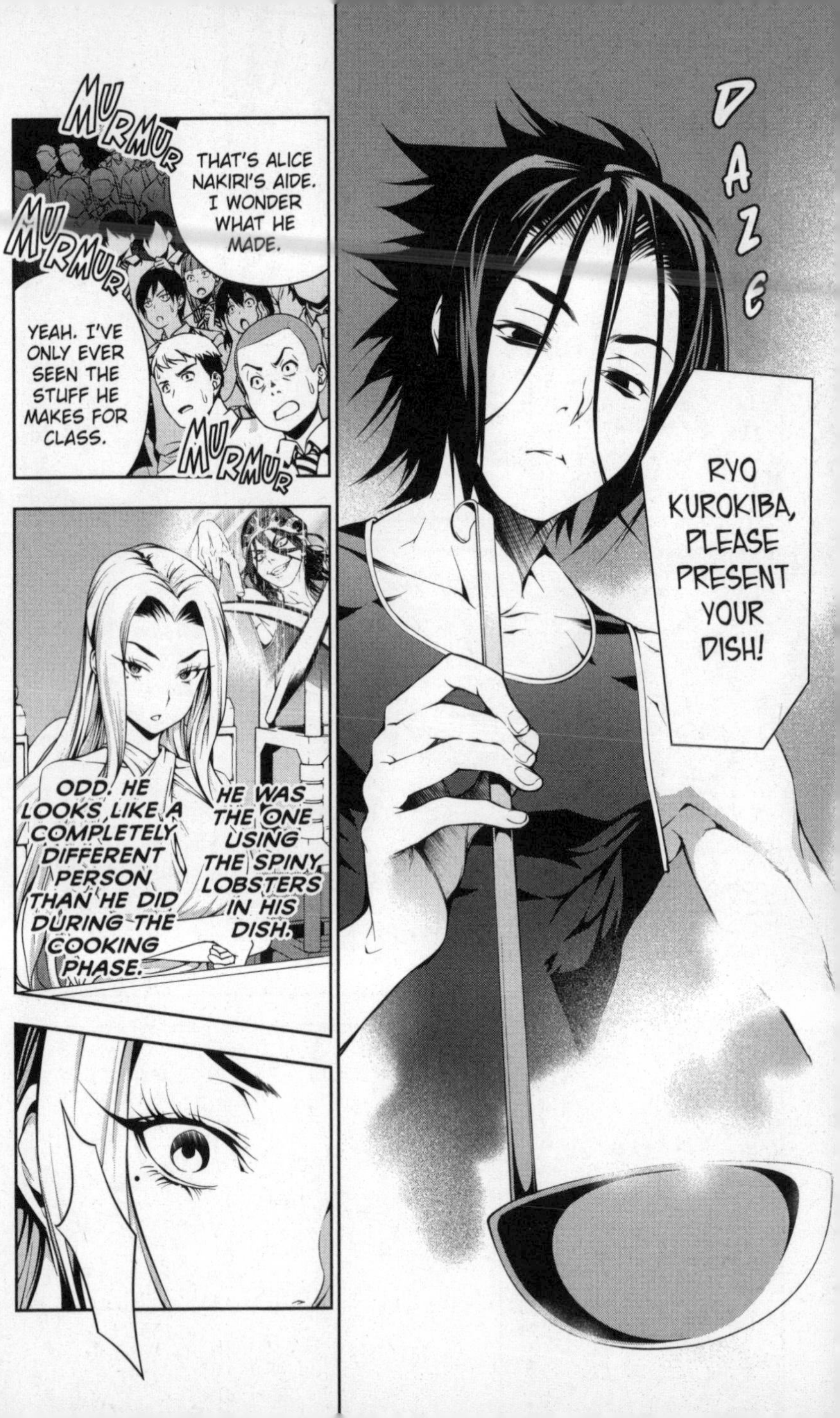
DAZE
RYO KUROKIBA, PLEASE PRESENT YOUR DISH!
MURMUR
THAT'S ALICE NAKIRI'S AIDE. I WONDER WHAT HE MADE.
MURMUR
YEAH. I'VE ONLY EVER SEEN THE STUFF HE MAKES FOR CLASS.
MURMUR
HE WAS THE ONE USING THE SPINY LOBSTERS IN HIS DISH.
ODD. HE LOOKS LIKE A COMPLETELY DIFFERENT PERSON THAN HE DID DURING THE COOKING PHASE.

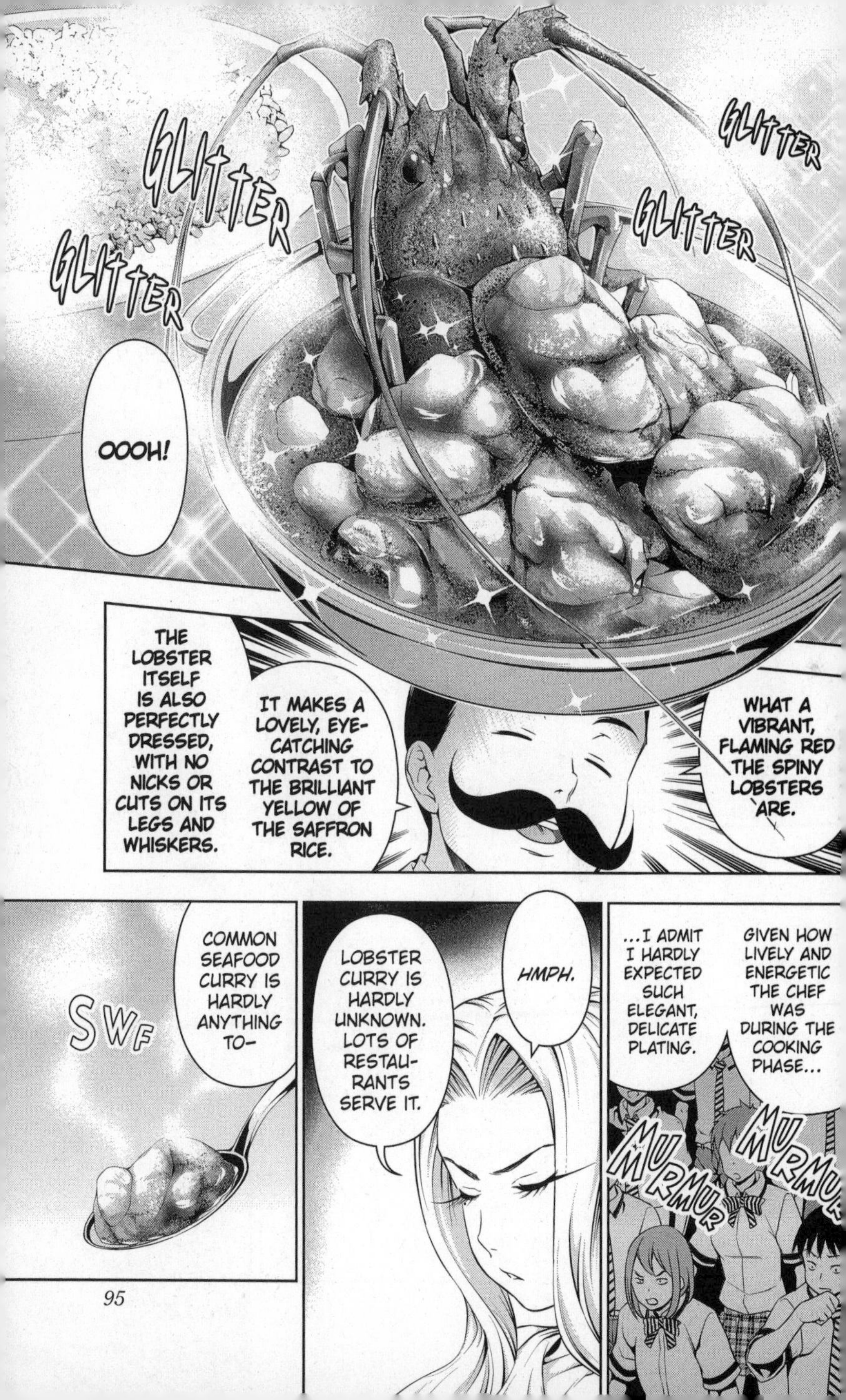
GLITTER
GLITTER
GLITTER
GLITTER
OOOH!
WHAT A VIBRANT, FLAMING RED THE SPINY LOBSTERS ARE.
IT MAKES A LOVELY, EYE-CATCHING CONTRAST TO THE BRILLIANT YELLOW OF THE SAFFRON RICE.
THE LOBSTER ITSELF IS ALSO PERFECTLY DRESSED, WITH NO NICKS OR CUTS ON ITS LEGS AND WHISKERS.
GIVEN HOW LIVELY AND ENERGETIC THE CHEF WAS DURING THE COOKING PHASE...
...I ADMIT I HARDLY EXPECTED SUCH ELEGANT, DELICATE PLATING.
MURMUR
MURMUR
HMPH.
LOBSTER CURRY IS HARDLY UNKNOWN. LOTS OF RESTAU-RANTS SERVE IT.
COMMON SEAFOOD CURRY IS HARDLY ANYTHING TO-
SWF

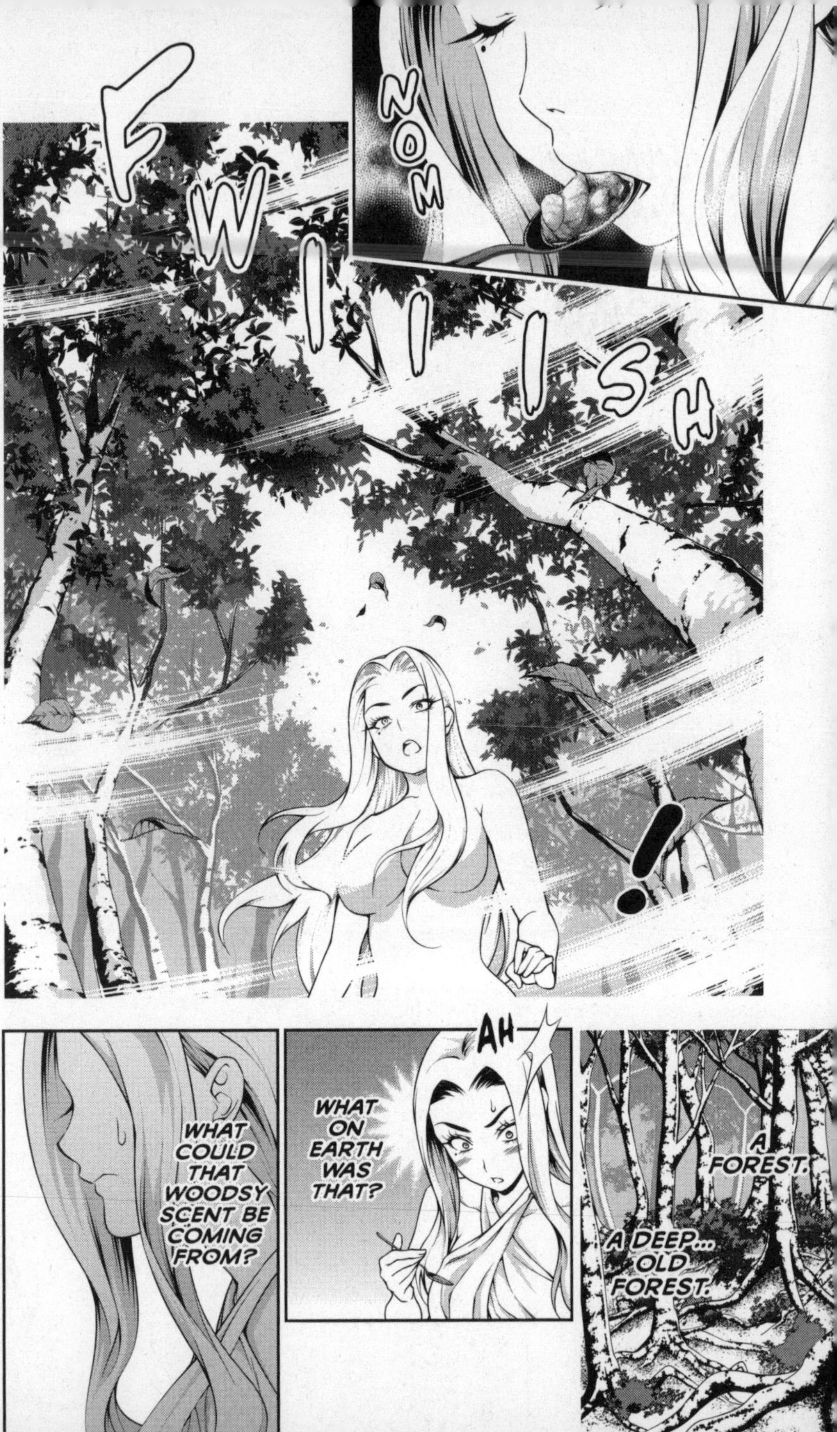
NOM NOM
FWIIISH
!
A FOREST.
A DEEP... OLD FOREST.
AH
WHAT ON EARTH WAS THAT?
WHAT COULD THAT WOODSY SCENT BE COMING FROM?

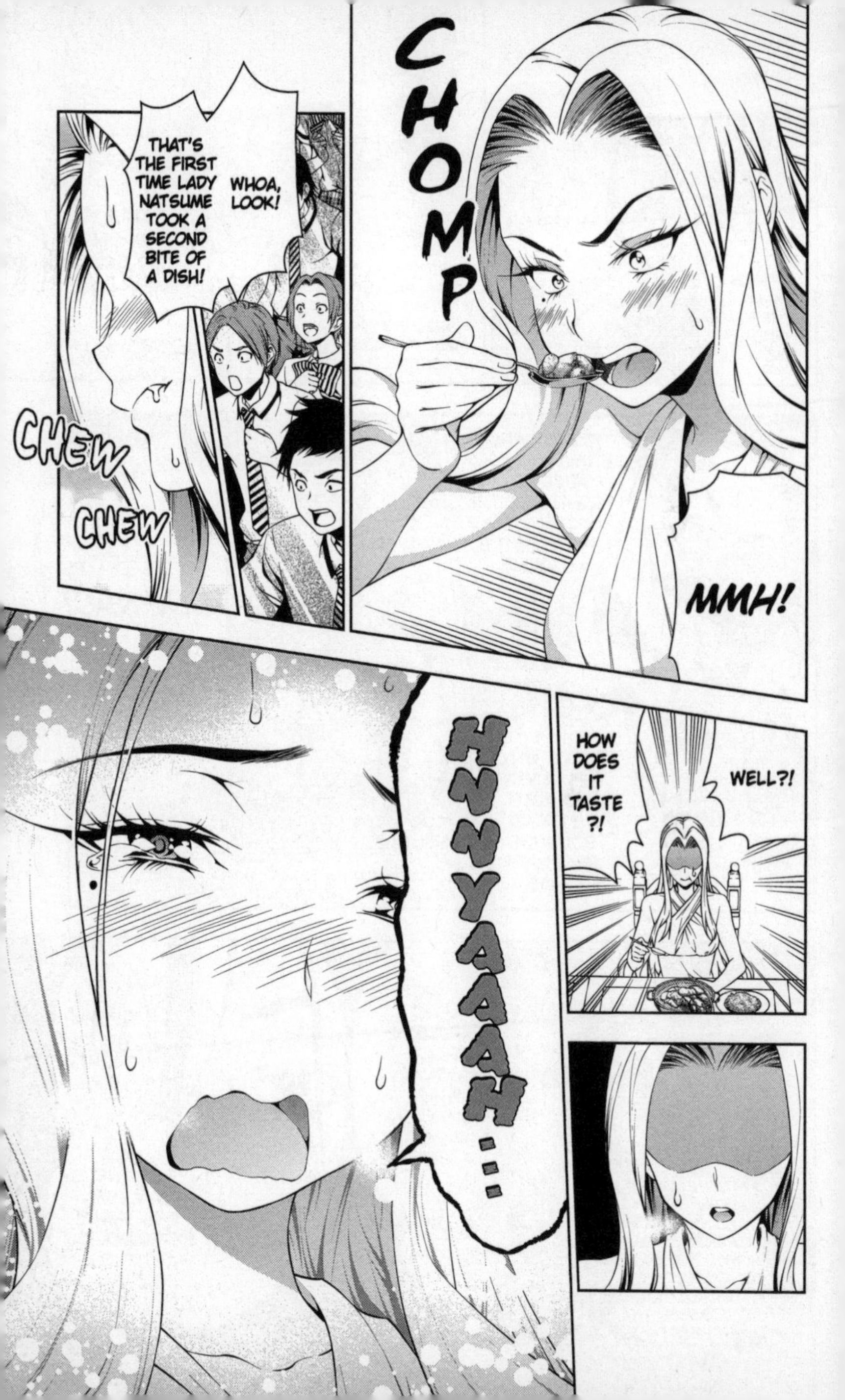
CHOMP
MMH!
WHOA, LOOK!
THAT'S THE FIRST TIME LADY NATSUME TOOK A SECOND BITE OF A DISH!
CHEW
CHEW
WELL?!
HOW DOES IT TASTE?!
HNNYAAAH...

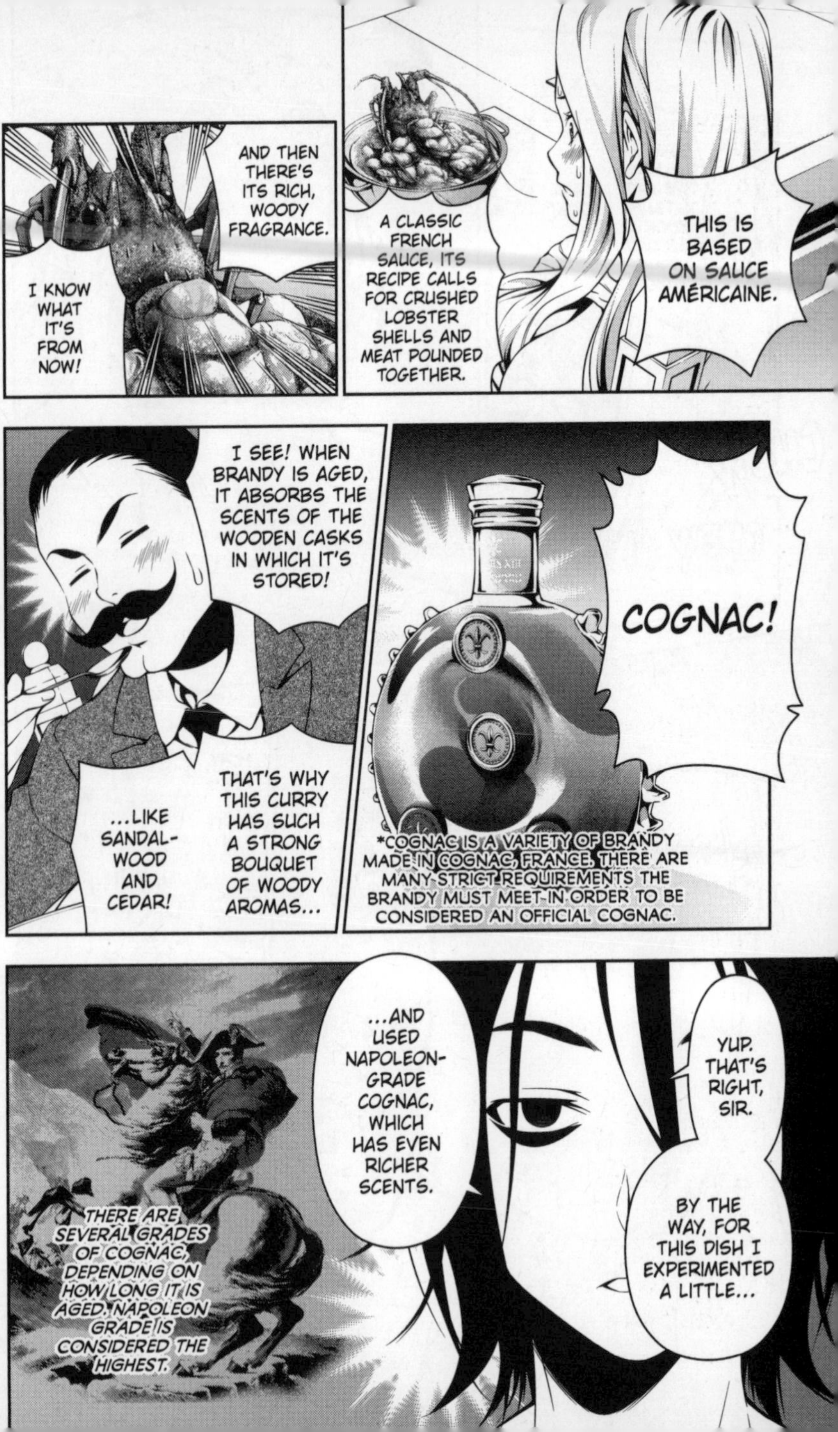
THIS IS BASED ON SAUCE AMÉRICAINE.
A CLASSIC FRENCH SAUCE, ITS RECIPE CALLS FOR CRUSHED LOBSTER SHELLS AND MEAT POUNDED TOGETHER.
AND THEN THERE'S ITS RICH, WOODY FRAGRANCE.
I KNOW WHAT IT'S FROM NOW!
COGNAC!
*COGNAC IS A VARIETY OF BRANDY MADE IN COGNAC, FRANCE. THERE ARE MANY STRICT REQUIREMENTS THE BRANDY MUST MEET IN ORDER TO BE CONSIDERED AN OFFICIAL COGNAC.
I SEE! WHEN BRANDY IS AGED, IT ABSORBS THE SCENTS OF THE WOODEN CASKS IN WHICH IT'S STORED!
THAT'S WHY THIS CURRY HAS SUCH A STRONG BOUQUET OF WOODY AROMAS...
...LIKE SANDAL-WOOD AND CEDAR!
YUP. THAT'S RIGHT, SIR.
BY THE WAY, FOR THIS DISH I EXPERIMENTED A LITTLE...
...AND USED NAPOLEON-GRADE COGNAC, WHICH HAS EVEN RICHER SCENTS.
THERE ARE SEVERAL GRADES OF COGNAC, DEPENDING ON HOW LONG IT IS AGED. NAPOLEON GRADE IS CONSIDERED THE HIGHEST.

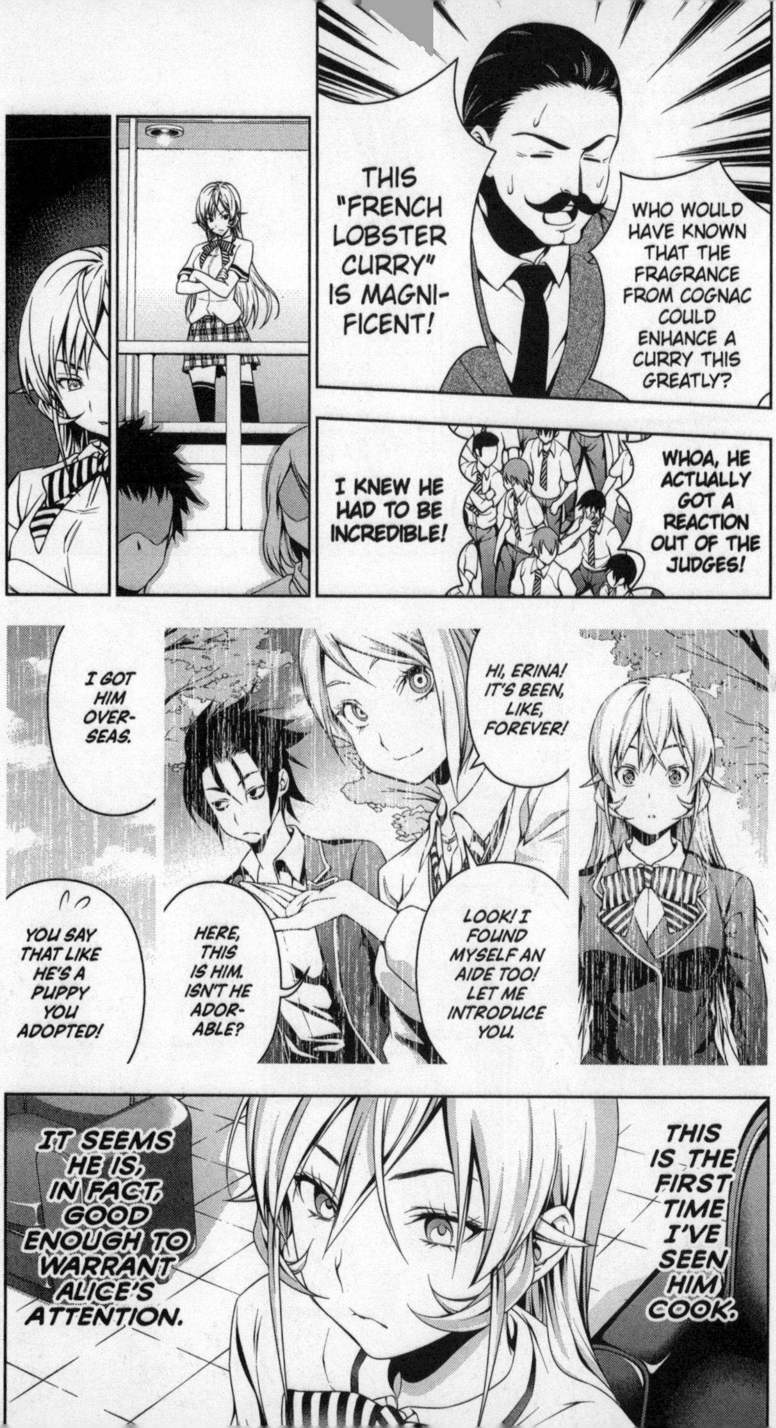
WHO WOULD HAVE KNOWN THAT THE FRAGRANCE FROM COGNAC COULD ENHANCE A CURRY THIS GREATLY?
THIS "FRENCH LOBSTER CURRY" IS MAGNIFICENT!
WHOA, HE ACTUALLY GOT A REACTION OUT OF THE JUDGES!
I KNEW HE HAD TO BE INCREDIBLE!
HI, ERINA! IT'S BEEN, LIKE, FOREVER!
LOOK! I FOUND MYSELF AN AIDE TOO! LET ME INTRODUCE YOU.
HERE, THIS IS HIM. ISN'T HE ADORABLE?
I GOT HIM OVERSEAS.
YOU SAY THAT LIKE HE'S A PUPPY YOU ADOPTED!
THIS IS THE FIRST TIME I'VE SEEN HIM COOK.
IT SEEMS HE IS, IN FACT, GOOD ENOUGH TO WARRANT ALICE'S ATTENTION.

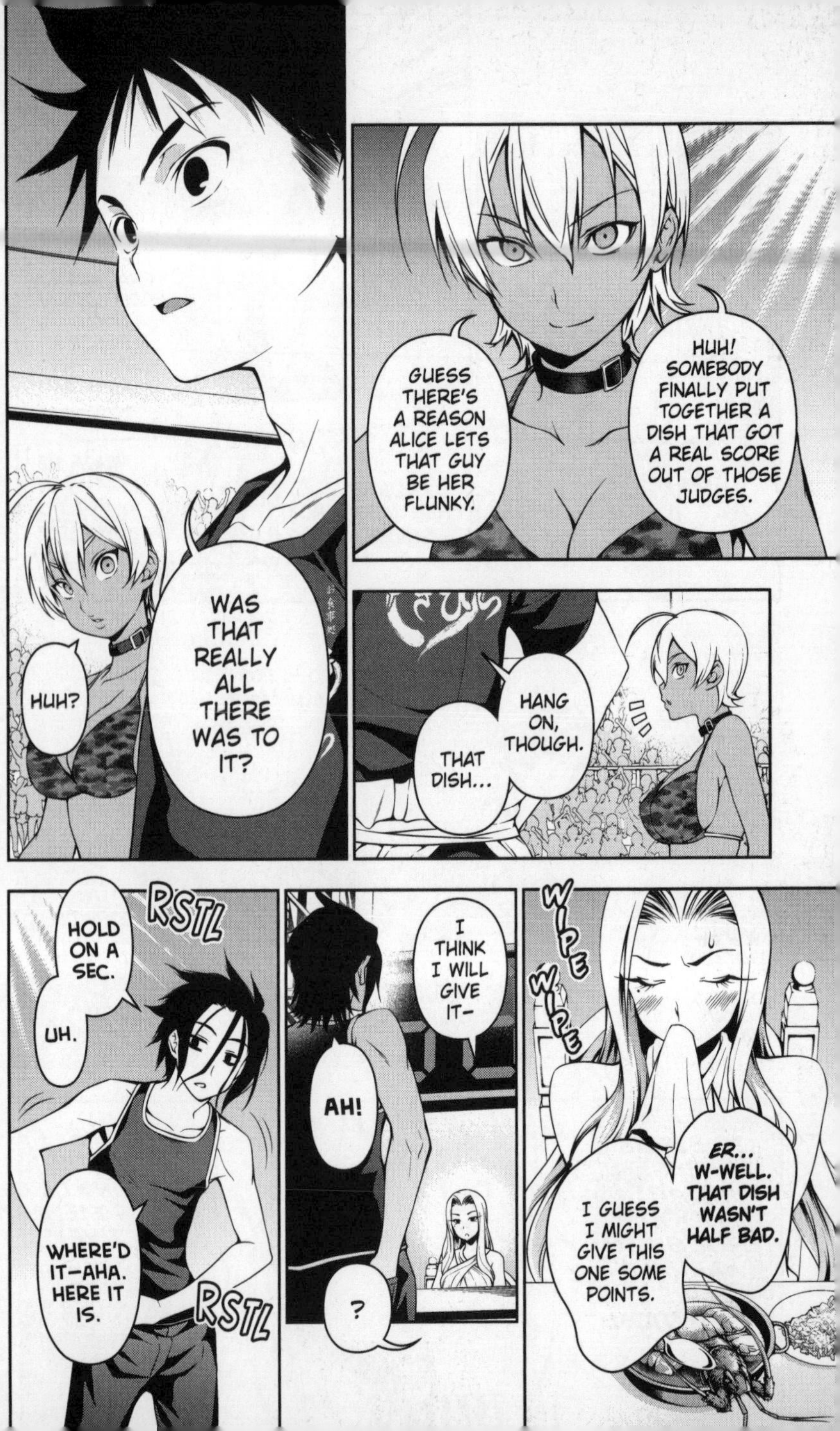
HUH! SOMEBODY FINALLY PUT TOGETHER A DISH THAT GOT A REAL SCORE OUT OF THOSE JUDGES.
GUESS THERE'S A REASON ALICE LETS THAT GUY BE HER FLUNKY.
HANG ON, THOUGH.
THAT DISH...
WAS THAT REALLY ALL THERE WAS TO IT?
HUH?
WIPE WIPE
ER... W-WELL. THAT DISH WASN'T HALF BAD.
I GUESS I MIGHT GIVE THIS ONE SOME POINTS.
I THINK I WILL GIVE IT–
AH!
?
RSTL
HOLD ON A SEC.
UH.
WHERE'D IT—AHA. HERE IT IS.
RSTL

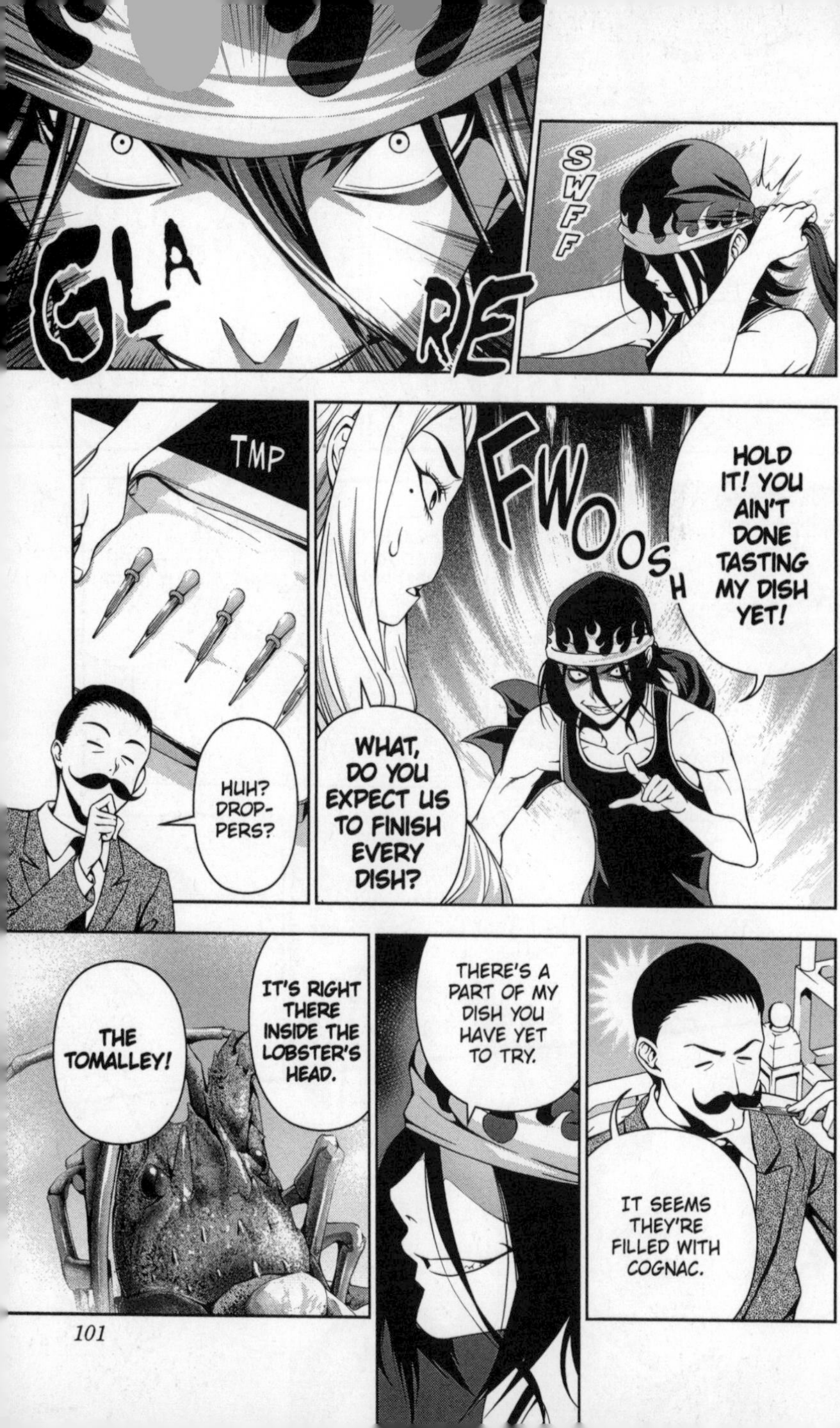
SWFF
GLARE
FWOOSH
HOLD IT! YOU AIN'T DONE TASTING MY DISH YET!
WHAT, DO YOU EXPECT US TO FINISH EVERY DISH?
TMP
HUH? DROP-PERS?
IT SEEMS THEY'RE FILLED WITH COGNAC.
THERE'S A PART OF MY DISH YOU HAVE YET TO TRY.
IT'S RIGHT THERE INSIDE THE LOBSTER'S HEAD.
THE TOMALLEY!

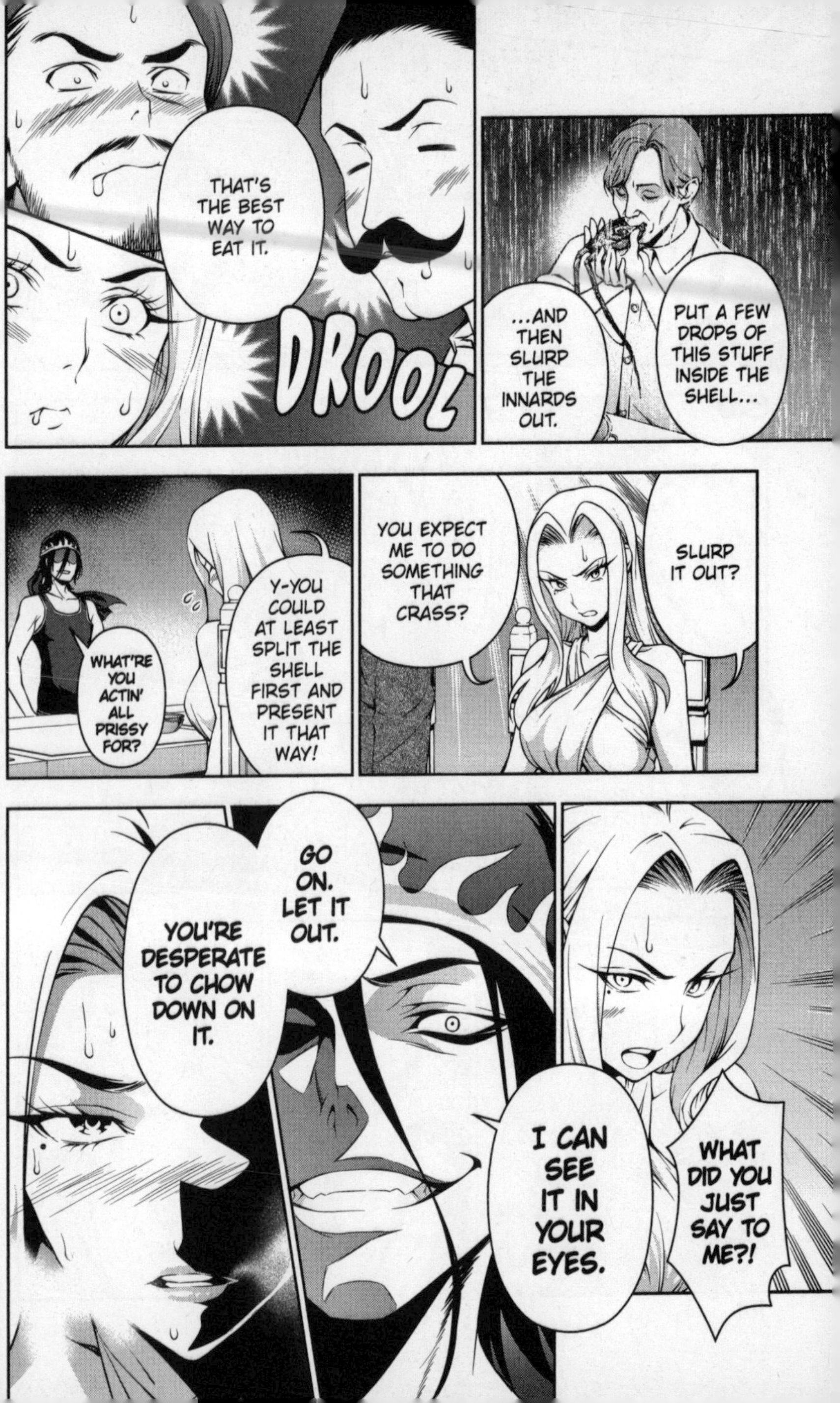
PUT A FEW DROPS OF THIS STUFF INSIDE THE SHELL...
...AND THEN SLURP THE INNARDS OUT.
THAT'S THE BEST WAY TO EAT IT.
DROOL
SLURP IT OUT?
YOU EXPECT ME TO DO SOMETHING THAT CRASS?
Y-YOU COULD AT LEAST SPLIT THE SHELL FIRST AND PRESENT IT THAT WAY!
WHAT'RE YOU ACTIN' ALL PRISSY FOR?
WHAT DID YOU JUST SAY TO ME?!
GO ON. LET IT OUT.
YOU'RE DESPERATE TO CHOW DOWN ON IT.
I CAN SEE IT IN YOUR EYES.

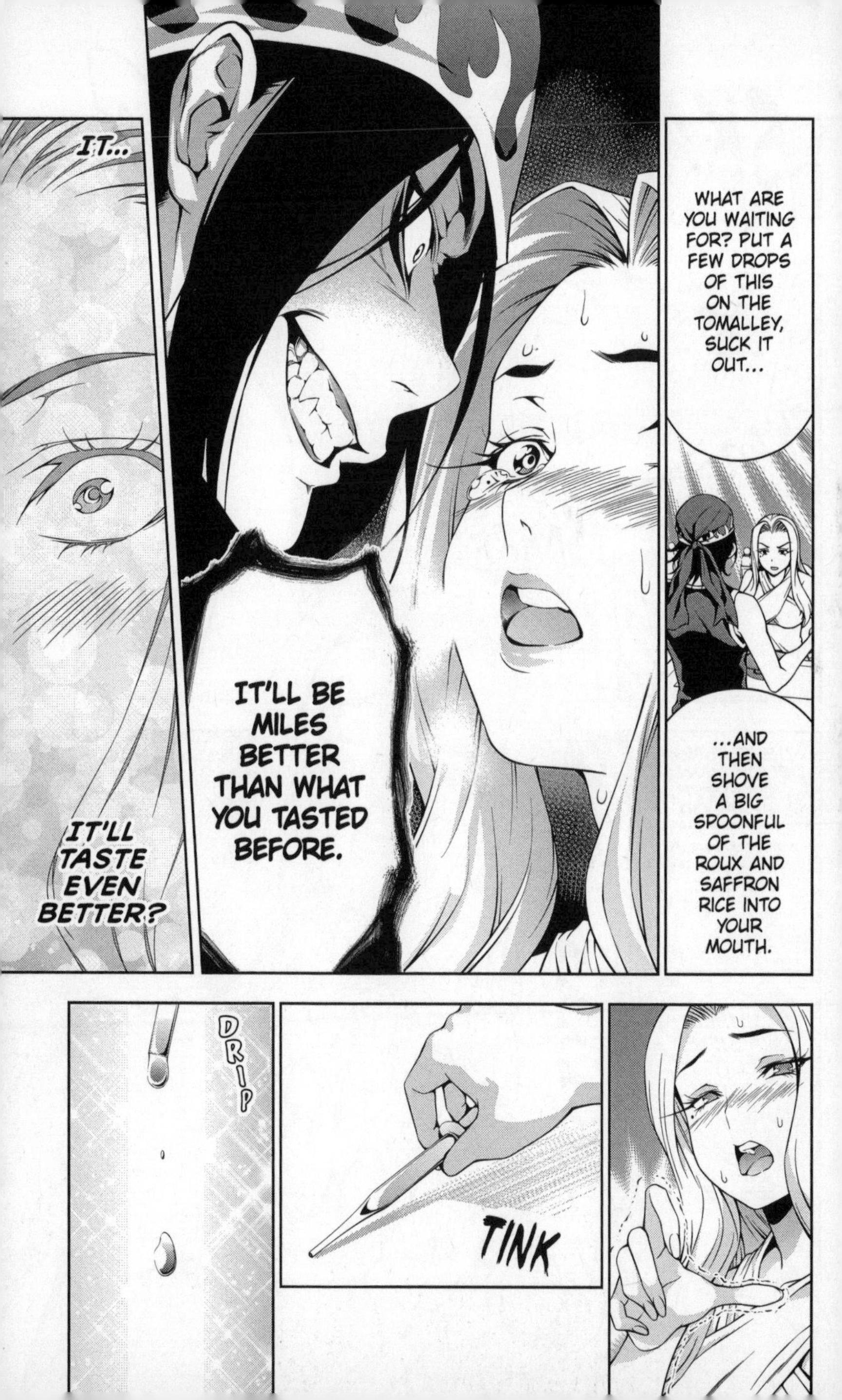
WHAT ARE YOU WAITING FOR? PUT A FEW DROPS OF THIS ON THE TOMALLEY, SUCK IT OUT...
...AND THEN SHOVE A BIG SPOONFUL OF THE ROUX AND SAFFRON RICE INTO YOUR MOUTH.
IT'LL BE MILES BETTER THAN WHAT YOU TASTED BEFORE.
IT...
IT'LL TASTE EVEN BETTER?
TINK
DRIP

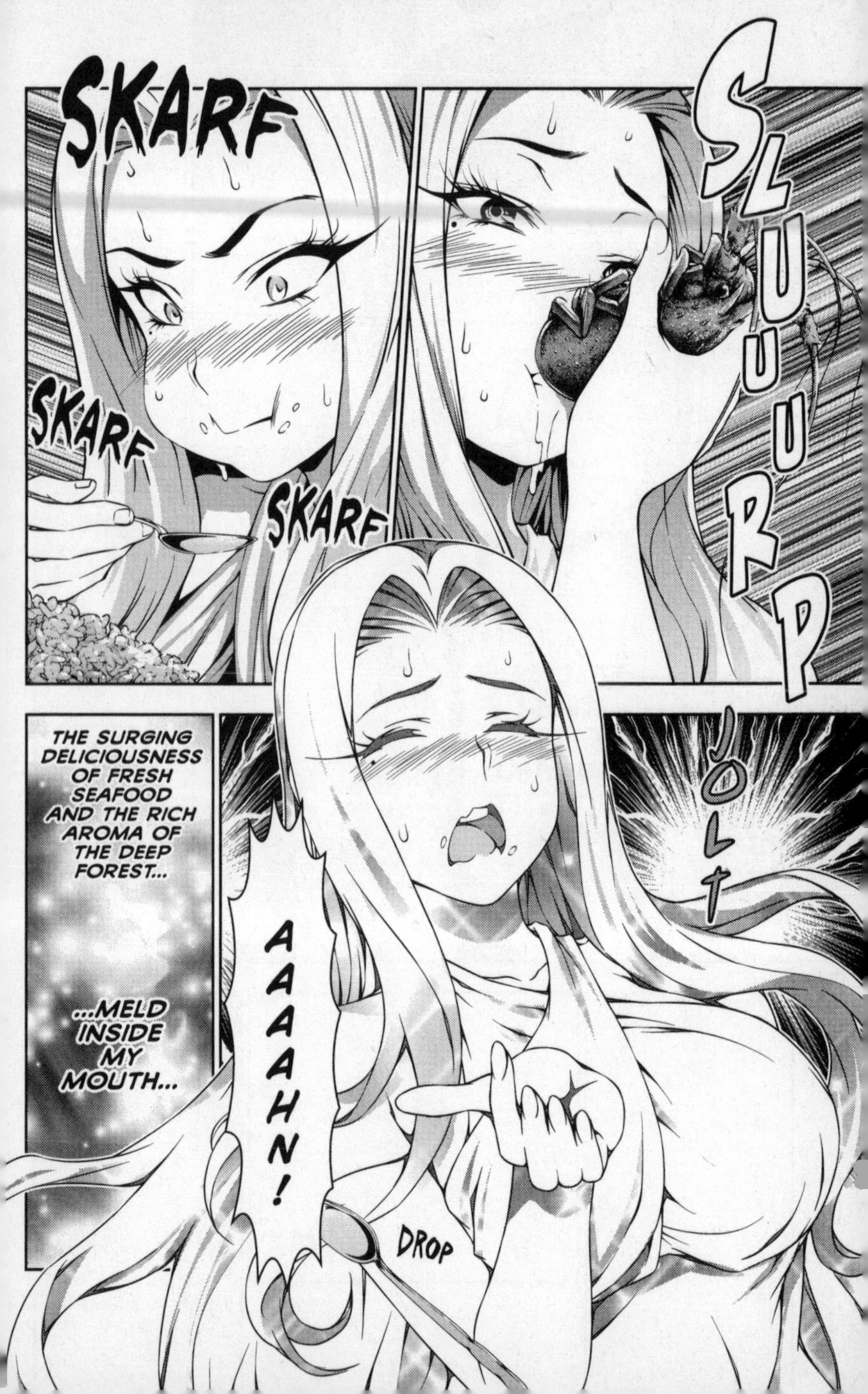
SLUUURP
SKARF
SKARF
SKARF
JOLT
AAAAAHN!
DROP
THE SURGING DELICIOUSNESS OF FRESH SEAFOOD AND THE RICH AROMA OF THE DEEP FOREST...
...MELD INSIDE MY MOUTH...

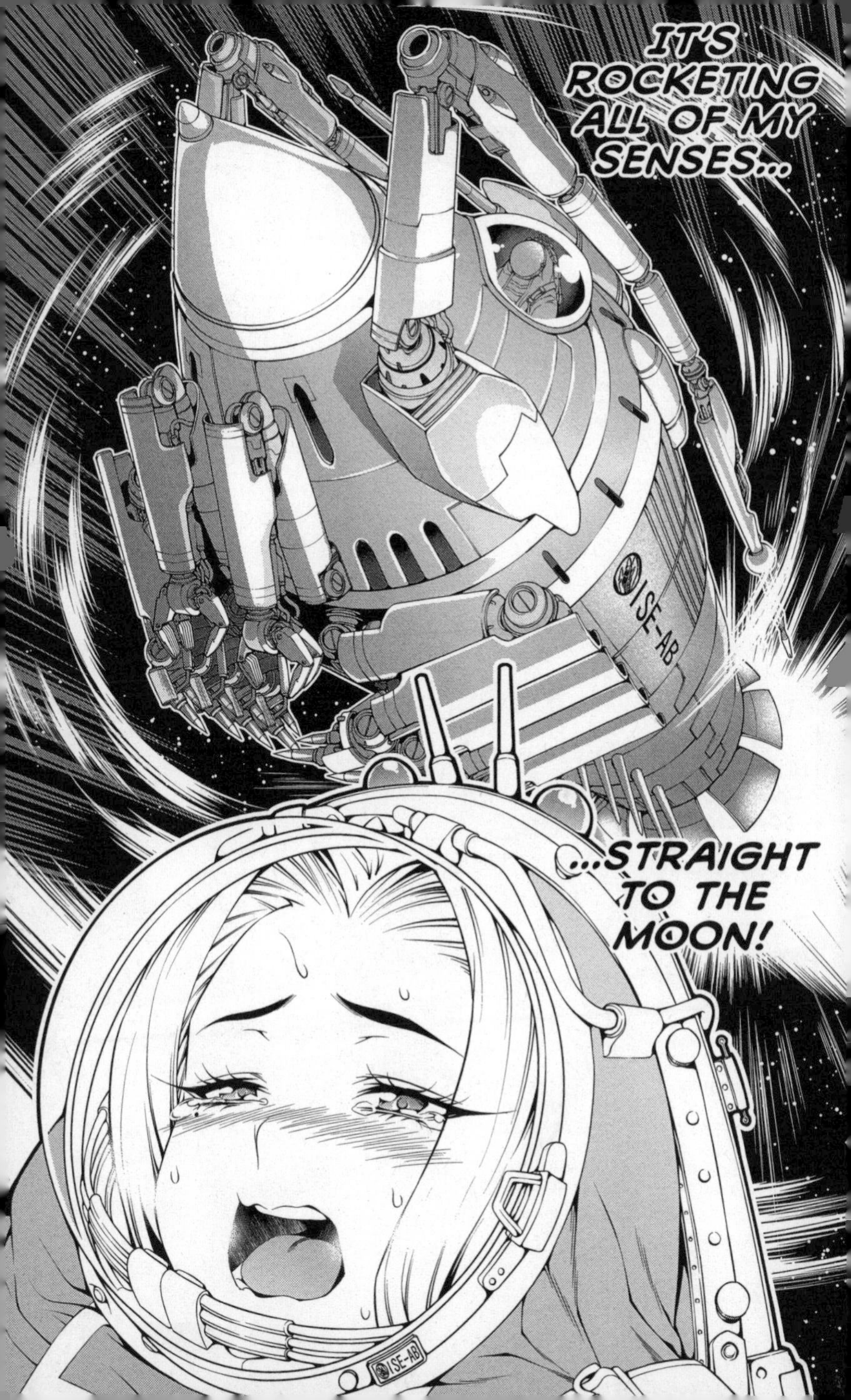
IT'S ROCKETING ALL OF MY SENSES...
...STRAIGHT TO THE MOON!
ISE-AB

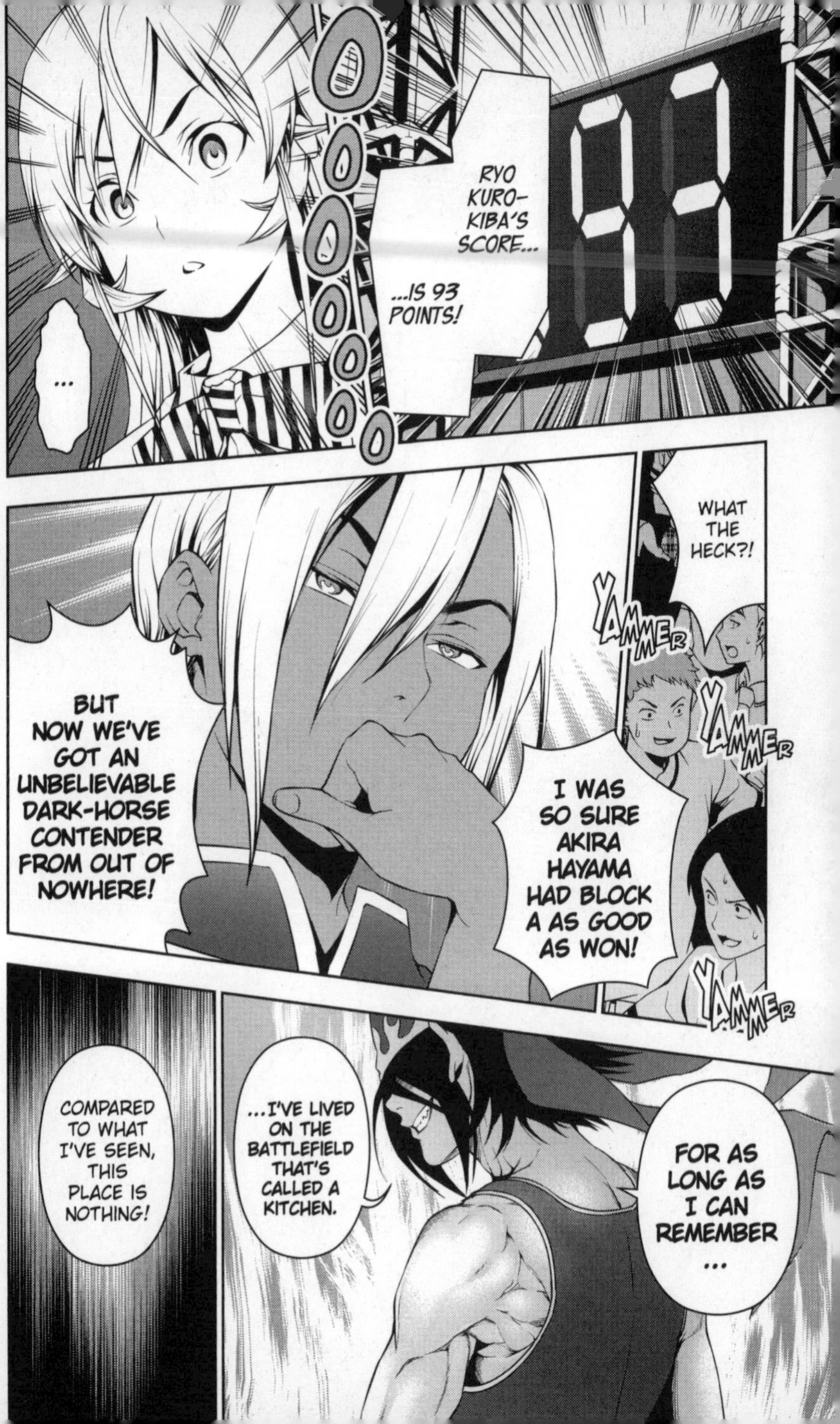
RYO KURO-KIBA'S SCORE...
...IS 93 POINTS!
...
WHAT THE HECK?!
YAMMER
YAMMER
I WAS SO SURE AKIRA HAYAMA HAD BLOCK A AS GOOD AS WON!
YAMMER
BUT NOW WE'VE GOT AN UNBELIEVABLE DARK-HORSE CONTENDER FROM OUT OF NOWHERE!
FOR AS LONG AS I CAN REMEMBER...
...I'VE LIVED ON THE BATTLEFIELD THAT'S CALLED A KITCHEN.
COMPARED TO WHAT I'VE SEEN, THIS PLACE IS NOTHING!

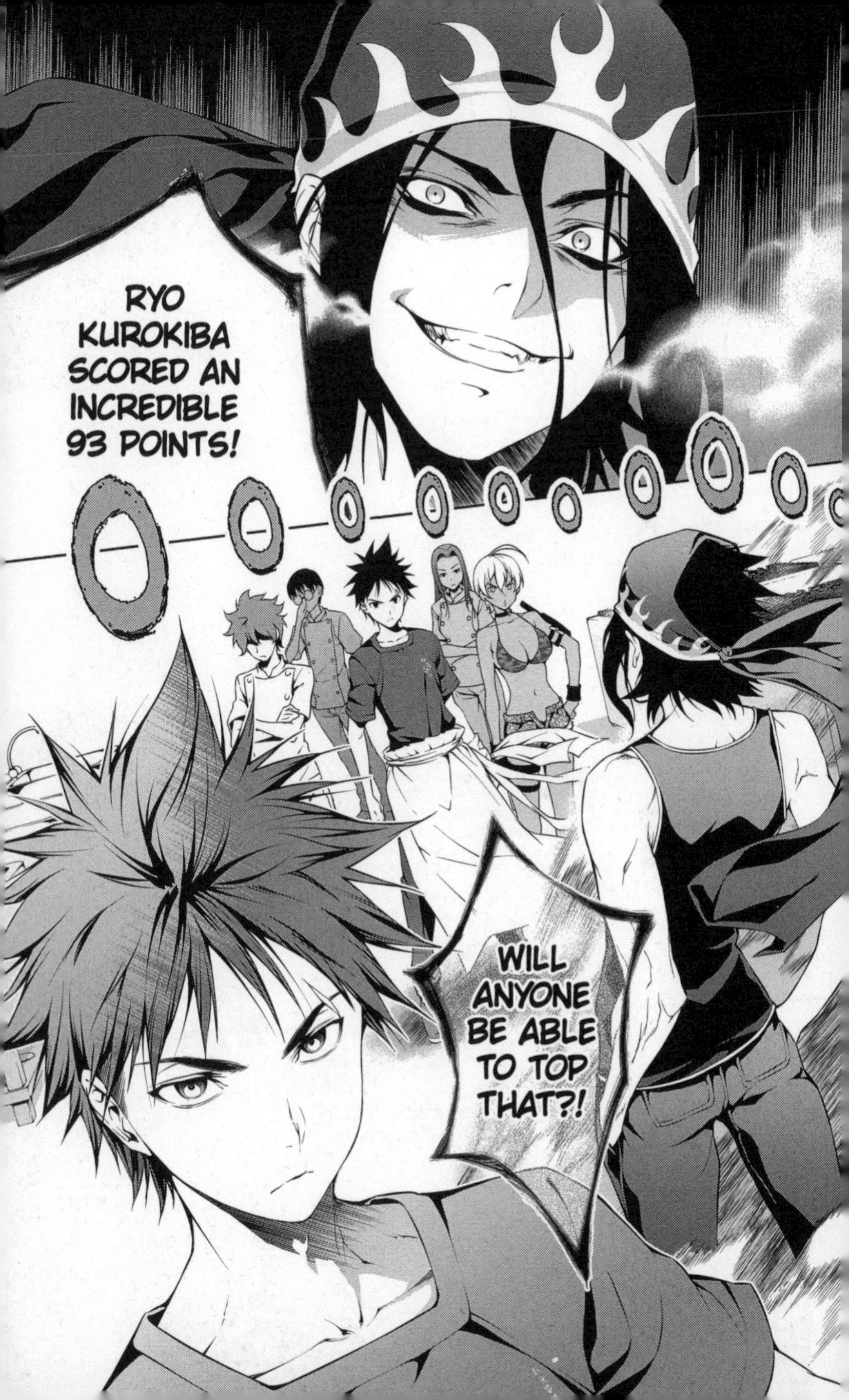
RYO KUROKIBA SCORED AN INCREDIBLE 93 POINTS!
WILL ANYONE BE ABLE TO TOP THAT?!

BING BONG DING DONG

ATTENTION—

IN THE ORIGINAL WEEKLY JUMP MAGAZINE, THE SIDE STORY "ERINA'S SUMMER VACATION" WAS RUN ALONGSIDE CHAPTER 53, "THE MAN FROM THE FROZEN NORTH." HOWEVER, DUE TO PAGE CONSTRAINTS, WE WERE UNABLE TO INCLUDE IT IN VOLUME 7. WE DO INTEND TO ADD IT TO A VOLUME AT SOME POINT. ERINA FANS, PLEASE HAVE A LITTLE MORE PATIENCE.

SORRY.

NOW BACK TO OUR REGULARLY SCHEDULED STORY...

DING DONG BING BONG

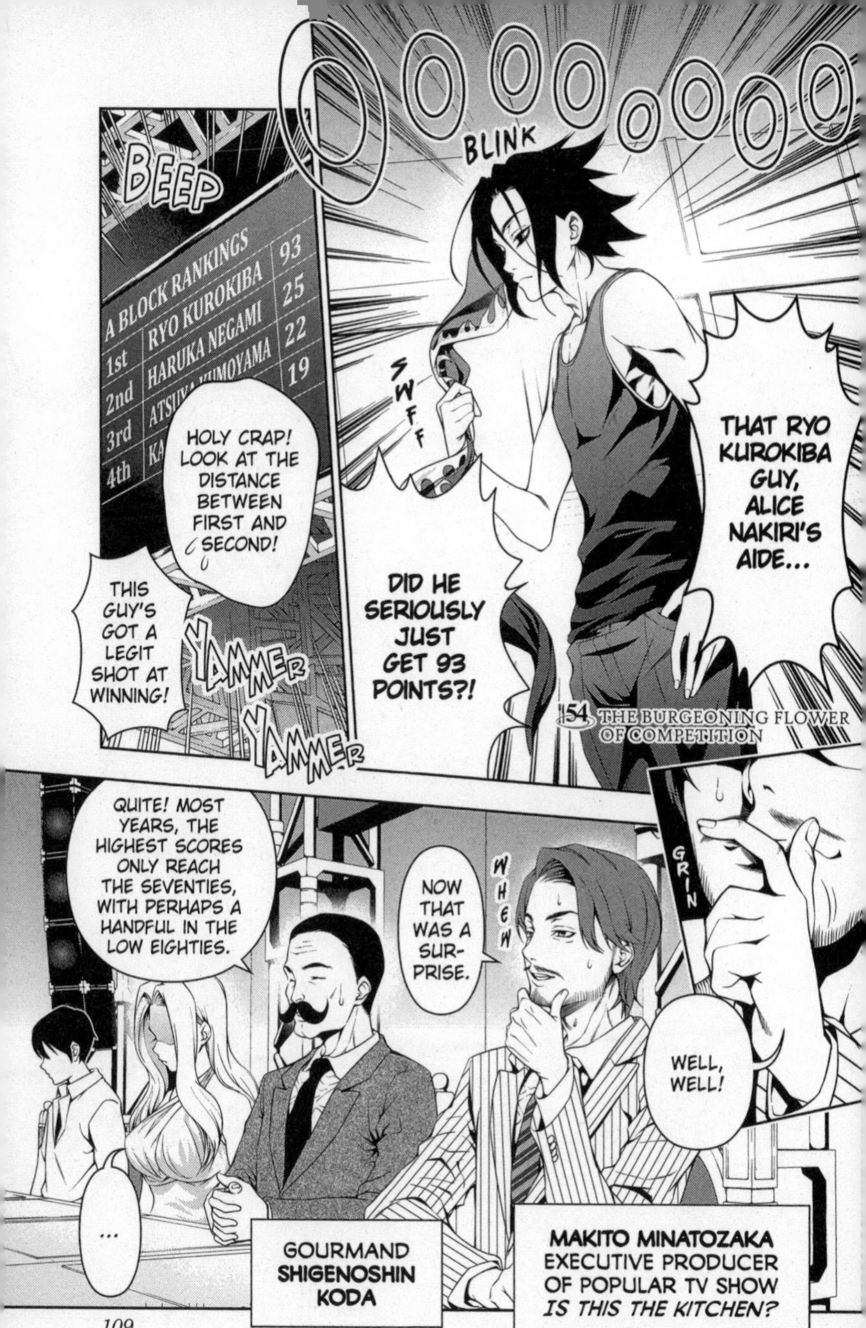
OOOOOOOOO
BLINK
THAT RYO KUROKIBA GUY, ALICE NAKIRI'S AIDE...
DID HE SERIOUSLY JUST GET 93 POINTS?!
SWFF
BEEP
A BLOCK RANKINGS
1st RYO KUROKIBA 93
2nd HARUKA NEGAMI 25
3rd ATSUYA 22
4th KA 19
HOLY CRAP! LOOK AT THE DISTANCE BETWEEN FIRST AND SECOND!
THIS GUY'S GOT A LEGIT SHOT AT WINNING!
YAMMER YAMMER
54 THE BURGEONING FLOWER OF COMPETITION
GRIN
WELL, WELL!
MAKITO MINATOZAKA EXECUTIVE PRODUCER OF POPULAR TV SHOW *IS THIS THE KITCHEN?*
WHEW
NOW THAT WAS A SUR-PRISE.
QUITE! MOST YEARS, THE HIGHEST SCORES ONLY REACH THE SEVENTIES, WITH PERHAPS A HANDFUL IN THE LOW EIGHTIES.
GOURMAND SHIGENOSHIN KODA
...

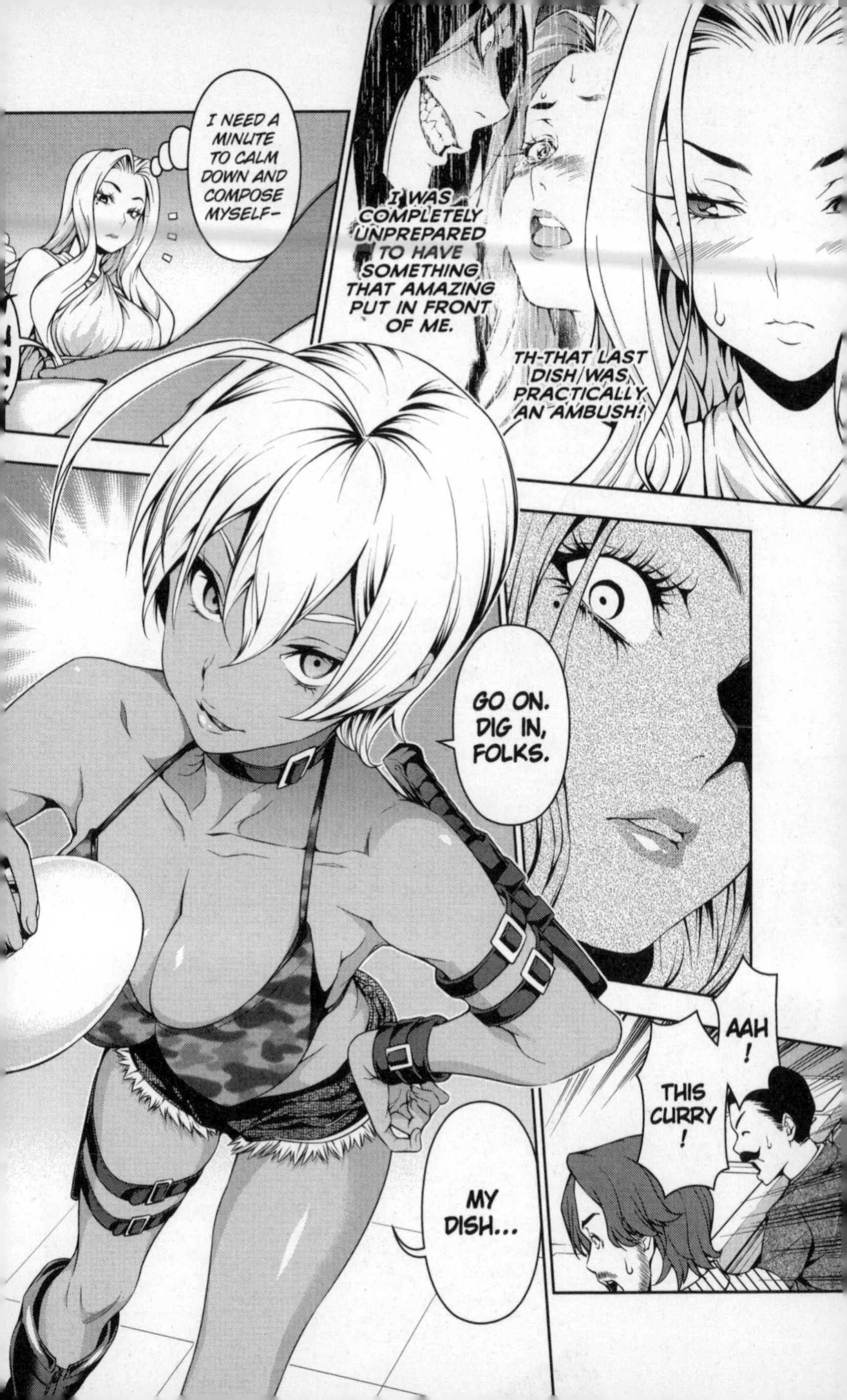
I WAS COMPLETELY UNPREPARED TO HAVE SOMETHING THAT AMAZING PUT IN FRONT OF ME.
TH-THAT LAST DISH WAS PRACTICALLY AN AMBUSH!
I NEED A MINUTE TO CALM DOWN AND COMPOSE MYSELF-
GO ON. DIG IN, FOLKS.
AAH!
THIS CURRY!
MY DISH...

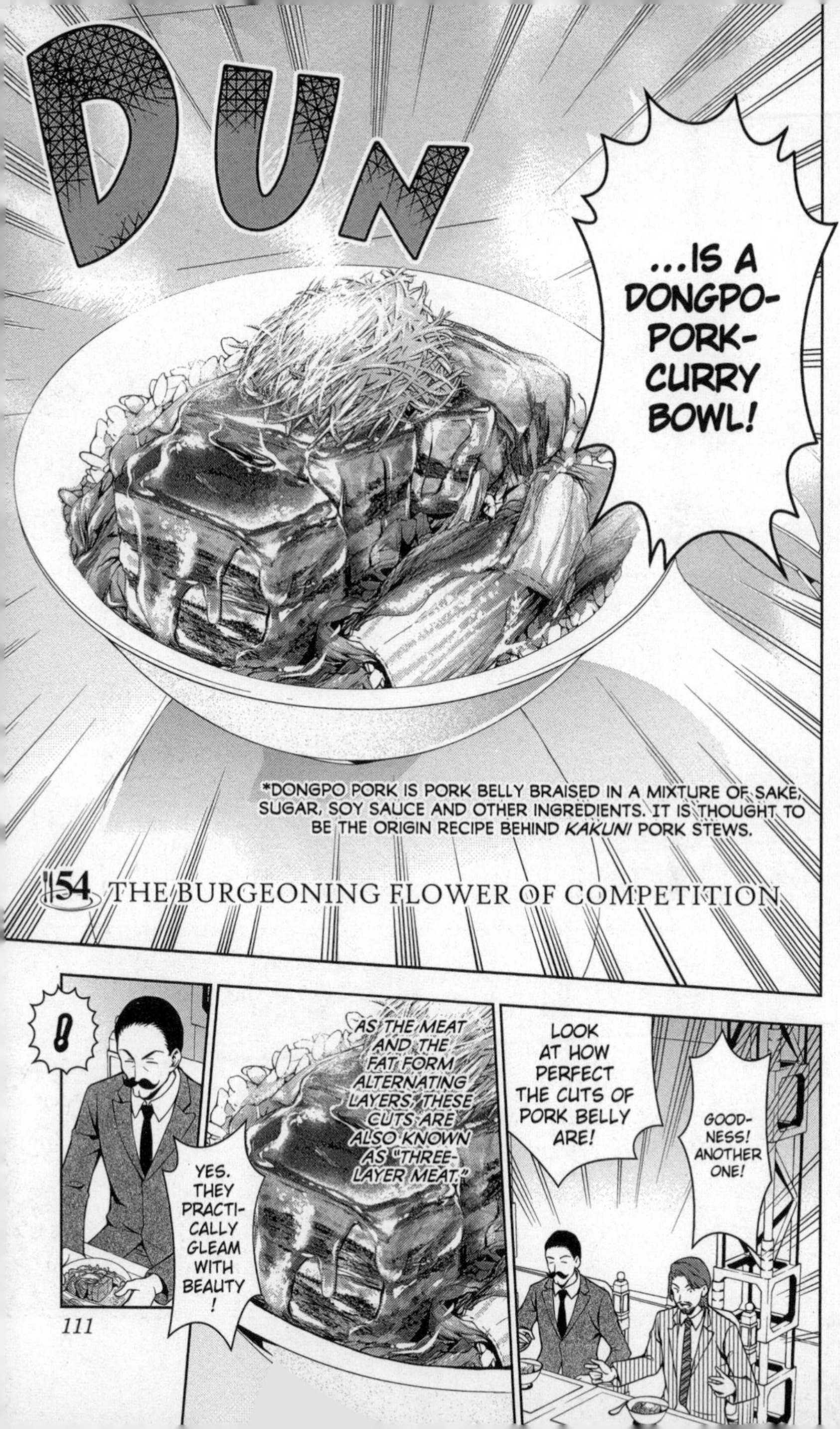
DUN
...IS A DONGPO-PORK-CURRY BOWL!
*DONGPO PORK IS PORK BELLY BRAISED IN A MIXTURE OF SAKE, SUGAR, SOY SAUCE AND OTHER INGREDIENTS. IT IS THOUGHT TO BE THE ORIGIN RECIPE BEHIND *KAKUNI* PORK STEWS.
54 THE BURGEONING FLOWER OF COMPETITION
GOODNESS! ANOTHER ONE!
LOOK AT HOW PERFECT THE CUTS OF PORK BELLY ARE!
AS THE MEAT AND THE FAT FORM ALTERNATING LAYERS, THESE CUTS ARE ALSO KNOWN AS "THREE-LAYER MEAT."
!
YES. THEY PRACTICALLY GLEAM WITH BEAUTY!

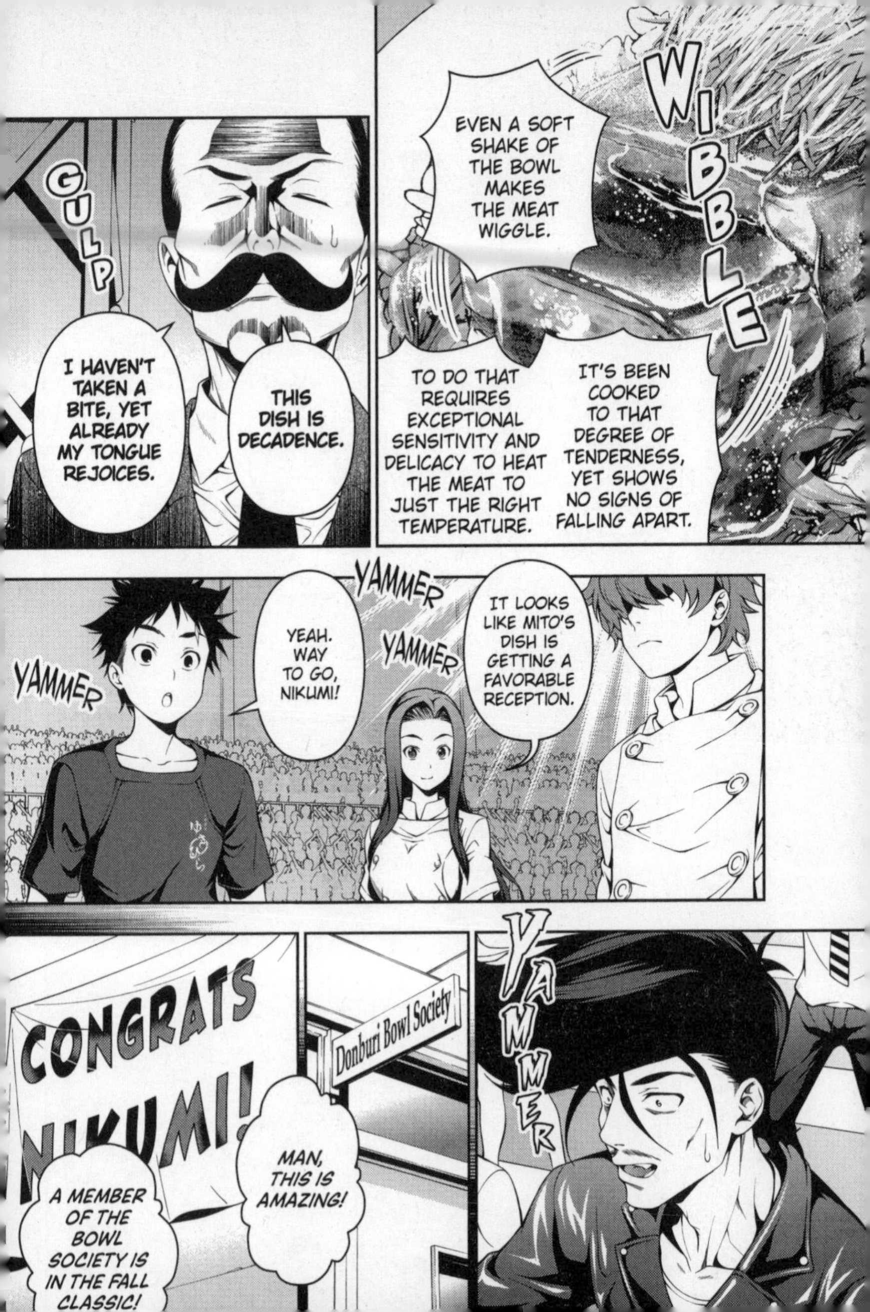
WIBBLE
EVEN A SOFT SHAKE OF THE BOWL MAKES THE MEAT WIGGLE.
IT'S BEEN COOKED TO THAT DEGREE OF TENDERNESS, YET SHOWS NO SIGNS OF FALLING APART.
TO DO THAT REQUIRES EXCEPTIONAL SENSITIVITY AND DELICACY TO HEAT THE MEAT TO JUST THE RIGHT TEMPERATURE.
GULP
THIS DISH IS DECADENCE.
I HAVEN'T TAKEN A BITE, YET ALREADY MY TONGUE REJOICES.
IT LOOKS LIKE MITO'S DISH IS GETTING A FAVORABLE RECEPTION.
YAMMER
YAMMER
YEAH. WAY TO GO, NIKUMI!
YAMMER
YAMMER
Donburi Bowl Society
MAN, THIS IS AMAZING!
CONGRATS NIKUMI!
A MEMBER OF THE BOWL SOCIETY IS IN THE FALL CLASSIC!

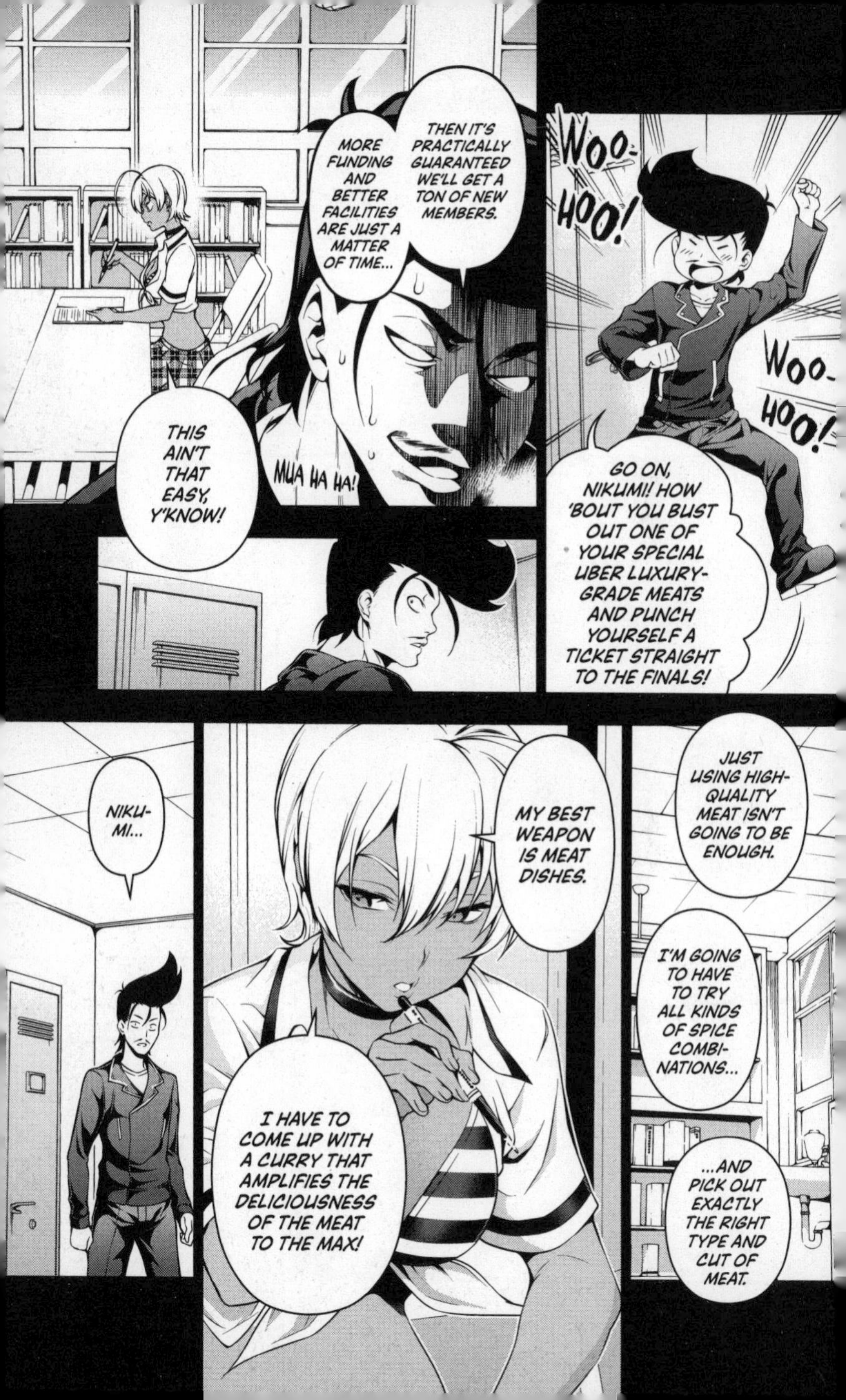
WOO-HOO!
WOO-HOO!
GO ON, NIKUMI! HOW 'BOUT YOU BUST OUT ONE OF YOUR SPECIAL UBER LUXURY-GRADE MEATS AND PUNCH YOURSELF A TICKET STRAIGHT TO THE FINALS!
THEN IT'S PRACTICALLY GUARANTEED WE'LL GET A TON OF NEW MEMBERS.
MORE FUNDING AND BETTER FACILITIES ARE JUST A MATTER OF TIME...
MUA HA HA!
THIS AIN'T THAT EASY, Y'KNOW!
JUST USING HIGH-QUALITY MEAT ISN'T GOING TO BE ENOUGH.
I'M GOING TO HAVE TO TRY ALL KINDS OF SPICE COMBI-NATIONS...
...AND PICK OUT EXACTLY THE RIGHT TYPE AND CUT OF MEAT.
MY BEST WEAPON IS MEAT DISHES.
I HAVE TO COME UP WITH A CURRY THAT AMPLIFIES THE DELICIOUSNESS OF THE MEAT TO THE MAX!
NIKU-MI...

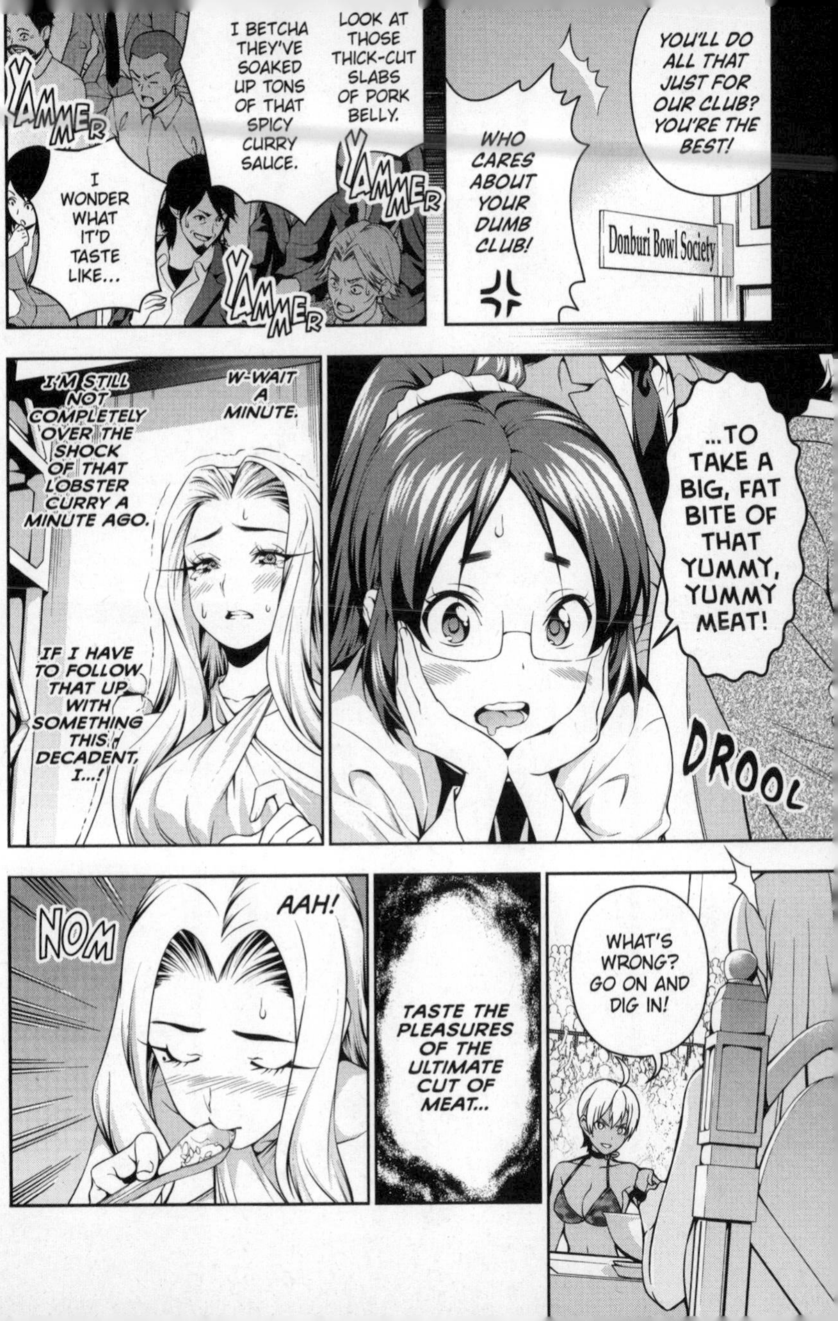
YOU'LL DO ALL THAT JUST FOR OUR CLUB? YOU'RE THE BEST!
Donburi Bowl Society
WHO CARES ABOUT YOUR DUMB CLUB!
LOOK AT THOSE THICK-CUT SLABS OF PORK BELLY.
YAMMER
I BETCHA THEY'VE SOAKED UP TONS OF THAT SPICY CURRY SAUCE.
YAMMER
YAMMER
I WONDER WHAT IT'D TASTE LIKE...
...TO TAKE A BIG, FAT BITE OF THAT YUMMY, YUMMY MEAT!
DROOL
W-WAIT A MINUTE.
I'M STILL NOT COMPLETELY OVER THE SHOCK OF THAT LOBSTER CURRY A MINUTE AGO.
IF I HAVE TO FOLLOW THAT UP WITH SOMETHING THIS DECADENT, I...!
WHAT'S WRONG? GO ON AND DIG IN!
TASTE THE PLEASURES OF THE ULTIMATE CUT OF MEAT...
AAH!
NOM

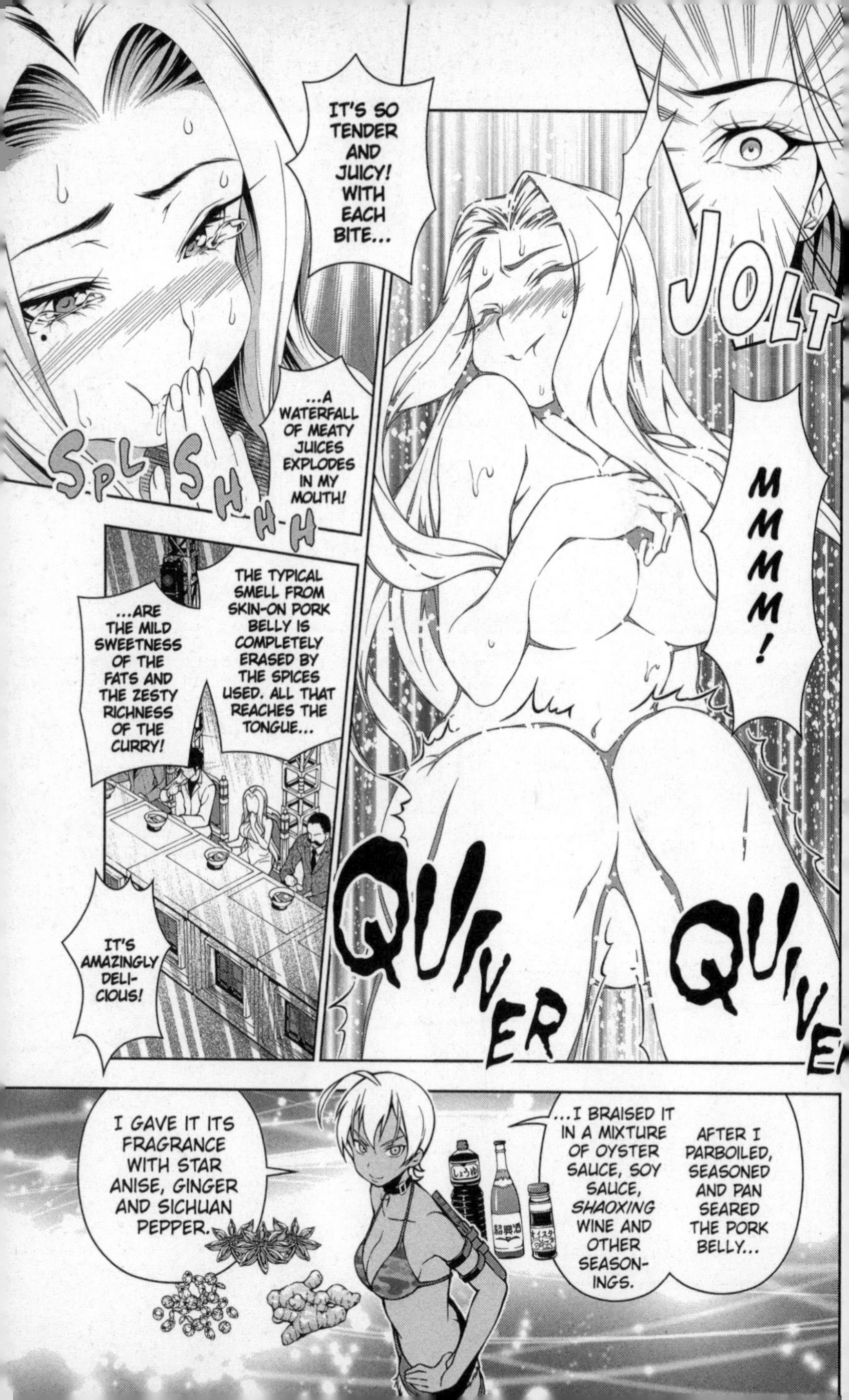
JOLT
MMMM!
QUIVER
QUIVER
IT'S SO TENDER AND JUICY! WITH EACH BITE...
SPLSHHH
...A WATERFALL OF MEATY JUICES EXPLODES IN MY MOUTH!
THE TYPICAL SMELL FROM SKIN-ON PORK BELLY IS COMPLETELY ERASED BY THE SPICES USED. ALL THAT REACHES THE TONGUE...
...ARE THE MILD SWEETNESS OF THE FATS AND THE ZESTY RICHNESS OF THE CURRY!
IT'S AMAZINGLY DELICIOUS!
AFTER I PARBOILED, SEASONED AND PAN SEARED THE PORK BELLY...
...I BRAISED IT IN A MIXTURE OF OYSTER SAUCE, SOY SAUCE, *SHAOXING* WINE AND OTHER SEASONINGS.
I GAVE IT ITS FRAGRANCE WITH STAR ANISE, GINGER AND SICHUAN PEPPER.

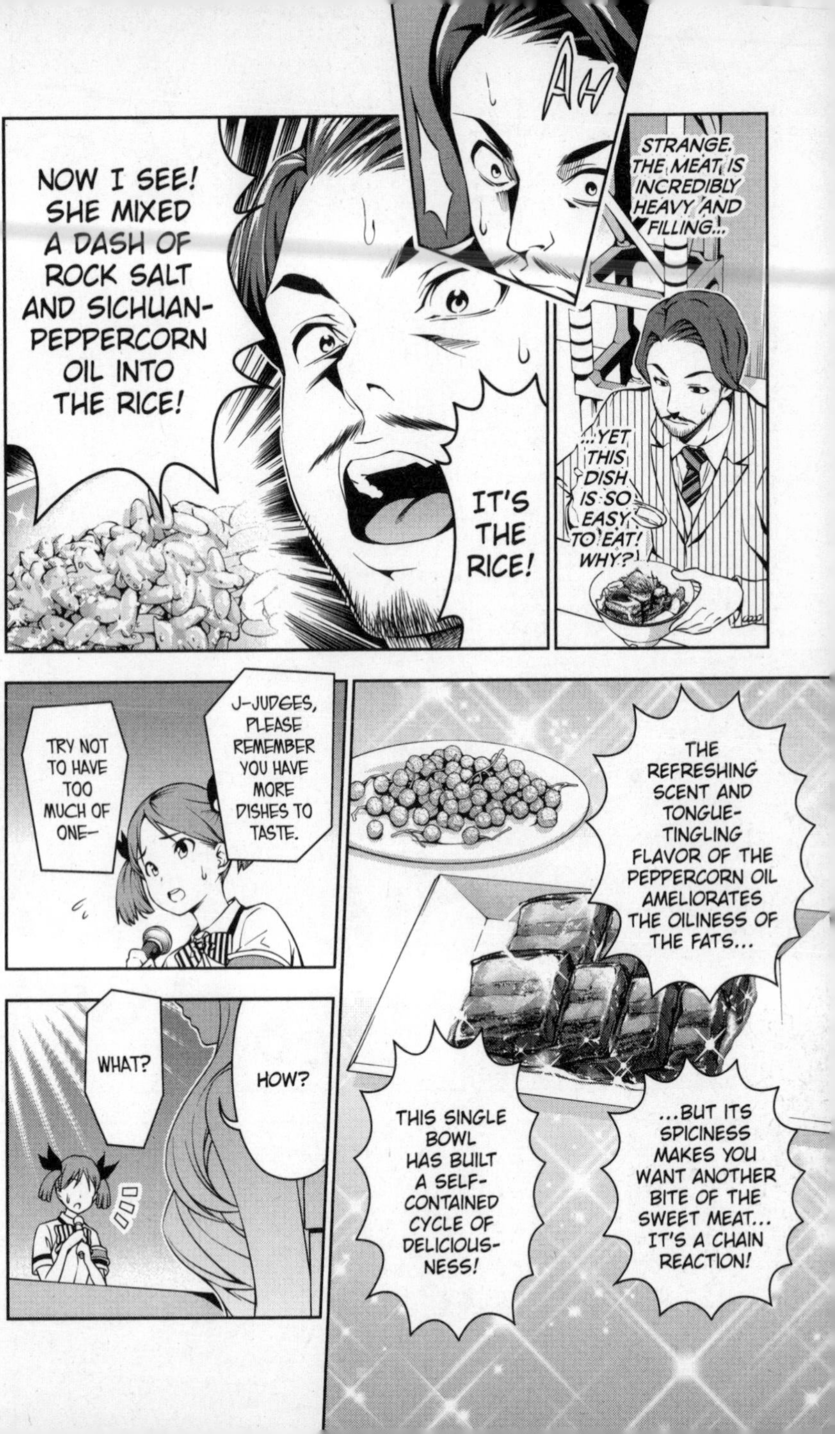
AH
STRANGE. THE MEAT IS INCREDIBLY HEAVY AND FILLING...
...YET THIS DISH IS SO EASY TO EAT! WHY?
IT'S THE RICE!
NOW I SEE! SHE MIXED A DASH OF ROCK SALT AND SICHUAN-PEPPERCORN OIL INTO THE RICE!
THE REFRESHING SCENT AND TONGUE-TINGLING FLAVOR OF THE PEPPERCORN OIL AMELIORATES THE OILINESS OF THE FATS...
...BUT ITS SPICINESS MAKES YOU WANT ANOTHER BITE OF THE SWEET MEAT... IT'S A CHAIN REACTION!
THIS SINGLE BOWL HAS BUILT A SELF-CONTAINED CYCLE OF DELICIOUS-NESS!
J-JUDGES, PLEASE REMEMBER YOU HAVE MORE DISHES TO TASTE.
TRY NOT TO HAVE TOO MUCH OF ONE—
HOW?
WHAT?

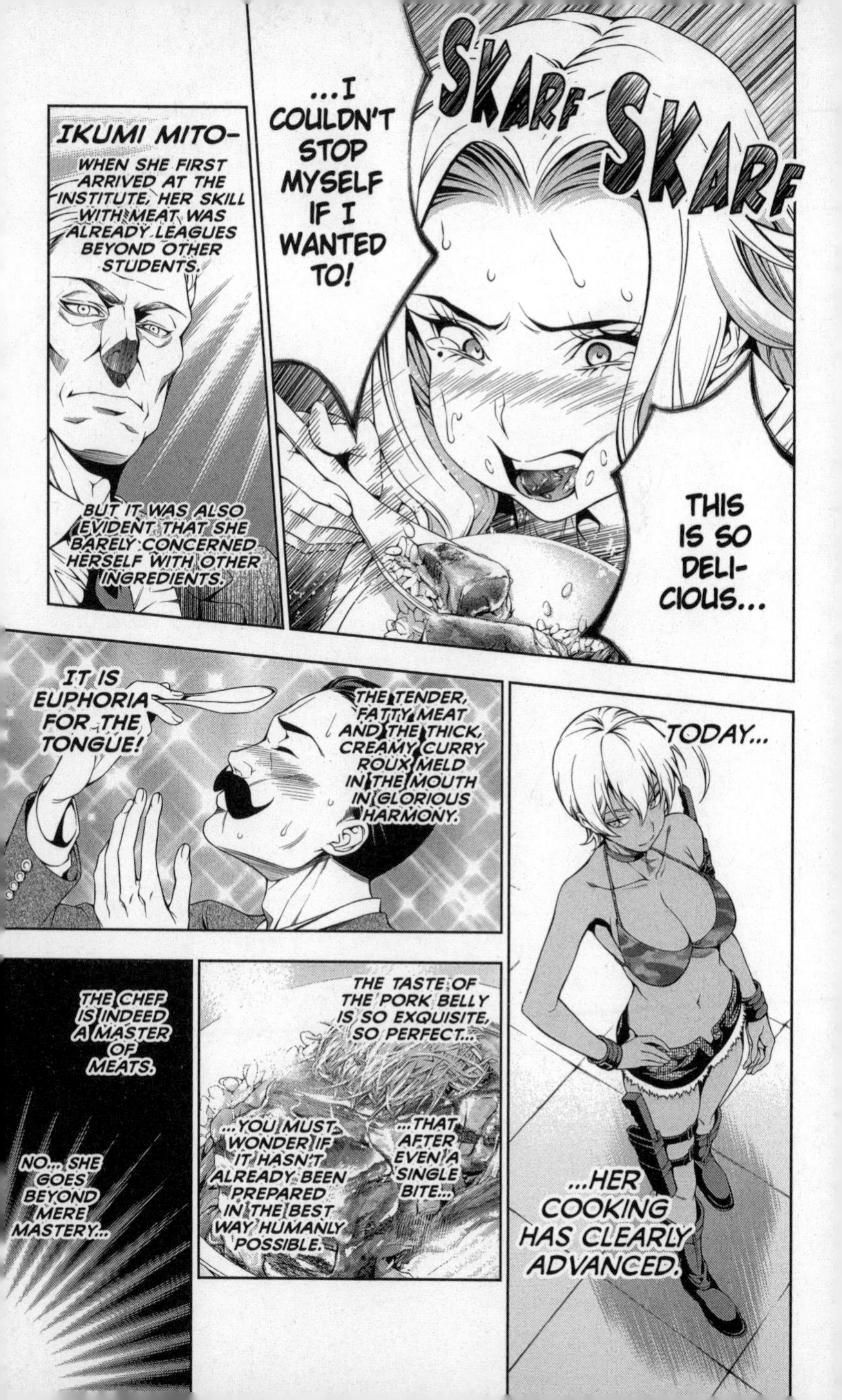
SKARF SKARF
...I COULDN'T STOP MYSELF IF I WANTED TO!
THIS IS SO DELICIOUS...
IKUMI MITO-
WHEN SHE FIRST ARRIVED AT THE INSTITUTE, HER SKILL WITH MEAT WAS ALREADY LEAGUES BEYOND OTHER STUDENTS.
BUT IT WAS ALSO EVIDENT THAT SHE BARELY CONCERNED HERSELF WITH OTHER INGREDIENTS.
TODAY...
...HER COOKING HAS CLEARLY ADVANCED.
THE TENDER, FATTY MEAT AND THE THICK, CREAMY CURRY ROUX MELD IN THE MOUTH IN GLORIOUS HARMONY.
IT IS EUPHORIA FOR THE TONGUE!
THE TASTE OF THE PORK BELLY IS SO EXQUISITE, SO PERFECT...
...THAT AFTER EVEN A SINGLE BITE...
...YOU MUST WONDER IF IT HASN'T ALREADY BEEN PREPARED IN THE BEST WAY HUMANLY POSSIBLE.
THE CHEF IS INDEED A MASTER OF MEATS.
NO... SHE GOES BEYOND MERE MASTERY...

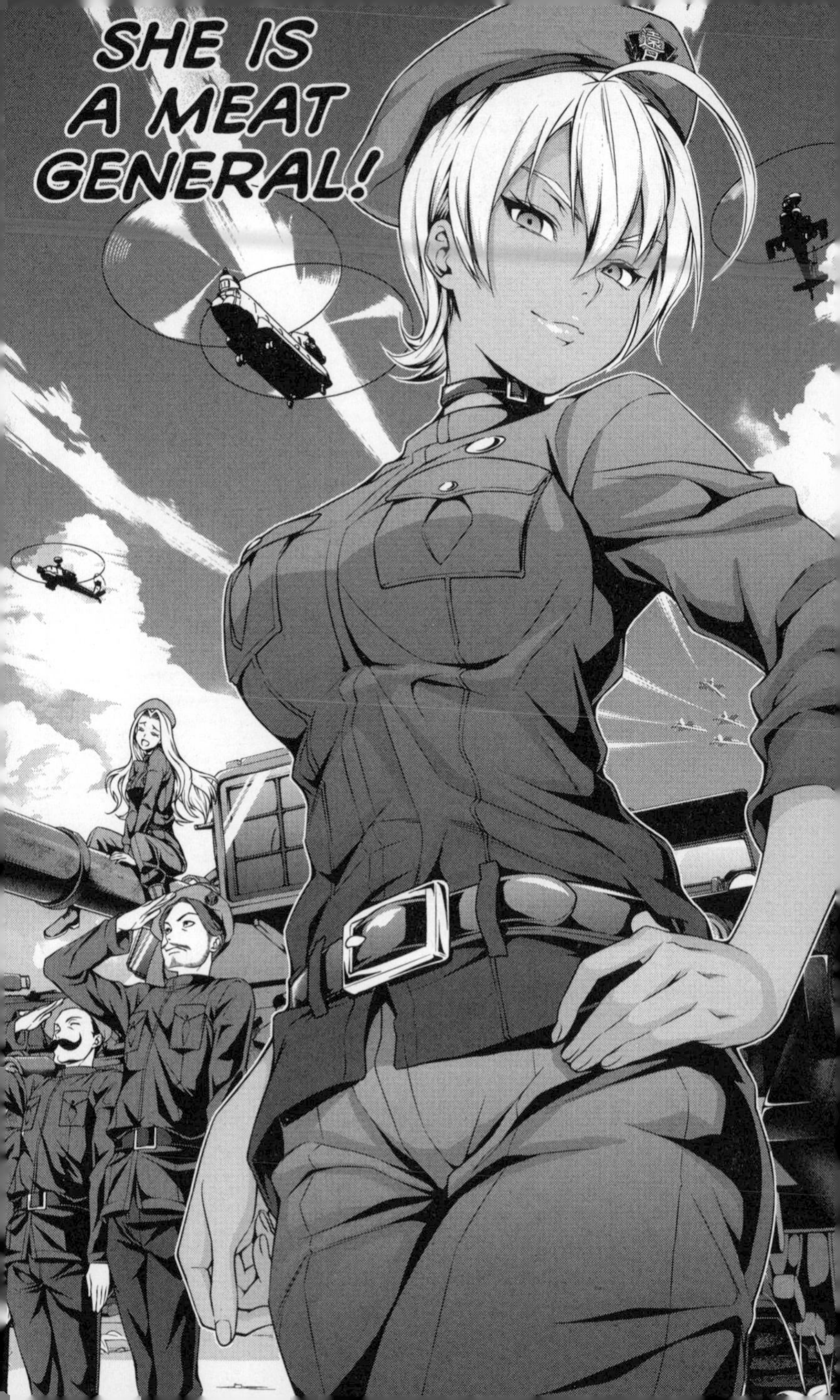
SHE IS A MEAT GENERAL!

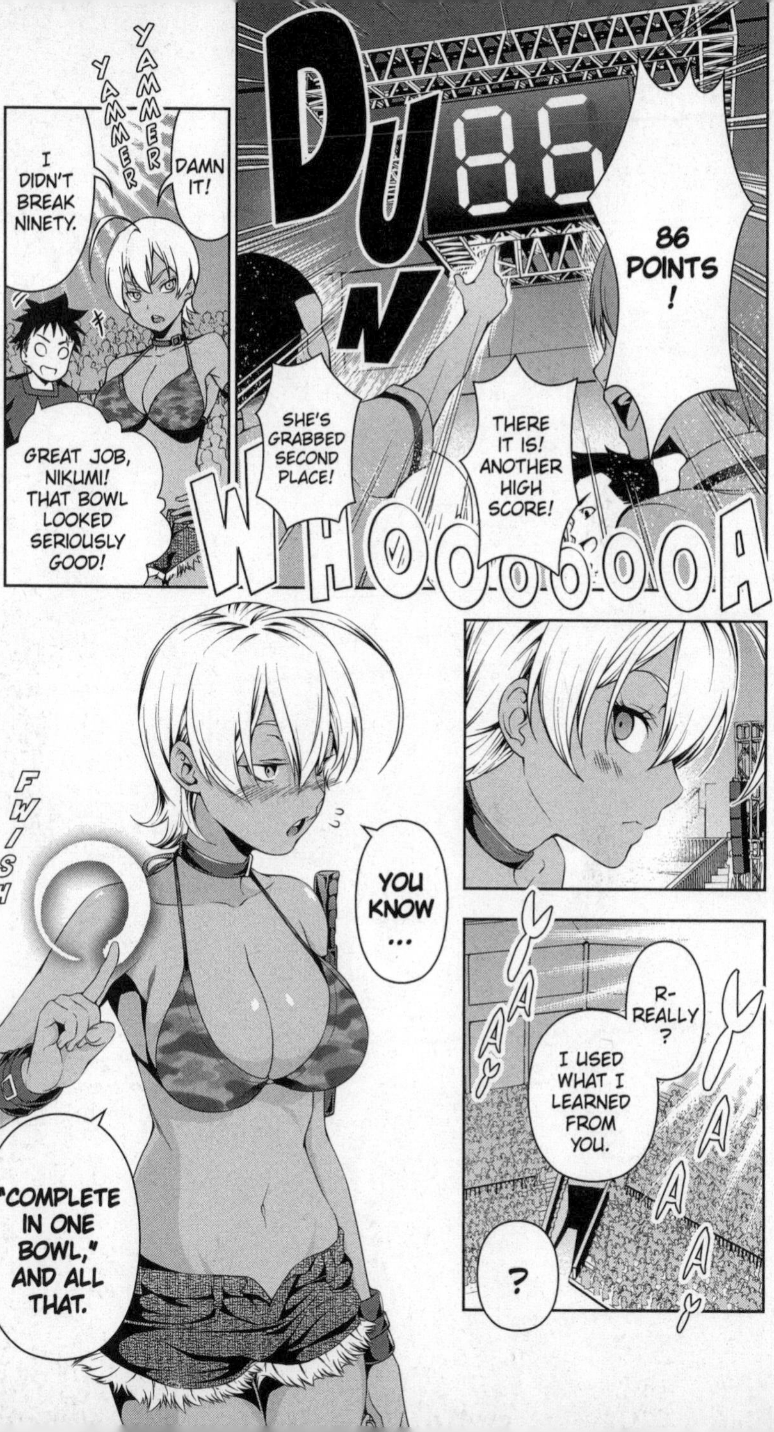
DUN
86
86 POINTS!
THERE IT IS! ANOTHER HIGH SCORE!
SHE'S GRABBED SECOND PLACE!
WHOOOOOOOA
YAMMER YAMMER
DAMN IT!
I DIDN'T BREAK NINETY.
GREAT JOB, NIKUMI! THAT BOWL LOOKED SERIOUSLY GOOD!
YAAAY
YAAAAAY
R-REALLY?
I USED WHAT I LEARNED FROM YOU.
?
FWISH
YOU KNOW...
"COMPLETE IN ONE BOWL," AND ALL THAT.

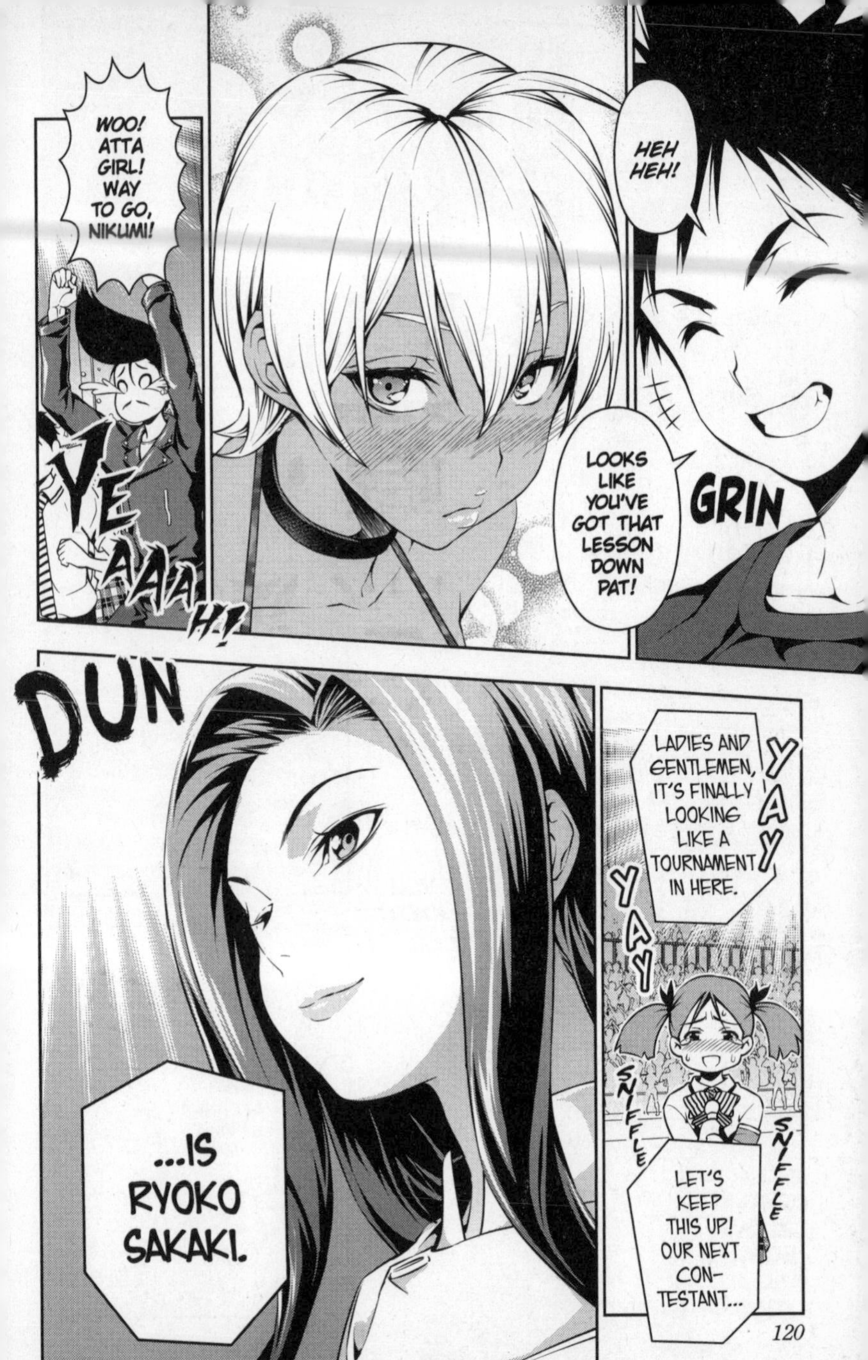
HEH HEH!
LOOKS LIKE YOU'VE GOT THAT LESSON DOWN PAT!
GRIN
WOO! ATTA GIRL! WAY TO GO, NIKUMI!
YEAAAAH!
LADIES AND GENTLEMEN, IT'S FINALLY LOOKING LIKE A TOURNAMENT IN HERE.
YAY
YAY
SNIFFLE
SNIFFLE
LET'S KEEP THIS UP! OUR NEXT CON-TESTANT...
DUN
...IS RYOKO SAKAKI.

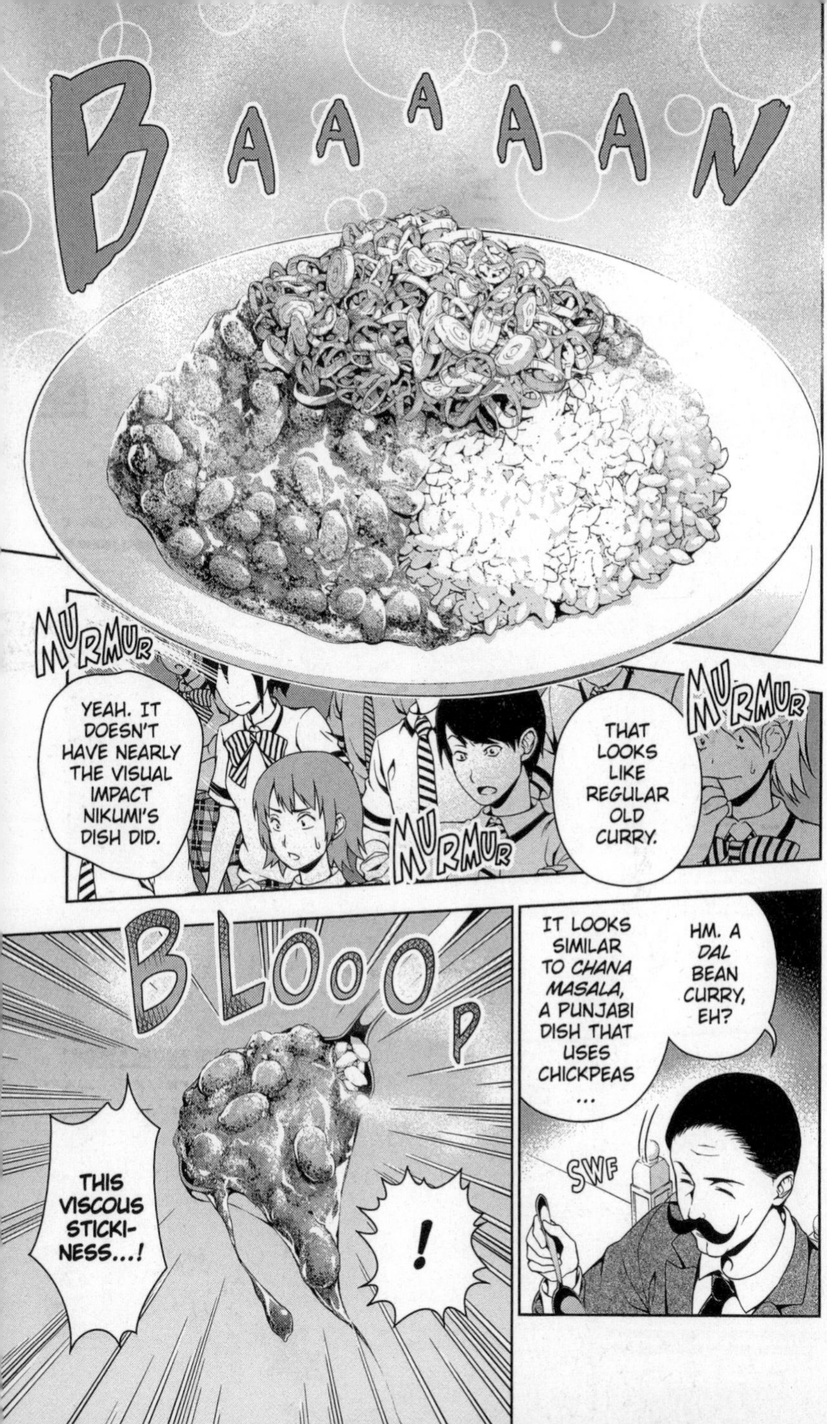
BAAAAAN
MURMUR
THAT LOOKS LIKE REGULAR OLD CURRY.
MURMUR
YEAH. IT DOESN'T HAVE NEARLY THE VISUAL IMPACT NIKUMI'S DISH DID.
MURMUR
HM. A *DAL* BEAN CURRY, EH?
IT LOOKS SIMILAR TO *CHANA MASALA*, A PUNJABI DISH THAT USES CHICKPEAS...
SWF
BLOOOP
!
THIS VISCOUS STICKI-NESS...!

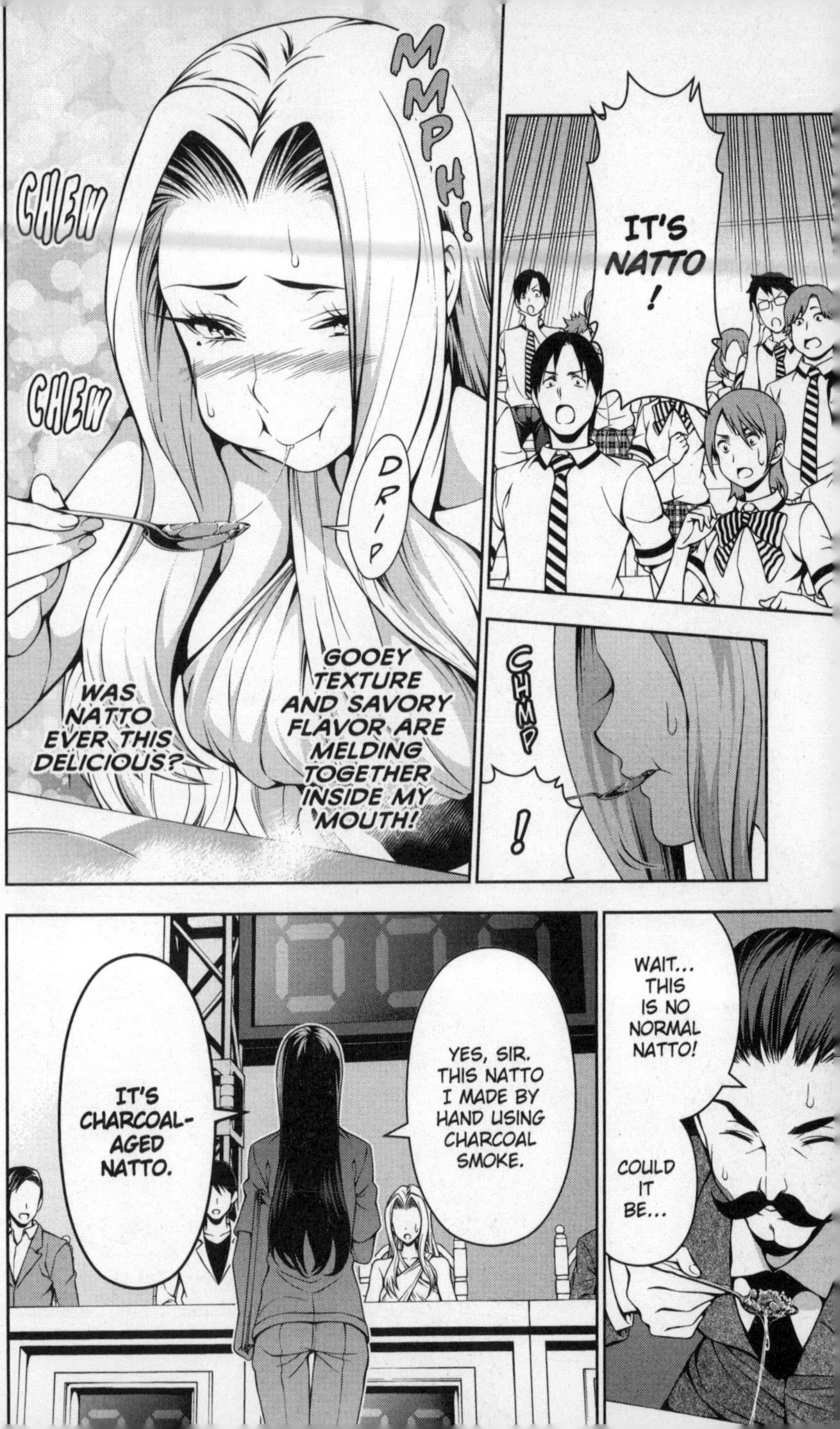
IT'S NATTO!
CHMP
!
MMPH!
CHEW
CHEW
DRIP
GOOEY TEXTURE AND SAVORY FLAVOR ARE MELDING TOGETHER INSIDE MY MOUTH!
WAS NATTO EVER THIS DELICIOUS?
WAIT... THIS IS NO NORMAL NATTO!
COULD IT BE...
YES, SIR. THIS NATTO I MADE BY HAND USING CHARCOAL SMOKE.
IT'S CHARCOAL-AGED NATTO.

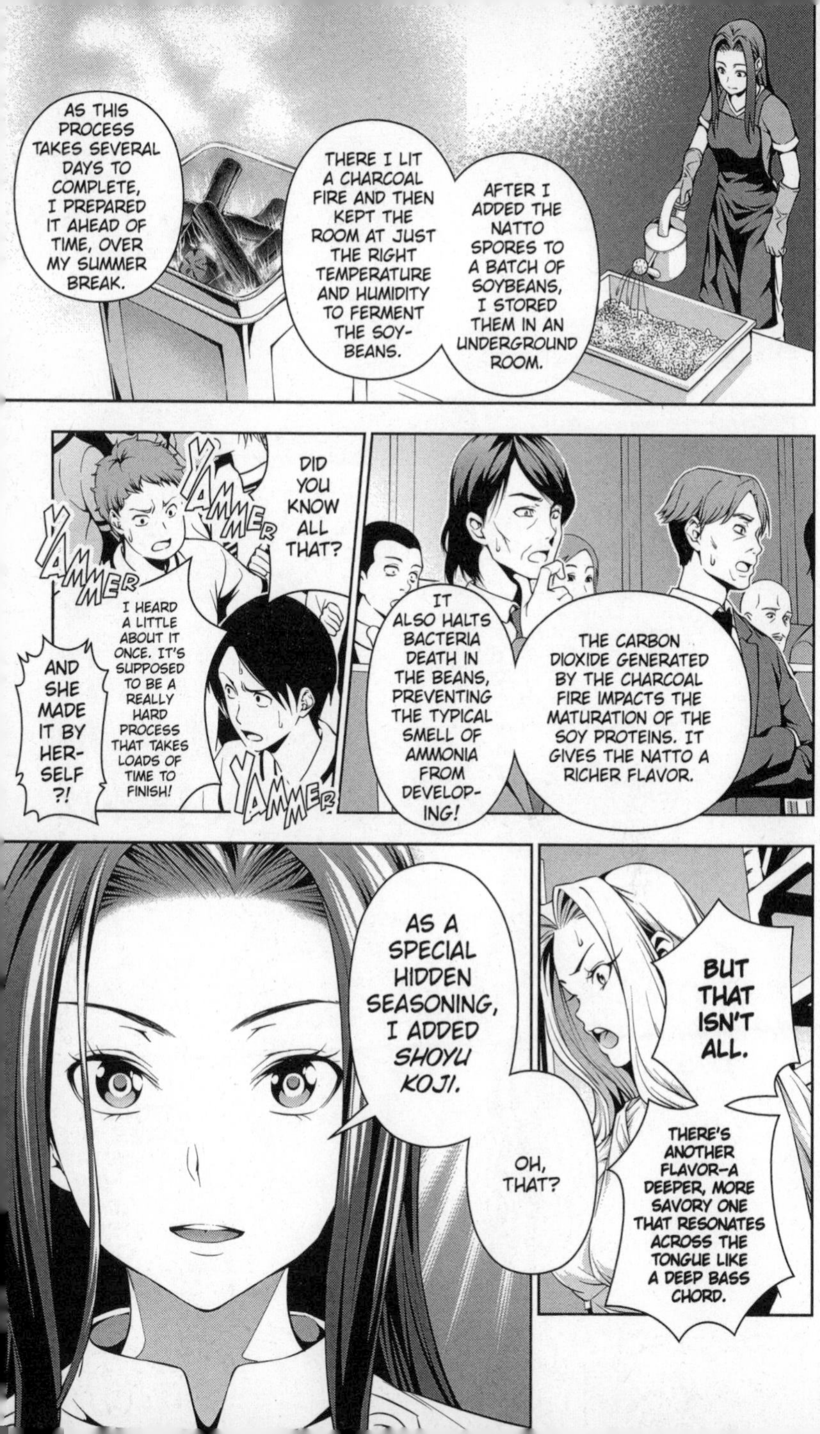
AFTER I ADDED THE NATTO SPORES TO A BATCH OF SOYBEANS, I STORED THEM IN AN UNDERGROUND ROOM.
THERE I LIT A CHARCOAL FIRE AND THEN KEPT THE ROOM AT JUST THE RIGHT TEMPERATURE AND HUMIDITY TO FERMENT THE SOY-BEANS.
AS THIS PROCESS TAKES SEVERAL DAYS TO COMPLETE, I PREPARED IT AHEAD OF TIME, OVER MY SUMMER BREAK.
THE CARBON DIOXIDE GENERATED BY THE CHARCOAL FIRE IMPACTS THE MATURATION OF THE SOY PROTEINS. IT GIVES THE NATTO A RICHER FLAVOR.
IT ALSO HALTS BACTERIA DEATH IN THE BEANS, PREVENTING THE TYPICAL SMELL OF AMMONIA FROM DEVELOP-ING!
YAMMER
DID YOU KNOW ALL THAT?
YAMMER
I HEARD A LITTLE ABOUT IT ONCE. IT'S SUPPOSED TO BE A REALLY HARD PROCESS THAT TAKES LOADS OF TIME TO FINISH!
AND SHE MADE IT BY HER-SELF?!
YAMMER
BUT THAT ISN'T ALL.
THERE'S ANOTHER FLAVOR—A DEEPER, MORE SAVORY ONE THAT RESONATES ACROSS THE TONGUE LIKE A DEEP BASS CHORD.
OH, THAT?
AS A SPECIAL HIDDEN SEASONING, I ADDED *SHOYU KOJI*.

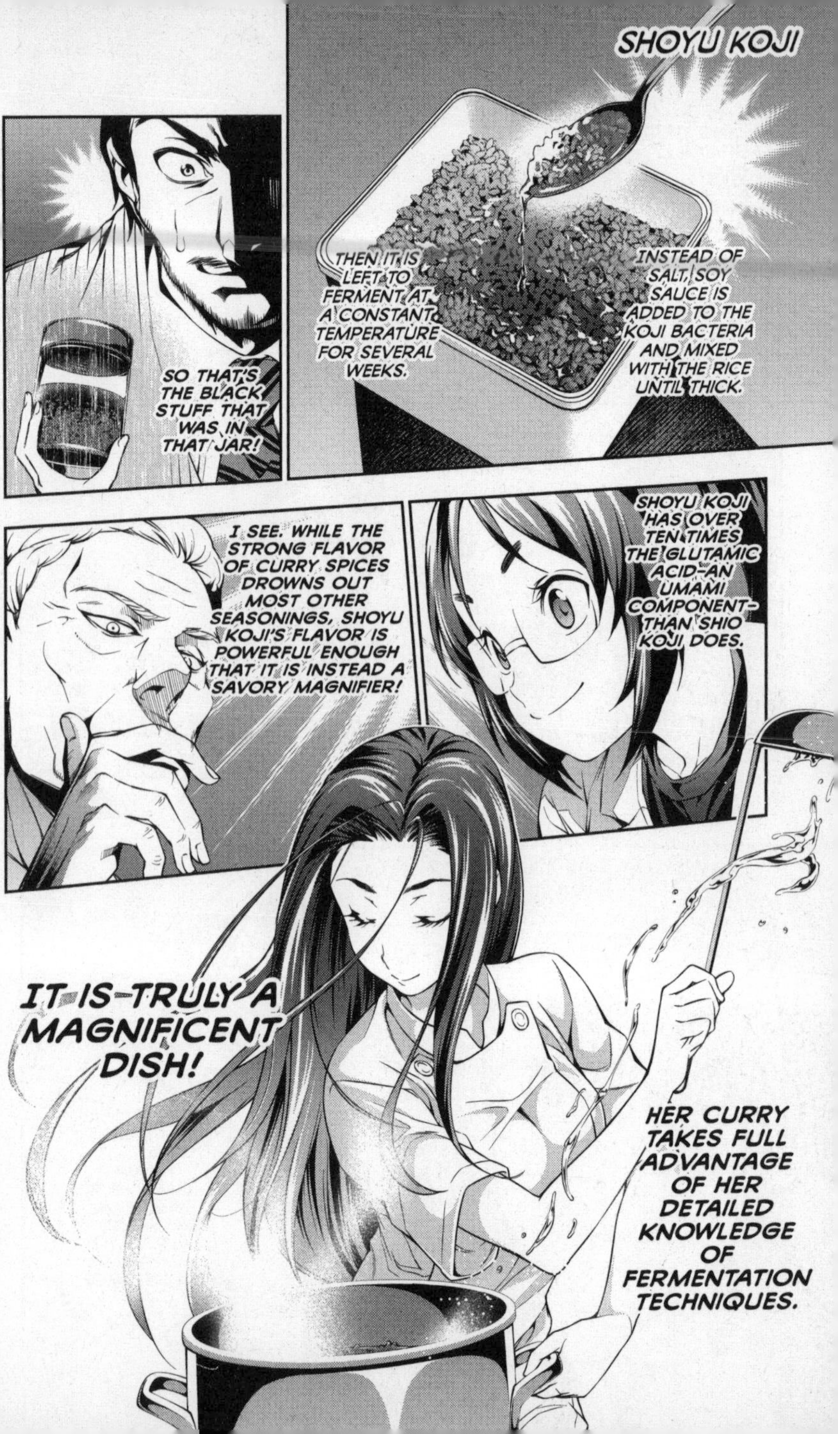
SHOYU KOJI
INSTEAD OF SALT, SOY SAUCE IS ADDED TO THE KOJI BACTERIA AND MIXED WITH THE RICE UNTIL THICK.
THEN IT IS LEFT TO FERMENT AT A CONSTANT TEMPERATURE FOR SEVERAL WEEKS.
SO THAT'S THE BLACK STUFF THAT WAS IN THAT JAR!
SHOYU KOJI HAS OVER TEN TIMES THE GLUTAMIC ACID—AN UMAMI COMPONENT—THAN SHIO KOJI DOES.
I SEE. WHILE THE STRONG FLAVOR OF CURRY SPICES DROWNS OUT MOST OTHER SEASONINGS, SHOYU KOJI'S FLAVOR IS POWERFUL ENOUGH THAT IT IS INSTEAD A SAVORY MAGNIFIER!
IT IS TRULY A MAGNIFICENT DISH!
HER CURRY TAKES FULL ADVANTAGE OF HER DETAILED KNOWLEDGE OF FERMENTATION TECHNIQUES.

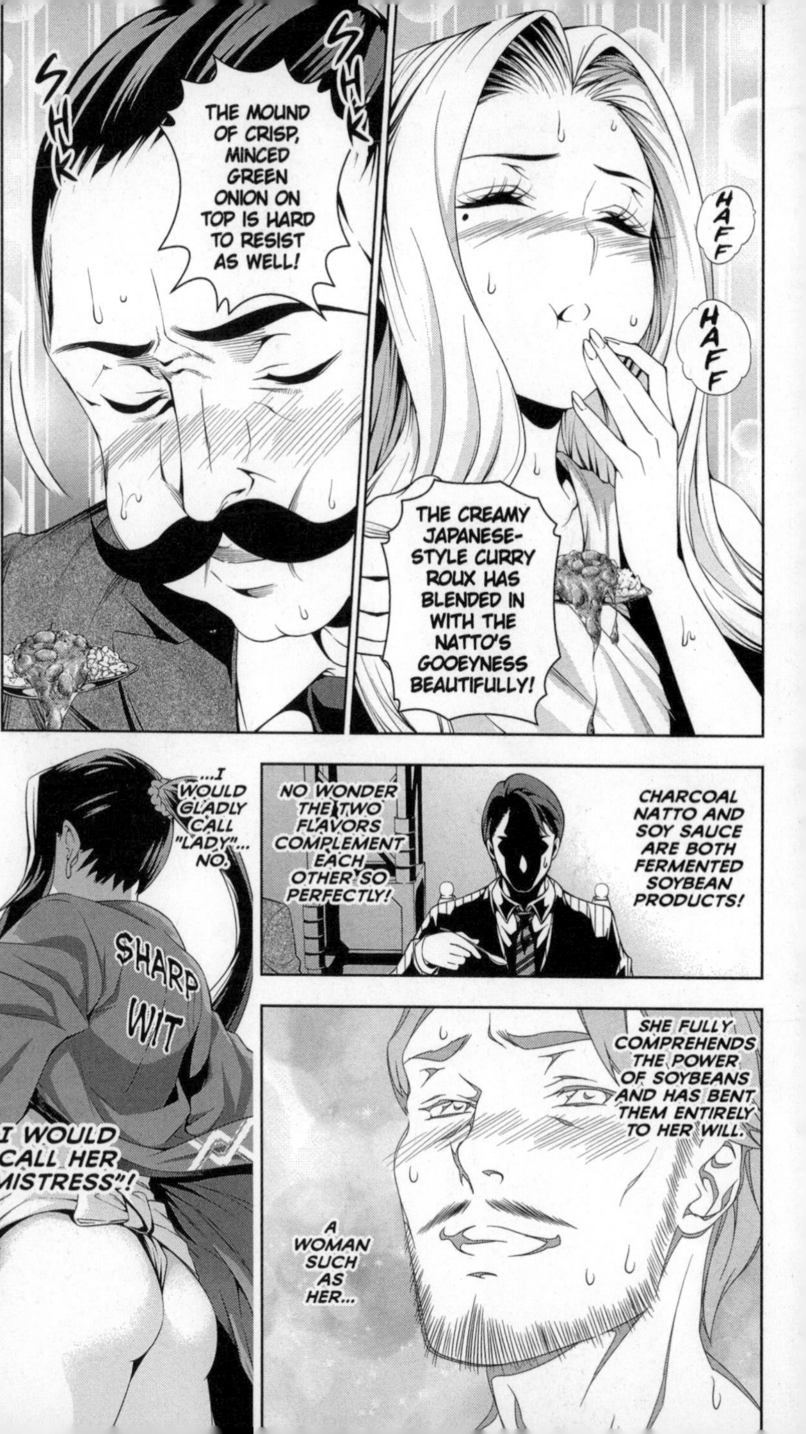
HAFF
HAFF
THE CREAMY JAPANESE-STYLE CURRY ROUX HAS BLENDED IN WITH THE NATTO'S GOOEYNESS BEAUTIFULLY!
SHK
THE MOUND OF CRISP, MINCED GREEN ONION ON TOP IS HARD TO RESIST AS WELL!
SHK
CHARCOAL NATTO AND SOY SAUCE ARE BOTH FERMENTED SOYBEAN PRODUCTS!
NO WONDER THE TWO FLAVORS COMPLEMENT EACH OTHER SO PERFECTLY!
SHE FULLY COMPREHENDS THE POWER OF SOYBEANS AND HAS BENT THEM ENTIRELY TO HER WILL.
A WOMAN SUCH AS HER...
...I WOULD GLADLY CALL "LADY"... NO,
SHARP WIT
I WOULD CALL HER "MISTRESS"!

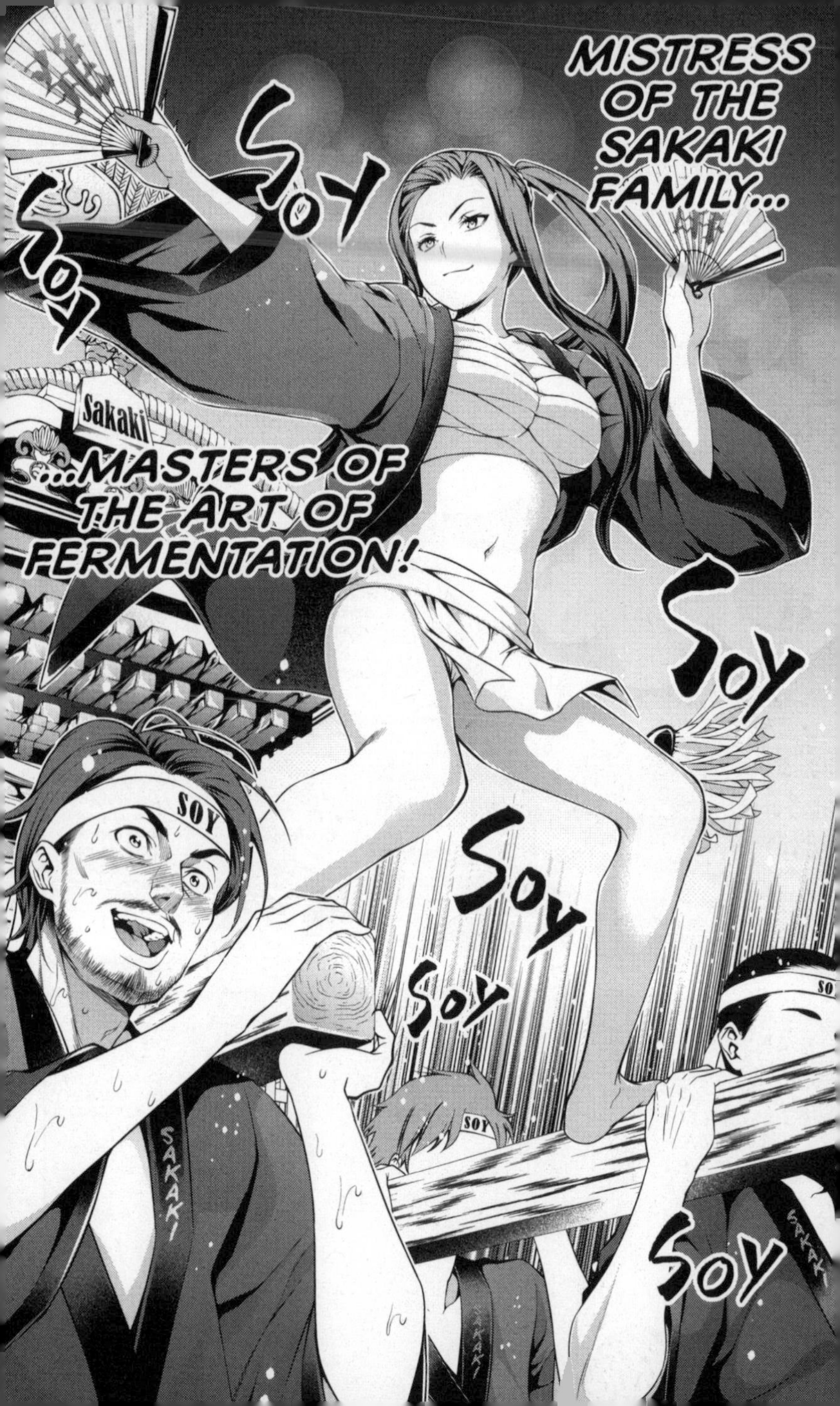
MISTRESS OF THE SAKAKI FAMILY...
SOY
SOY
Sakaki
...MASTERS OF THE ART OF FERMENTATION!
SOY
SOY
SOY
SOY
SOY
SOY
SAKAKI
SOY

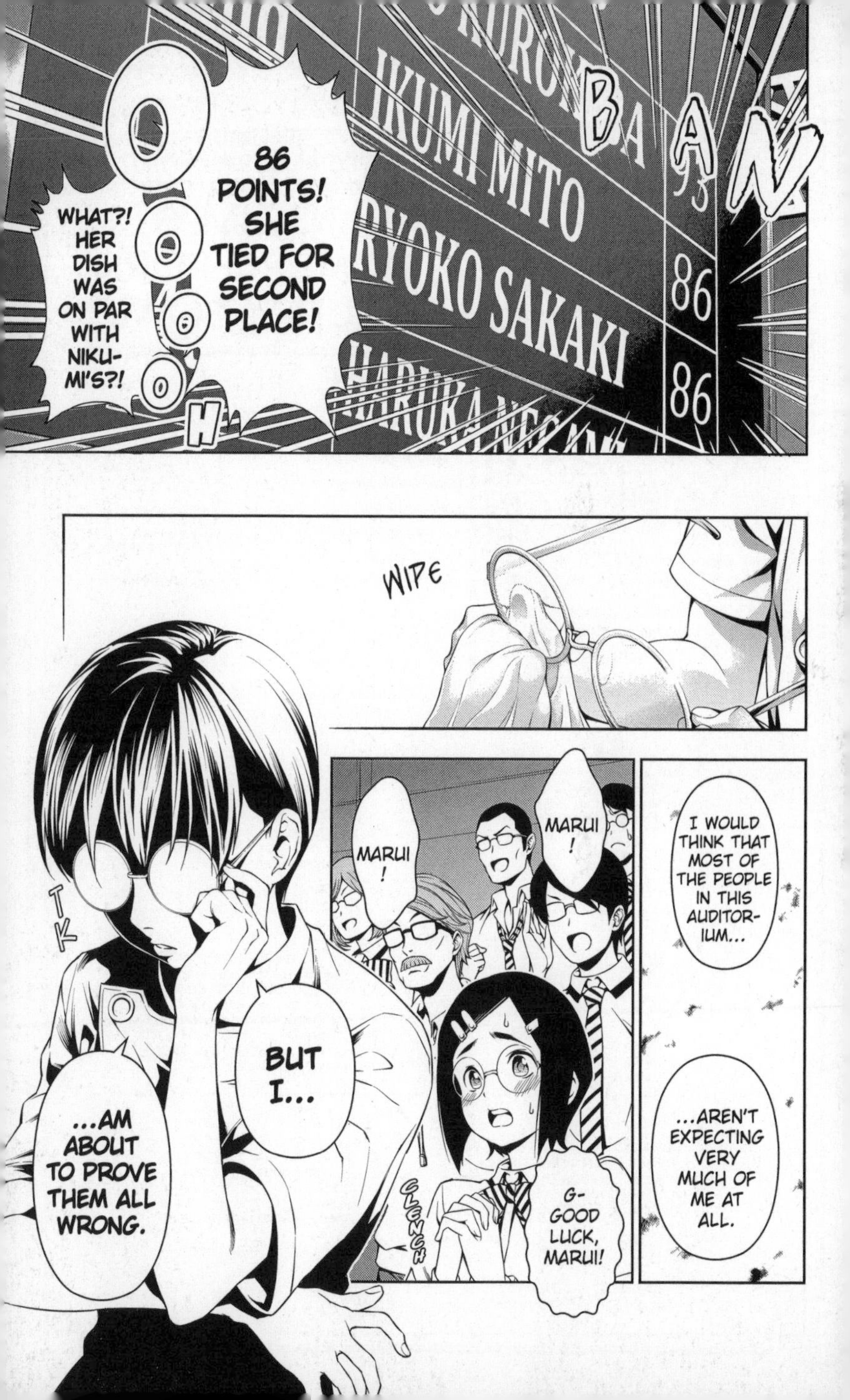
BAAN
IKUMI MITO
RYOKO SAKAKI
86
86
86 POINTS! SHE TIED FOR SECOND PLACE!
OOOOH
WHAT?! HER DISH WAS ON PAR WITH NIKU-MI'S?!
WIPE
I WOULD THINK THAT MOST OF THE PEOPLE IN THIS AUDITOR-IUM...
...AREN'T EXPECTING VERY MUCH OF ME AT ALL.
MARUI!
MARUI!
G-GOOD LUCK, MARUI!
CLENCH
TK
BUT I...
...AM ABOUT TO PROVE THEM ALL WRONG.

RECIPE BY: YUKI MORISAKI

PRACTICAL RECIPE #1

VOLUME 7
SPECIAL SUPPLEMENT!

# NIKUMI'S DONGPO-PORK-CURRY BOWL

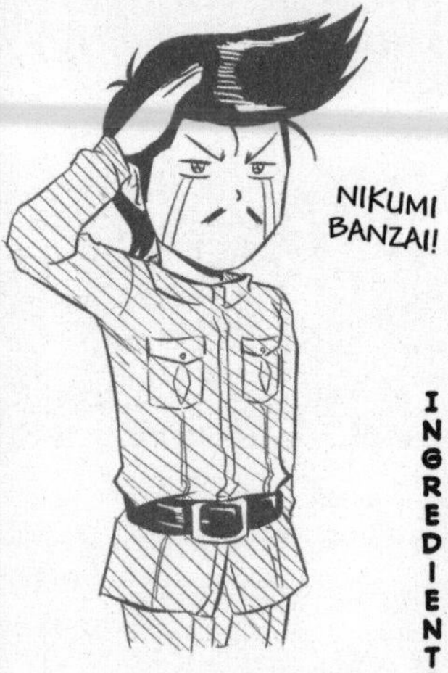
NIKUMI BANZAI!

ARTIST: YUTO TSUKUDA

## INGREDIENTS

SERVES 2

- 300 GRAMS PORK BELLY
- 1 TABLESPOON CANOLA OIL
- [A]
  - 1000 CC WATER
  - 1/2 TABLESPOON CHICKEN BOUILLON
- 1 LARGE SPRING ONION
- 1 HEAD BOK CHOY
- 2 THUMBS GINGER ROOT
- 1 PIECE STAR ANISE
- 5 SICHUAN PEPPERCORNS
- [B]
  - 100 CC SHAOXING WINE
  - 2 TABLESPOONS EACH SUGAR AND SOY SAUCE
  - 1 TABLESPOON EACH OYSTER SAUCE AND CURRY POWDER
- 2 BOWLS COOKED RICE
- SOY SAUCE, OYSTER SAUCE, POTATO STARCH
- ROCK SALT, SICHUAN PEPPERCORN OIL

1. CUT THE PORK BELLY INTO FIVE-CENTIMETER BLOCKS. SUBMERGE IN PLENTY OF WATER AND BOIL FOR TEN MINUTES UNTIL SOFT.

2. CUT OFF THE GREEN PART OF THE SPRING ONION AND FINELY CHOP IT. JULIENNE THE WHITE PART AND SOAK IN COLD WATER FOR TEN MINUTES. THINLY SLICE THE GINGER. CHOP THE BOK CHOY INTO QUARTERS AND BLANCH.

3. SEAR THE PORK BELLY FROM (1) IN A FRYING PAN UNTIL THE EDGES ARE GOLDEN BROWN.

4. PUT (A) IN A PRESSURE COOKER AND HEAT UNTIL BOILING. ADD THE MEAT FROM (3), THE SLICED GINGER, THE STAR ANISE, THE SICHUAN PEPPERCORNS AND THE CHOPPED GREEN PART OF THE SPRING ONION, AND THEN CLOSE THE LID AND SIMMER UNDER PRESSURE FOR TWENTY MINUTES.

5. OPEN THE LID, ADD (B), CLOSE AND SIMMER FOR ANOTHER FIFTEEN MINUTES. SEASON TO TASTE WITH SOY SAUCE AND OYSTER SAUCE. THICKEN WITH POTATO STARCH.

6. SEASON THE RICE TO TASTE WITH ROCK SALT AND PEPPERCORN FLAVORING OIL. PUT EVEN PORTIONS IN TWO BOWLS AND TOP WITH (5). GARNISH WITH JULIENNED SPRING ONION AND BOK CHOY. DONE!

155 BRIDGING THE GAP WITH KNOWLEDGE

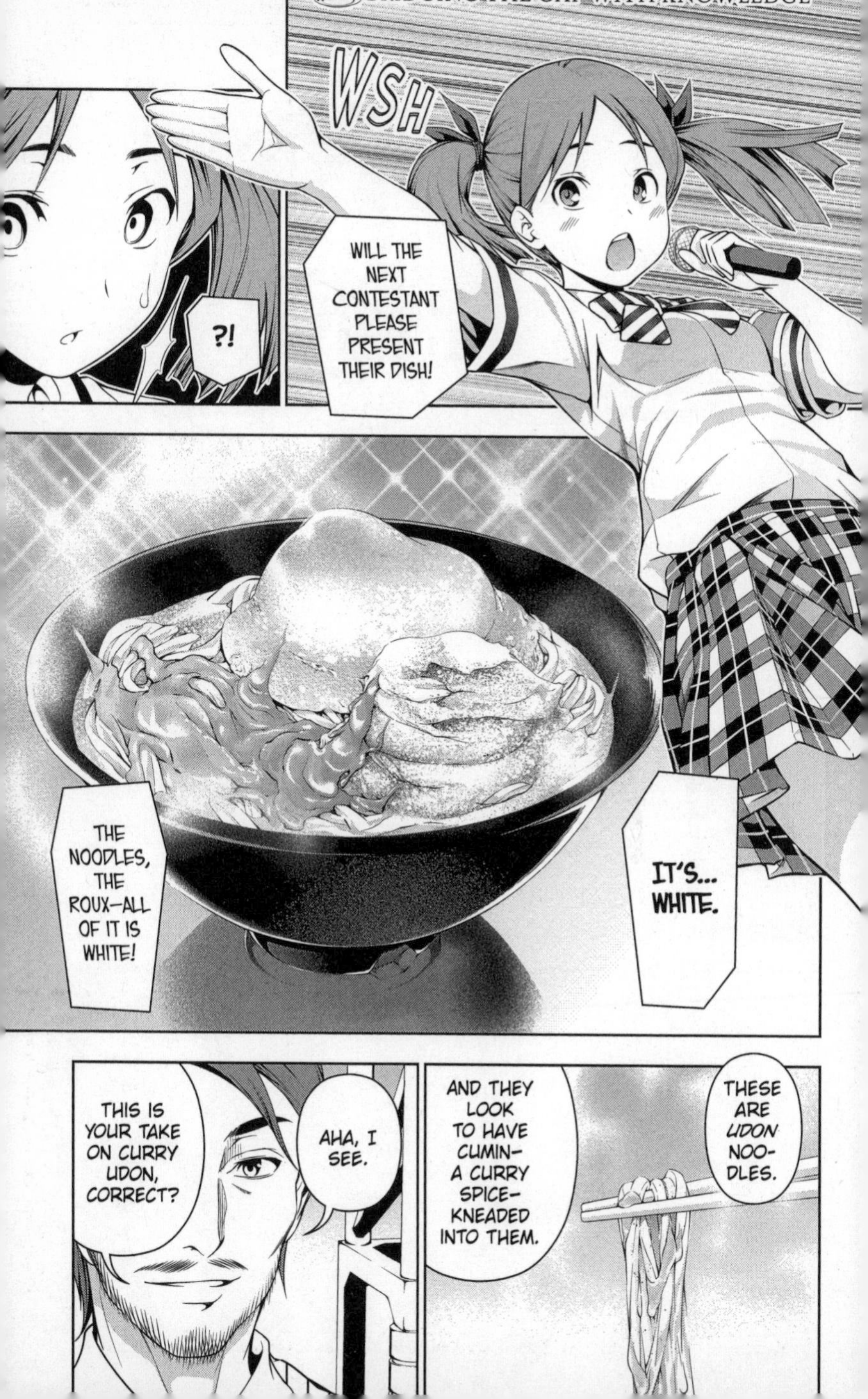
WSH
WILL THE NEXT CONTESTANT PLEASE PRESENT THEIR DISH!
?!
IT'S... WHITE.
THE NOODLES, THE ROUX—ALL OF IT IS WHITE!
THESE ARE *UDON* NOODLES.
AND THEY LOOK TO HAVE CUMIN—A CURRY SPICE—KNEADED INTO THEM.
AHA, I SEE.
THIS IS YOUR TAKE ON CURRY UDON, CORRECT?

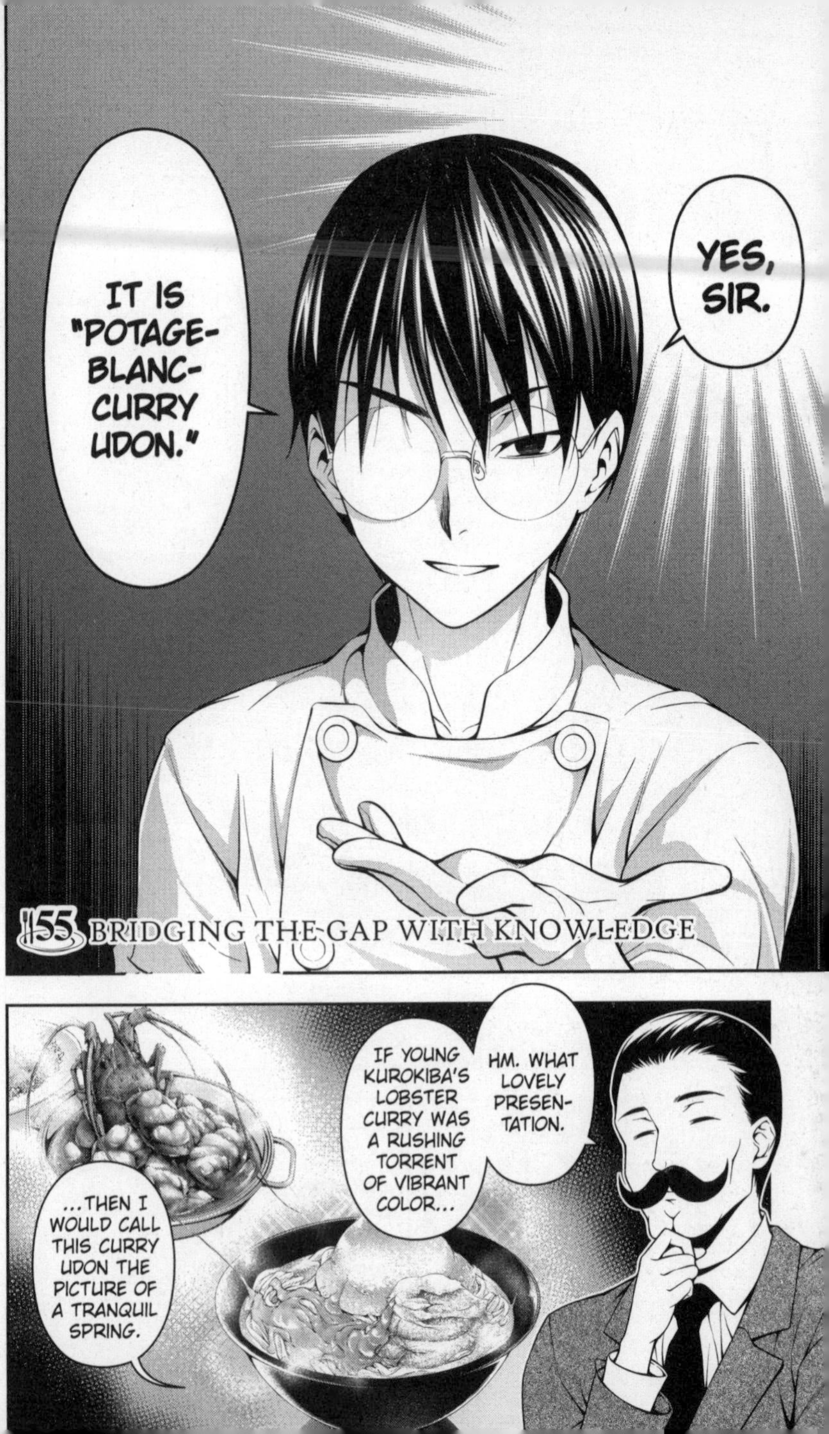
YES, SIR.
IT IS "POTAGE-BLANC-CURRY UDON."
55 BRIDGING THE GAP WITH KNOWLEDGE
HM. WHAT LOVELY PRESEN-TATION.
IF YOUNG KUROKIBA'S LOBSTER CURRY WAS A RUSHING TORRENT OF VIBRANT COLOR...
...THEN I WOULD CALL THIS CURRY UDON THE PICTURE OF A TRANQUIL SPRING.

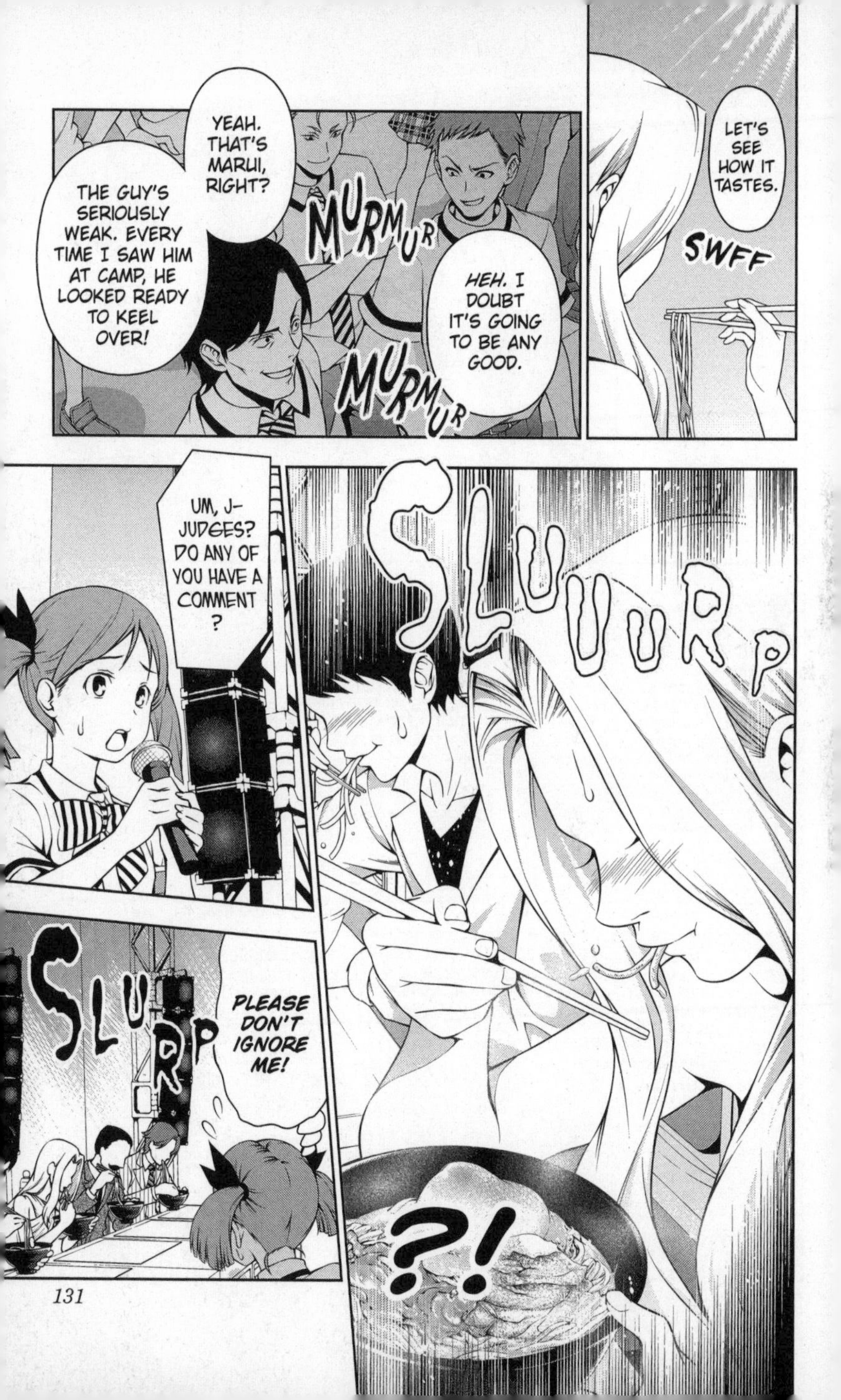
LET'S SEE HOW IT TASTES.
SWFF
YEAH. THAT'S MARUI, RIGHT?
THE GUY'S SERIOUSLY WEAK. EVERY TIME I SAW HIM AT CAMP, HE LOOKED READY TO KEEL OVER!
MURMUR
HEH. I DOUBT IT'S GOING TO BE ANY GOOD.
MURMUR
SLUUURP
?!
UM, J-JUDGES? DO ANY OF YOU HAVE A COMMENT?
SLURP
PLEASE DON'T IGNORE ME!

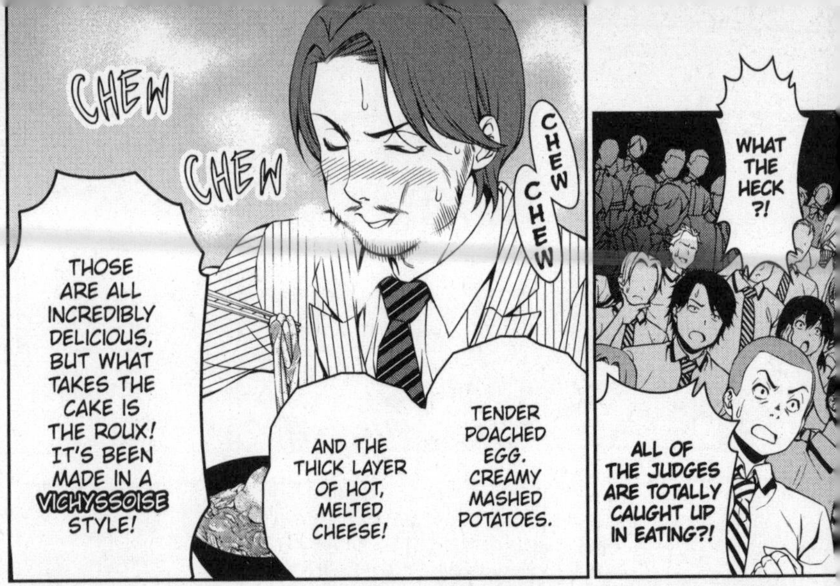
WHAT THE HECK?!
ALL OF THE JUDGES ARE TOTALLY CAUGHT UP IN EATING?!
CHEW CHEW
CHEW
CHEW
TENDER POACHED EGG. CREAMY MASHED POTATOES.
AND THE THICK LAYER OF HOT, MELTED CHEESE!
THOSE ARE ALL INCREDIBLY DELICIOUS, BUT WHAT TAKES THE CAKE IS THE ROUX! IT'S BEEN MADE IN A VICHYSSOISE STYLE!

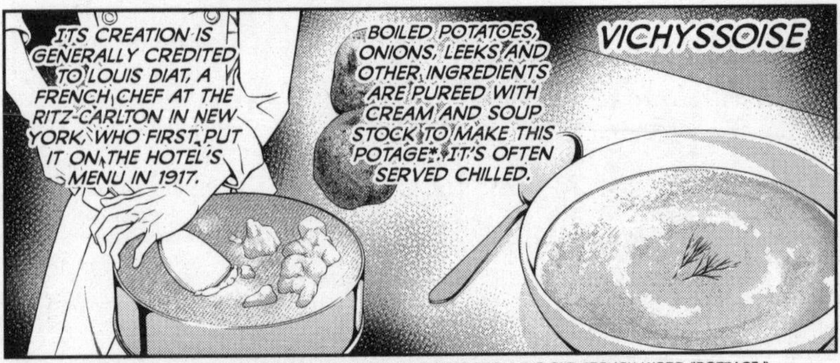
VICHYSSOISE
BOILED POTATOES, ONIONS, LEEKS AND OTHER INGREDIENTS ARE PUREED WITH CREAM AND SOUP STOCK TO MAKE THIS POTAGE*. IT'S OFTEN SERVED CHILLED.
ITS CREATION IS GENERALLY CREDITED TO LOUIS DIAT, A FRENCH CHEF AT THE RITZ-CARLTON IN NEW YORK, WHO FIRST PUT IT ON THE HOTEL'S MENU IN 1917.

*POTAGE IS A CATEGORY OF THICK SOUPS AND STEWS. IT COMES FROM THE OLD-FRENCH WORD "POTTAGE."

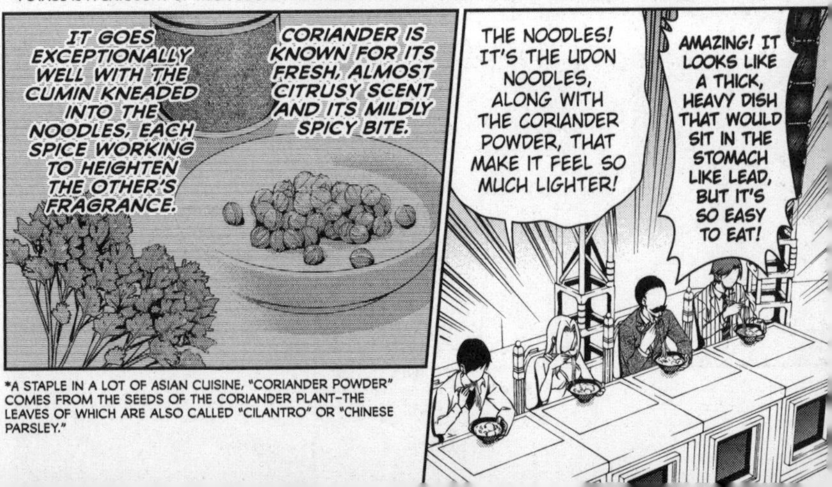
AMAZING! IT LOOKS LIKE A THICK, HEAVY DISH THAT WOULD SIT IN THE STOMACH LIKE LEAD, BUT IT'S SO EASY TO EAT!
THE NOODLES! IT'S THE UDON NOODLES, ALONG WITH THE CORIANDER POWDER, THAT MAKE IT FEEL SO MUCH LIGHTER!
CORIANDER IS KNOWN FOR ITS FRESH, ALMOST CITRUSY SCENT AND ITS MILDLY SPICY BITE.
IT GOES EXCEPTIONALLY WELL WITH THE CUMIN KNEADED INTO THE NOODLES, EACH SPICE WORKING TO HEIGHTEN THE OTHER'S FRAGRANCE.

*A STAPLE IN A LOT OF ASIAN CUISINE, "CORIANDER POWDER" COMES FROM THE SEEDS OF THE CORIANDER PLANT–THE LEAVES OF WHICH ARE ALSO CALLED "CILANTRO" OR "CHINESE PARSLEY."

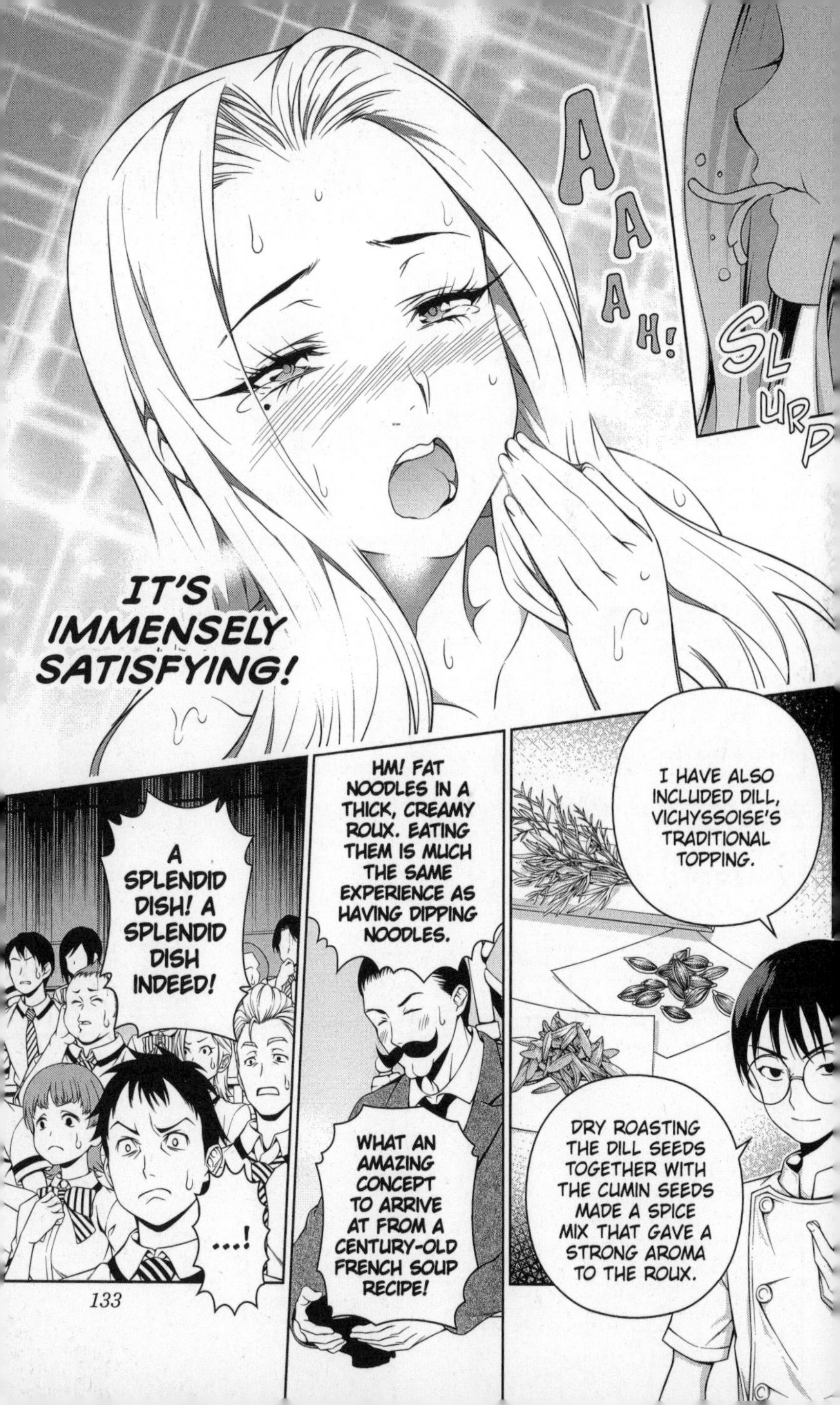
SLURP
AAAH!
IT'S IMMENSELY SATISFYING!
I HAVE ALSO INCLUDED DILL, VICHYSSOISE'S TRADITIONAL TOPPING.
DRY ROASTING THE DILL SEEDS TOGETHER WITH THE CUMIN SEEDS MADE A SPICE MIX THAT GAVE A STRONG AROMA TO THE ROUX.
HM! FAT NOODLES IN A THICK, CREAMY ROUX. EATING THEM IS MUCH THE SAME EXPERIENCE AS HAVING DIPPING NOODLES.
WHAT AN AMAZING CONCEPT TO ARRIVE AT FROM A CENTURY-OLD FRENCH SOUP RECIPE!
A SPLENDID DISH! A SPLENDID DISH INDEED!
...!

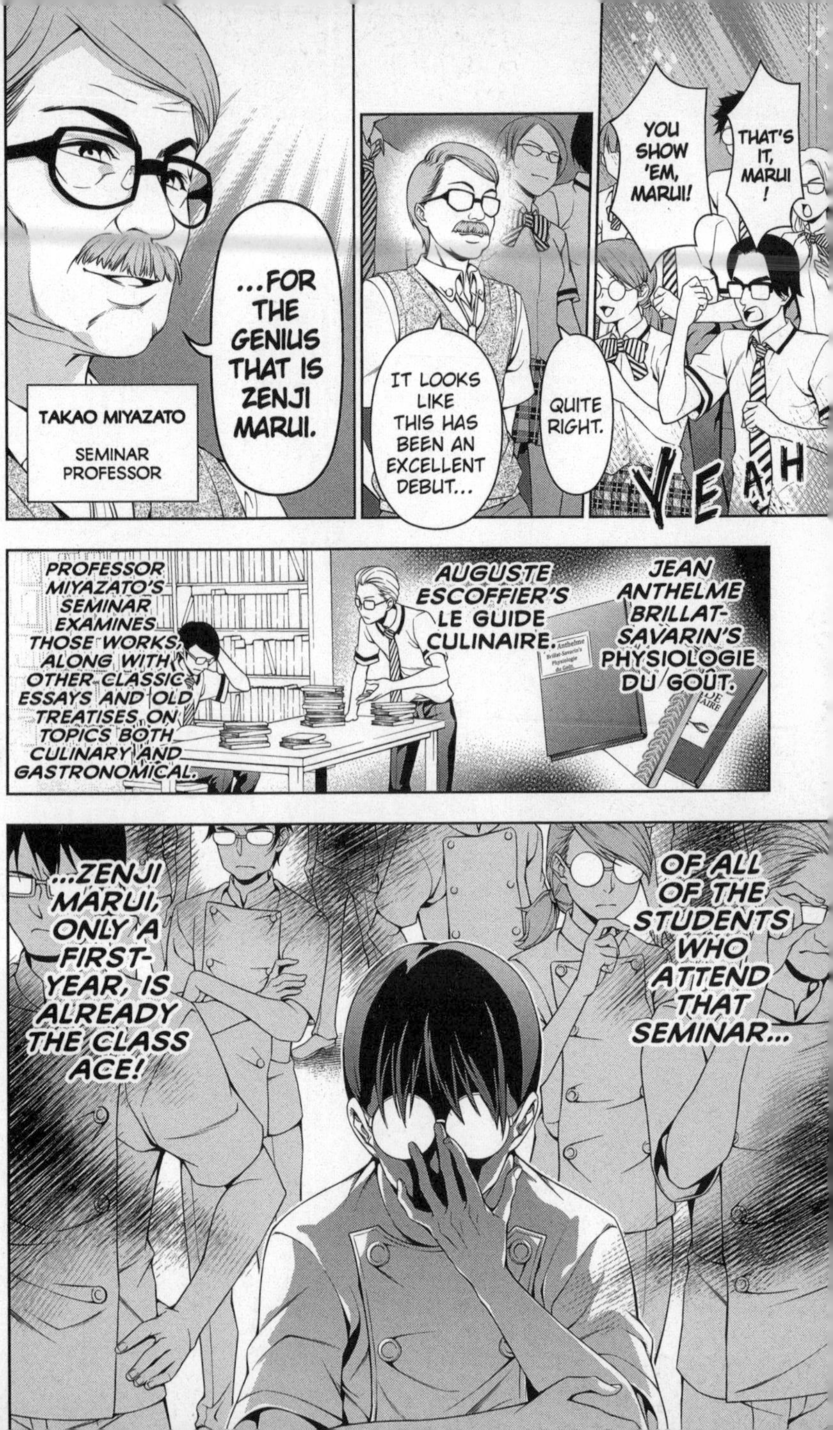
THAT'S IT, MARUI!
YOU SHOW 'EM, MARUI!
YEAH
QUITE RIGHT.
IT LOOKS LIKE THIS HAS BEEN AN EXCELLENT DEBUT...
...FOR THE GENIUS THAT IS ZENJI MARUI.
TAKAO MIYAZATO
SEMINAR PROFESSOR
JEAN ANTHELME BRILLAT-SAVARIN'S PHYSIOLOGIE DU GOÛT.
AUGUSTE ESCOFFIER'S LE GUIDE CULINAIRE.
PROFESSOR MIYAZATO'S SEMINAR EXAMINES THOSE WORKS, ALONG WITH OTHER CLASSIC ESSAYS AND OLD TREATISES ON TOPICS BOTH CULINARY AND GASTRONOMICAL.
OF ALL OF THE STUDENTS WHO ATTEND THAT SEMINAR...
...ZENJI MARUI, ONLY A FIRST-YEAR, IS ALREADY THE CLASS ACE!

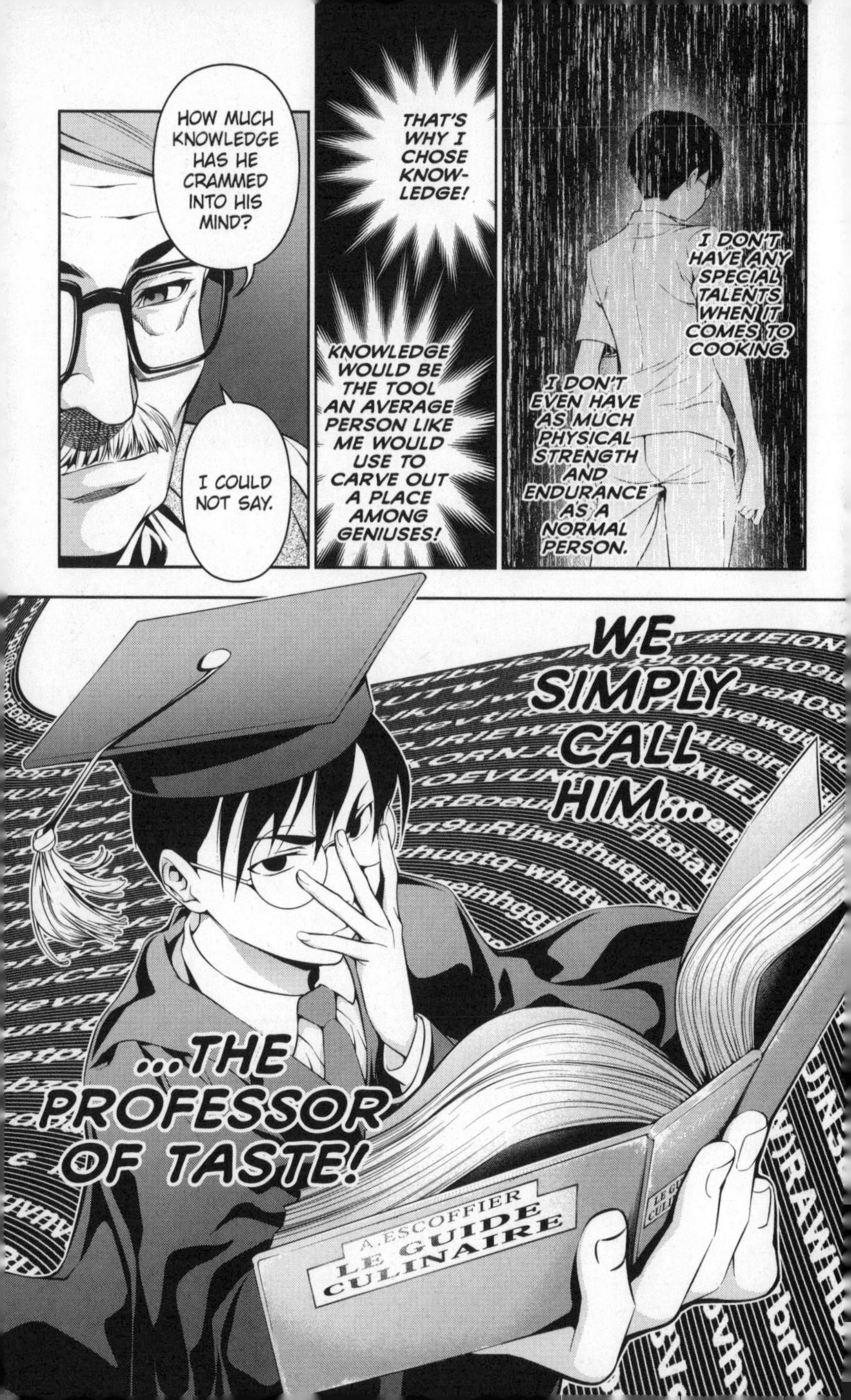
I DON'T HAVE ANY SPECIAL TALENTS WHEN IT COMES TO COOKING.
I DON'T EVEN HAVE AS MUCH PHYSICAL STRENGTH AND ENDURANCE AS A NORMAL PERSON.
THAT'S WHY I CHOSE KNOW-LEDGE!
KNOWLEDGE WOULD BE THE TOOL AN AVERAGE PERSON LIKE ME WOULD USE TO CARVE OUT A PLACE AMONG GENIUSES!
HOW MUCH KNOWLEDGE HAS HE CRAMMED INTO HIS MIND?
I COULD NOT SAY.
WE SIMPLY CALL HIM...
...THE PROFESSOR OF TASTE!
A. ESCOFFIER
LE GUIDE CULINAIRE

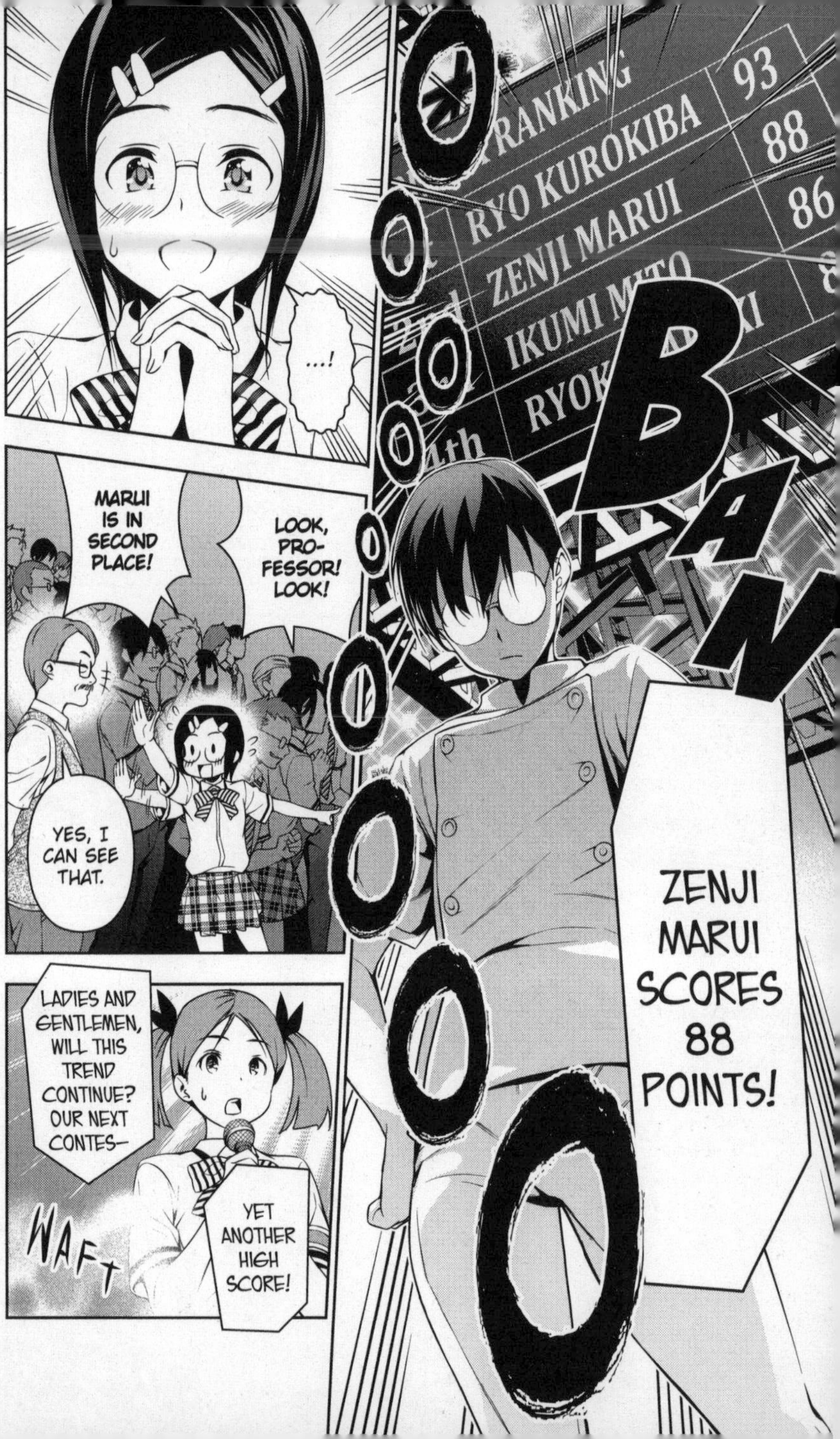

RANKING
RYO KUROKIBA
ZENJI MARUI
IKUMI MITO
93
88
86
BAN
ZENJI MARUI SCORES 88 POINTS!
...!
LOOK, PRO-FESSOR! LOOK!
MARUI IS IN SECOND PLACE!
YES, I CAN SEE THAT.
LADIES AND GENTLEMEN, WILL THIS TREND CONTINUE? OUR NEXT CONTES—
YET ANOTHER HIGH SCORE!
WAFT

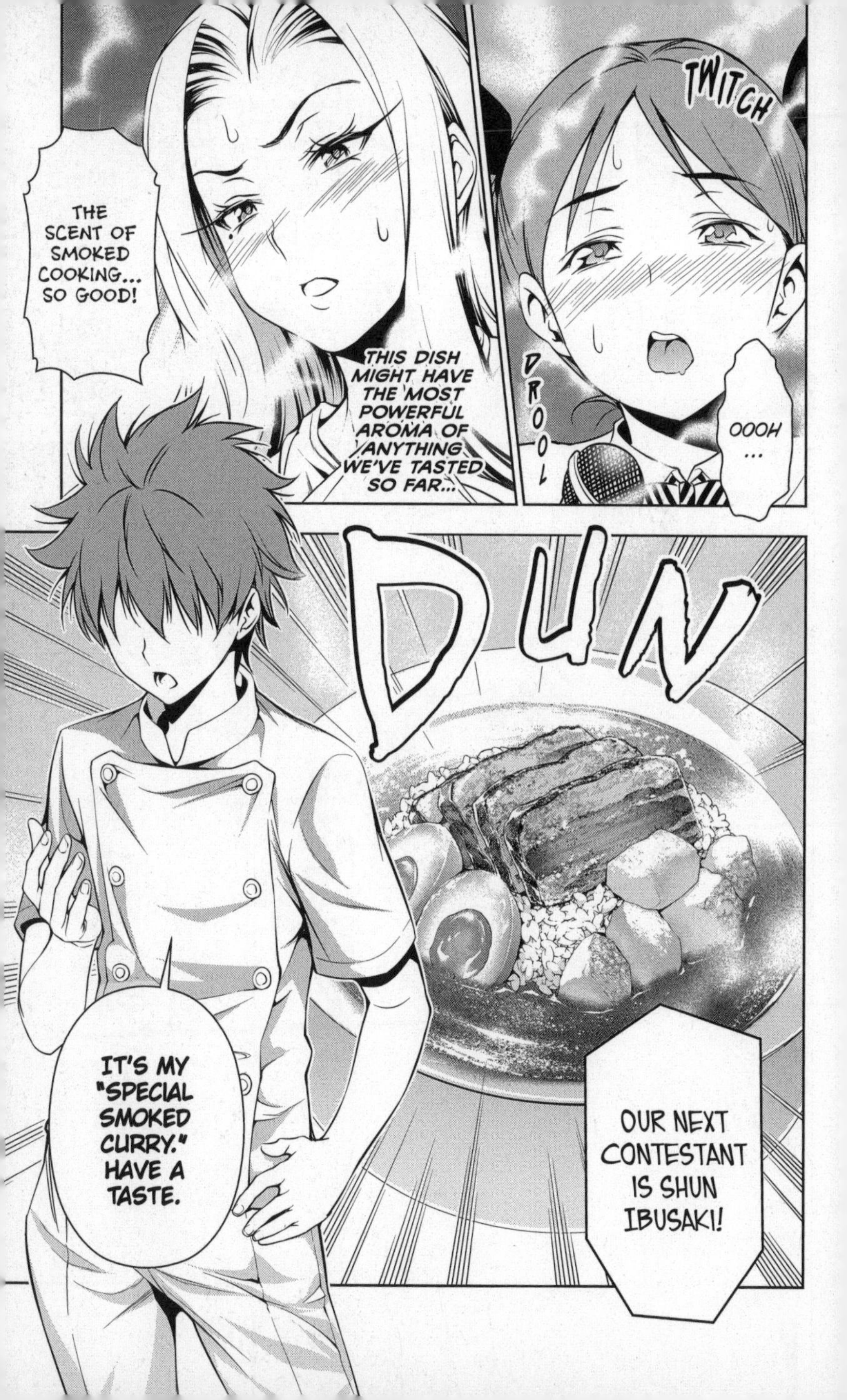
TWITCH
OOOH ...
DROOL
THE SCENT OF SMOKED COOKING... SO GOOD!
THIS DISH MIGHT HAVE THE MOST POWERFUL AROMA OF ANYTHING WE'VE TASTED SO FAR...
DUN
OUR NEXT CONTESTANT IS SHUN IBUSAKI!
IT'S MY "SPECIAL SMOKED CURRY." HAVE A TASTE.

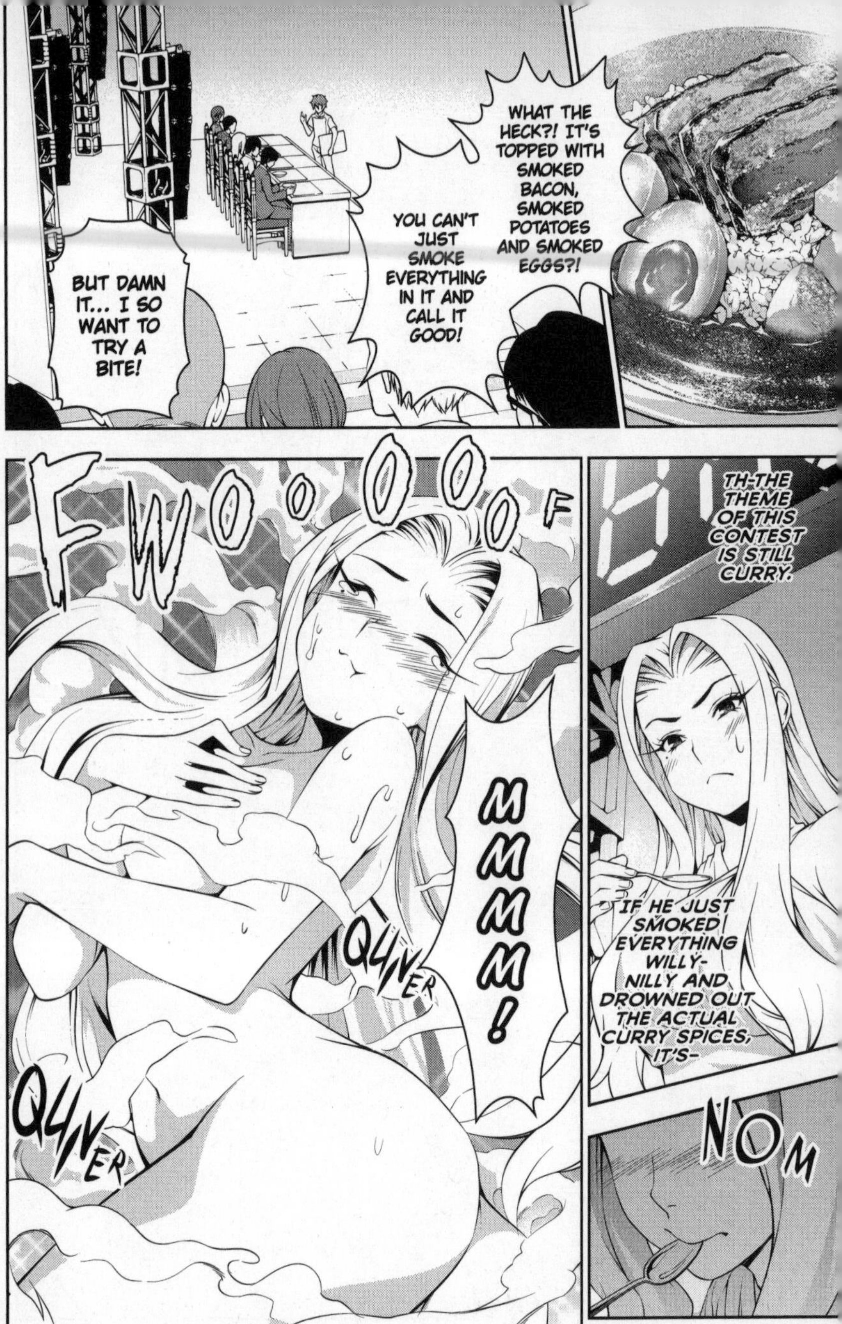
WHAT THE HECK?! IT'S TOPPED WITH SMOKED BACON, SMOKED POTATOES AND SMOKED EGGS?!
YOU CAN'T JUST SMOKE EVERYTHING IN IT AND CALL IT GOOD!
BUT DAMN IT... I SO WANT TO TRY A BITE!
TH-THE THEME OF THIS CONTEST IS STILL CURRY.
IF HE JUST SMOKED EVERYTHING WILLY-NILLY AND DROWNED OUT THE ACTUAL CURRY SPICES, IT'S-
NOM
FWOOOOOF
MMMMMM!
QUIVER
QUIVER

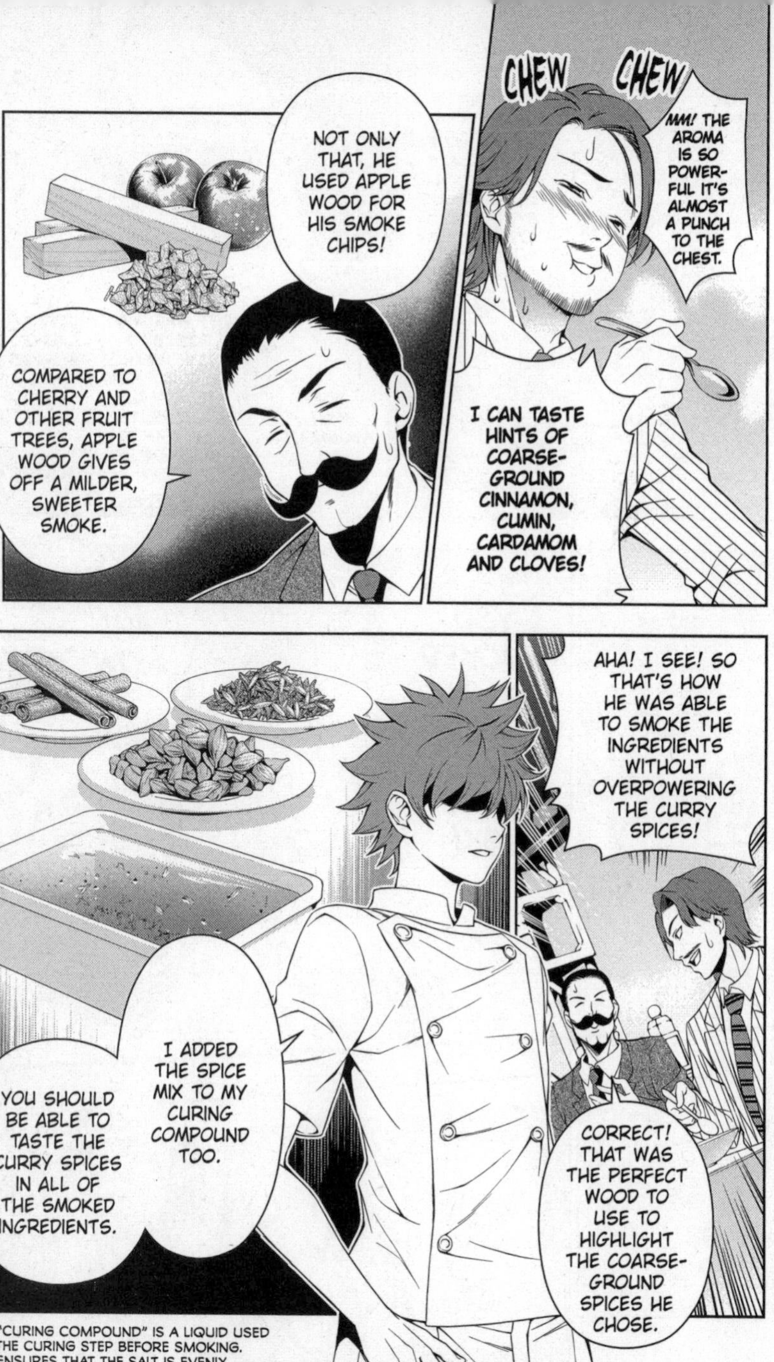
CHEW CHEW
MM! THE AROMA IS SO POWERFUL IT'S ALMOST A PUNCH TO THE CHEST.
I CAN TASTE HINTS OF COARSE-GROUND CINNAMON, CUMIN, CARDAMOM AND CLOVES!
NOT ONLY THAT, HE USED APPLE WOOD FOR HIS SMOKE CHIPS!
COMPARED TO CHERRY AND OTHER FRUIT TREES, APPLE WOOD GIVES OFF A MILDER, SWEETER SMOKE.
AHA! I SEE! SO THAT'S HOW HE WAS ABLE TO SMOKE THE INGREDIENTS WITHOUT OVERPOWERING THE CURRY SPICES!
CORRECT! THAT WAS THE PERFECT WOOD TO USE TO HIGHLIGHT THE COARSE-GROUND SPICES HE CHOSE.
I ADDED THE SPICE MIX TO MY CURING COMPOUND TOO.
YOU SHOULD BE ABLE TO TASTE THE CURRY SPICES IN ALL OF THE SMOKED INGREDIENTS.

*A "CURING COMPOUND" IS A LIQUID USED IN THE CURING STEP BEFORE SMOKING. IT ENSURES THAT THE SALT IS EVENLY DISTRIBUTED THROUGHOUT THE INGREDIENT.

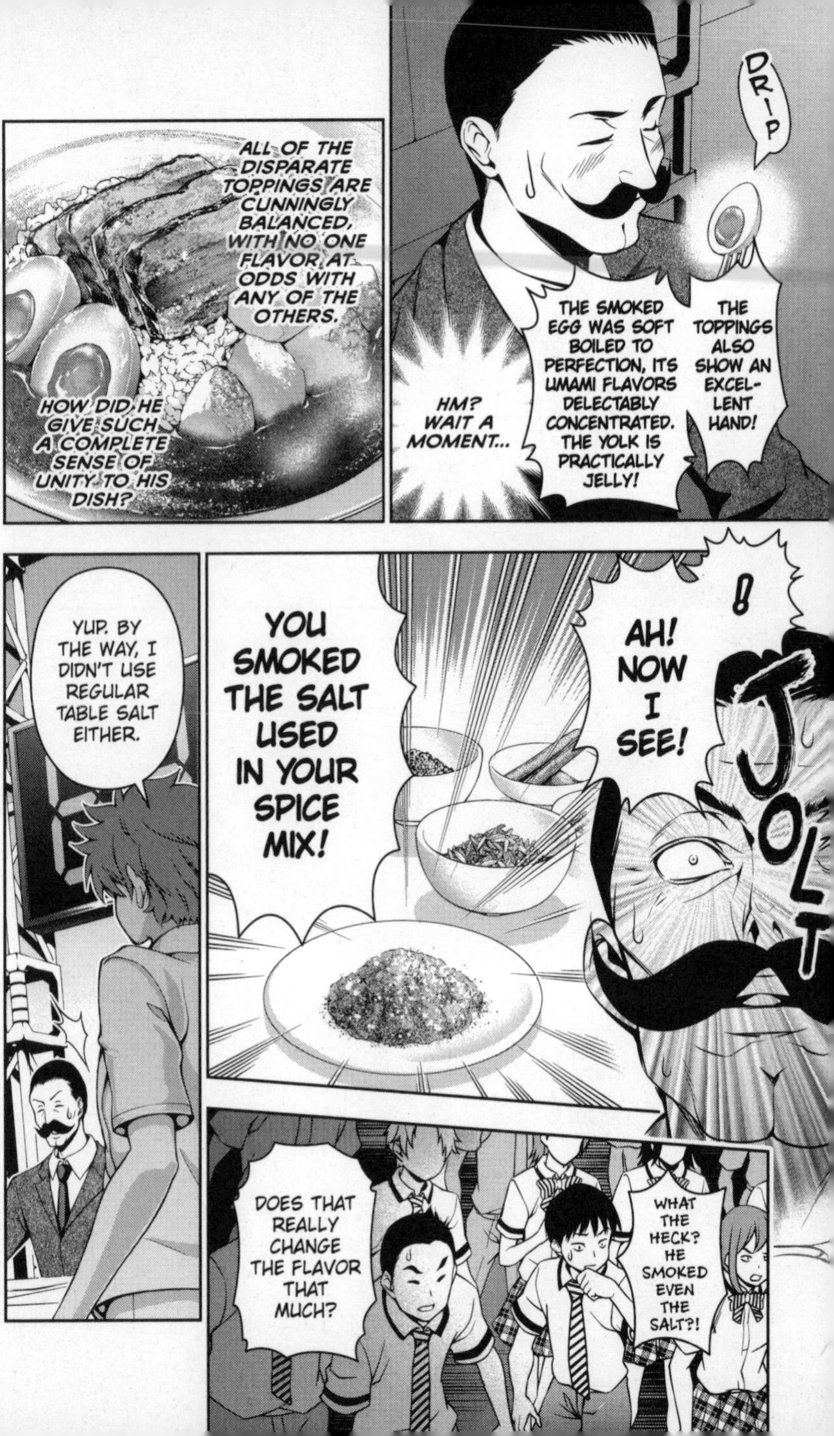
DRIP
THE TOPPINGS ALSO SHOW AN EXCEL-LENT HAND!
THE SMOKED EGG WAS SOFT BOILED TO PERFECTION, ITS UMAMI FLAVORS DELECTABLY CONCENTRATED. THE YOLK IS PRACTICALLY JELLY!
HM? WAIT A MOMENT...
ALL OF THE DISPARATE TOPPINGS ARE CUNNINGLY BALANCED, WITH NO ONE FLAVOR AT ODDS WITH ANY OF THE OTHERS.
HOW DID HE GIVE SUCH A COMPLETE SENSE OF UNITY TO HIS DISH?
!
AH! NOW I SEE!
JOLT
YOU SMOKED THE SALT USED IN YOUR SPICE MIX!
WHAT THE HECK? HE SMOKED EVEN THE SALT?!
DOES THAT REALLY CHANGE THE FLAVOR THAT MUCH?
YUP. BY THE WAY, I DIDN'T USE REGULAR TABLE SALT EITHER.

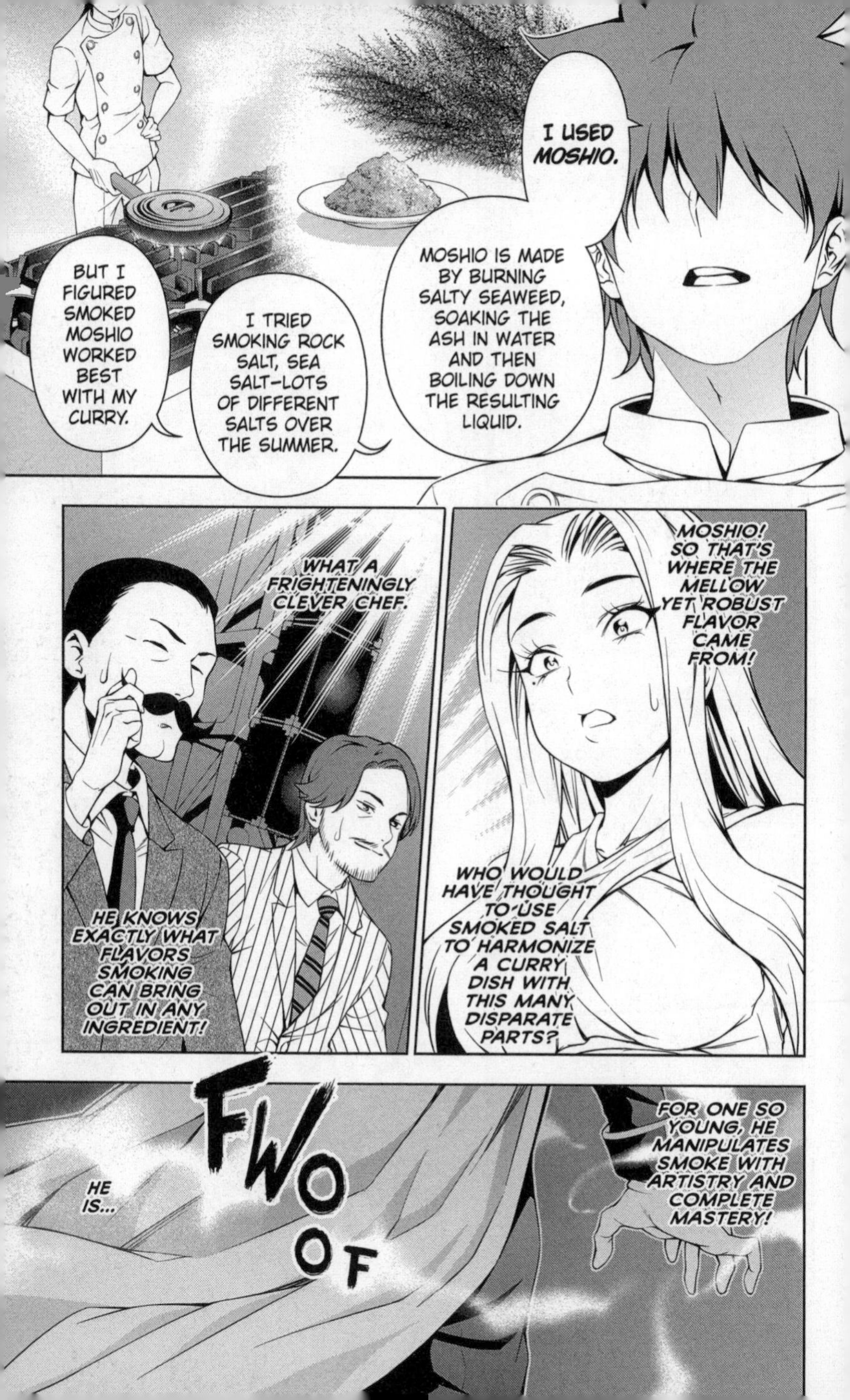
I USED *MOSHIO.*
MOSHIO IS MADE BY BURNING SALTY SEAWEED, SOAKING THE ASH IN WATER AND THEN BOILING DOWN THE RESULTING LIQUID.
I TRIED SMOKING ROCK SALT, SEA SALT—LOTS OF DIFFERENT SALTS OVER THE SUMMER.
BUT I FIGURED SMOKED MOSHIO WORKED BEST WITH MY CURRY.
MOSHIO! SO THAT'S WHERE THE MELLOW YET ROBUST FLAVOR CAME FROM!
WHO WOULD HAVE THOUGHT TO USE SMOKED SALT TO HARMONIZE A CURRY DISH WITH THIS MANY DISPARATE PARTS?
WHAT A FRIGHTENINGLY CLEVER CHEF.
HE KNOWS EXACTLY WHAT FLAVORS SMOKING CAN BRING OUT IN ANY INGREDIENT!
FOR ONE SO YOUNG, HE MANIPULATES SMOKE WITH ARTISTRY AND COMPLETE MASTERY!
FWOOF
HE IS...

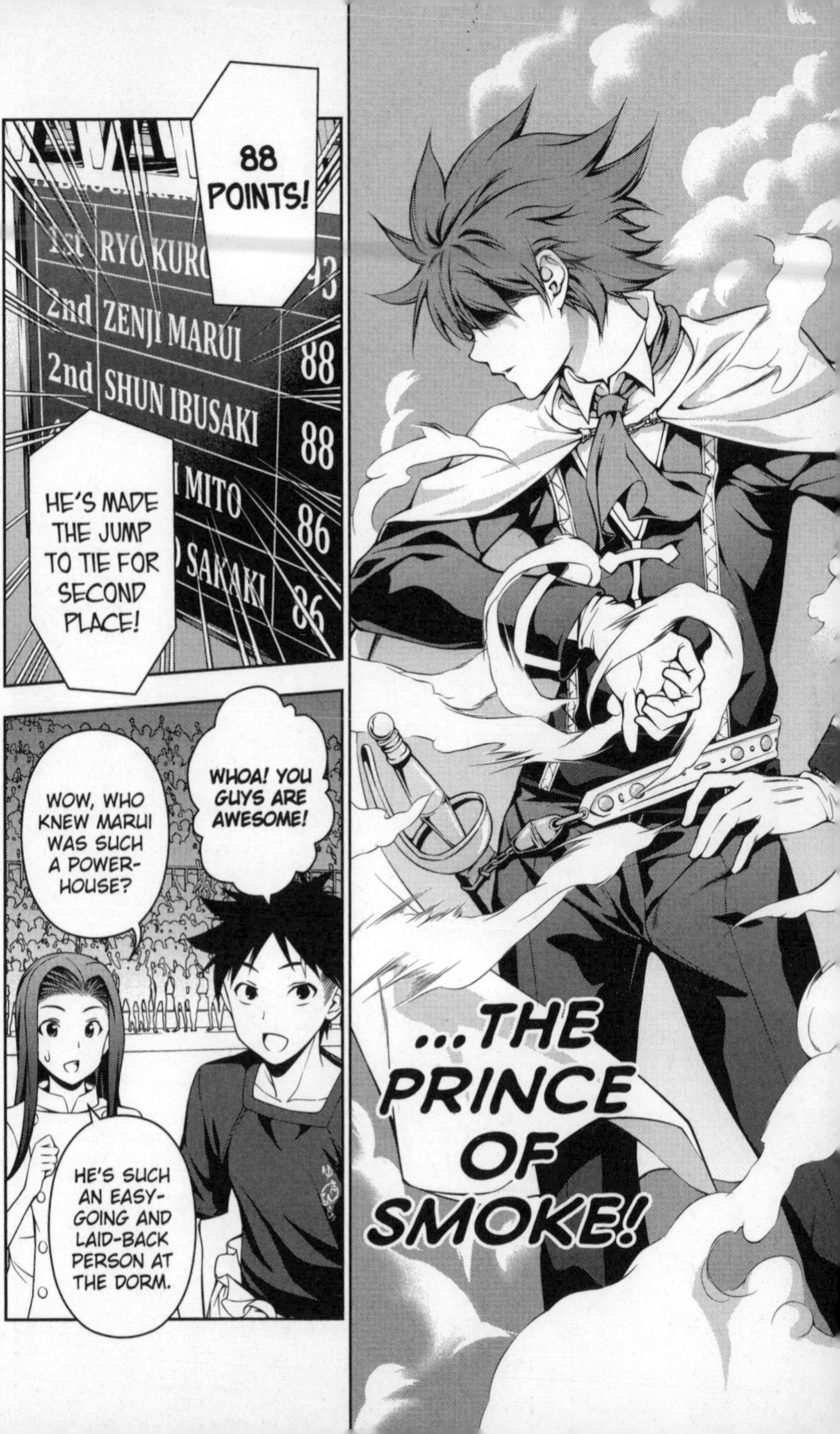
...THE PRINCE OF SMOKE!
88 POINTS!
2nd ZENJI MARUI 88
2nd SHUN IBUSAKI 88
HE'S MADE THE JUMP TO TIE FOR SECOND PLACE!
WHOA! YOU GUYS ARE AWESOME!
WOW, WHO KNEW MARUI WAS SUCH A POWER-HOUSE?
HE'S SUCH AN EASY-GOING AND LAID-BACK PERSON AT THE DORM.

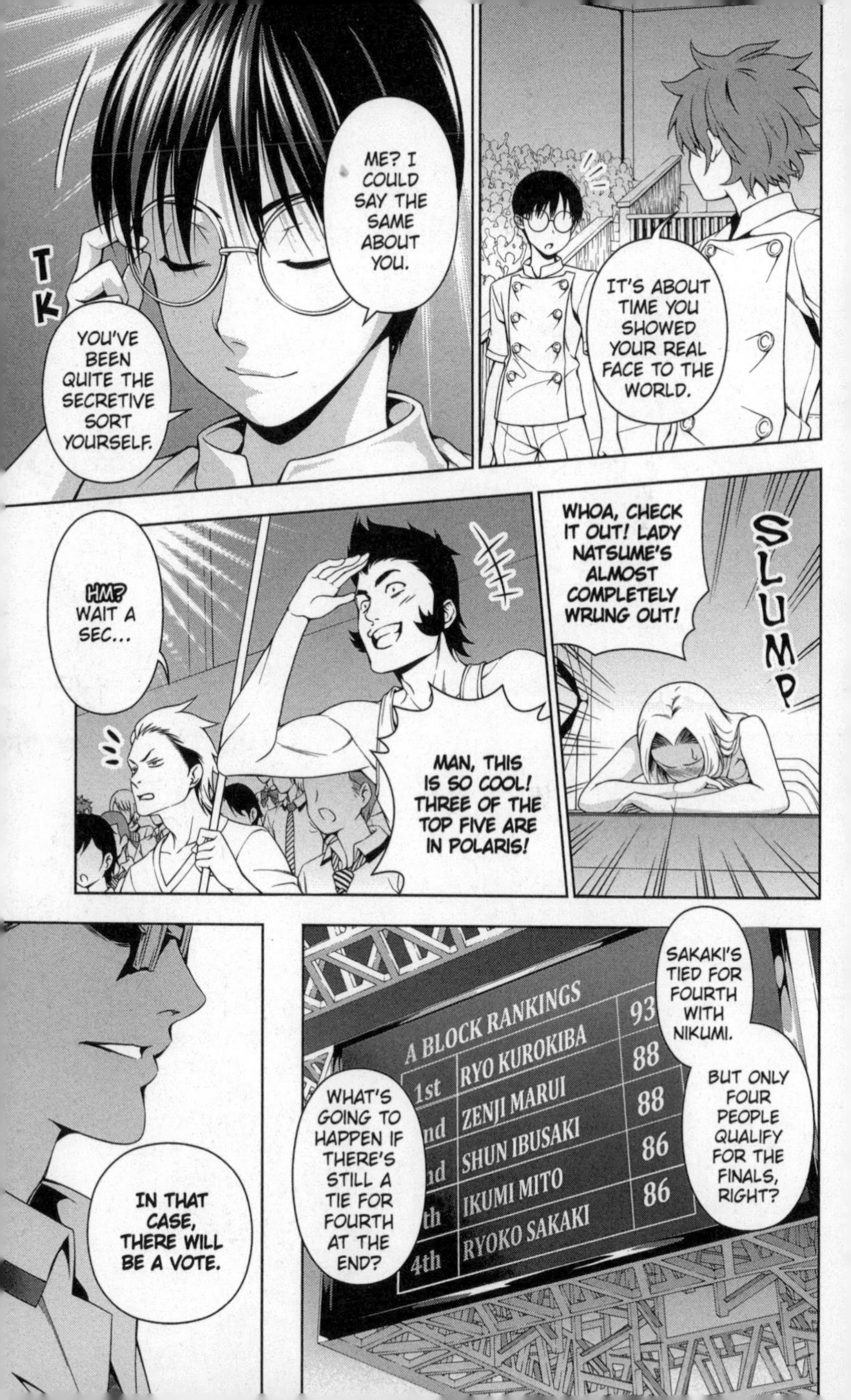
IT'S ABOUT TIME YOU SHOWED YOUR REAL FACE TO THE WORLD.
ME? I COULD SAY THE SAME ABOUT YOU.
TK
YOU'VE BEEN QUITE THE SECRETIVE SORT YOURSELF.
SLUMP
WHOA, CHECK IT OUT! LADY NATSUME'S ALMOST COMPLETELY WRUNG OUT!
MAN, THIS IS SO COOL! THREE OF THE TOP FIVE ARE IN POLARIS!
HM? WAIT A SEC...
SAKAKI'S TIED FOR FOURTH WITH NIKUMI.
BUT ONLY FOUR PEOPLE QUALIFY FOR THE FINALS, RIGHT?
A BLOCK RANKINGS
1st RYO KUROKIBA 93
2nd ZENJI MARUI 88
3rd SHUN IBUSAKI 88
4th IKUMI MITO 86
4th RYOKO SAKAKI 86
WHAT'S GOING TO HAPPEN IF THERE'S STILL A TIE FOR FOURTH AT THE END?
IN THAT CASE, THERE WILL BE A VOTE.

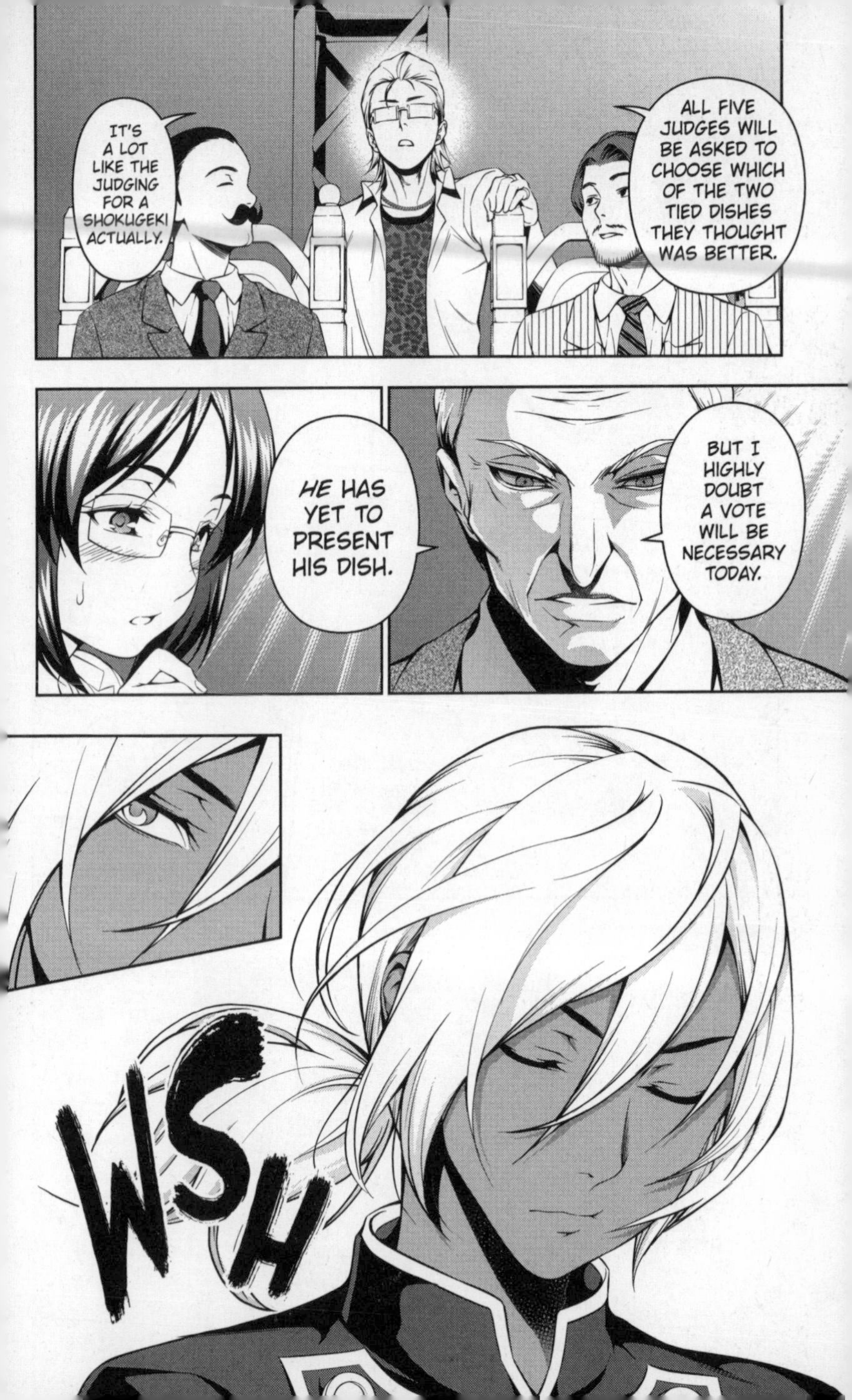
ALL FIVE JUDGES WILL BE ASKED TO CHOOSE WHICH OF THE TWO TIED DISHES THEY THOUGHT WAS BETTER.
IT'S A LOT LIKE THE JUDGING FOR A SHOKUGEKI ACTUALLY.
BUT I HIGHLY DOUBT A VOTE WILL BE NECESSARY TODAY.
*HE* HAS YET TO PRESENT HIS DISH.
WSH

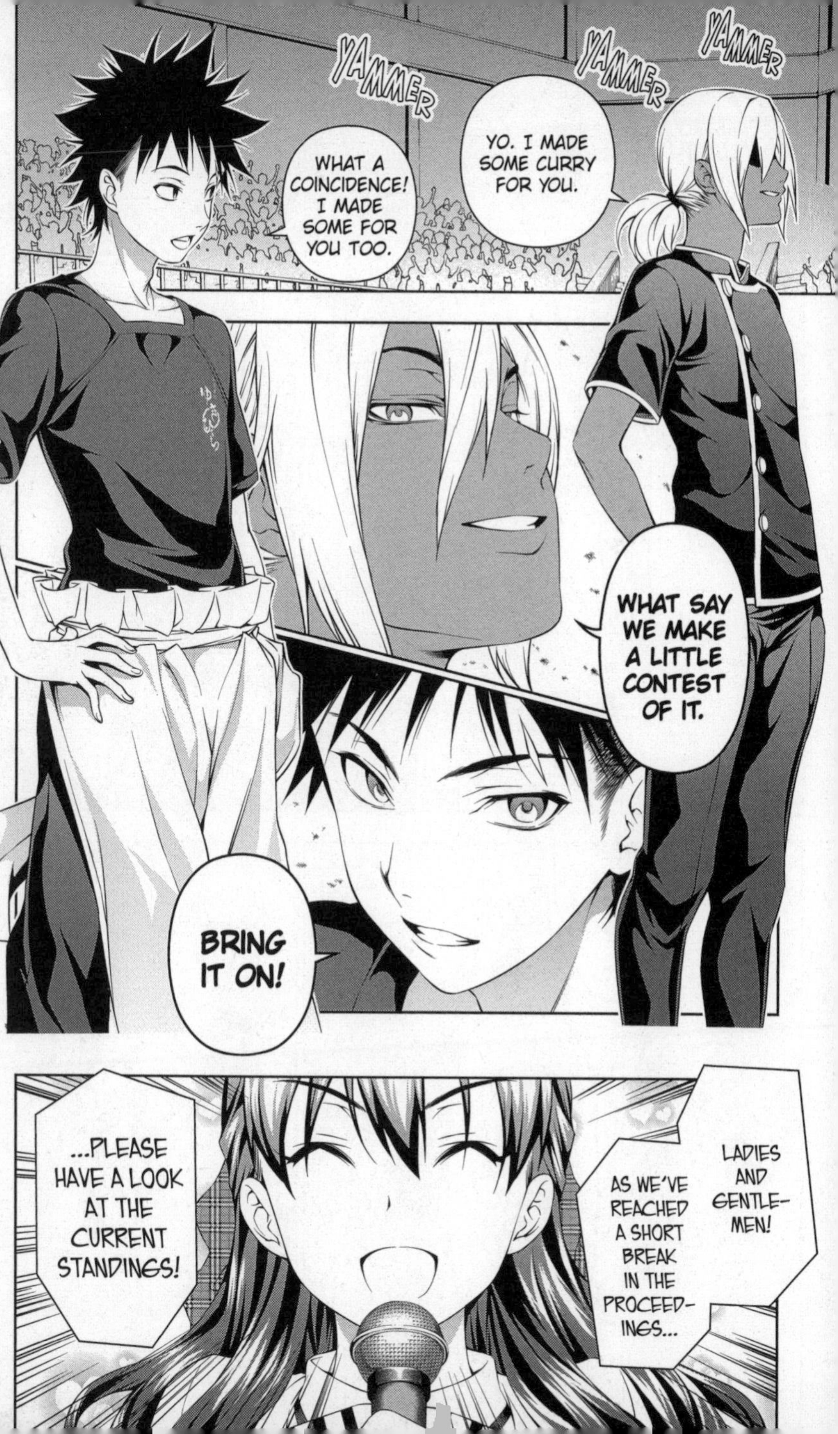
YAMMER
YAMMER
YAMMER
YO. I MADE SOME CURRY FOR YOU.
WHAT A COINCIDENCE! I MADE SOME FOR YOU TOO.
WHAT SAY WE MAKE A LITTLE CONTEST OF IT.
BRING IT ON!
LADIES AND GENTLEMEN!
AS WE'VE REACHED A SHORT BREAK IN THE PROCEEDINGS...
...PLEASE HAVE A LOOK AT THE CURRENT STANDINGS!

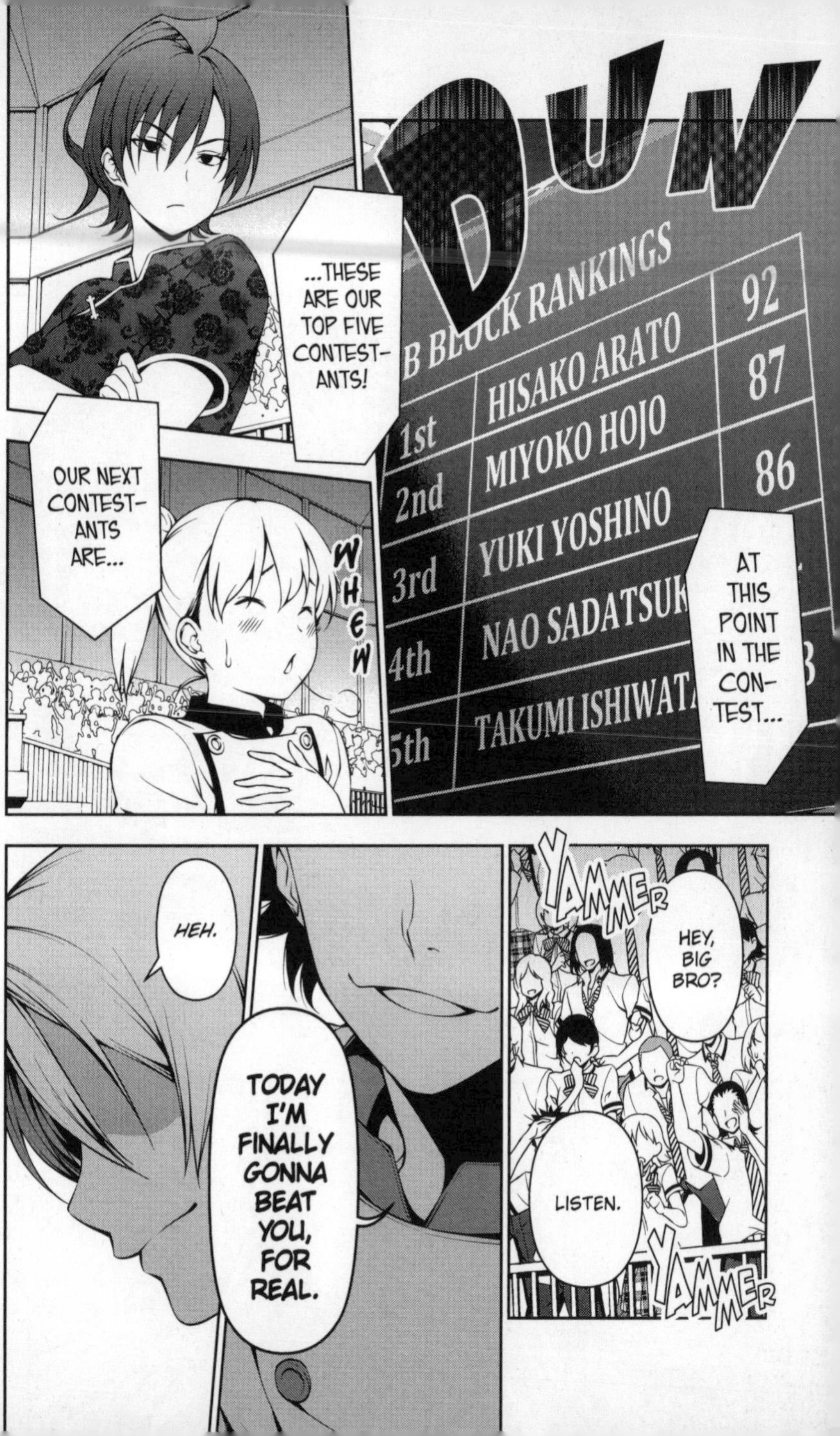
DUN
B BLOCK RANKINGS
1st HISAKO ARATO 92
2nd MIYOKO HOJO 87
3rd YUKI YOSHINO 86
4th NAO SADATSUK
5th TAKUMI ISHIWATA
AT THIS POINT IN THE CONTEST...
...THESE ARE OUR TOP FIVE CONTESTANTS!
OUR NEXT CONTESTANTS ARE...
WHEW
YAMMER
HEY, BIG BRO?
LISTEN.
YAMMER
HEH.
TODAY I'M FINALLY GONNA BEAT YOU, FOR REAL.

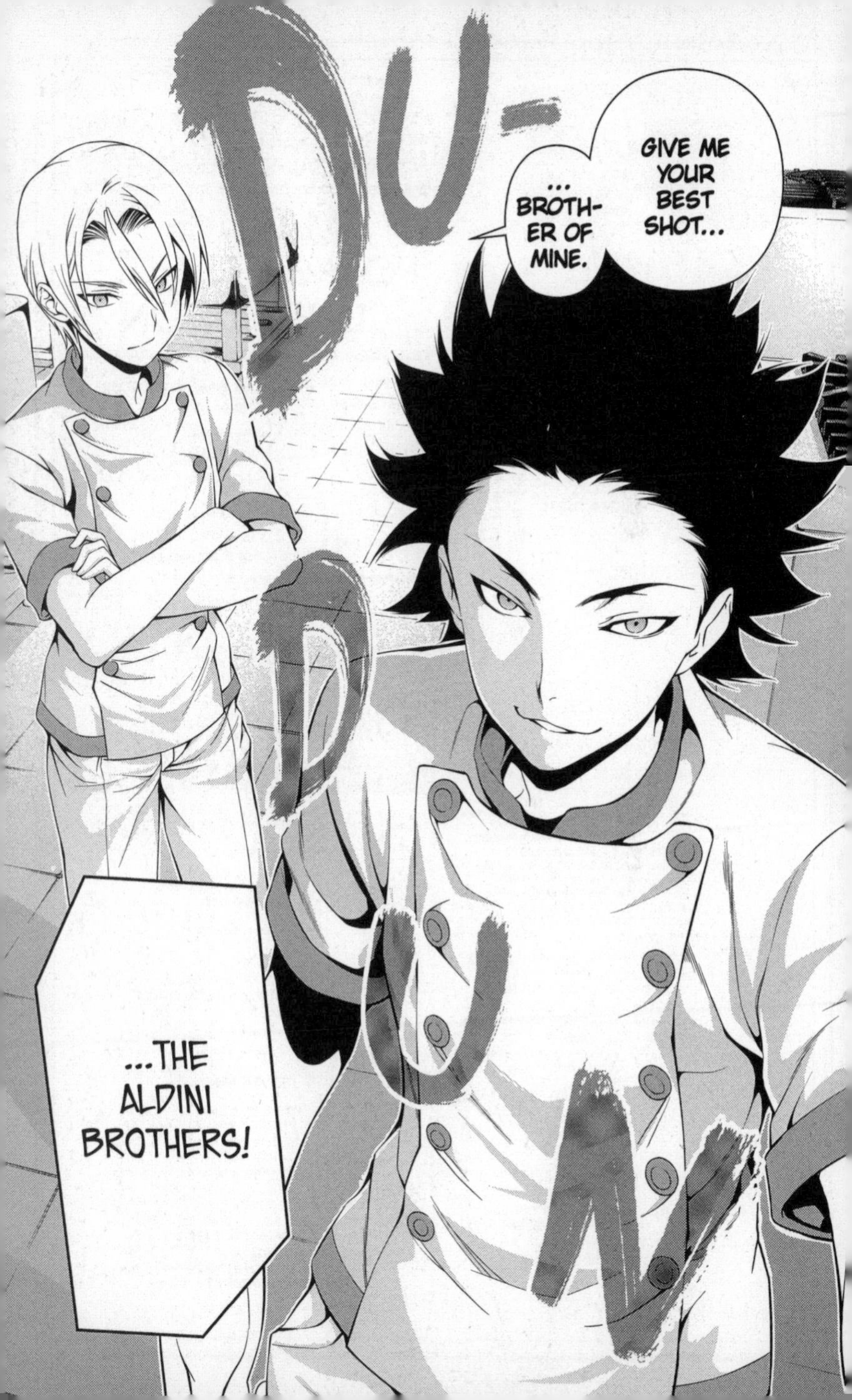
DU-DUN
GIVE ME YOUR BEST SHOT...
...BROTH-ER OF MINE.
...THE ALDINI BROTHERS!

RECIPE BY: YUKI MORISAKI

PRACTICAL RECIPE #2

VOLUME 7
SPECIAL SUPPLEMENT!

# MARUI'S POTAGE-BLANC-CURRY UDON

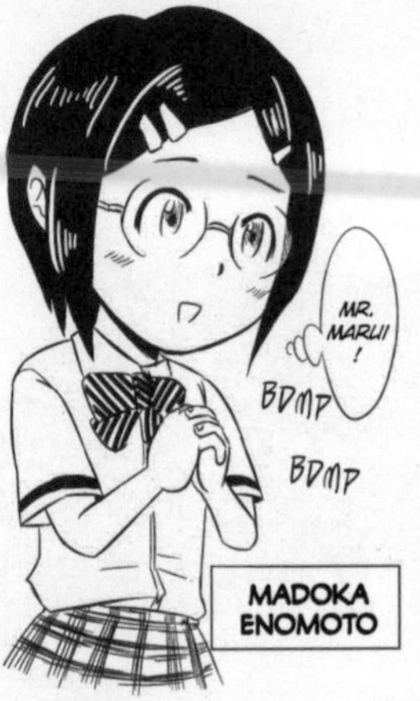
MR. MARUI!
BDMP
BDMP
MADOKA ENOMOTO

ARTIST: YUTO TSUKUDA

## INGREDIENTS
SERVES 2

- 2 BUNDLES UDON NOODLES
- DILL, POWDERED CHEESE, PEPPER

★ **THE BROTH**
- 2 POTATOES
- 1/2 ONION
- 2 TABLESPOONS BUTTER
- 1 TABLESPOON CURRY POWDER
- 2 TEASPOONS GRANULATED CONSOMMÉ
- 400 CC EACH OF WATER AND MILK
- 200 CC CREAM
- SALT, PEPPER

★ **THE MASHED POTATOES**
- 2 POTATOES
- 100 CC MILK
- 4 TABLESPOONS CREAM
- 1/4 TEASPOON CUMIN POWDER
- 1 TABLESPOON BUTTER
- SALT, PEPPER

★ **THE POACHED EGG**
- 2 EGGS
- 1 TEASPOON SALT
- 1 TABLESPOON VINEGAR
- 1000 CC WATER

1. **MAKE THE MASHED POTATOES**
   PEEL AND SLICE THE POTATOES.
2. PUT (1) IN A POT AND ADD ENOUGH WATER TO JUST COVER THE POTATOES. BOIL FOR SEVEN MINUTES OR UNTIL TENDER.
3. DRAIN THE WATER FROM (2). MASH THE POTATOES WHILE STILL HOT, ADDING THE CUMIN POWDER, MILK AND CREAM. PUT ON MEDIUM HEAT UNTIL THE MASHED POTATOES REACH THE DESIRED THICKNESS. REMOVE FROM HEAT AND ADD BUTTER, SALT AND PEPPER TO TASTE.
4. **MAKE THE BROTH**
   PEEL AND SLICE THE POTATOES. THINLY SLICE THE ONION.
5. HEAT THE BUTTER IN A POT. ADD THE ONIONS, POTATOES AND CURRY POWDER AND SAUTÉ UNTIL TRANSLUCENT. ADD THE WATER AND GRANULATED CONSOMMÉ AND SIMMER FOR SEVEN MINUTES.
6. PUT (5) IN A MIXER, ADD THE MILK AND BLEND UNTIL SMOOTH. RETURN MIXTURE TO THE POT.
7. ADD THE CREAM TO (6) AND SEASON TO TASTE WITH SALT AND PEPPER.
8. **MAKE THE POACHED EGG**
   BOIL THE WATER IN A SMALL POT, AND THEN ADD THE SALT AND VINEGAR. CRACK THE EGGS INTO A BOWL AND EASE INTO THE WATER ONE AT A TIME.
9. GENTLY SWIRL TO KEEP THE EGG WHITE FROM FEATHERING OUT AND BOIL FOR THREE MINUTES. REMOVE FROM THE WATER WITH A STRAINER AND DRY ANY EXCESS MOISTURE.
10. BOIL THE UDON NOODLES IN A SEPARATE POT AND DRAIN. PUT THEM IN A BOWL AND POUR THE BROTH OVER TOP. ADD THE MASHED POTATOES AND POACHED EGG ON TOP. GARNISH WITH POWDERED CHEESE, PEPPER AND DILL. DONE!

BING BONG DING DONG

ATTENTION–
THE RESULTS OF THE FIRST FOOD WARS!: SHOKUGEKI NO SOMA CHARACTER AND RECIPE POPULARITY POLL WERE ORIGINALLY RUN IN WEEKLY SHONEN JUMP ALONGSIDE THE MANGA'S FIFTY-SIXTH CHAPTER. DUE TO PAGE CONSTRAINTS IN THE VOLUME, THE RESULTS OF THE POLL WILL BE ADDED AT THE END. ELEVENTH THROUGH THIRTIETH PLACE, WHICH WERE NOT RUN IN THE ANTHOLOGY, HAVE ALSO BEEN INCLUDED.

LOOK FORWARD TO IT!

DING DONG BING BONG

# 56 TUSCANY MOON

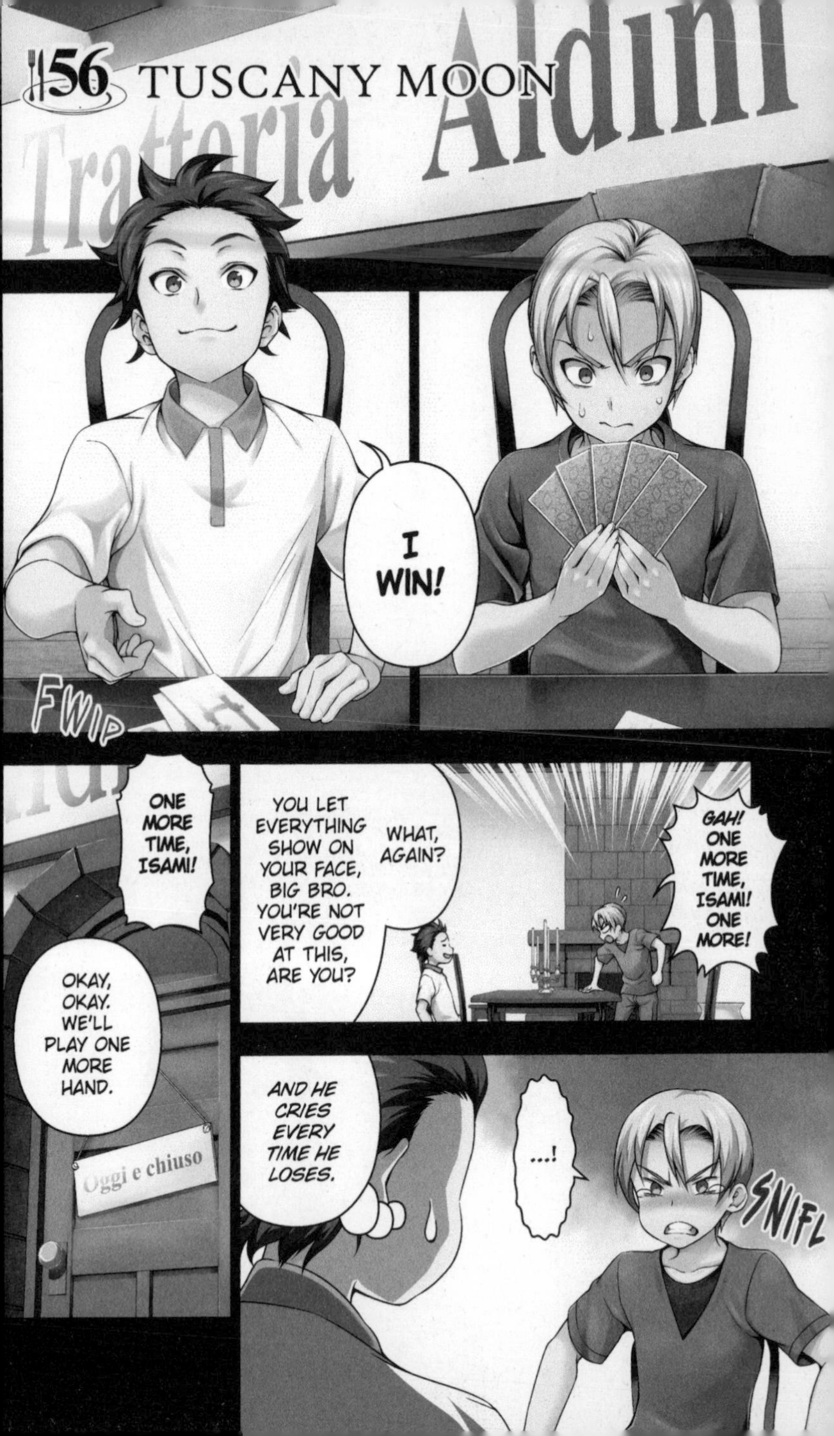

Trattoria Aldini
I WIN!
FWIP
GAH! ONE MORE TIME, ISAMI! ONE MORE!
WHAT, AGAIN?
YOU LET EVERYTHING SHOW ON YOUR FACE, BIG BRO. YOU'RE NOT VERY GOOD AT THIS, ARE YOU?
...!
SNIFL
AND HE CRIES EVERY TIME HE LOSES.
ONE MORE TIME, ISAMI!
OKAY, OKAY. WE'LL PLAY ONE MORE HAND.
Oggi e chiuso

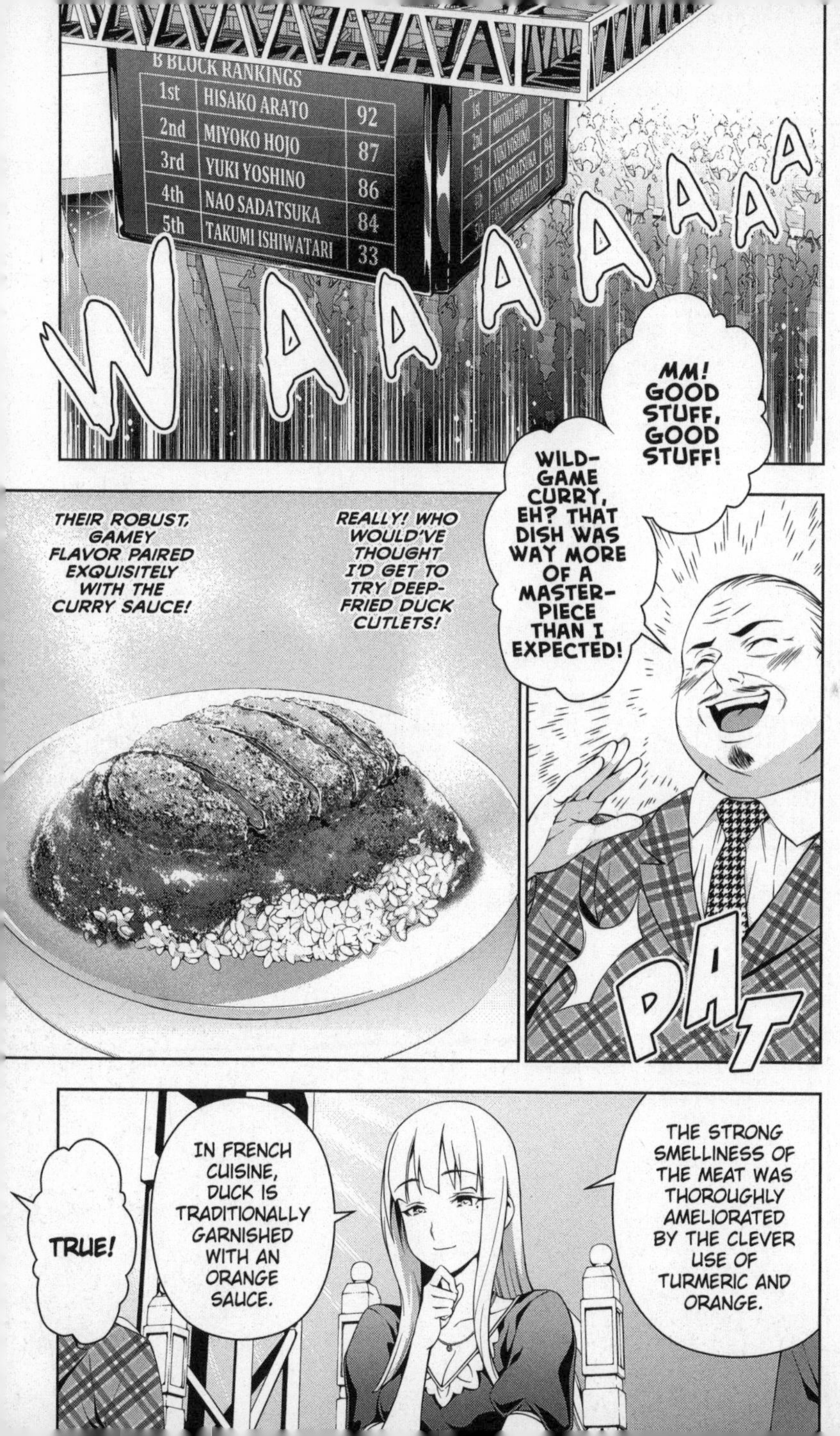
B BLOCK RANKINGS
1st HISAKO ARATO 92
2nd MIYOKO HOJO 87
3rd YUKI YOSHINO 86
4th NAO SADATSUKA 84
5th TAKUMI ISHIWATARI 33
WAAAAAAAA
MM! GOOD STUFF, GOOD STUFF!
WILD-GAME CURRY, EH? THAT DISH WAS WAY MORE OF A MASTERPIECE THAN I EXPECTED!
PAT
REALLY! WHO WOULD'VE THOUGHT I'D GET TO TRY DEEP-FRIED DUCK CUTLETS!
THEIR ROBUST, GAMEY FLAVOR PAIRED EXQUISITELY WITH THE CURRY SAUCE!
THE STRONG SMELLINESS OF THE MEAT WAS THOROUGHLY AMELIORATED BY THE CLEVER USE OF TURMERIC AND ORANGE.
IN FRENCH CUISINE, DUCK IS TRADITIONALLY GARNISHED WITH AN ORANGE SAUCE.
TRUE!

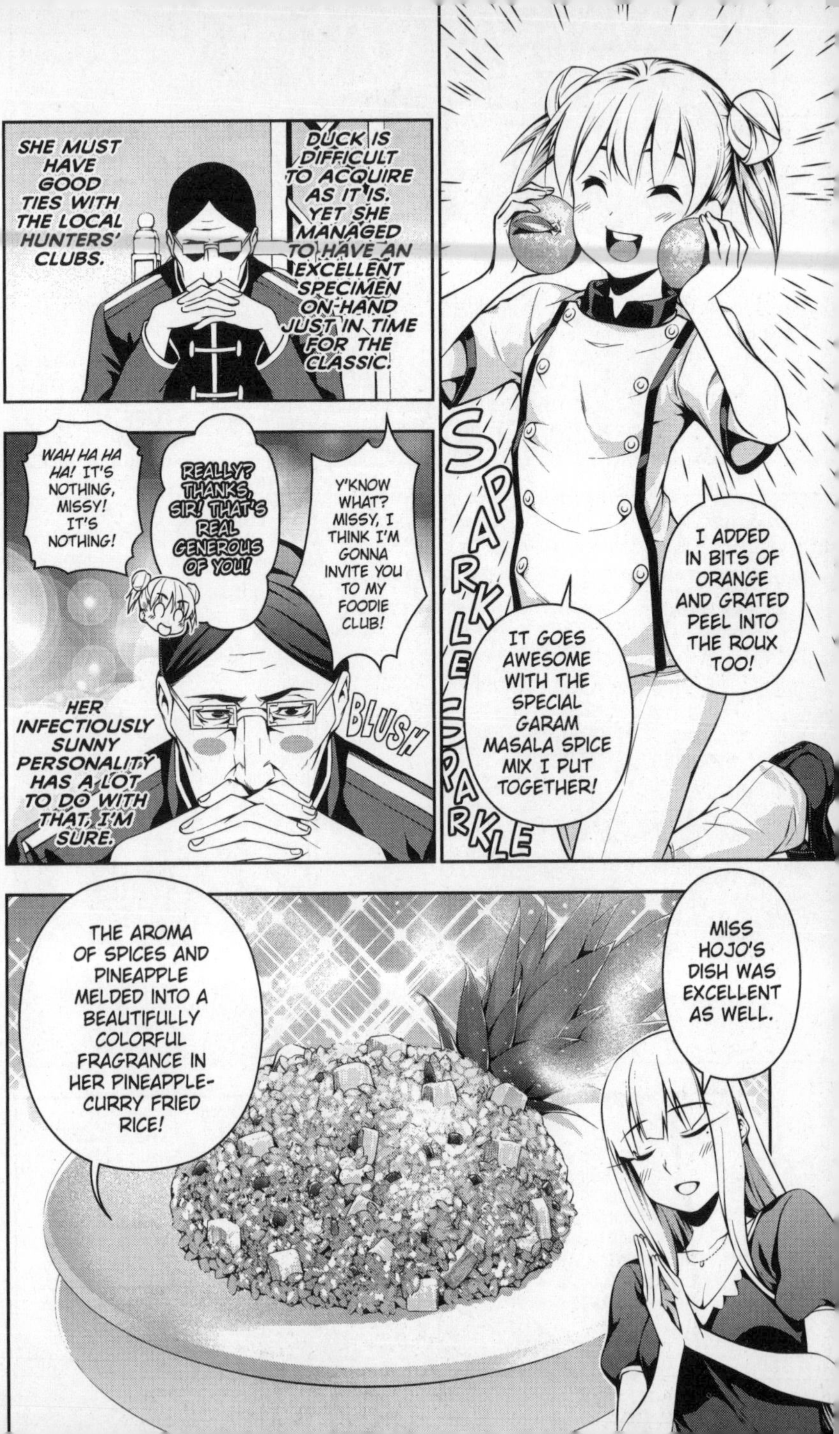
I ADDED IN BITS OF ORANGE AND GRATED PEEL INTO THE ROUX TOO!
IT GOES AWESOME WITH THE SPECIAL GARAM MASALA SPICE MIX I PUT TOGETHER!
SPARKLE SPARKLE
DUCK IS DIFFICULT TO ACQUIRE AS IT IS. YET SHE MANAGED TO HAVE AN EXCELLENT SPECIMEN ON-HAND JUST IN TIME FOR THE CLASSIC.
SHE MUST HAVE GOOD TIES WITH THE LOCAL HUNTERS' CLUBS.
Y'KNOW WHAT? MISSY, I THINK I'M GONNA INVITE YOU TO MY FOODIE CLUB!
REALLY? THANKS, SIR! THAT'S REAL GENEROUS OF YOU!
WAH HA HA HA! IT'S NOTHING, MISSY! IT'S NOTHING!
BLUSH
HER INFECTIOUSLY SUNNY PERSONALITY HAS A LOT TO DO WITH THAT, I'M SURE.
MISS HOJO'S DISH WAS EXCELLENT AS WELL.
THE AROMA OF SPICES AND PINEAPPLE MELDED INTO A BEAUTIFULLY COLORFUL FRAGRANCE IN HER PINEAPPLE-CURRY FRIED RICE!

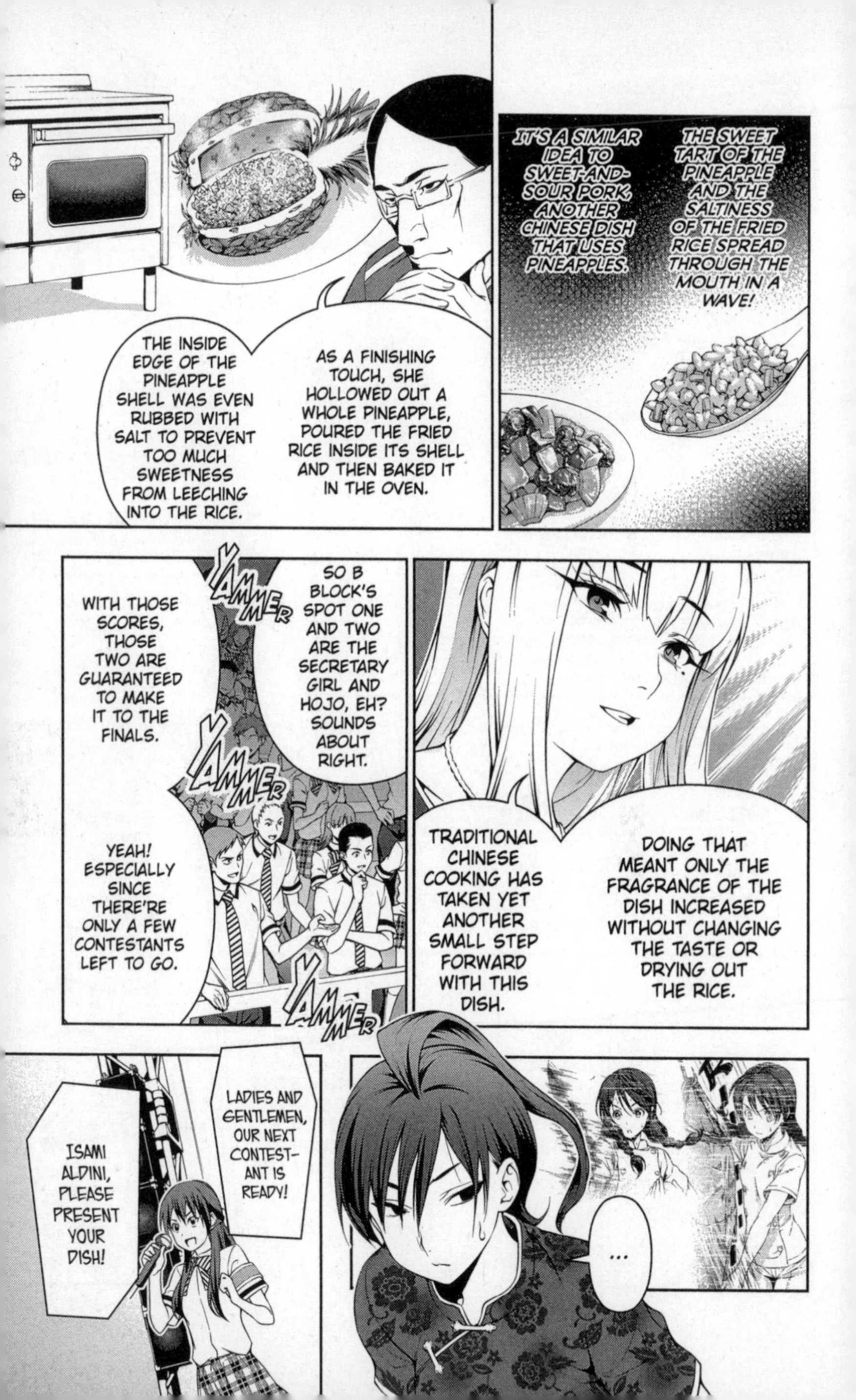
THE SWEET TART OF THE PINEAPPLE AND THE SALTINESS OF THE FRIED RICE SPREAD THROUGH THE MOUTH IN A WAVE!
IT'S A SIMILAR IDEA TO SWEET-AND-SOUR PORK, ANOTHER CHINESE DISH THAT USES PINEAPPLES.
AS A FINISHING TOUCH, SHE HOLLOWED OUT A WHOLE PINEAPPLE, POURED THE FRIED RICE INSIDE ITS SHELL AND THEN BAKED IT IN THE OVEN.
THE INSIDE EDGE OF THE PINEAPPLE SHELL WAS EVEN RUBBED WITH SALT TO PREVENT TOO MUCH SWEETNESS FROM LEECHING INTO THE RICE.
DOING THAT MEANT ONLY THE FRAGRANCE OF THE DISH INCREASED WITHOUT CHANGING THE TASTE OR DRYING OUT THE RICE.
TRADITIONAL CHINESE COOKING HAS TAKEN YET ANOTHER SMALL STEP FORWARD WITH THIS DISH.
SO B BLOCK'S SPOT ONE AND TWO ARE THE SECRETARY GIRL AND HOJO, EH? SOUNDS ABOUT RIGHT.
YAMMER
WITH THOSE SCORES, THOSE TWO ARE GUARANTEED TO MAKE IT TO THE FINALS.
YAMMER
YEAH! ESPECIALLY SINCE THERE'RE ONLY A FEW CONTESTANTS LEFT TO GO.
YAMMER
...
LADIES AND GENTLEMEN, OUR NEXT CONTEST-ANT IS READY!
ISAMI ALDINI, PLEASE PRESENT YOUR DISH!

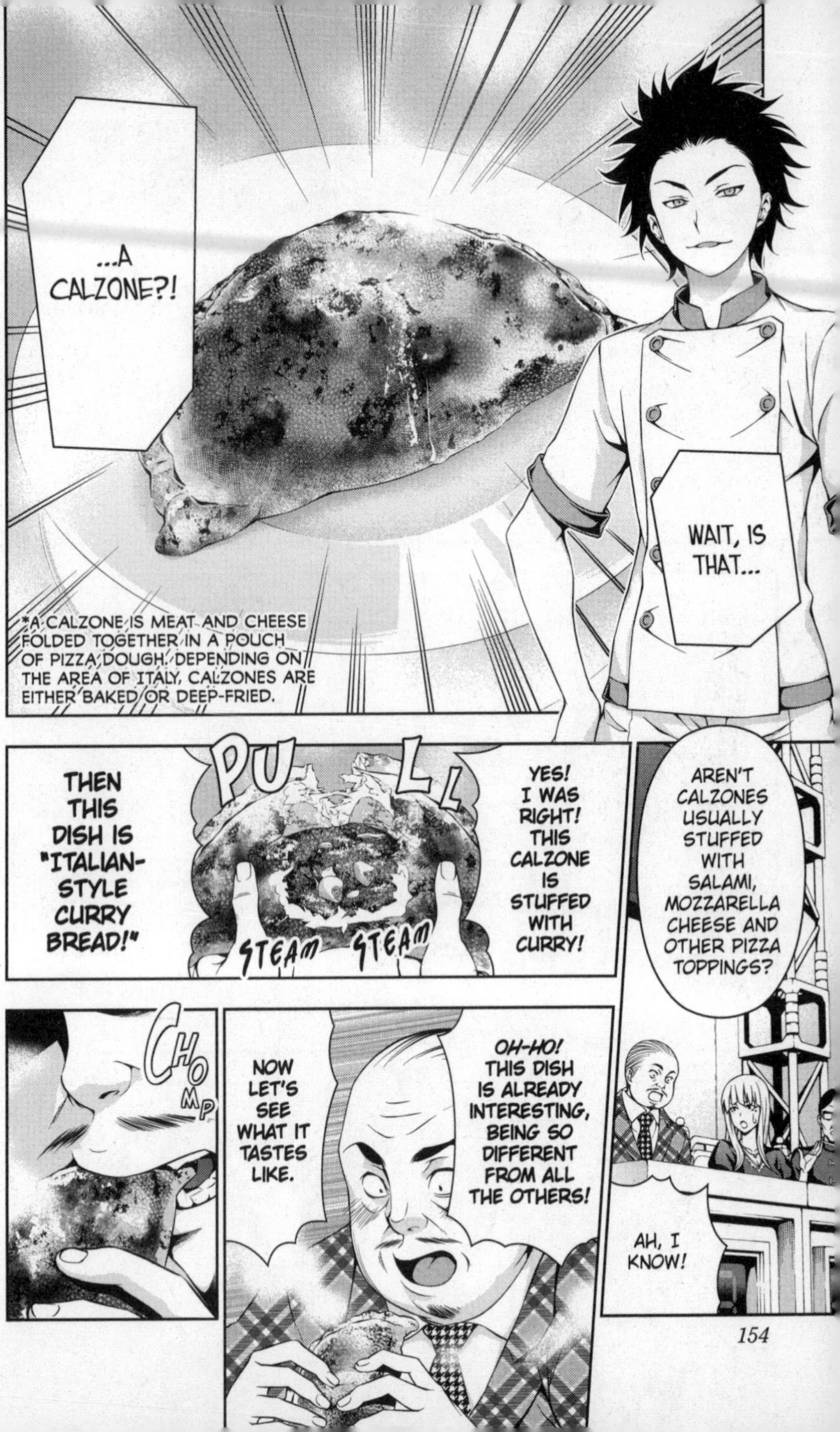
WAIT, IS THAT...
...A CALZONE?!
*A CALZONE IS MEAT AND CHEESE FOLDED TOGETHER IN A POUCH OF PIZZA DOUGH. DEPENDING ON THE AREA OF ITALY, CALZONES ARE EITHER BAKED OR DEEP-FRIED.
AREN'T CALZONES USUALLY STUFFED WITH SALAMI, MOZZARELLA CHEESE AND OTHER PIZZA TOPPINGS?
AH, I KNOW!
YES! I WAS RIGHT! THIS CALZONE IS STUFFED WITH CURRY!
PULL
STEAM STEAM
THEN THIS DISH IS "ITALIAN-STYLE CURRY BREAD!"
OH-HO! THIS DISH IS ALREADY INTERESTING, BEING SO DIFFERENT FROM ALL THE OTHERS!
NOW LET'S SEE WHAT IT TASTES LIKE.
CHOMP

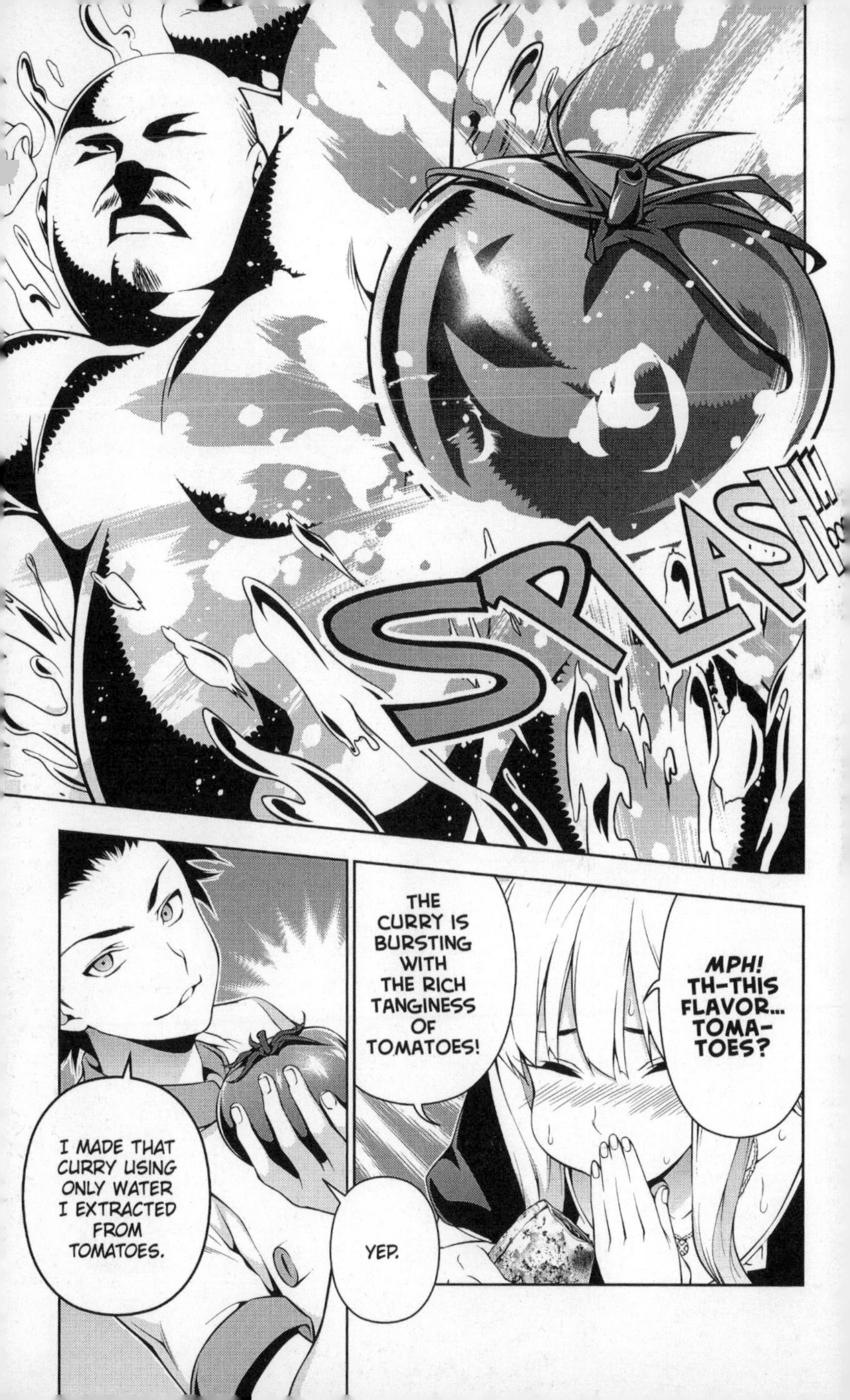
SPLASH!!
MPH! TH-THIS FLAVOR... TOMA-TOES?
THE CURRY IS BURSTING WITH THE RICH TANGINESS OF TOMATOES!
YEP.
I MADE THAT CURRY USING ONLY WATER I EXTRACTED FROM TOMATOES.

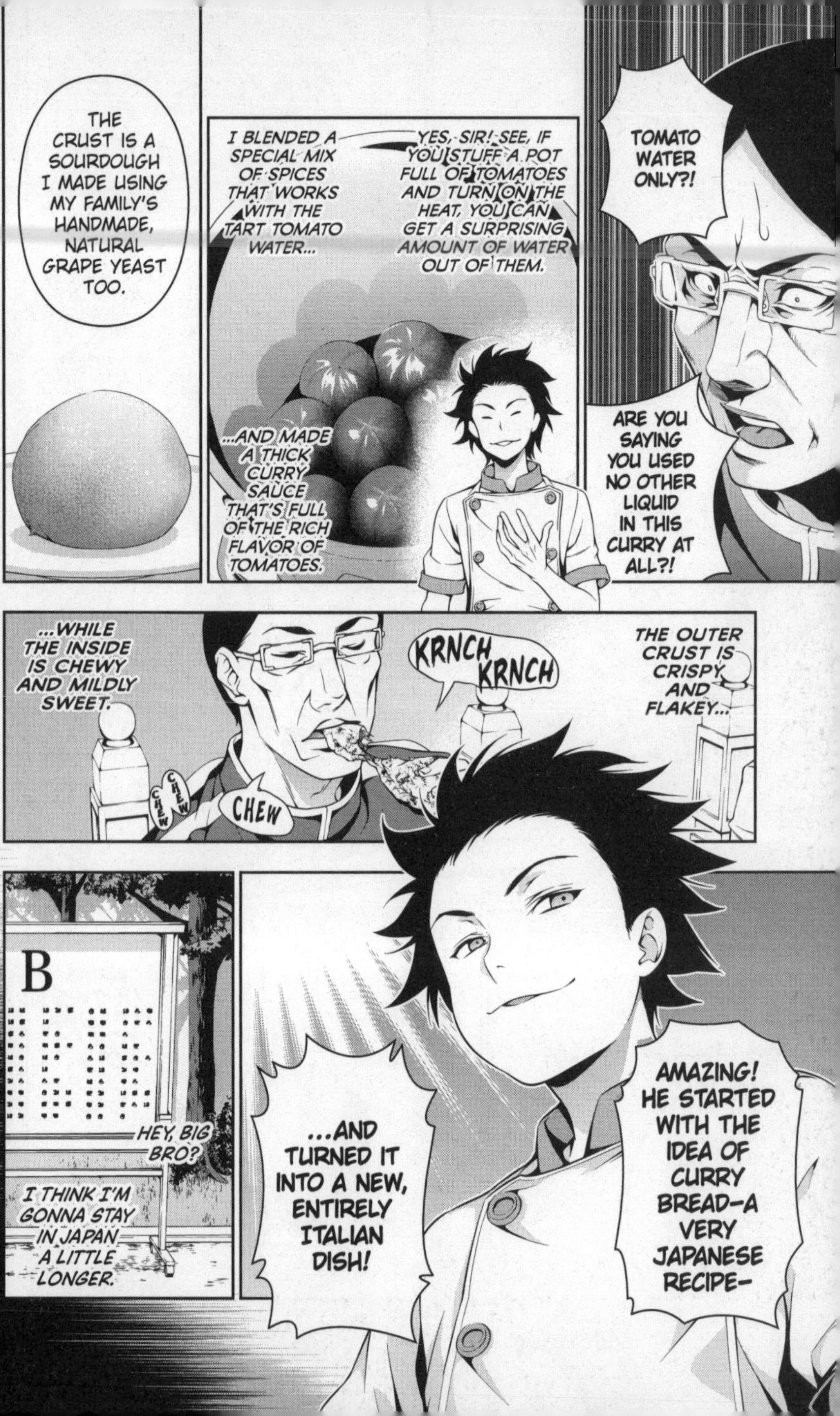
TOMATO WATER ONLY?!
ARE YOU SAYING YOU USED NO OTHER LIQUID IN THIS CURRY AT ALL?!
YES, SIR! SEE, IF YOU STUFF A POT FULL OF TOMATOES AND TURN ON THE HEAT, YOU CAN GET A SURPRISING AMOUNT OF WATER OUT OF THEM.
I BLENDED A SPECIAL MIX OF SPICES THAT WORKS WITH THE TART TOMATO WATER...
...AND MADE A THICK CURRY SAUCE THAT'S FULL OF THE RICH FLAVOR OF TOMATOES.
THE CRUST IS A SOURDOUGH I MADE USING MY FAMILY'S HANDMADE, NATURAL GRAPE YEAST TOO.
THE OUTER CRUST IS CRISPY AND FLAKEY...
KRNCH KRNCH
...WHILE THE INSIDE IS CHEWY AND MILDLY SWEET.
CHEW
CHEW
CHEW
AMAZING! HE STARTED WITH THE IDEA OF CURRY BREAD—A VERY JAPANESE RECIPE—
...AND TURNED IT INTO A NEW, ENTIRELY ITALIAN DISH!
B
HEY, BIG BRO?
I THINK I'M GONNA STAY IN JAPAN A LITTLE LONGER.

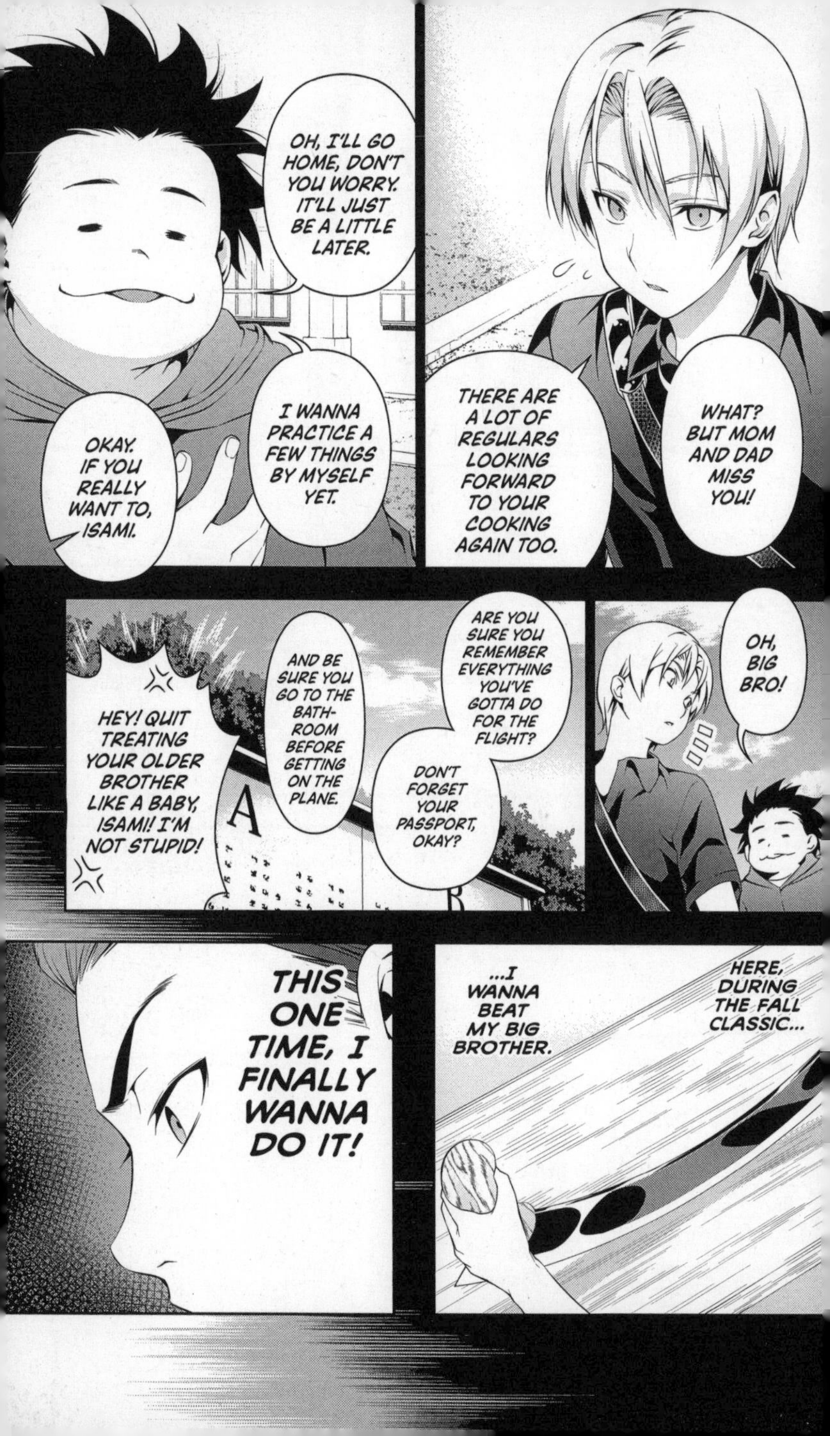
WHAT? BUT MOM AND DAD MISS YOU!
THERE ARE A LOT OF REGULARS LOOKING FORWARD TO YOUR COOKING AGAIN TOO.
OH, I'LL GO HOME, DON'T YOU WORRY. IT'LL JUST BE A LITTLE LATER.
I WANNA PRACTICE A FEW THINGS BY MYSELF YET.
OKAY. IF YOU REALLY WANT TO, ISAMI.
OH, BIG BRO!
ARE YOU SURE YOU REMEMBER EVERYTHING YOU'VE GOTTA DO FOR THE FLIGHT?
DON'T FORGET YOUR PASSPORT, OKAY?
AND BE SURE YOU GO TO THE BATH-ROOM BEFORE GETTING ON THE PLANE.
HEY! QUIT TREATING YOUR OLDER BROTHER LIKE A BABY, ISAMI! I'M NOT STUPID!
HERE, DURING THE FALL CLASSIC...
...I WANNA BEAT MY BIG BROTHER.
THIS ONE TIME, I FINALLY WANNA DO IT!

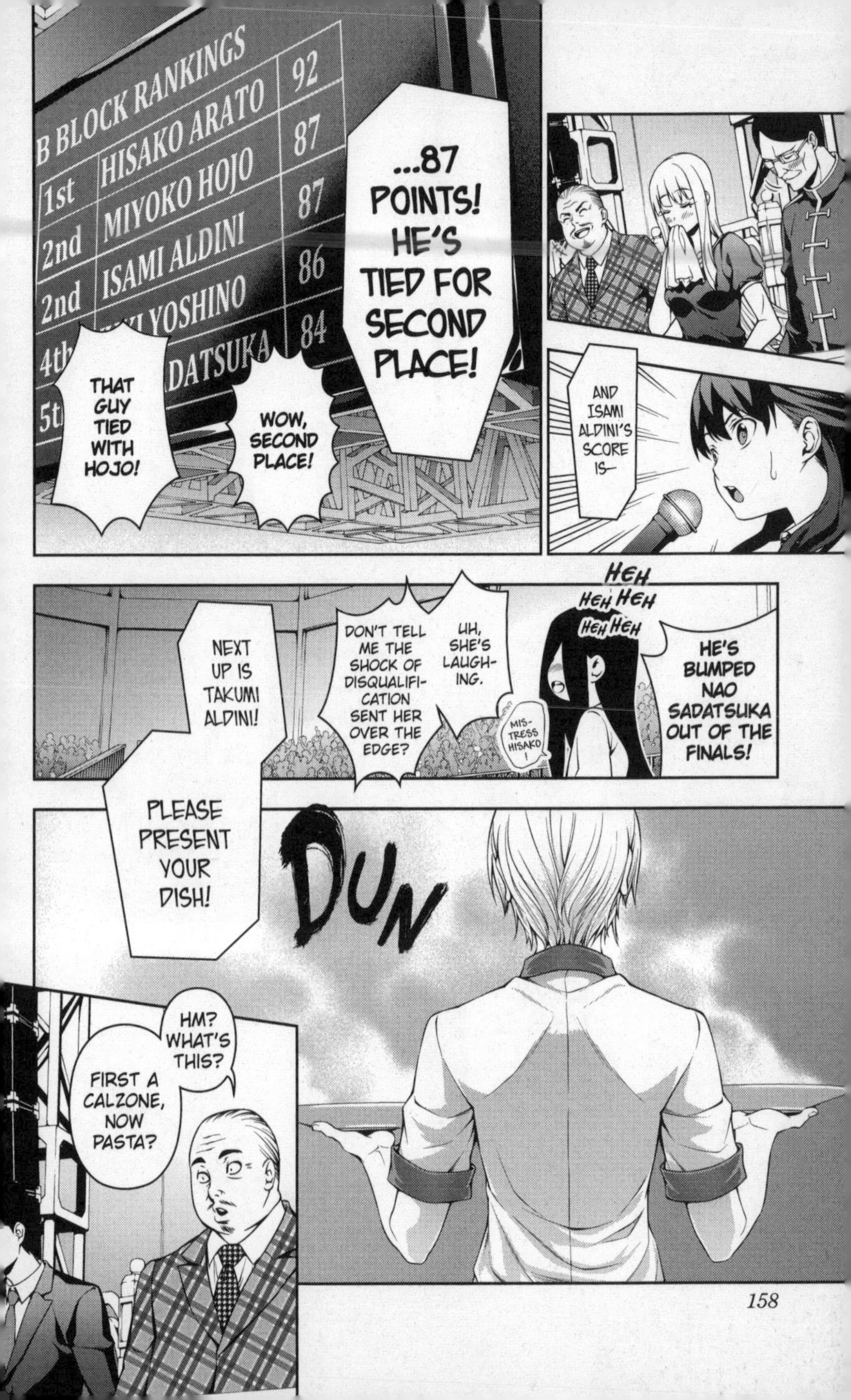
AND ISAMI ALDINI'S SCORE IS—
B BLOCK RANKINGS
1st HISAKO ARATO 92
2nd MIYOKO HOJO 87
2nd ISAMI ALDINI 87
4th YOSHINO 86
5th DATSUKA 84
...87 POINTS! HE'S TIED FOR SECOND PLACE!
WOW, SECOND PLACE!
THAT GUY TIED WITH HOJO!
HEH HEH HEH HEH HEH
HE'S BUMPED NAO SADATSUKA OUT OF THE FINALS!
MISTRESS HISAKO!
UH, SHE'S LAUGHING.
DON'T TELL ME THE SHOCK OF DISQUALIFICATION SENT HER OVER THE EDGE?
NEXT UP IS TAKUMI ALDINI!
PLEASE PRESENT YOUR DISH!
DUN
HM? WHAT'S THIS?
FIRST A CALZONE, NOW PASTA?

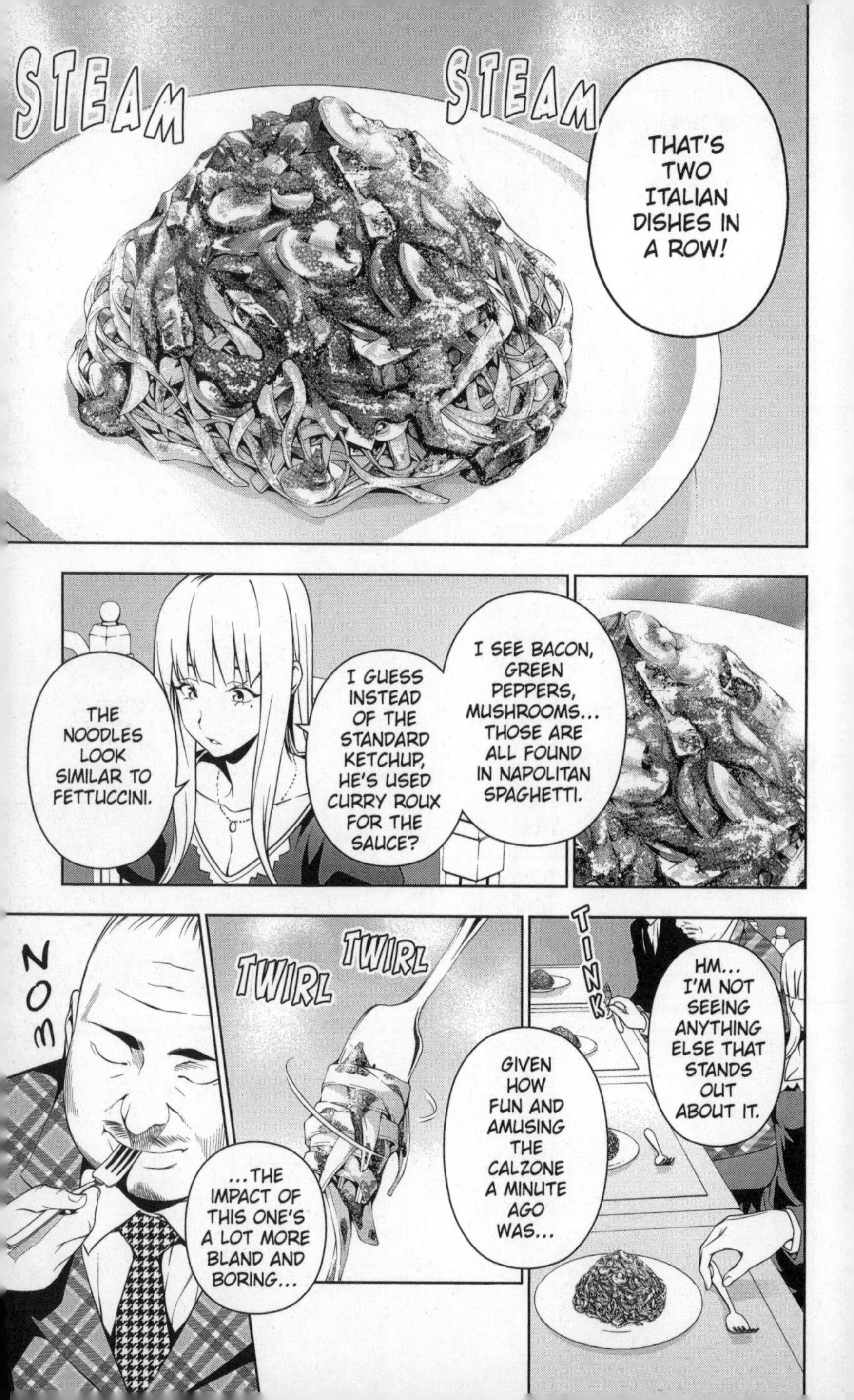
THAT'S TWO ITALIAN DISHES IN A ROW!
STEAM
STEAM
I SEE BACON, GREEN PEPPERS, MUSHROOMS... THOSE ARE ALL FOUND IN NAPOLITAN SPAGHETTI.
I GUESS INSTEAD OF THE STANDARD KETCHUP, HE'S USED CURRY ROUX FOR THE SAUCE?
THE NOODLES LOOK SIMILAR TO FETTUCCINI.
TINK
HM... I'M NOT SEEING ANYTHING ELSE THAT STANDS OUT ABOUT IT.
GIVEN HOW FUN AND AMUSING THE CALZONE A MINUTE AGO WAS...
TWIRL
TWIRL
...THE IMPACT OF THIS ONE'S A LOT MORE BLAND AND BORING...
NOM

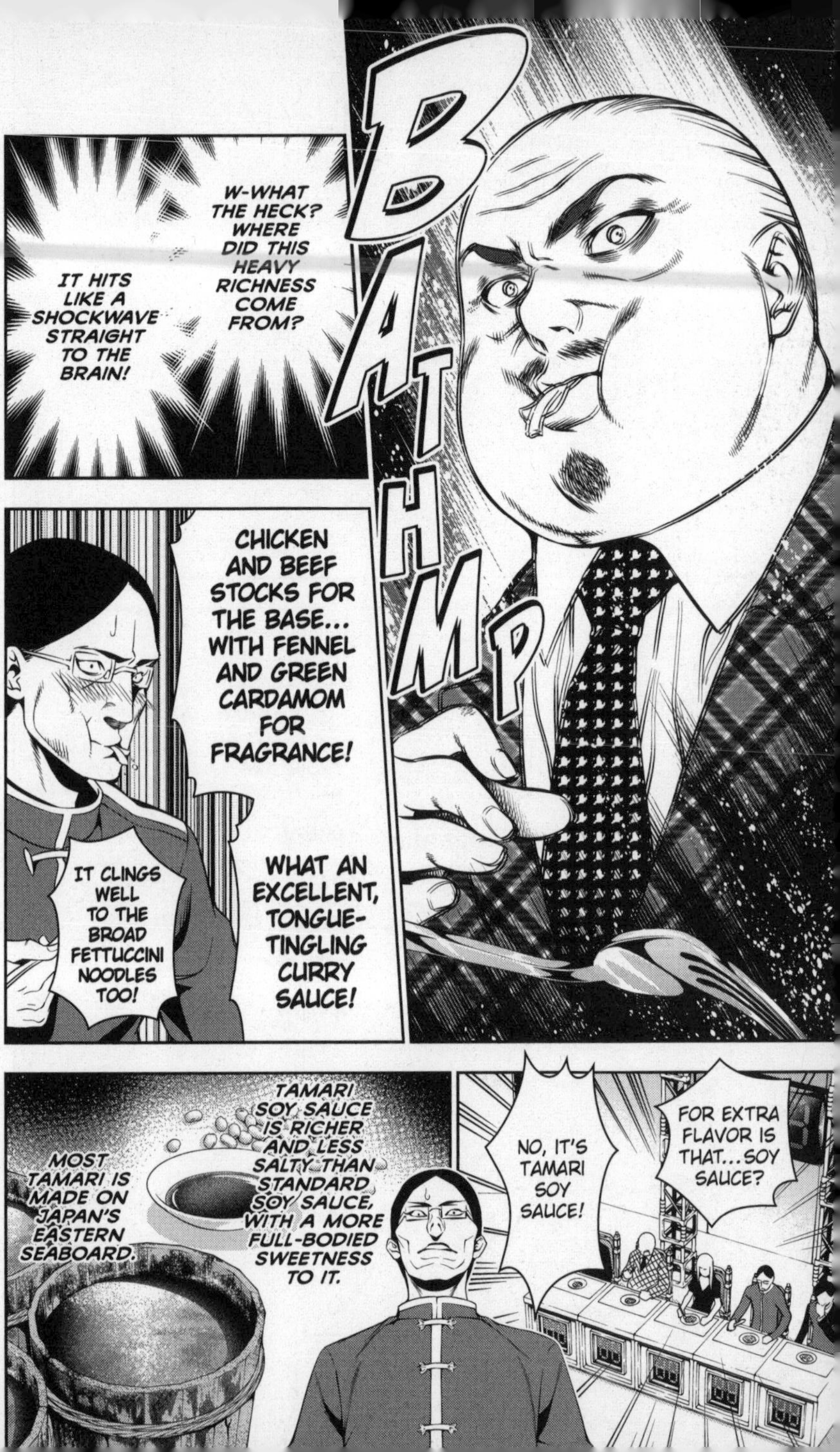
BATHMP
W-WHAT THE HECK? WHERE DID THIS HEAVY RICHNESS COME FROM?
IT HITS LIKE A SHOCKWAVE STRAIGHT TO THE BRAIN!
CHICKEN AND BEEF STOCKS FOR THE BASE... WITH FENNEL AND GREEN CARDAMOM FOR FRAGRANCE!
WHAT AN EXCELLENT, TONGUE-TINGLING CURRY SAUCE!
IT CLINGS WELL TO THE BROAD FETTUCCINI NOODLES TOO!
FOR EXTRA FLAVOR IS THAT...SOY SAUCE?
NO, IT'S TAMARI SOY SAUCE!
TAMARI SOY SAUCE IS RICHER AND LESS SALTY THAN STANDARD SOY SAUCE, WITH A MORE FULL-BODIED SWEETNESS TO IT.
MOST TAMARI IS MADE ON JAPAN'S EASTERN SEABOARD.

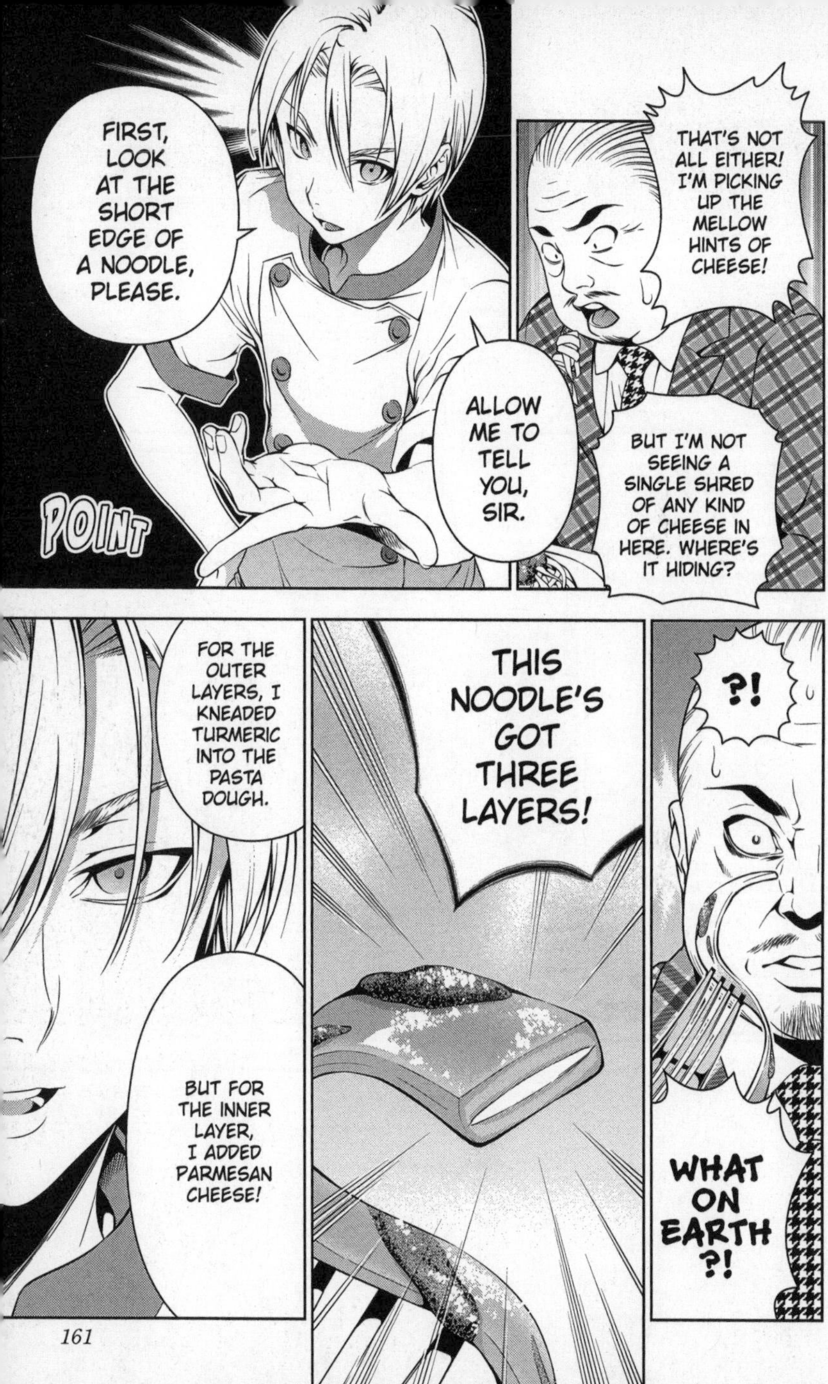
THAT'S NOT ALL EITHER! I'M PICKING UP THE MELLOW HINTS OF CHEESE!
BUT I'M NOT SEEING A SINGLE SHRED OF ANY KIND OF CHEESE IN HERE. WHERE'S IT HIDING?
ALLOW ME TO TELL YOU, SIR.
FIRST, LOOK AT THE SHORT EDGE OF A NOODLE, PLEASE.
POINT
?!
WHAT ON EARTH ?!
THIS NOODLE'S GOT THREE LAYERS!
FOR THE OUTER LAYERS, I KNEADED TURMERIC INTO THE PASTA DOUGH.
BUT FOR THE INNER LAYER, I ADDED PARMESAN CHEESE!

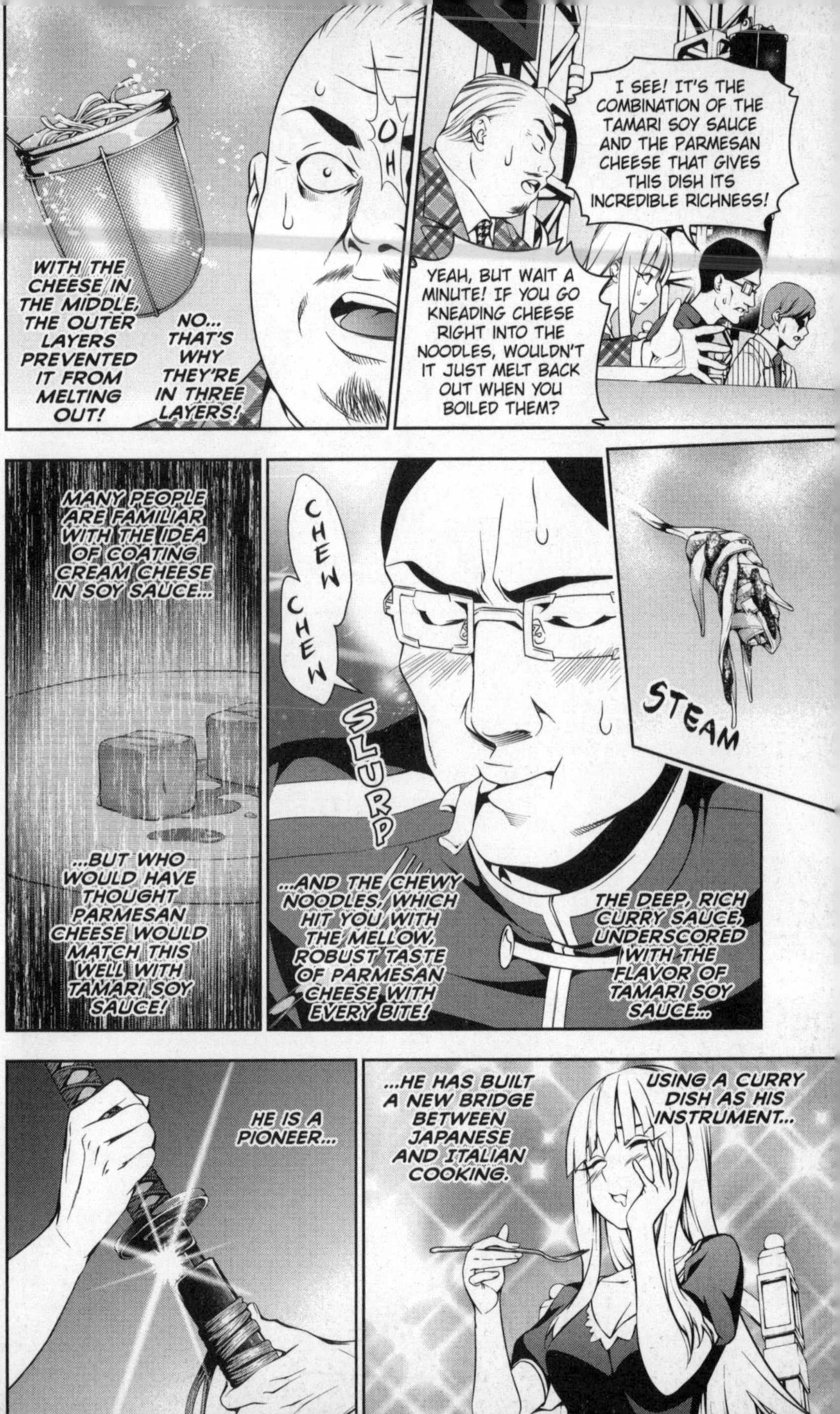
I SEE! IT'S THE COMBINATION OF THE TAMARI SOY SAUCE AND THE PARMESAN CHEESE THAT GIVES THIS DISH ITS INCREDIBLE RICHNESS!
YEAH, BUT WAIT A MINUTE! IF YOU GO KNEADING CHEESE RIGHT INTO THE NOODLES, WOULDN'T IT JUST MELT BACK OUT WHEN YOU BOILED THEM?
OH
NO... THAT'S WHY THEY'RE IN THREE LAYERS!
WITH THE CHEESE IN THE MIDDLE, THE OUTER LAYERS PREVENTED IT FROM MELTING OUT!
STEAM
THE DEEP, RICH CURRY SAUCE, UNDERSCORED WITH THE FLAVOR OF TAMARI SOY SAUCE...
...AND THE CHEWY NOODLES, WHICH HIT YOU WITH THE MELLOW, ROBUST TASTE OF PARMESAN CHEESE WITH EVERY BITE!
CHEW CHEW CHEW
SLURP
MANY PEOPLE ARE FAMILIAR WITH THE IDEA OF COATING CREAM CHEESE IN SOY SAUCE...
...BUT WHO WOULD HAVE THOUGHT PARMESAN CHEESE WOULD MATCH THIS WELL WITH TAMARI SOY SAUCE!
USING A CURRY DISH AS HIS INSTRUMENT...
...HE HAS BUILT A NEW BRIDGE BETWEEN JAPANESE AND ITALIAN COOKING.
HE IS A PIONEER...

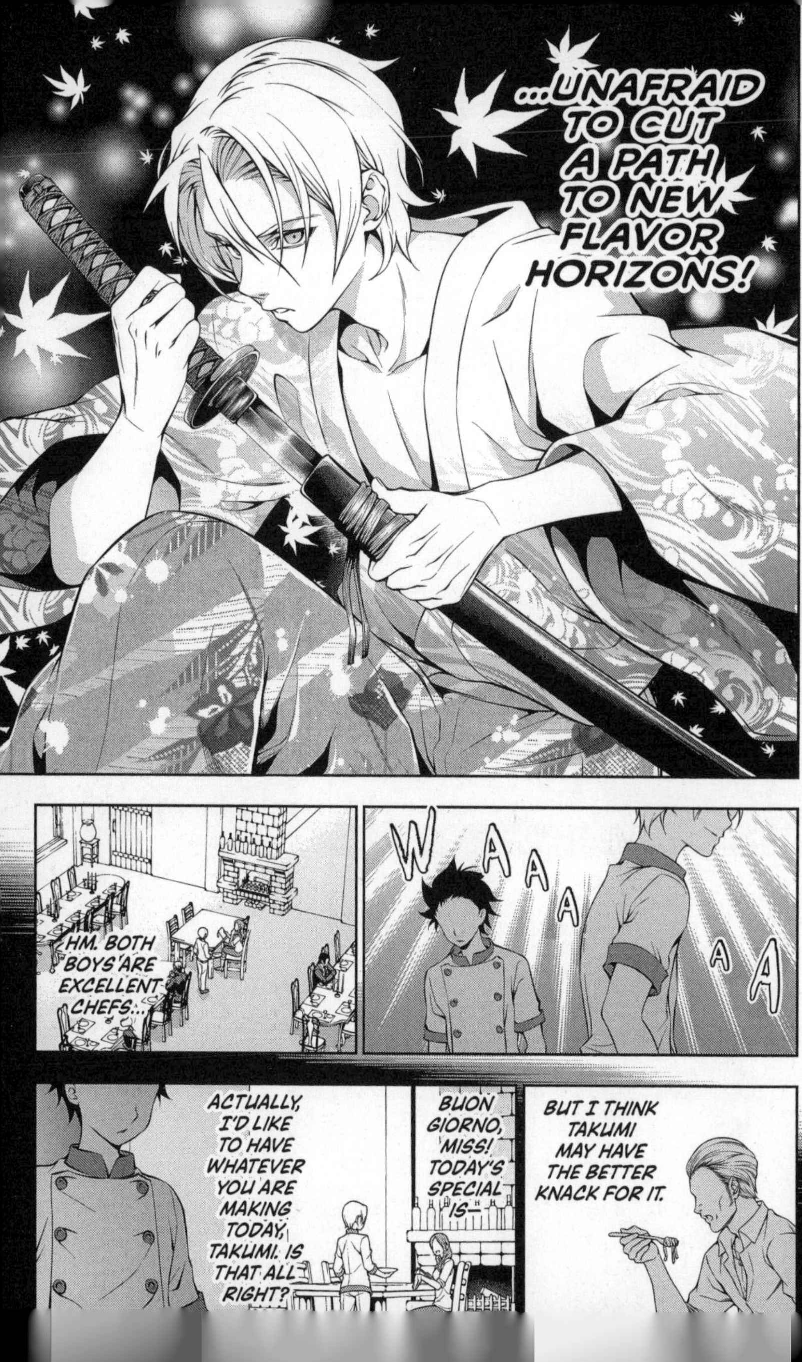
...UNAFRAID TO CUT A PATH TO NEW FLAVOR HORIZONS!
WAAAAA
HM. BOTH BOYS ARE EXCELLENT CHEFS...
BUT I THINK TAKUMI MAY HAVE THE BETTER KNACK FOR IT.
BUON GIORNO, MISS! TODAY'S SPECIAL IS—
ACTUALLY, I'D LIKE TO HAVE WHATEVER YOU ARE MAKING TODAY, TAKUMI. IS THAT ALL RIGHT?

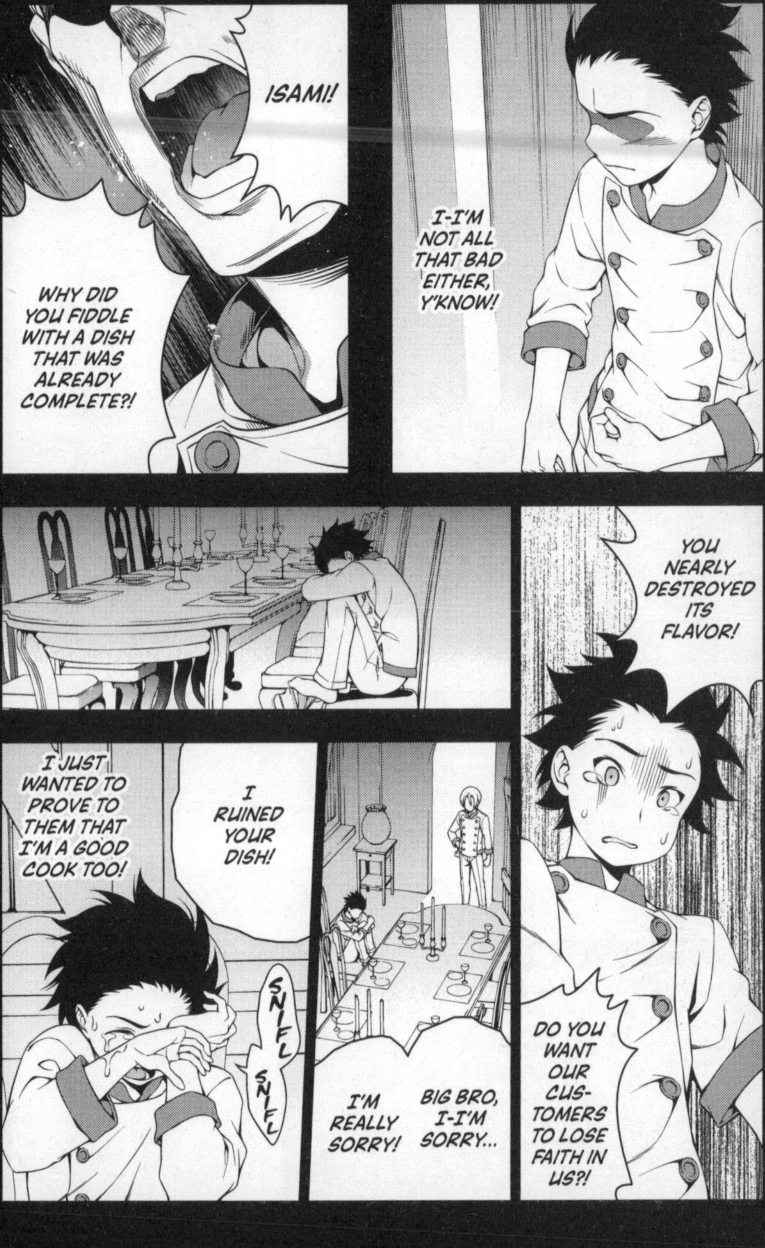
I-I'M NOT ALL THAT BAD EITHER, Y'KNOW!
ISAMI!
WHY DID YOU FIDDLE WITH A DISH THAT WAS ALREADY COMPLETE?!
YOU NEARLY DESTROYED ITS FLAVOR!
DO YOU WANT OUR CUS-TOMERS TO LOSE FAITH IN US?!
BIG BRO, I-I'M SORRY...
I'M REALLY SORRY!
I RUINED YOUR DISH!
I JUST WANTED TO PROVE TO THEM THAT I'M A GOOD COOK TOO!
SNIFL
SNIFL

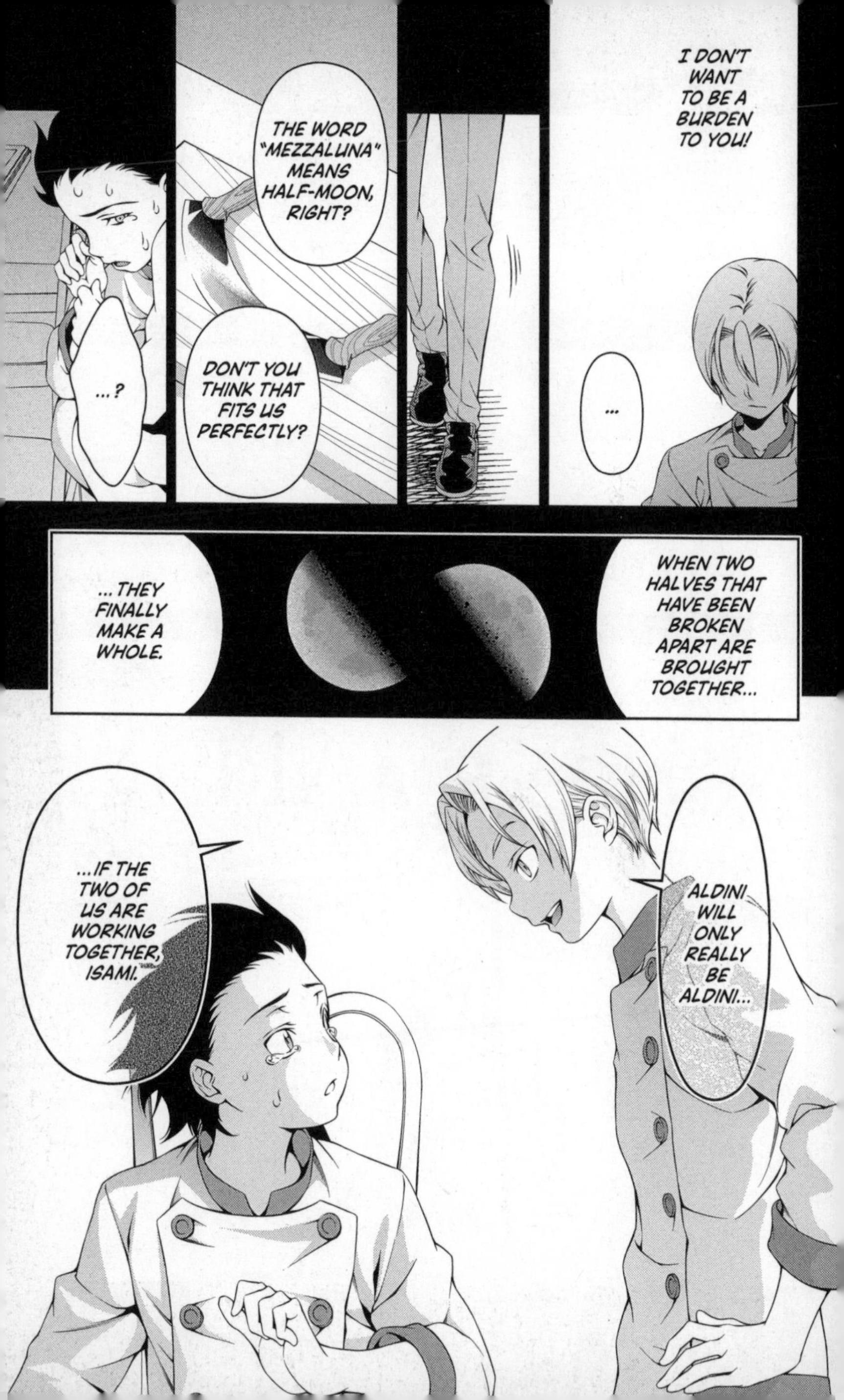
I DON'T WANT TO BE A BURDEN TO YOU!
...
THE WORD "MEZZALUNA" MEANS HALF-MOON, RIGHT?
DON'T YOU THINK THAT FITS US PERFECTLY?
...?
WHEN TWO HALVES THAT HAVE BEEN BROKEN APART ARE BROUGHT TOGETHER...
...THEY FINALLY MAKE A WHOLE.
ALDINI WILL ONLY REALLY BE ALDINI...
...IF THE TWO OF US ARE WORKING TOGETHER, ISAMI.

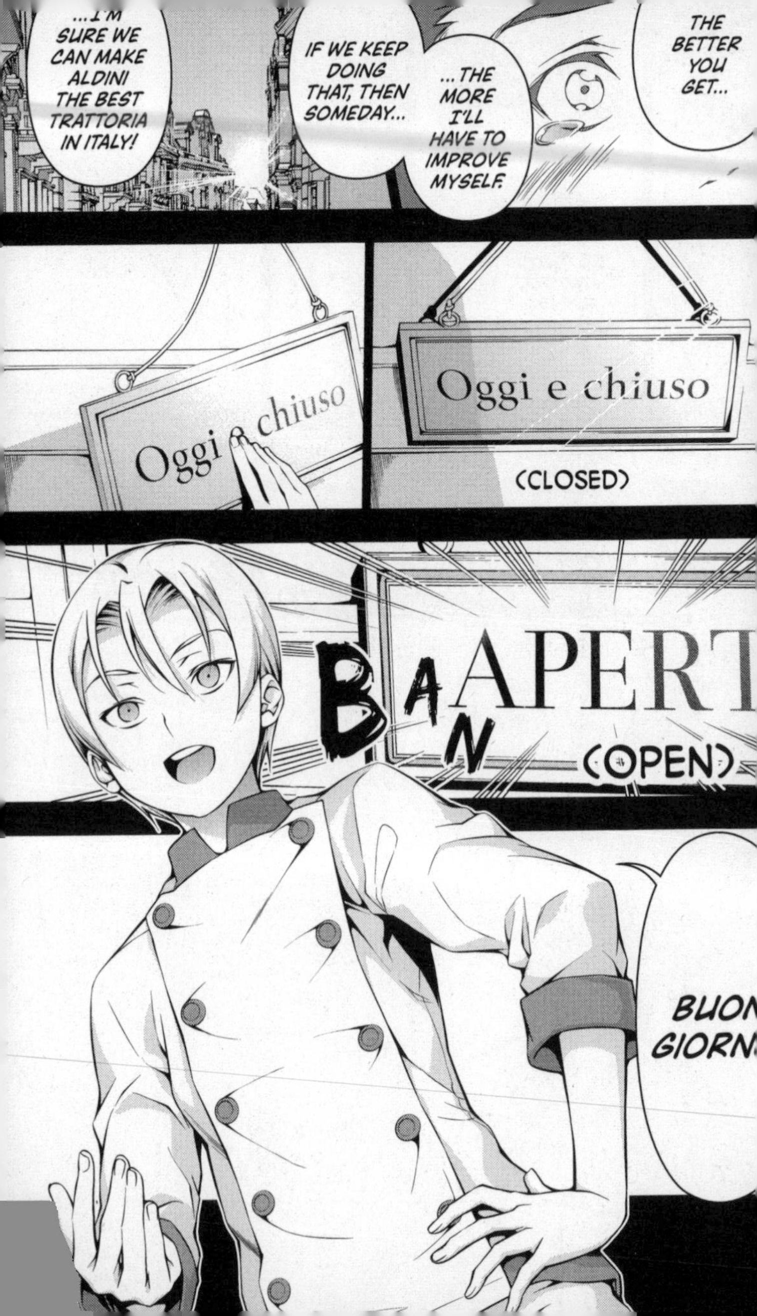
THE BETTER YOU GET...
...THE MORE I'LL HAVE TO IMPROVE MYSELF.
IF WE KEEP DOING THAT, THEN SOMEDAY...
...I'M SURE WE CAN MAKE ALDINI THE BEST TRATTORIA IN ITALY!
Oggi e chiuso
(CLOSED)
Oggi e chiuso
APERT
(OPEN)
BAN
BUON GIORN

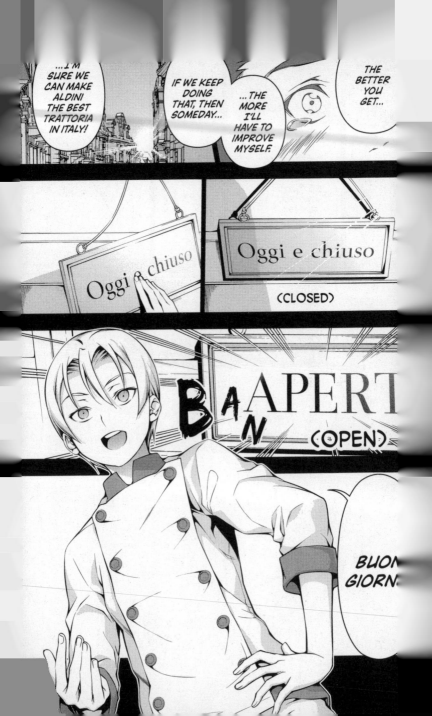

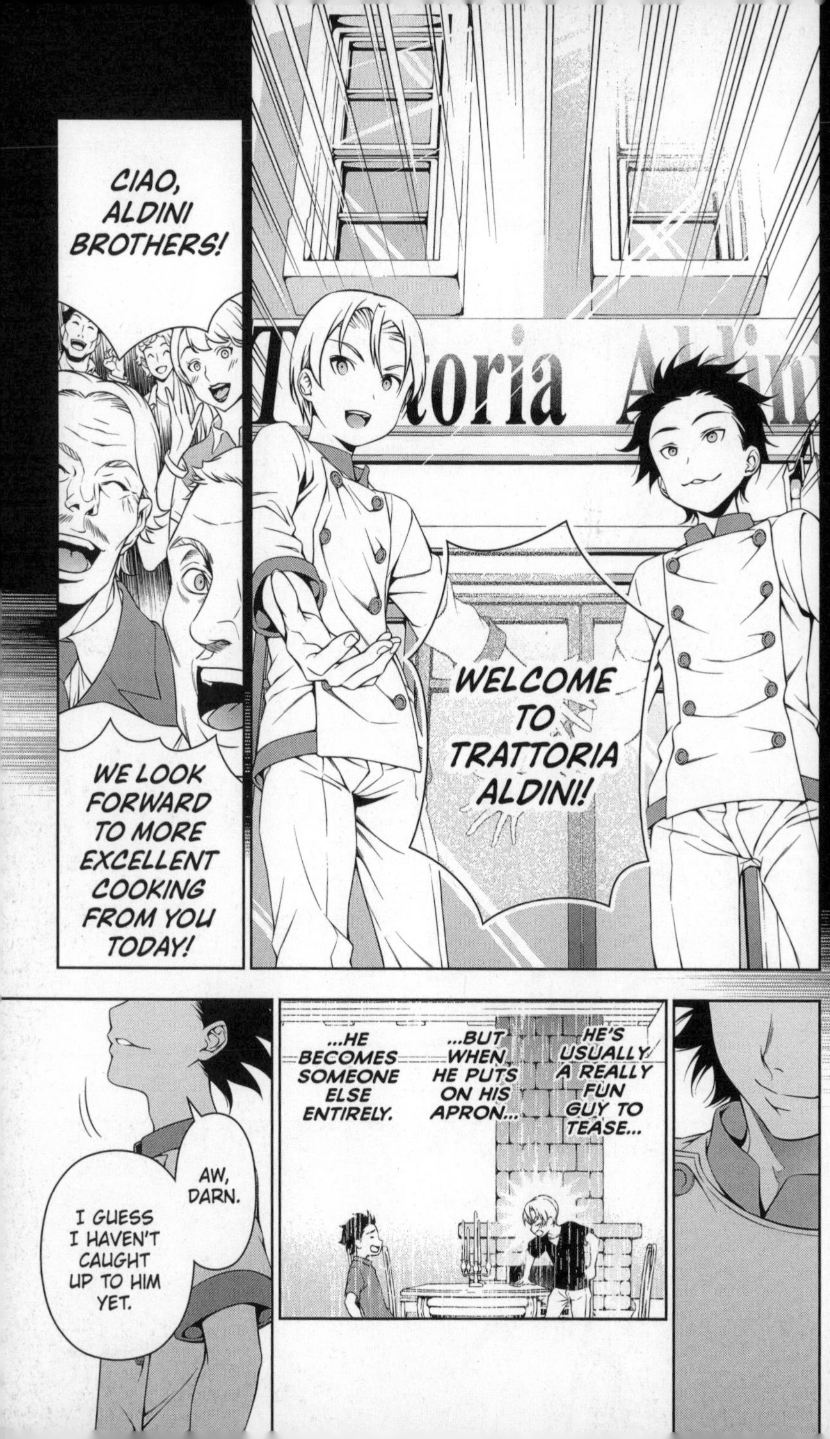
WELCOME TO TRATTORIA ALDINI!
CIAO, ALDINI BROTHERS!
WE LOOK FORWARD TO MORE EXCELLENT COOKING FROM YOU TODAY!
HE'S USUALLY A REALLY FUN GUY TO TEASE...
...BUT WHEN HE PUTS ON HIS APRON...
...HE BECOMES SOMEONE ELSE ENTIRELY.
AW, DARN.
I GUESS I HAVEN'T CAUGHT UP TO HIM YET.

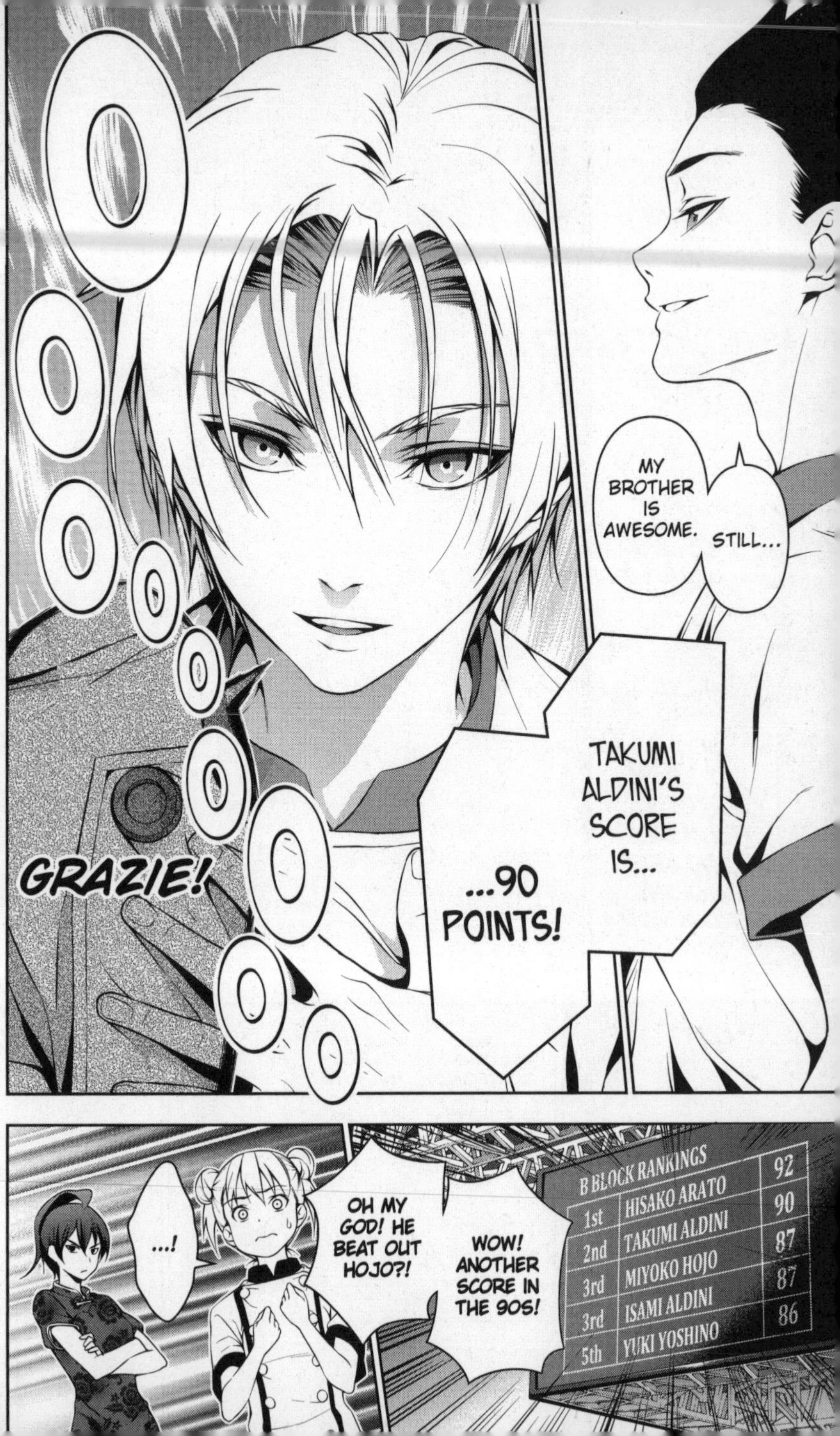
MY BROTHER IS AWESOME.
STILL...
TAKUMI ALDINI'S SCORE IS...
...90 POINTS!
GRAZIE!
B BLOCK RANKINGS
92
1st HISAKO ARATO
90
2nd TAKUMI ALDINI
87
3rd MIYOKO HOJO
87
3rd ISAMI ALDINI
86
5th YUKI YOSHINO
WOW! ANOTHER SCORE IN THE 90S!
OH MY GOD! HE BEAT OUT HOJO?!
...!

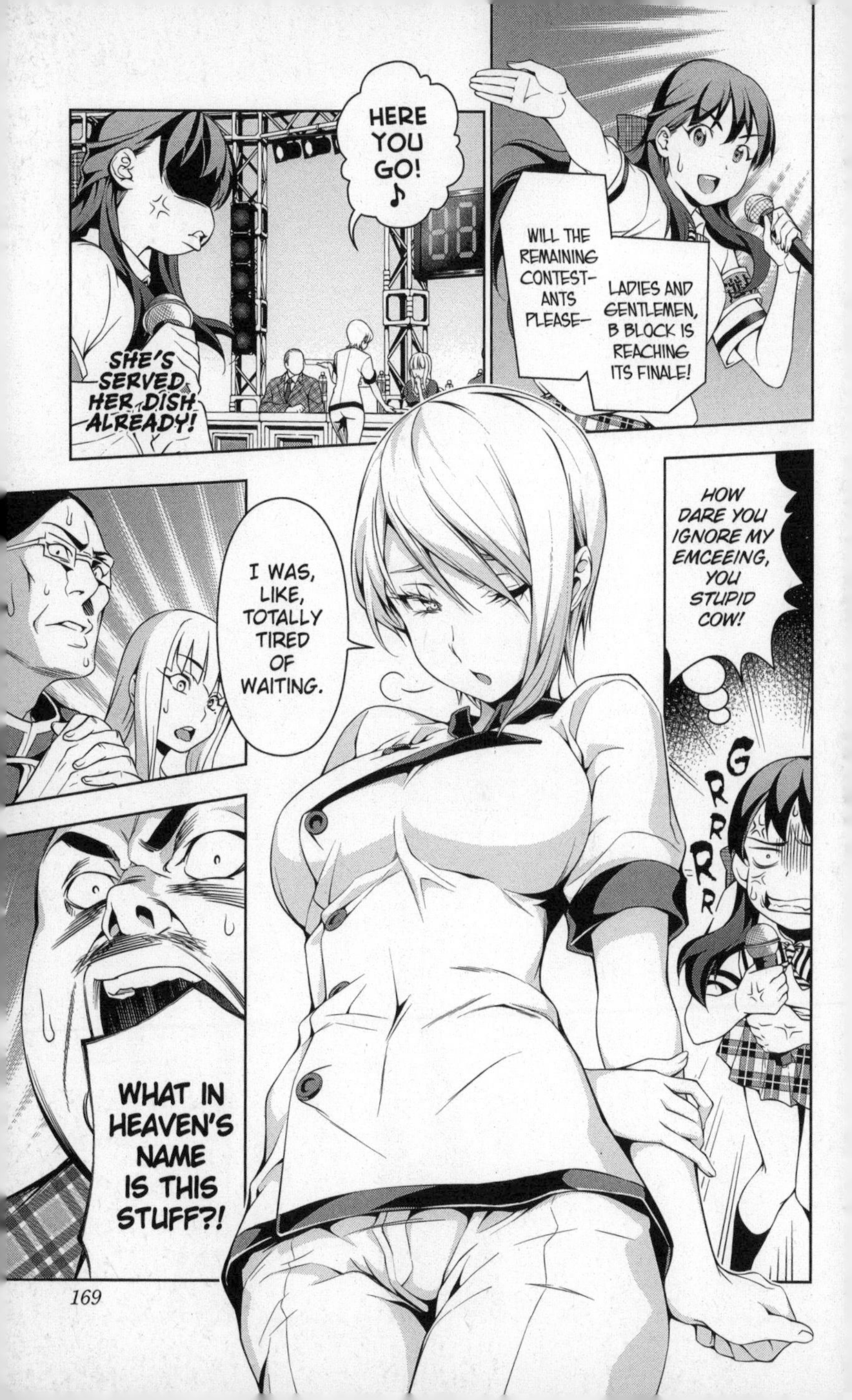
LADIES AND GENTLEMEN, B BLOCK IS REACHING ITS FINALE!
WILL THE REMAINING CONTEST-ANTS PLEASE—
HERE YOU GO! ♪
SHE'S SERVED HER DISH ALREADY!
HOW DARE YOU IGNORE MY EMCEEING, YOU STUPID COW!
GRRRRR
I WAS, LIKE, TOTALLY TIRED OF WAITING.
WHAT IN HEAVEN'S NAME IS THIS STUFF?!

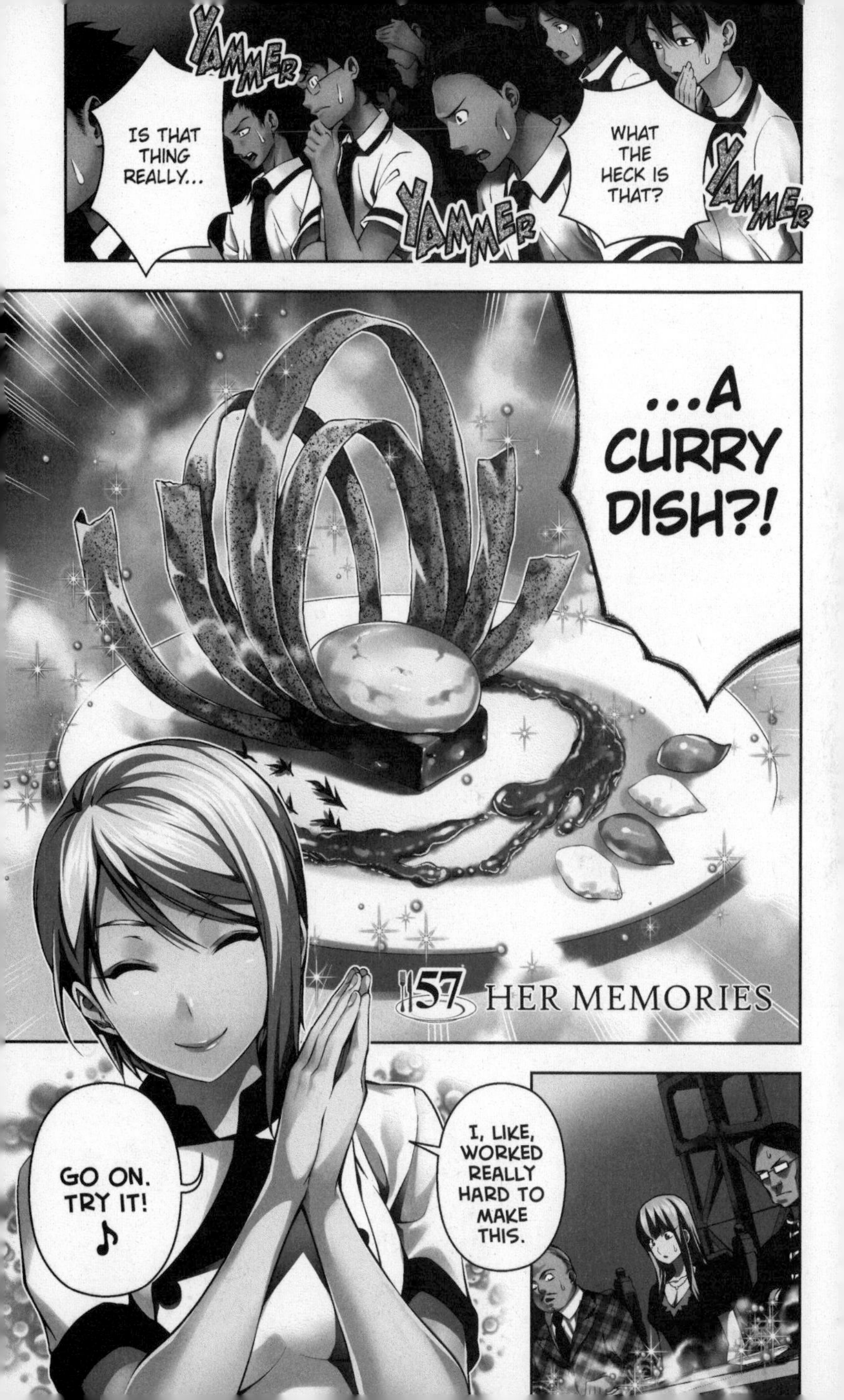
YAMMER
WHAT THE HECK IS THAT?
YAMMER
IS THAT THING REALLY...
YAMMER
...A CURRY DISH?!
57 HER MEMORIES
I, LIKE, WORKED REALLY HARD TO MAKE THIS.
GO ON. TRY IT! ♪

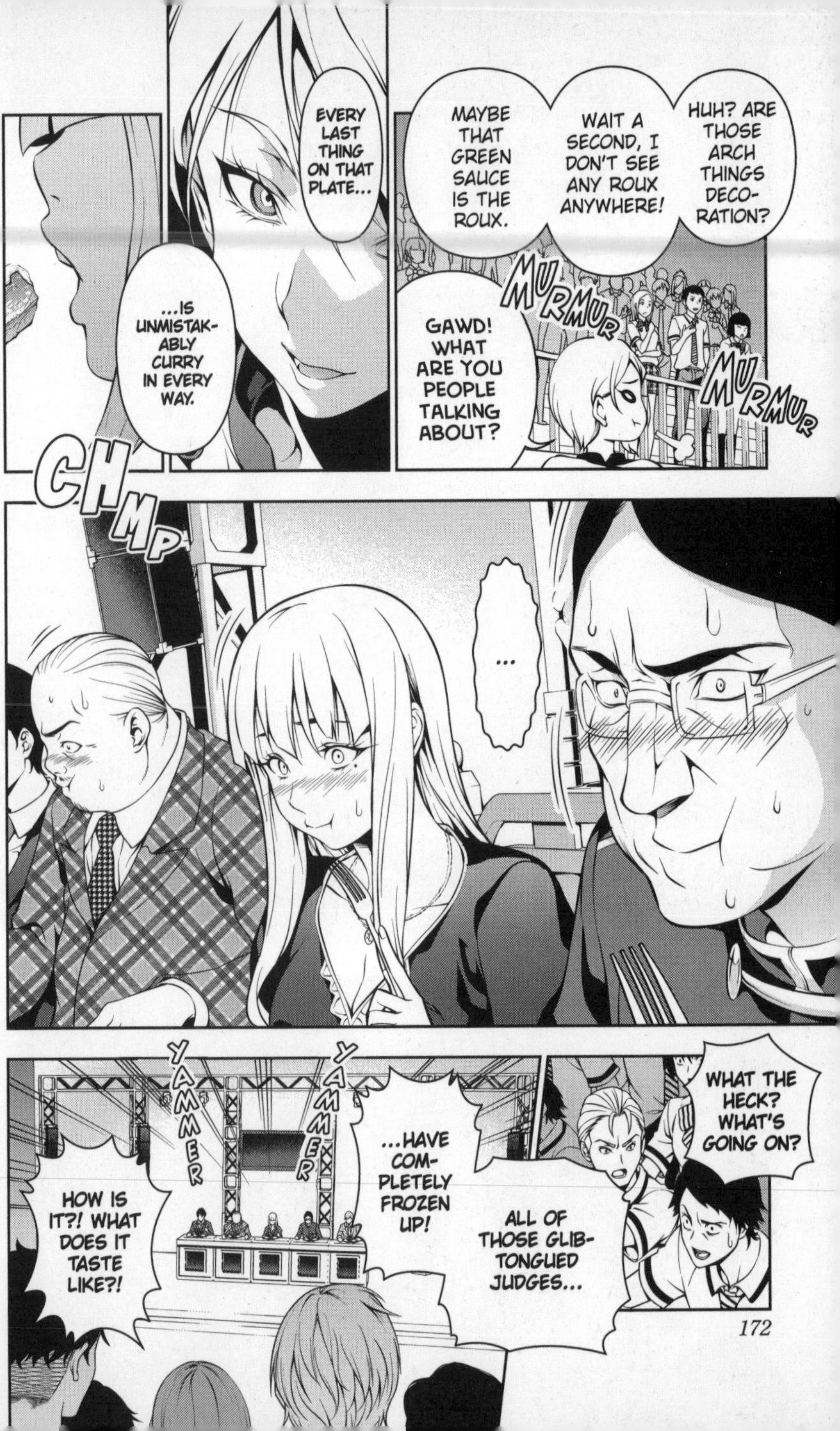

HUH? ARE THOSE ARCH THINGS DECORATION?
WAIT A SECOND, I DON'T SEE ANY ROUX ANYWHERE!
MAYBE THAT GREEN SAUCE IS THE ROUX.
MURMUR
MURMUR
GAWD! WHAT ARE YOU PEOPLE TALKING ABOUT?
EVERY LAST THING ON THAT PLATE...
...IS UNMISTAKABLY CURRY IN EVERY WAY.
CHMP
...
WHAT THE HECK? WHAT'S GOING ON?
YAMMER
YAMMER
ALL OF THOSE GLIB-TONGUED JUDGES...
...HAVE COMPLETELY FROZEN UP!
HOW IS IT?! WHAT DOES IT TASTE LIKE?!

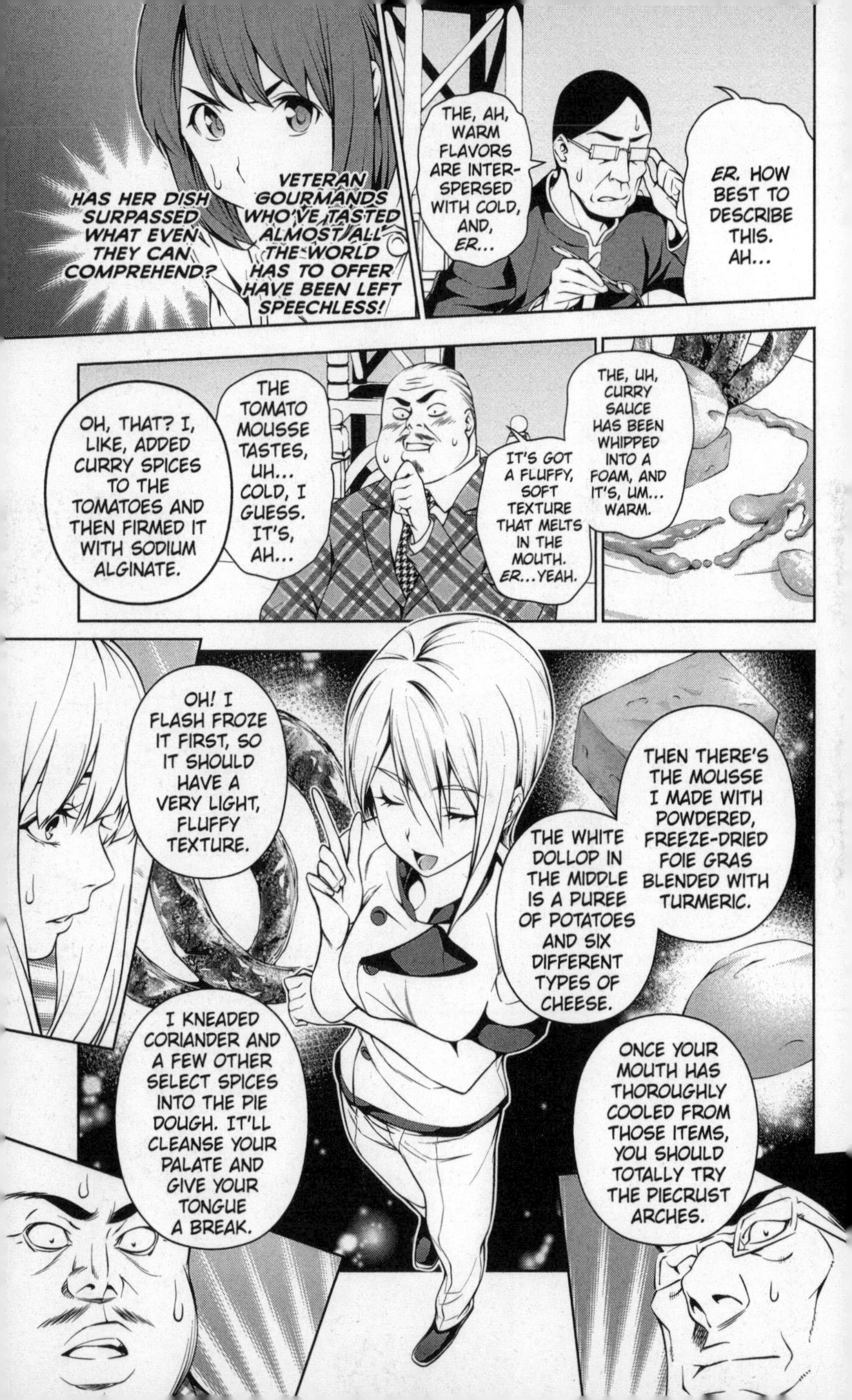
ER. HOW BEST TO DESCRIBE THIS. AH...
THE, AH, WARM FLAVORS ARE INTER-SPERSED WITH COLD, AND, ER...
VETERAN GOURMANDS WHO'VE TASTED ALMOST ALL THE WORLD HAS TO OFFER HAVE BEEN LEFT SPEECHLESS!
HAS HER DISH SURPASSED WHAT EVEN THEY CAN COMPREHEND?
THE, UH, CURRY SAUCE HAS BEEN WHIPPED INTO A FOAM, AND IT'S, UM... WARM.
IT'S GOT A FLUFFY, SOFT TEXTURE THAT MELTS IN THE MOUTH. ER...YEAH.
THE TOMATO MOUSSE TASTES, UH... COLD, I GUESS. IT'S, AH...
OH, THAT? I, LIKE, ADDED CURRY SPICES TO THE TOMATOES AND THEN FIRMED IT WITH SODIUM ALGINATE.
THEN THERE'S THE MOUSSE I MADE WITH POWDERED, FREEZE-DRIED FOIE GRAS BLENDED WITH TURMERIC.
THE WHITE DOLLOP IN THE MIDDLE IS A PUREE OF POTATOES AND SIX DIFFERENT TYPES OF CHEESE.
OH! I FLASH FROZE IT FIRST, SO IT SHOULD HAVE A VERY LIGHT, FLUFFY TEXTURE.
ONCE YOUR MOUTH HAS THOROUGHLY COOLED FROM THOSE ITEMS, YOU SHOULD TOTALLY TRY THE PIECRUST ARCHES.
I KNEADED CORIANDER AND A FEW OTHER SELECT SPICES INTO THE PIE DOUGH. IT'LL CLEANSE YOUR PALATE AND GIVE YOUR TONGUE A BREAK.

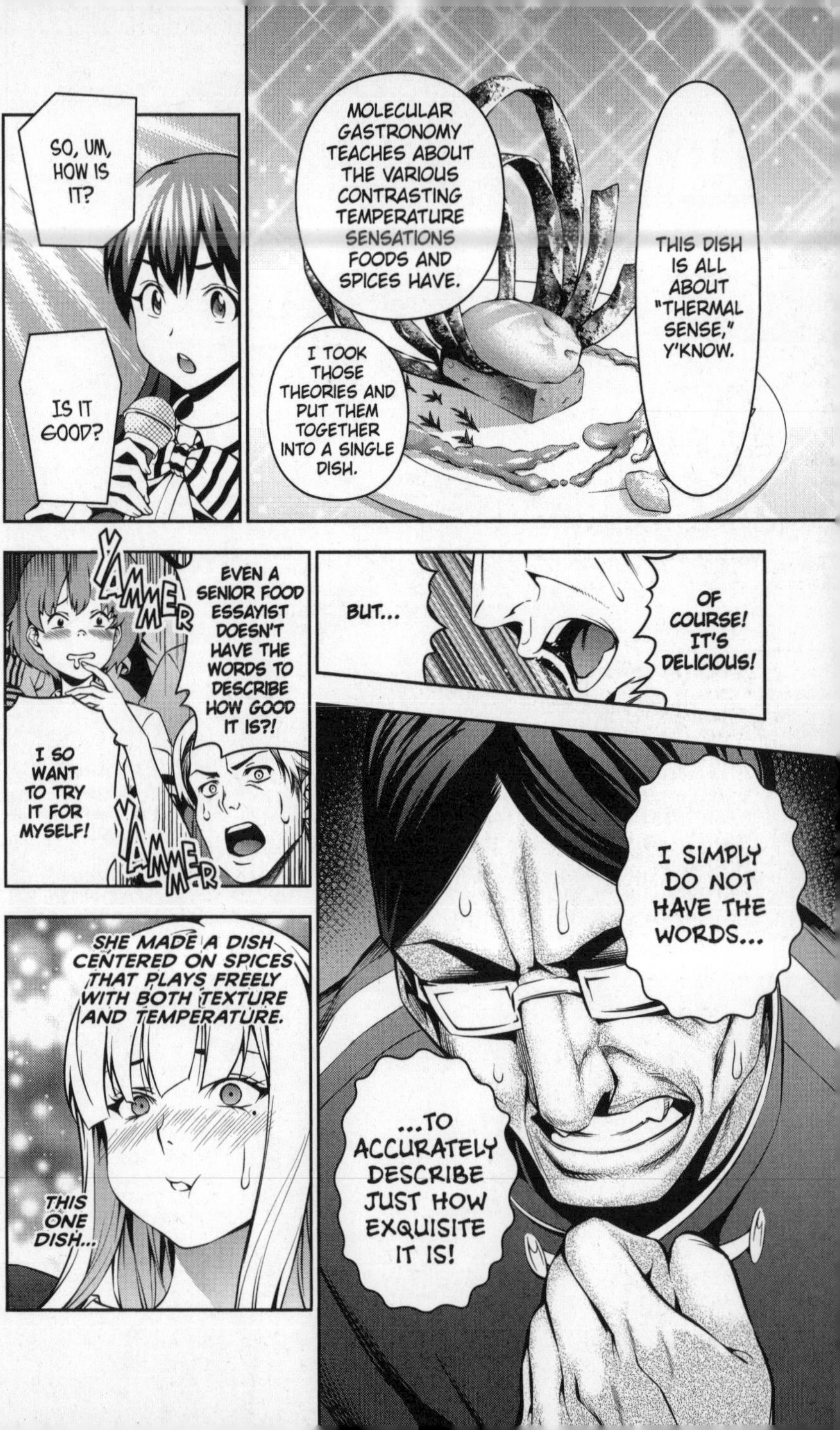
THIS DISH IS ALL ABOUT "THERMAL SENSE," Y'KNOW.
MOLECULAR GASTRONOMY TEACHES ABOUT THE VARIOUS CONTRASTING TEMPERATURE SENSATIONS FOODS AND SPICES HAVE.
I TOOK THOSE THEORIES AND PUT THEM TOGETHER INTO A SINGLE DISH.
SO, UM, HOW IS IT?
IS IT GOOD?
OF COURSE! IT'S DELICIOUS!
BUT...
I SIMPLY DO NOT HAVE THE WORDS...
...TO ACCURATELY DESCRIBE JUST HOW EXQUISITE IT IS!
YAMMER
EVEN A SENIOR FOOD ESSAYIST DOESN'T HAVE THE WORDS TO DESCRIBE HOW GOOD IT IS?!
I SO WANT TO TRY IT FOR MYSELF!
YAMMER
SHE MADE A DISH CENTERED ON SPICES THAT PLAYS FREELY WITH BOTH TEXTURE AND TEMPERATURE.
THIS ONE DISH...

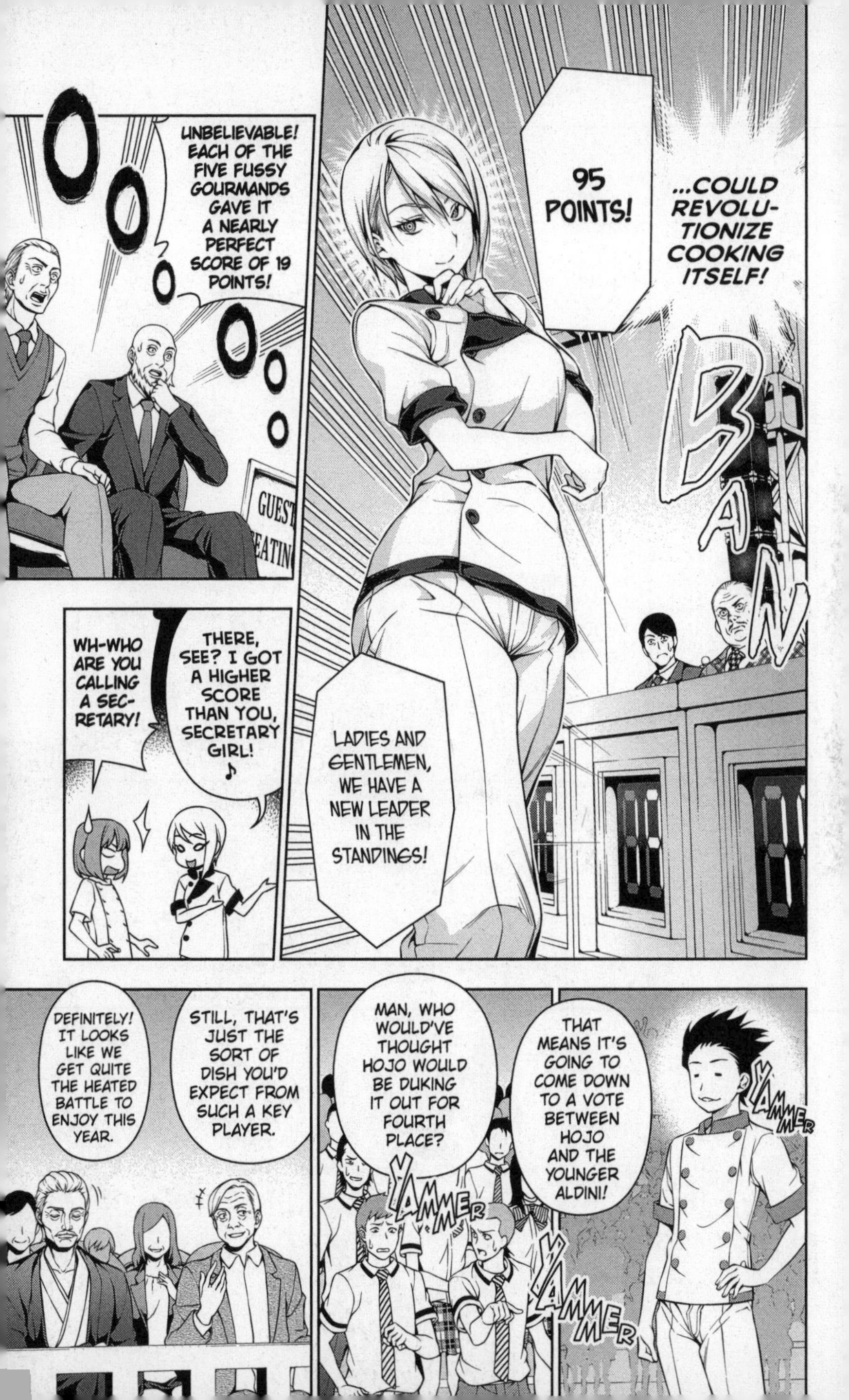
...COULD REVOLUTIONIZE COOKING ITSELF!
95 POINTS!
BAM
LADIES AND GENTLEMEN, WE HAVE A NEW LEADER IN THE STANDINGS!
OOOOOO
UNBELIEVABLE! EACH OF THE FIVE FUSSY GOURMANDS GAVE IT A NEARLY PERFECT SCORE OF 19 POINTS!
THERE, SEE? I GOT A HIGHER SCORE THAN YOU, SECRETARY GIRL! ♪
WH-WHO ARE YOU CALLING A SECRETARY!
YAMMER
THAT MEANS IT'S GOING TO COME DOWN TO A VOTE BETWEEN HOJO AND THE YOUNGER ALDINI!
MAN, WHO WOULD'VE THOUGHT HOJO WOULD BE DUKING IT OUT FOR FOURTH PLACE?
YAMMER
YAMMER
STILL, THAT'S JUST THE SORT OF DISH YOU'D EXPECT FROM SUCH A KEY PLAYER.
DEFINITELY! IT LOOKS LIKE WE GET QUITE THE HEATED BATTLE TO ENJOY THIS YEAR.

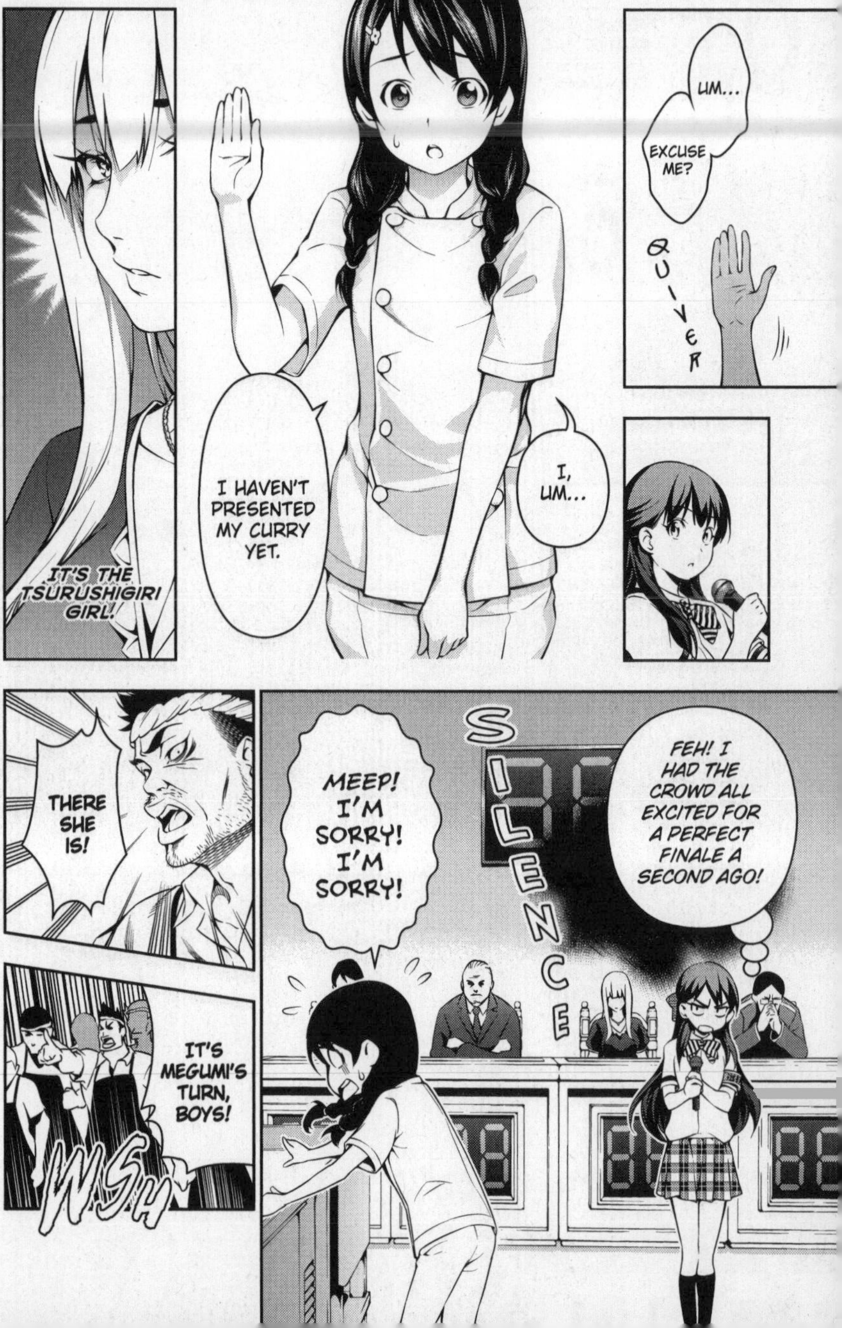
UM...
EXCUSE ME?
QUIVER
I, UM...
I HAVEN'T PRESENTED MY CURRY YET.
IT'S THE TSURUSHIGIRI GIRL!
FEH! I HAD THE CROWD ALL EXCITED FOR A PERFECT FINALE A SECOND AGO!
SILENCE
MEEP! I'M SORRY! I'M SORRY!
THERE SHE IS!
IT'S MEGUMI'S TURN, BOYS!
WSH

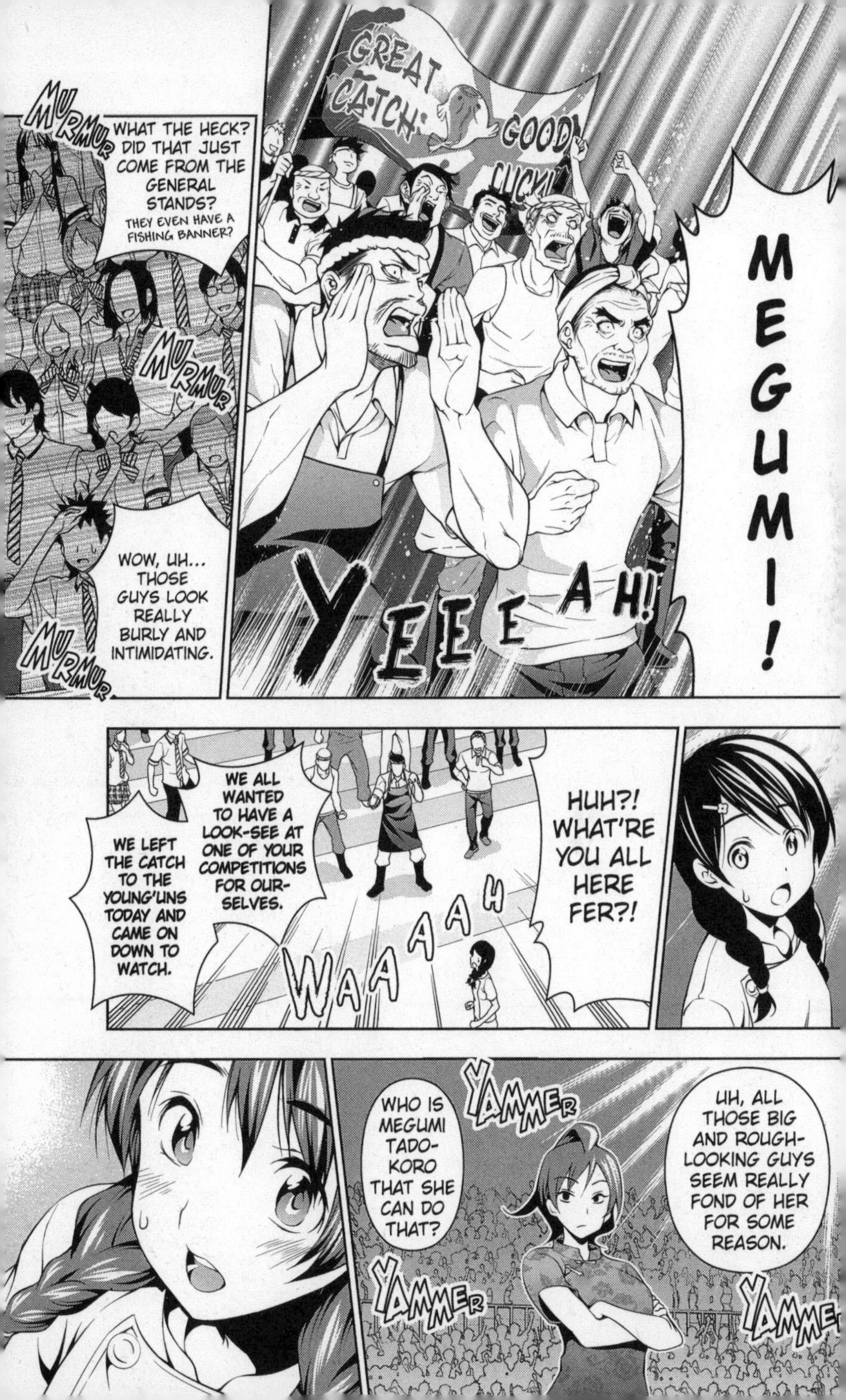

GREAT CATCH
GOOD
MEGUMI!
YEEEAH!
MURMUR
WHAT THE HECK? DID THAT JUST COME FROM THE GENERAL STANDS?
THEY EVEN HAVE A FISHING BANNER?
MURMUR
WOW, UH... THOSE GUYS LOOK REALLY BURLY AND INTIMIDATING.
MURMUR
HUH?! WHAT'RE YOU ALL HERE FER?!
WAAAAH
WE ALL WANTED TO HAVE A LOOK-SEE AT ONE OF YOUR COMPETITIONS FOR OURSELVES.
WE LEFT THE CATCH TO THE YOUNG'UNS TODAY AND CAME ON DOWN TO WATCH.
UH, ALL THOSE BIG AND ROUGH-LOOKING GUYS SEEM REALLY FOND OF HER FOR SOME REASON.
YAMMER
YAMMER
WHO IS MEGUMI TADOKORO THAT SHE CAN DO THAT?
YAMMER

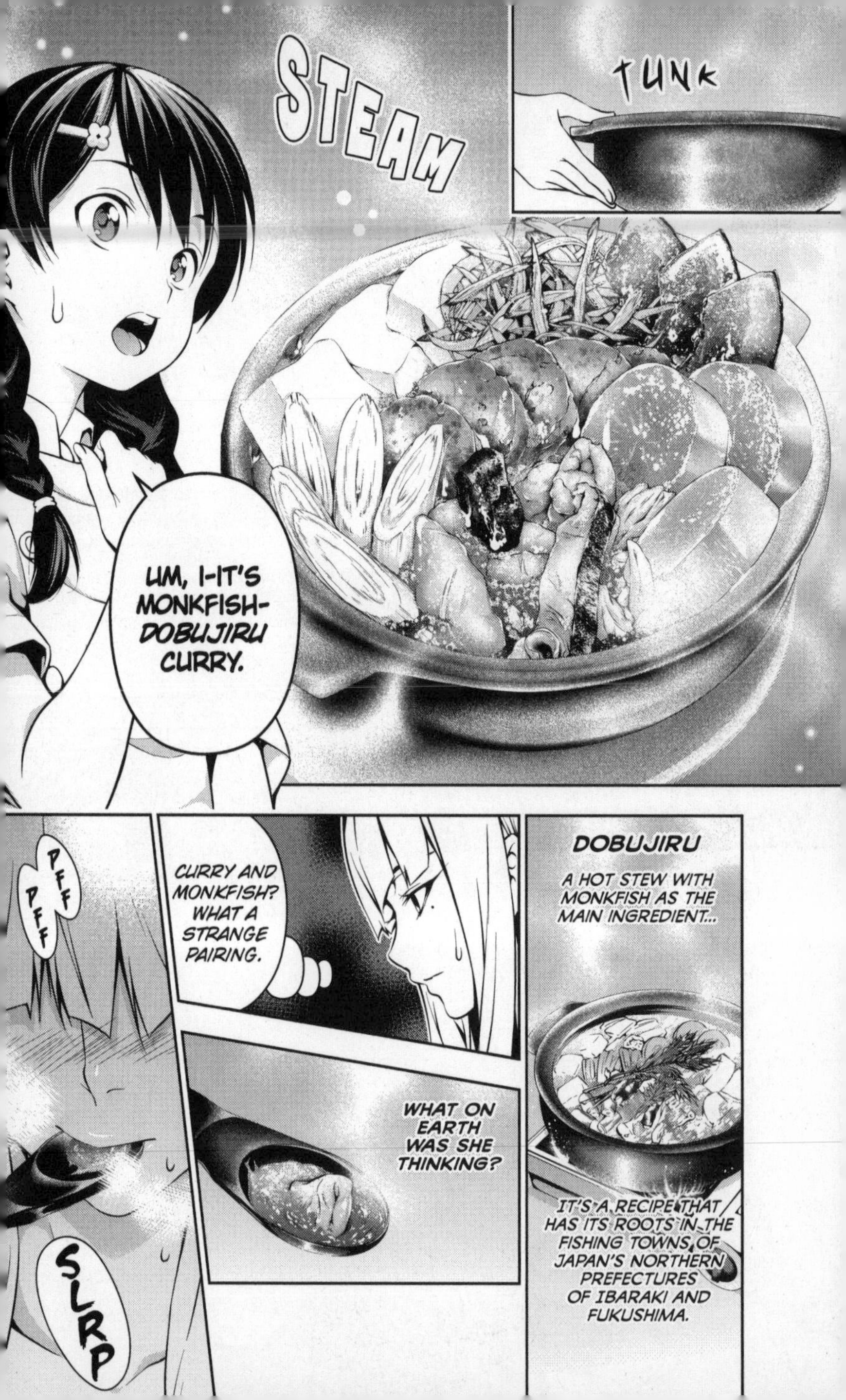
TUNK
STEAM
UM, I-IT'S MONKFISH-DOBUJIRU CURRY.
DOBUJIRU
A HOT STEW WITH MONKFISH AS THE MAIN INGREDIENT...
IT'S A RECIPE THAT HAS ITS ROOTS IN THE FISHING TOWNS OF JAPAN'S NORTHERN PREFECTURES OF IBARAKI AND FUKUSHIMA.
CURRY AND MONKFISH? WHAT A STRANGE PAIRING.
WHAT ON EARTH WAS SHE THINKING?
PFF PFF
SLRP

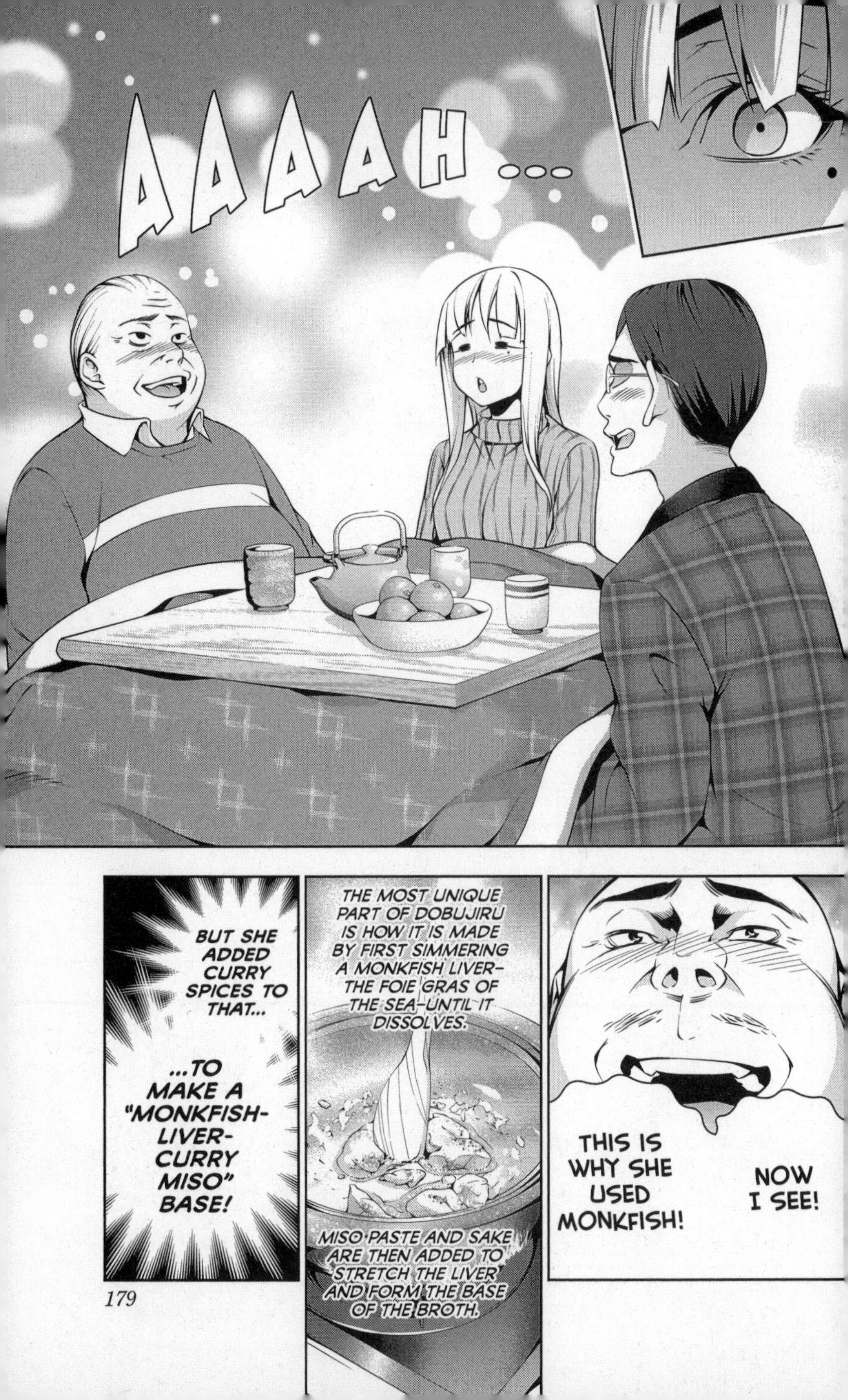
AAAAH...
NOW I SEE!
THIS IS WHY SHE USED MONKFISH!
THE MOST UNIQUE PART OF DOBUJIRU IS HOW IT IS MADE BY FIRST SIMMERING A MONKFISH LIVER–THE FOIE GRAS OF THE SEA–UNTIL IT DISSOLVES.
MISO PASTE AND SAKE ARE THEN ADDED TO STRETCH THE LIVER AND FORM THE BASE OF THE BROTH.
BUT SHE ADDED CURRY SPICES TO THAT...
...TO MAKE A "MONKFISH-LIVER-CURRY MISO" BASE!

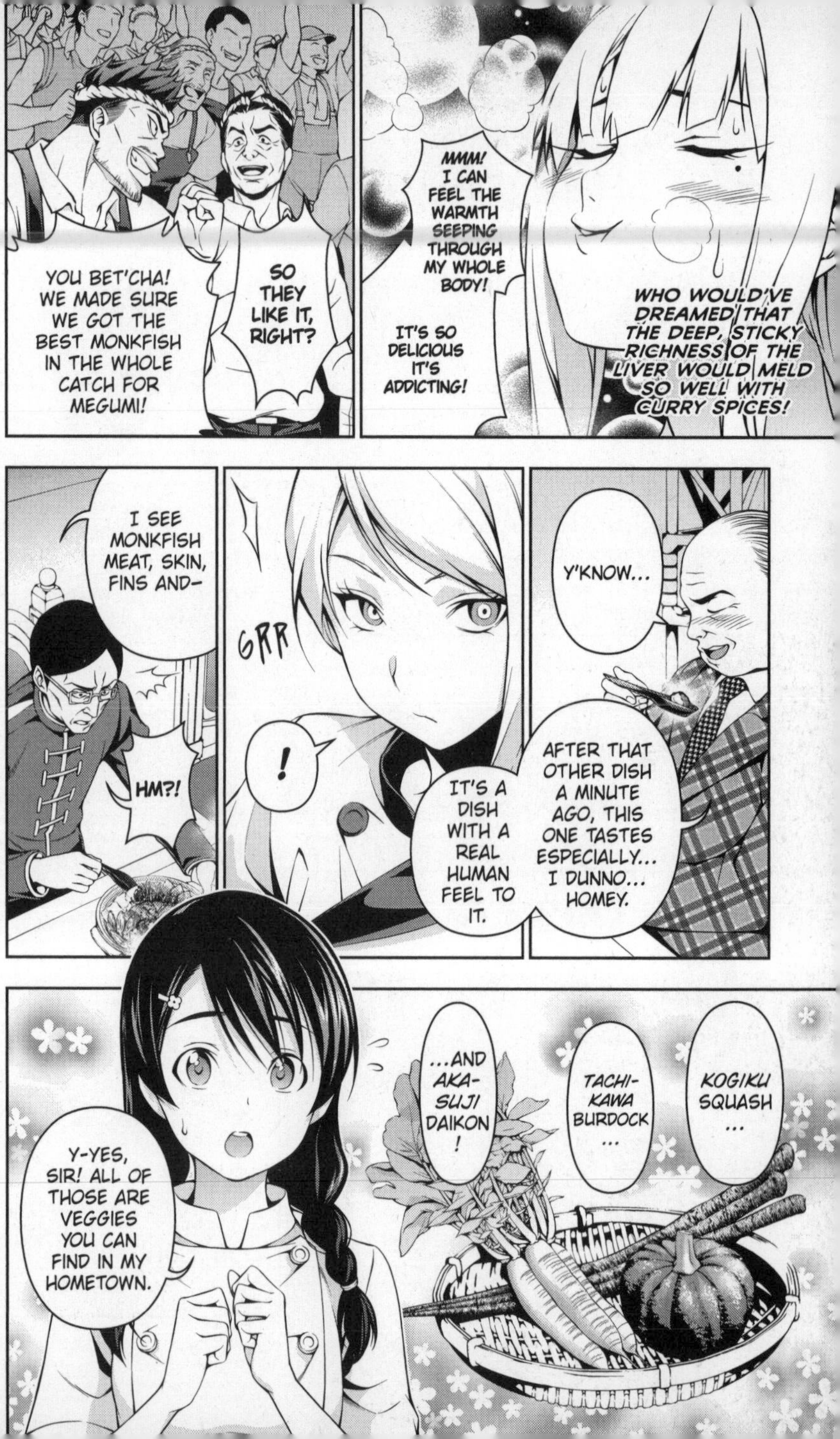
MMM! I CAN FEEL THE WARMTH SEEPING THROUGH MY WHOLE BODY!
WHO WOULD'VE DREAMED THAT THE DEEP, STICKY RICHNESS OF THE LIVER WOULD MELD SO WELL WITH CURRY SPICES!
IT'S SO DELICIOUS IT'S ADDICTING!
SO THEY LIKE IT, RIGHT?
YOU BET'CHA! WE MADE SURE WE GOT THE BEST MONKFISH IN THE WHOLE CATCH FOR MEGUMI!
Y'KNOW...
AFTER THAT OTHER DISH A MINUTE AGO, THIS ONE TASTES ESPECIALLY... I DUNNO... HOMEY.
IT'S A DISH WITH A REAL HUMAN FEEL TO IT.
GRR
!
I SEE MONKFISH MEAT, SKIN, FINS AND-
HM?!
KOGIKU SQUASH...
TACHIKAWA BURDOCK...
...AND AKASUJI DAIKON!
Y-YES, SIR! ALL OF THOSE ARE VEGGIES YOU CAN FIND IN MY HOMETOWN.

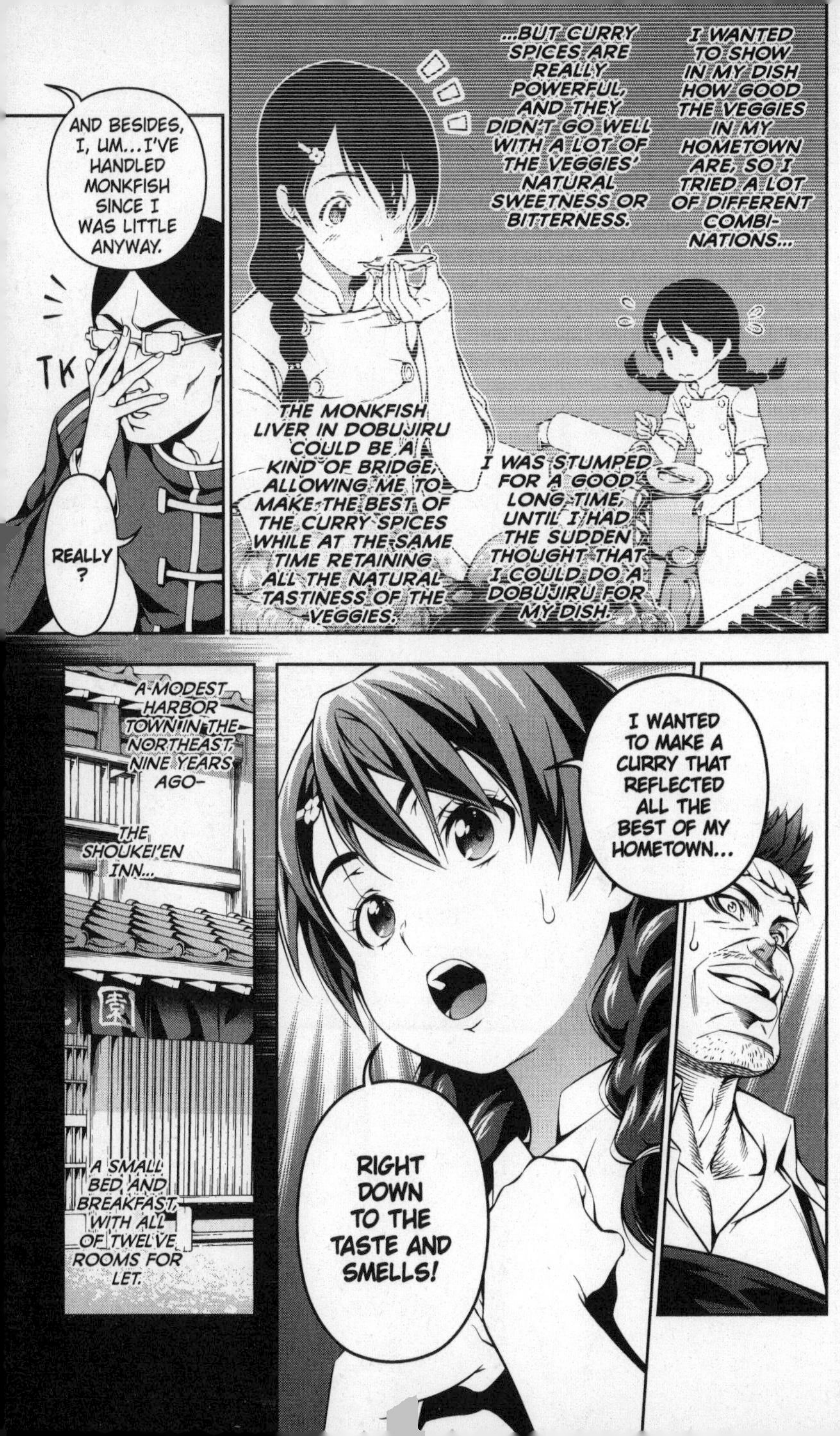
I WANTED TO SHOW IN MY DISH HOW GOOD THE VEGGIES IN MY HOMETOWN ARE, SO I TRIED A LOT OF DIFFERENT COMBI-NATIONS...
...BUT CURRY SPICES ARE REALLY POWERFUL, AND THEY DIDN'T GO WELL WITH A LOT OF THE VEGGIES' NATURAL SWEETNESS OR BITTERNESS.
I WAS STUMPED FOR A GOOD LONG TIME, UNTIL I HAD THE SUDDEN THOUGHT THAT I COULD DO A DOBUJIRU FOR MY DISH.
THE MONKFISH LIVER IN DOBUJIRU COULD BE A KIND OF BRIDGE, ALLOWING ME TO MAKE THE BEST OF THE CURRY SPICES WHILE AT THE SAME TIME RETAINING ALL THE NATURAL TASTINESS OF THE VEGGIES.
AND BESIDES, I, UM...I'VE HANDLED MONKFISH SINCE I WAS LITTLE ANYWAY.
TK
REALLY?
I WANTED TO MAKE A CURRY THAT REFLECTED ALL THE BEST OF MY HOMETOWN...
RIGHT DOWN TO THE TASTE AND SMELLS!
A MODEST HARBOR TOWN IN THE NORTHEAST, NINE YEARS AGO—
THE SHOUKEI'EN INN...
A SMALL BED AND BREAKFAST WITH ALL OF TWELVE ROOMS FOR LET.

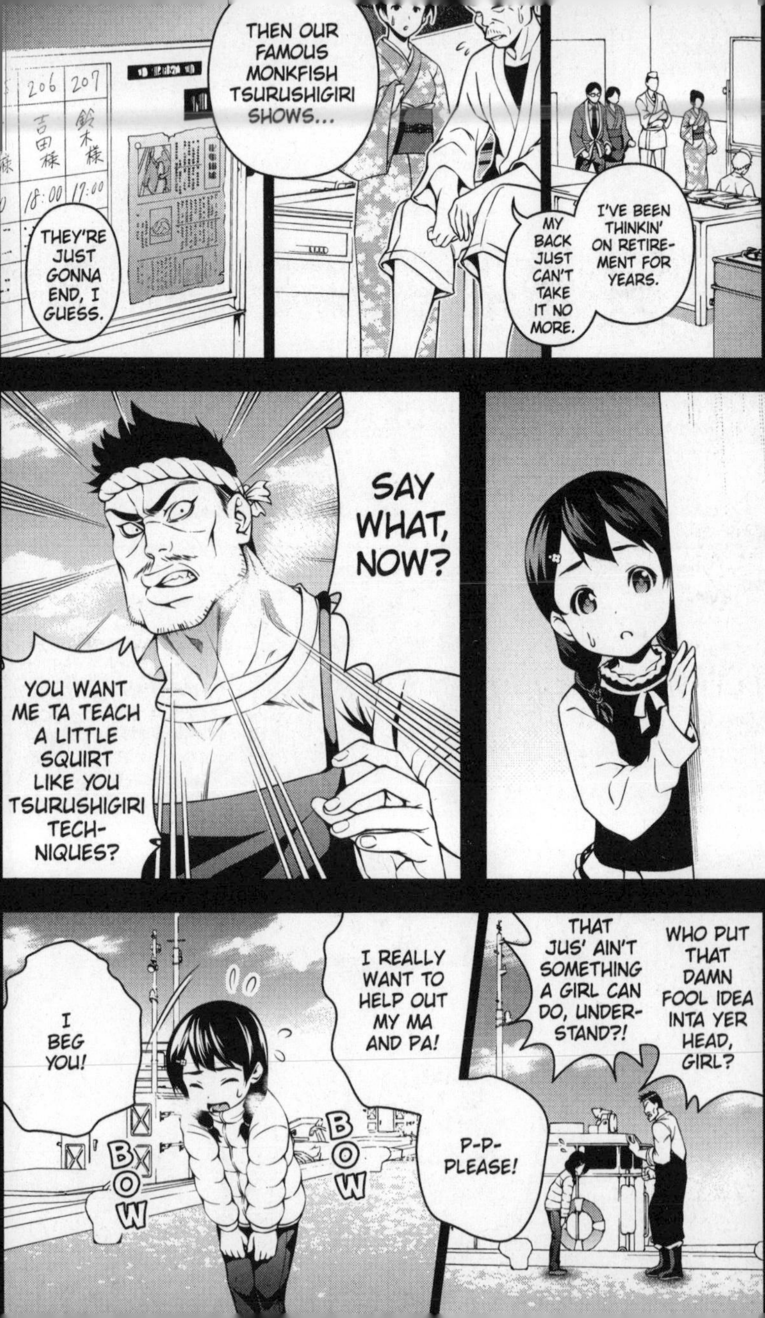
I'VE BEEN THINKIN' ON RETIRE-MENT FOR YEARS.
MY BACK JUST CAN'T TAKE IT NO MORE.
THEN OUR FAMOUS MONKFISH TSURUSHIGIRI SHOWS...
207 鈴木様 17:00
206 吉田様 18:00
THEY'RE JUST GONNA END, I GUESS.
SAY WHAT, NOW?
YOU WANT ME TA TEACH A LITTLE SQUIRT LIKE YOU TSURUSHIGIRI TECH-NIQUES?
WHO PUT THAT DAMN FOOL IDEA INTA YER HEAD, GIRL?
THAT JUS' AIN'T SOMETHING A GIRL CAN DO, UNDER-STAND?!
I REALLY WANT TO HELP OUT MY MA AND PA!
P-P-PLEASE!
BOW
BOW
I BEG YOU!

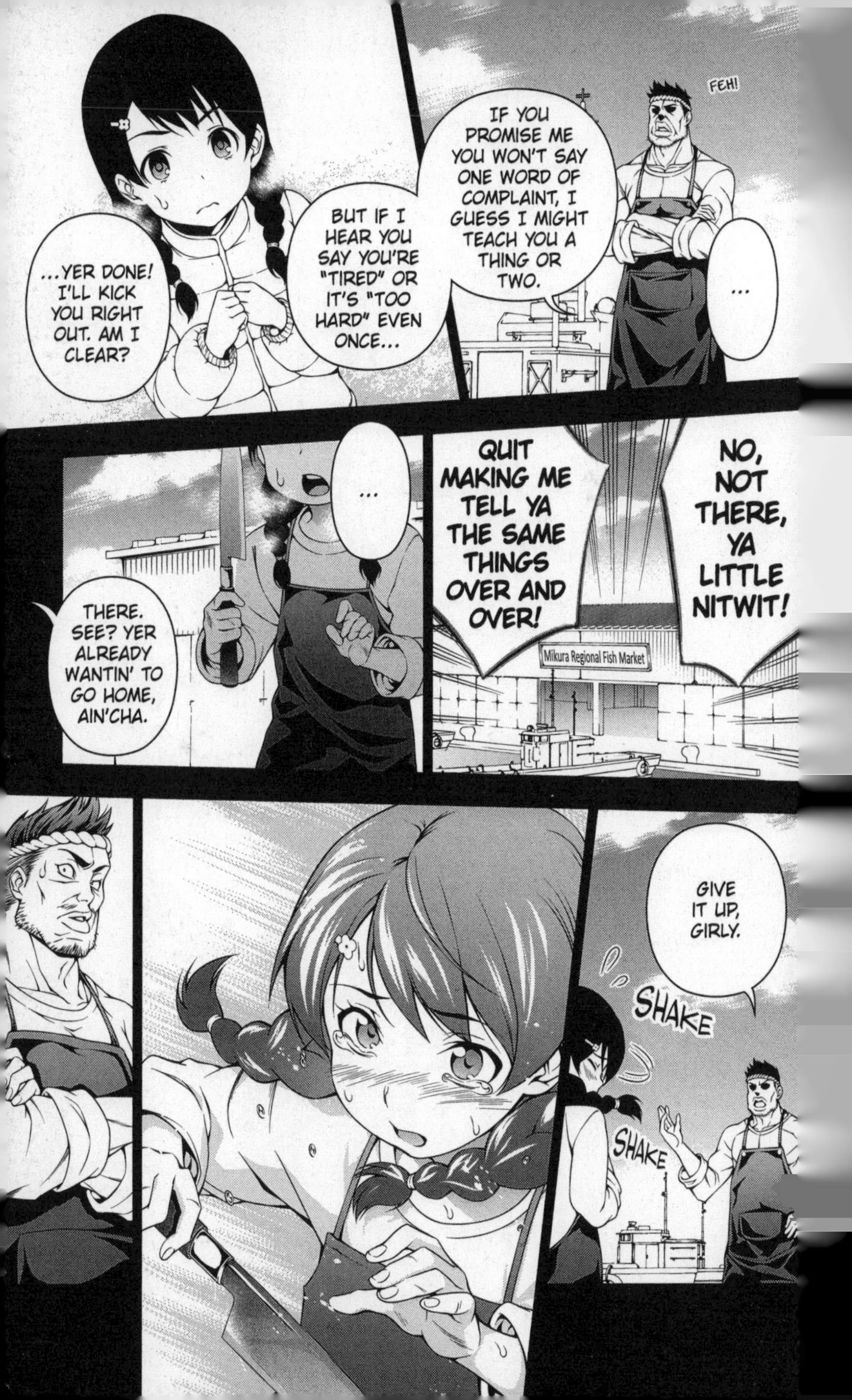
FEH!
...
IF YOU PROMISE ME YOU WON'T SAY ONE WORD OF COMPLAINT, I GUESS I MIGHT TEACH YOU A THING OR TWO.
BUT IF I HEAR YOU SAY YOU'RE "TIRED" OR IT'S "TOO HARD" EVEN ONCE...
...YER DONE! I'LL KICK YOU RIGHT OUT. AM I CLEAR?
NO, NOT THERE, YA LITTLE NITWIT!
QUIT MAKING ME TELL YA THE SAME THINGS OVER AND OVER!
Mikura Regional Fish Market
...
THERE. SEE? YER ALREADY WANTIN' TO GO HOME, AIN'CHA.
GIVE IT UP, GIRLY.
SHAKE
SHAKE

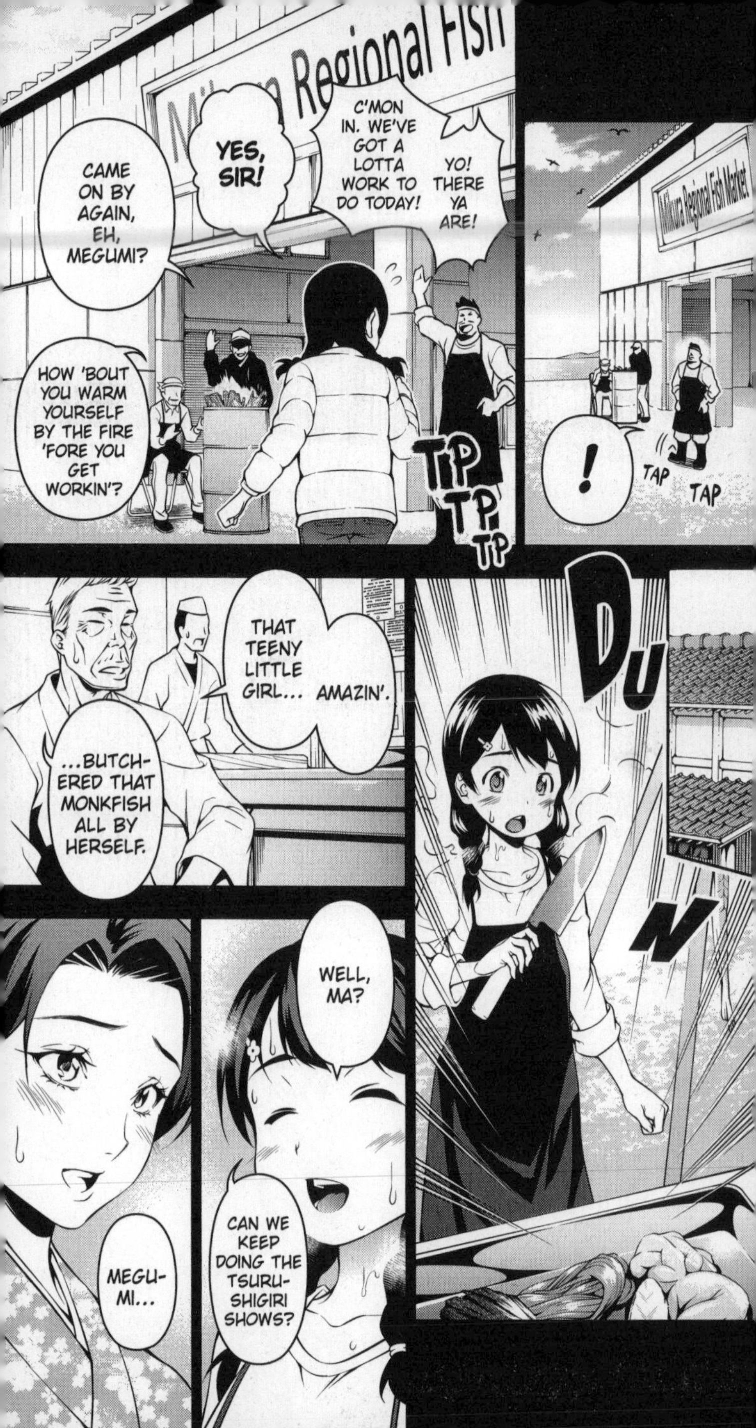
Mikura Regional Fish Market
!
TAP TAP
YO! THERE YA ARE!
C'MON IN. WE'VE GOT A LOTTA WORK TO DO TODAY!
YES, SIR!
CAME ON BY AGAIN, EH, MEGUMI?
HOW 'BOUT YOU WARM YOURSELF BY THE FIRE 'FORE YOU GET WORKIN'?
TP TP TP
DUN
THAT TEENY LITTLE GIRL... AMAZIN'.
...BUTCHERED THAT MONKFISH ALL BY HERSELF.
WELL, MA?
CAN WE KEEP DOING THE TSURU-SHIGIRI SHOWS?
MEGUMI...

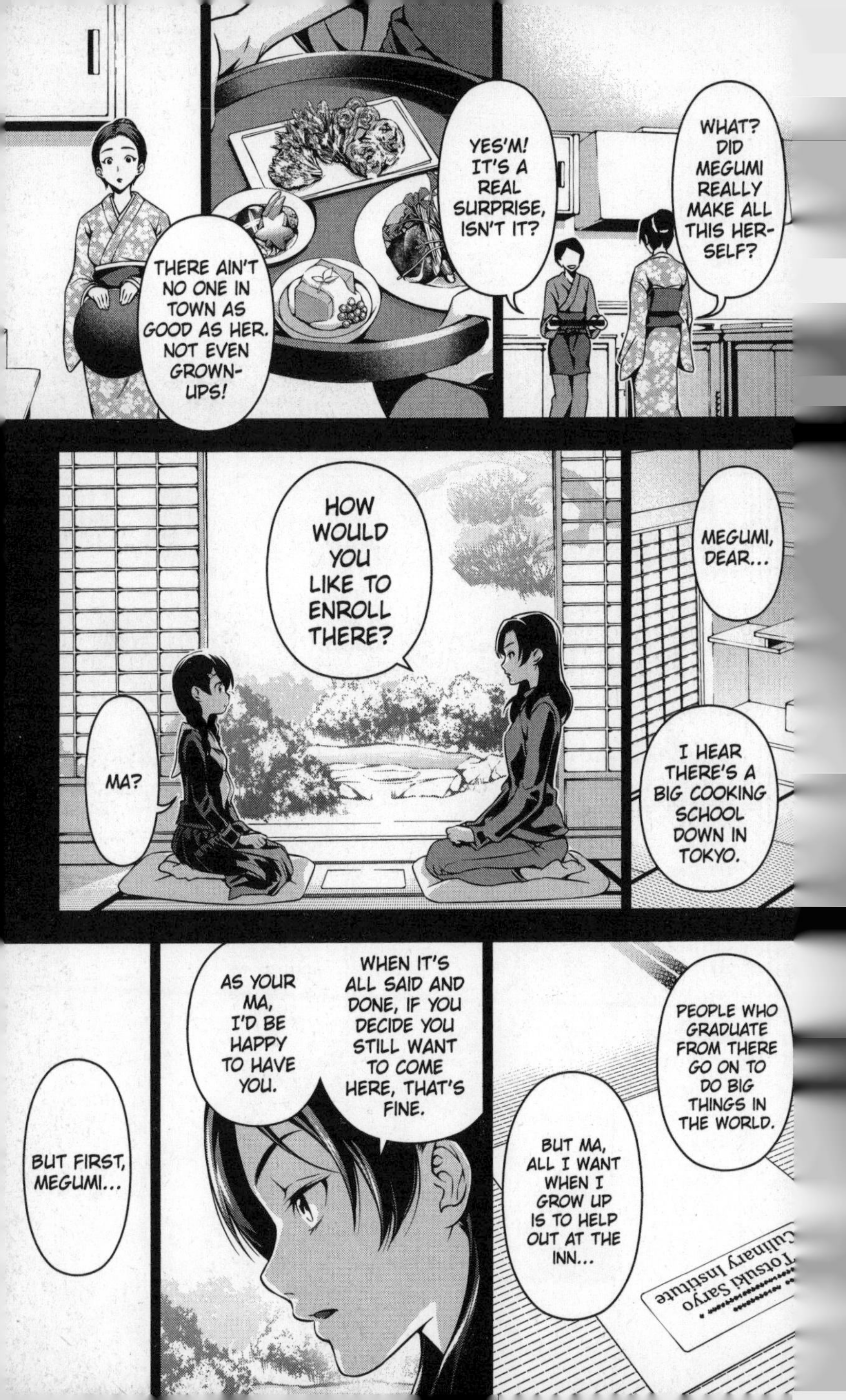
WHAT? DID MEGUMI REALLY MAKE ALL THIS HER-SELF?
YES'M! IT'S A REAL SURPRISE, ISN'T IT?
THERE AIN'T NO ONE IN TOWN AS GOOD AS HER. NOT EVEN GROWN-UPS!
MEGUMI, DEAR...
I HEAR THERE'S A BIG COOKING SCHOOL DOWN IN TOKYO.
HOW WOULD YOU LIKE TO ENROLL THERE?
MA?
PEOPLE WHO GRADUATE FROM THERE GO ON TO DO BIG THINGS IN THE WORLD.
BUT MA, ALL I WANT WHEN I GROW UP IS TO HELP OUT AT THE INN...
Totsuki Saryo Culinary Institute
WHEN IT'S ALL SAID AND DONE, IF YOU DECIDE YOU STILL WANT TO COME HERE, THAT'S FINE.
AS YOUR MA, I'D BE HAPPY TO HAVE YOU.
BUT FIRST, MEGUMI...

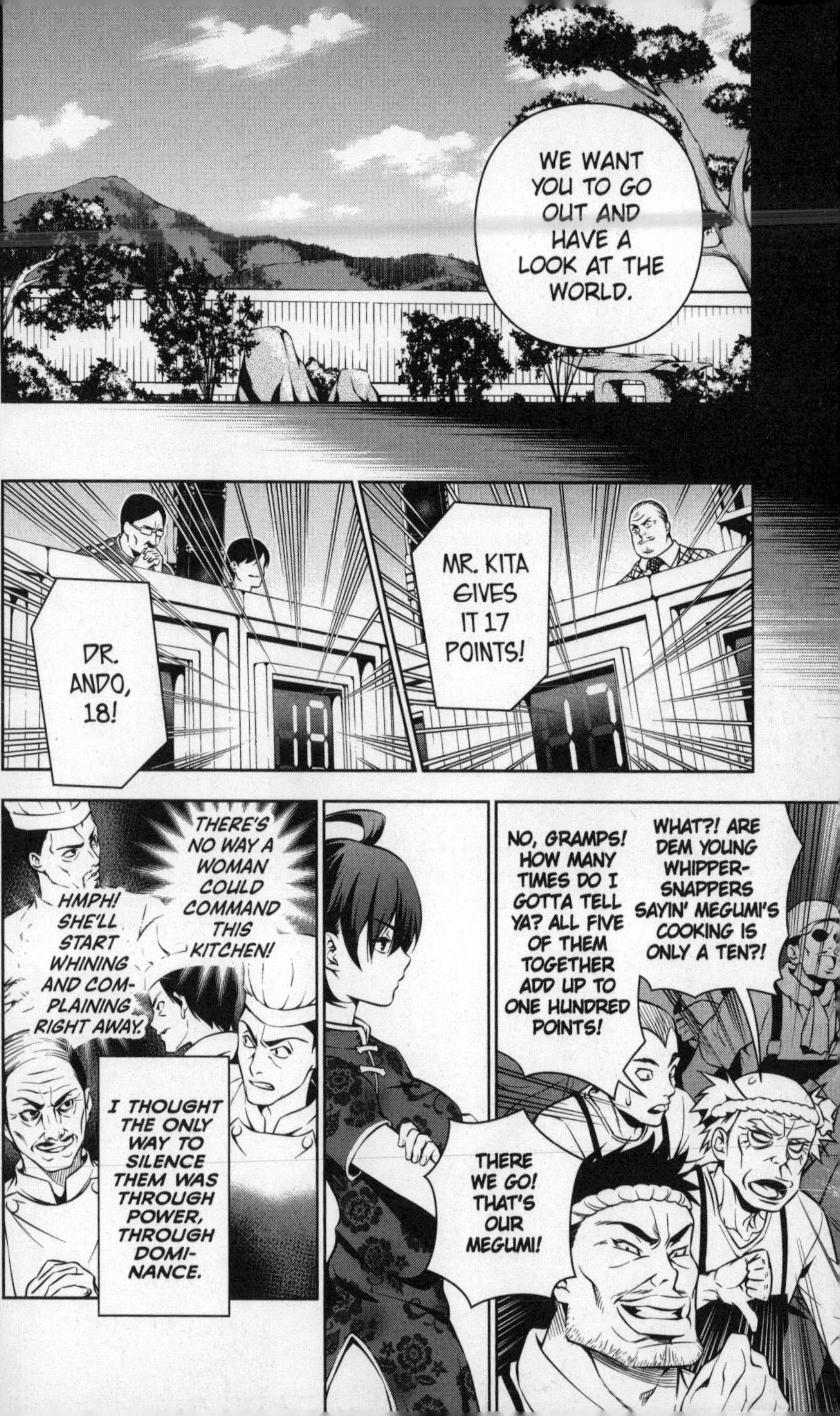
WE WANT YOU TO GO OUT AND HAVE A LOOK AT THE WORLD.
MR. KITA GIVES IT 17 POINTS!
DR. ANDO, 18!
WHAT?! ARE DEM YOUNG WHIPPER-SNAPPERS SAYIN' MEGUMI'S COOKING IS ONLY A TEN?!
NO, GRAMPS! HOW MANY TIMES DO I GOTTA TELL YA? ALL FIVE OF THEM TOGETHER ADD UP TO ONE HUNDRED POINTS!
THERE WE GO! THAT'S OUR MEGUMI!
THERE'S NO WAY A WOMAN COULD COMMAND THIS KITCHEN!
HMPH! SHE'LL START WHINING AND COMPLAINING RIGHT AWAY.
I THOUGHT THE ONLY WAY TO SILENCE THEM WAS THROUGH POWER, THROUGH DOMINANCE.

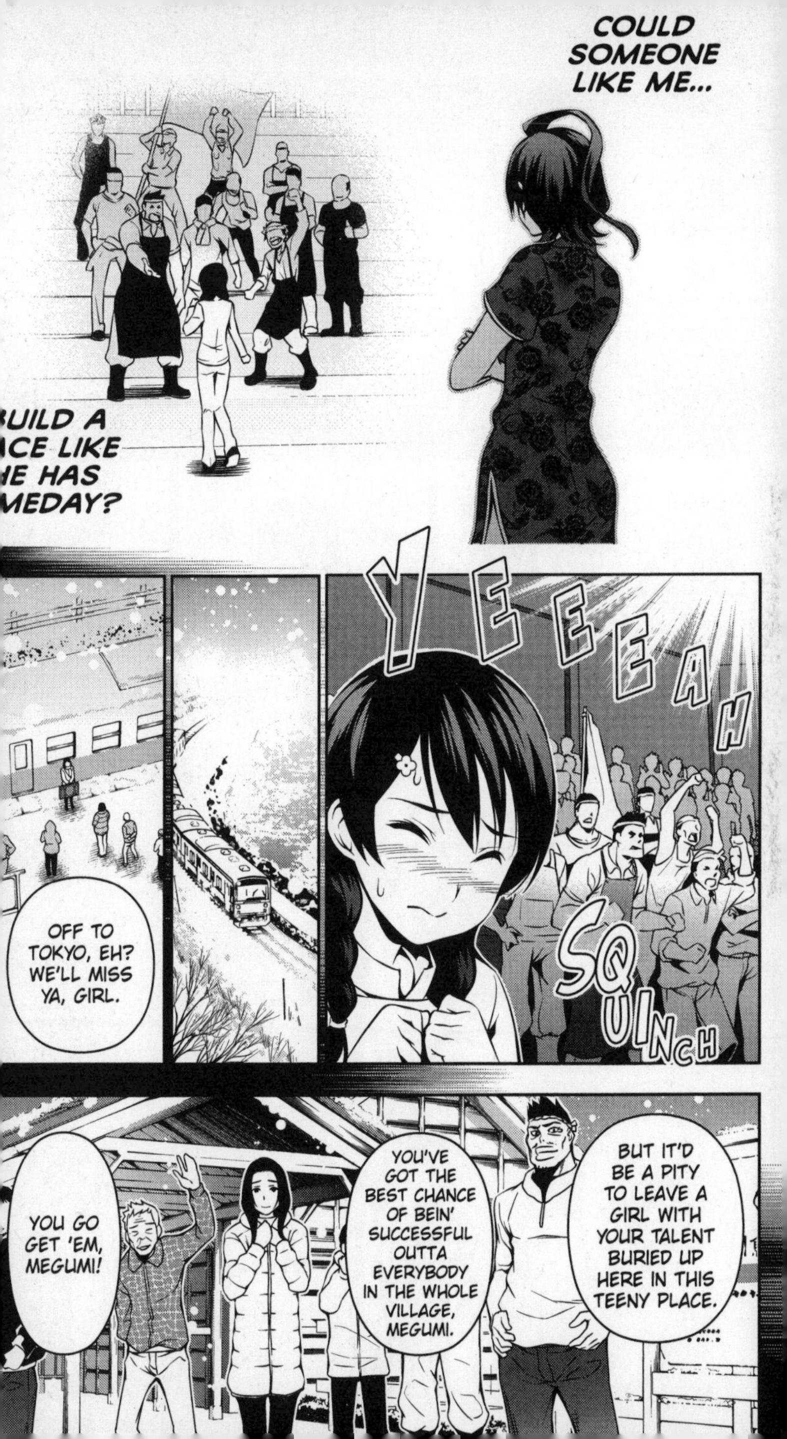
COULD SOMEONE LIKE ME...
UILD A CE LIKE HE HAS MEDAY?
YEEEEAH
SQUINCH
OFF TO TOKYO, EH? WE'LL MISS YA, GIRL.
BUT IT'D BE A PITY TO LEAVE A GIRL WITH YOUR TALENT BURIED UP HERE IN THIS TEENY PLACE.
YOU'VE GOT THE BEST CHANCE OF BEIN' SUCCESSFUL OUTTA EVERYBODY IN THE WHOLE VILLAGE, MEGUMI.
YOU GO GET 'EM, MEGUMI!

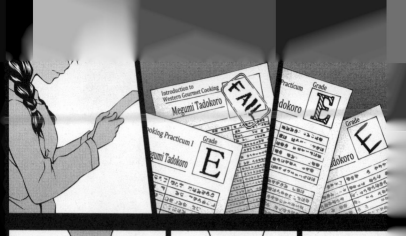

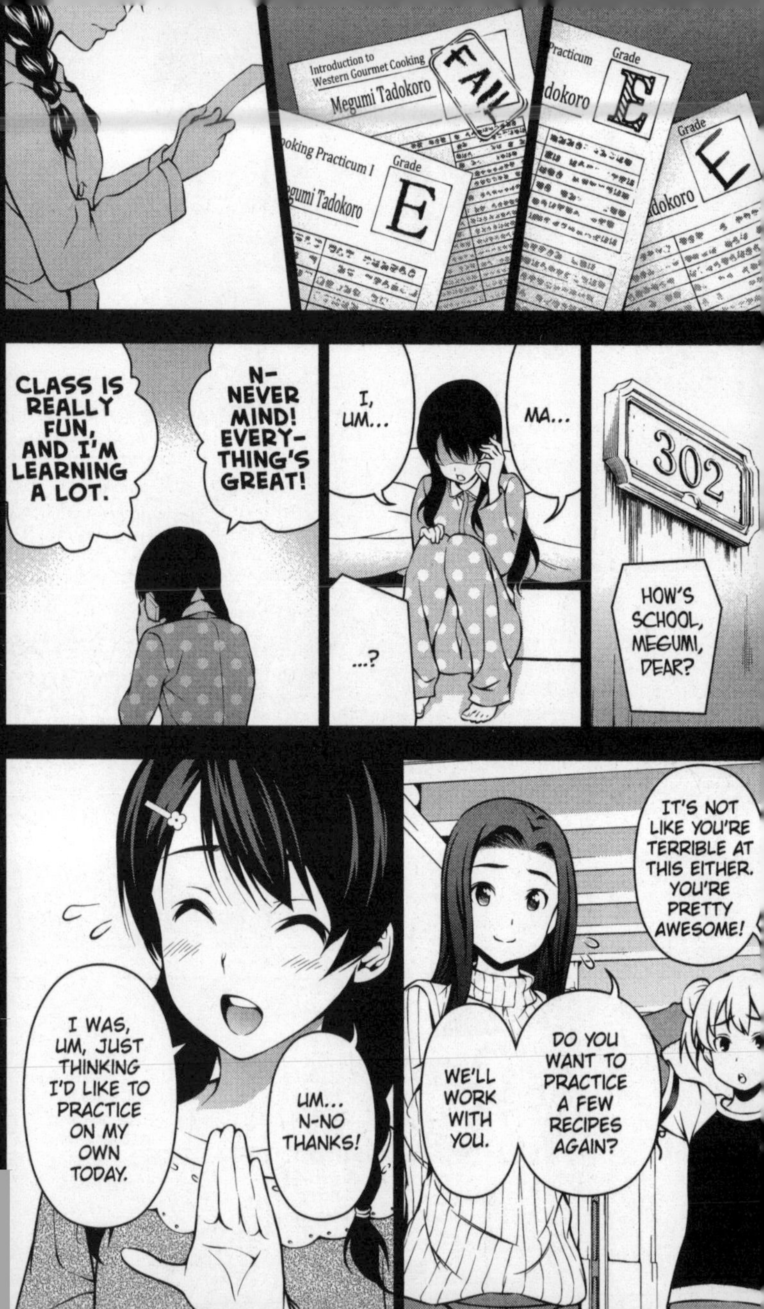
Grade
E
Tadokoro
Practicum Grade
Tadokoro
E
Introduction to Western Gourmet Cooking
Megumi Tadokoro
FAIL
Cooking Practicum I Grade
Megumi Tadokoro
E
302
HOW'S SCHOOL, MEGUMI, DEAR?
MA...
I, UM...
...?
N-NEVER MIND! EVERYTHING'S GREAT!
CLASS IS REALLY FUN, AND I'M LEARNING A LOT.
IT'S NOT LIKE YOU'RE TERRIBLE AT THIS EITHER. YOU'RE PRETTY AWESOME!
DO YOU WANT TO PRACTICE A FEW RECIPES AGAIN?
WE'LL WORK WITH YOU.
UM... N-NO THANKS!
I WAS, UM, JUST THINKING I'D LIKE TO PRACTICE ON MY OWN TODAY.

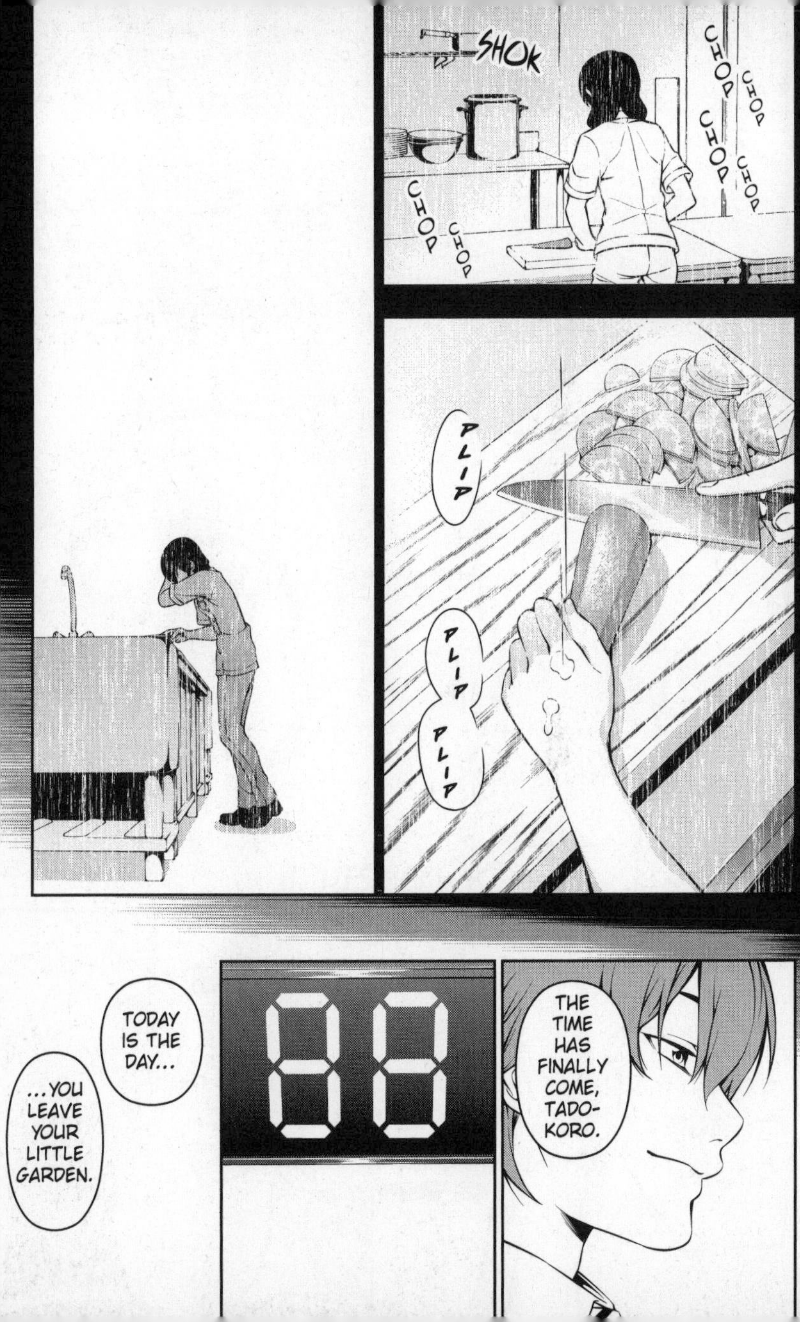
CHOP CHOP
CHOP CHOP
CHOP
SHOK
CHOP CHOP
PLIP
PLIP
PLIP
THE TIME HAS FINALLY COME, TADOKORO.
TODAY IS THE DAY...
...YOU LEAVE YOUR LITTLE GARDEN.

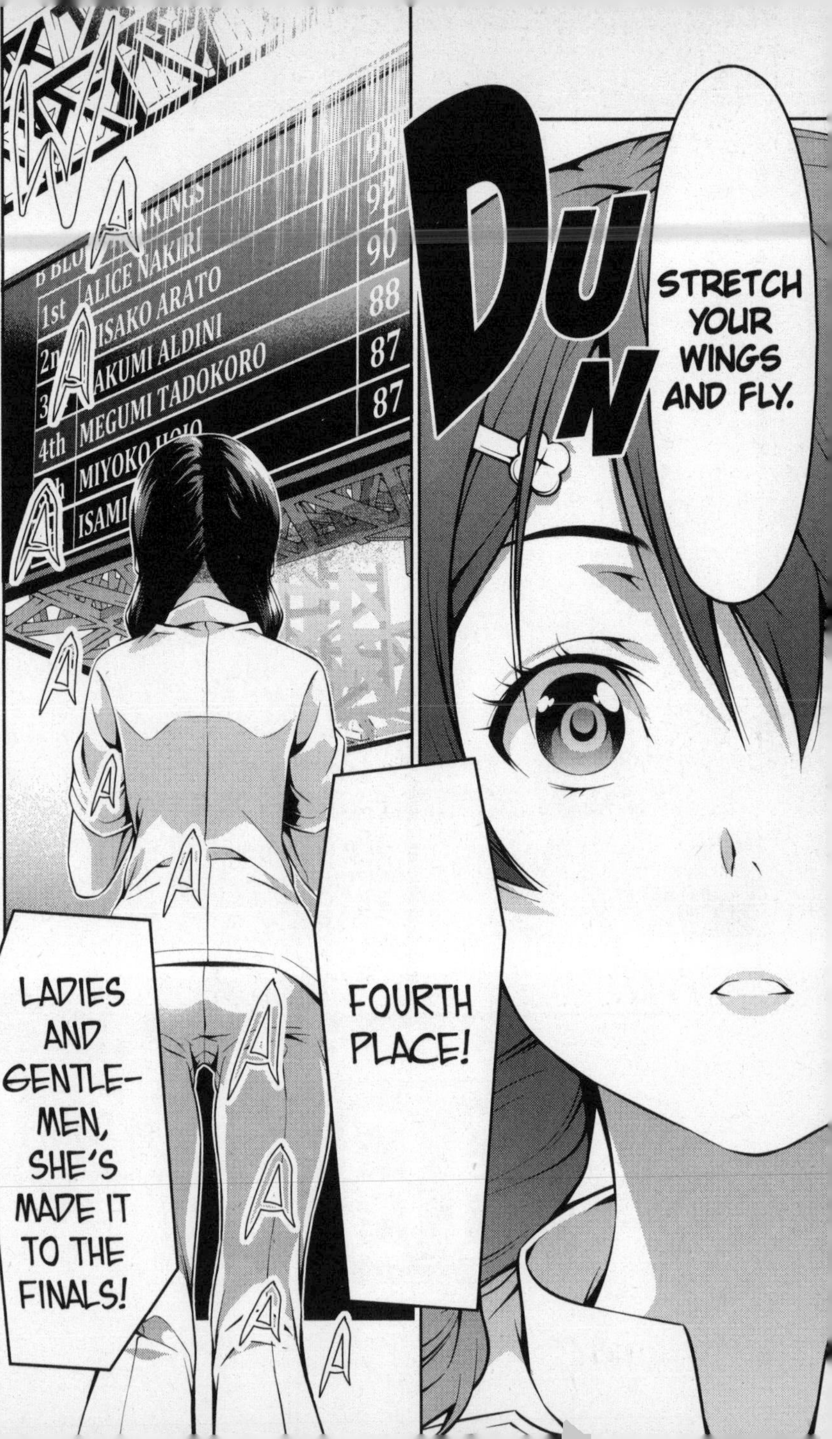
DUN
STRETCH YOUR WINGS AND FLY.
ALICE NAKIRI 90
MEGUMI TADOKORO 87
FOURTH PLACE!
LADIES AND GENTLE-MEN, SHE'S MADE IT TO THE FINALS!

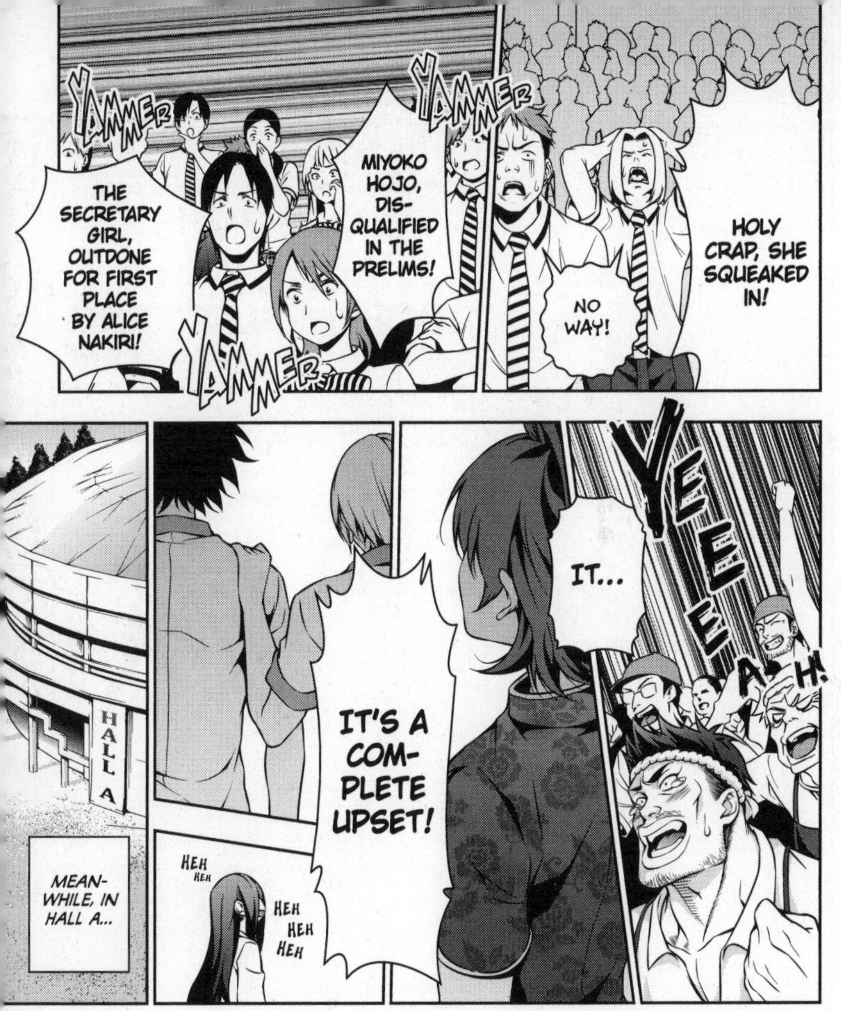
HOLY CRAP, SHE SQUEAKED IN!
NO WAY!
YAMMER
MIYOKO HOJO, DIS-QUALIFIED IN THE PRELIMS!
YAMMER
THE SECRETARY GIRL, OUTDONE FOR FIRST PLACE BY ALICE NAKIRI!
YAMMER
YAMMER
YEEEAH!
IT...
IT'S A COM-PLETE UPSET!
HEH HEH
HEH HEH HEH
HALL A
MEAN-WHILE, IN HALL A...

...BOTH AKIRA HAYAMA...

...AND SOMA YUKIHIRA...

...AWAIT THEIR TURN TO BE JUDGED.

WOLF PACK / END

RECIPE BY: YUKI MORISAKI

PRACTICAL RECIPE #3

VOLUME 7 SPECIAL SUPPLEMENT!

# MEGUMI'S MONKFISH-DOBUJIRU CURRY

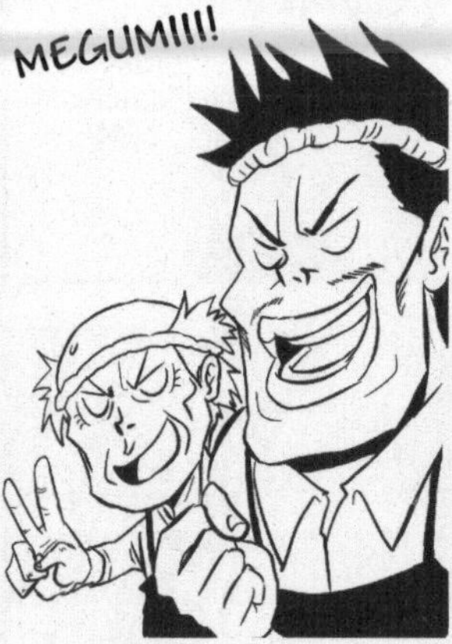
MEGUMIII!

ARTIST: YUTO TSUKUDA

## INGREDIENTS

SERVES 2

- 1 MONKFISH FILLET (APPROX. 500 GRAMS)
- 80 GRAMS MONKFISH LIVER
- 1/4 HEAD BOK CHOY
- 1/6 JAPANESE PUMPKIN
- 1 BURDOCK ROOT
- 1/6 DAIKON RADISH
- 1 PACK ENOKI MUSHROOMS
- 1 WHITE SCALLION
- 1/2 BLOCK GRILLED TOFU
- 1 LITER BONITO AND KELP SOUP STOCK
- 1 TABLESPOON CANOLA OIL
- 2 TABLESPOONS CURRY POWDER
- 4 TABLESPOONS EACH SOY SAUCE, AWASE MISO
- 100 CC SAKE
- 2 TABLESPOONS MIRIN
- 1 TEASPOON GRATED GINGER

★ FINISHING TOUCHES

- 2 SMALL BOWLS OF COOKED RICE
- 1 EGG, BEATEN
- CHOPPED SPRING ONION

1. BLANCH THE MONKFISH FILLET. DIP IT IN BOILING WATER FOR TWENTY SECONDS OR UNTIL THE SURFACE IS COMPLETELY WHITE. THEN QUICKLY DIP IT IN COLD WATER AND SET IT TO THE SIDE.

2. CUT THE BOK CHOY AND TOFU INTO BITE-SIZED PIECES. THINLY SLICE THE PUMPKIN AND BURDOCK ROOT. QUARTER THE DAIKON RADISH AND THEN SLICE THE QUARTERS. DIAGONALLY SLICE THE SCALLION. CUT THE BASE OFF THE ENOKI MUSHROOMS AND THEN SLICE IN HALF. FLATTEN THE MONKFISH LIVER WITH THE FLAT OF A KNIFE.

3. HEAT THE CANOLA OIL IN A POT. ADD THE MONKFISH LIVER AND CURRY POWDER AND SIMMER. ONCE THE FRAGRANCE OF THE CURRY POWDER HAS STRENGTHENED, ADD THE AWASE MISO, SAKE, MIRIN, SOUP STOCK, GRATED GINGER, AND SOY SAUCE TO MAKE THE BROTH. SEASON TO TASTE.

4. ADD THE MONKFISH FILLET, VEGETABLES AND TOFU. COVER AND BOIL FOR TEN MINUTES. DONE!

5. **FINISHING TOUCHES**

   ONCE MOST OF THE DOBUJIRU HAS BEEN EATEN, ADD THE COOKED RICE, BEATEN EGG AND CHOPPED SPRING ONION TO ANY LEFTOVER BROTH AND BITS OF FOOD IN THE POT. STIR TOGETHER TO MAKE ZOUSUI RICE GRUEL.

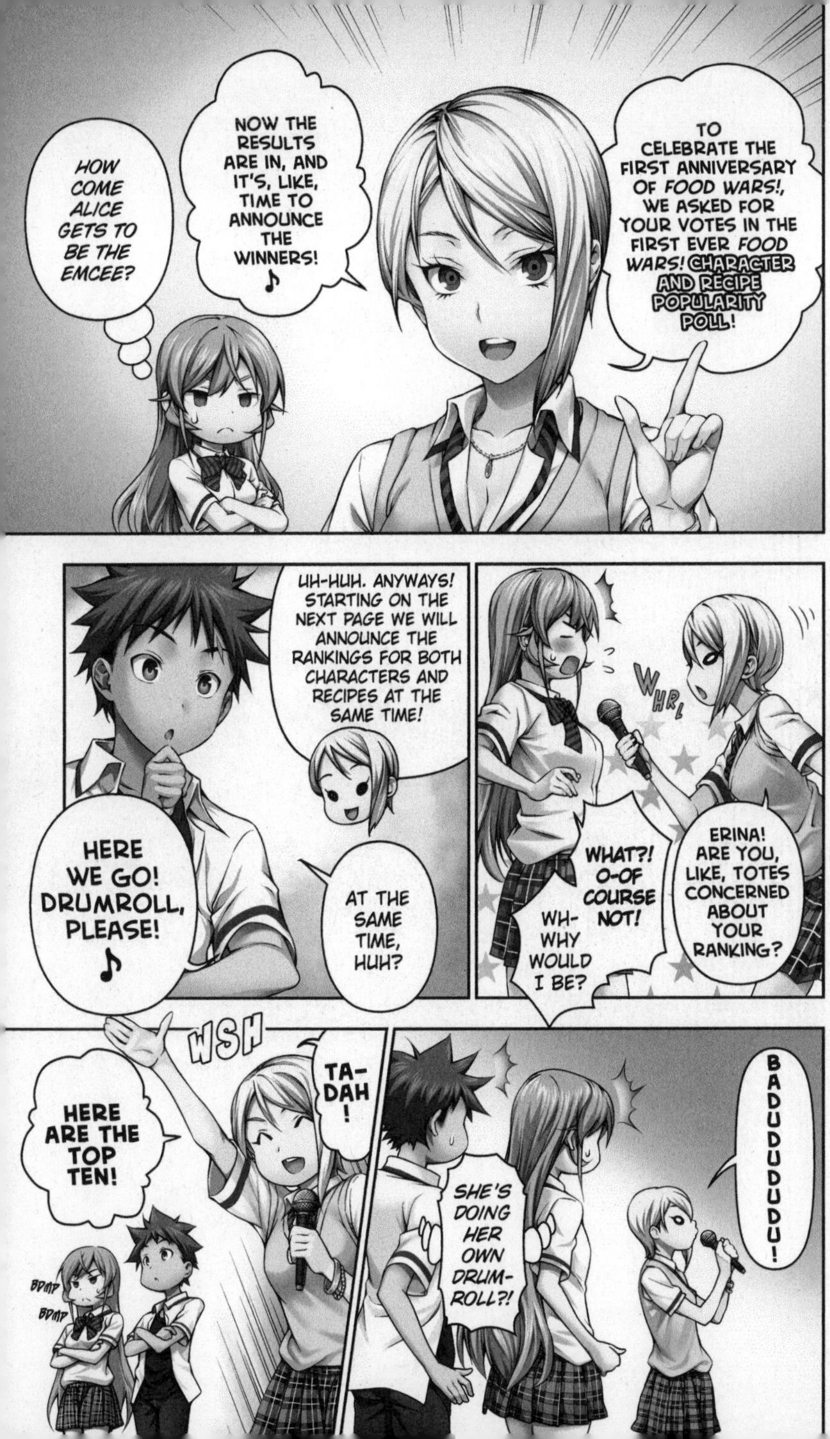
TO CELEBRATE THE FIRST ANNIVERSARY OF FOOD WARS!, WE ASKED FOR YOUR VOTES IN THE FIRST EVER FOOD WARS! CHARACTER AND RECIPE POPULARITY POLL!
NOW THE RESULTS ARE IN, AND IT'S, LIKE, TIME TO ANNOUNCE THE WINNERS! ♪
HOW COME ALICE GETS TO BE THE EMCEE?
ERINA! ARE YOU, LIKE, TOTES CONCERNED ABOUT YOUR RANKING?
WHRL
WHAT?! O-OF COURSE NOT!
WH-WHY WOULD I BE?
UH-HUH. ANYWAYS! STARTING ON THE NEXT PAGE WE WILL ANNOUNCE THE RANKINGS FOR BOTH CHARACTERS AND RECIPES AT THE SAME TIME!
AT THE SAME TIME, HUH?
HERE WE GO! DRUMROLL, PLEASE! ♪
BADUDUDUDUDU!
SHE'S DOING HER OWN DRUM-ROLL?!
TA-DAH!
WSH
HERE ARE THE TOP TEN!
BDMP
BDMP

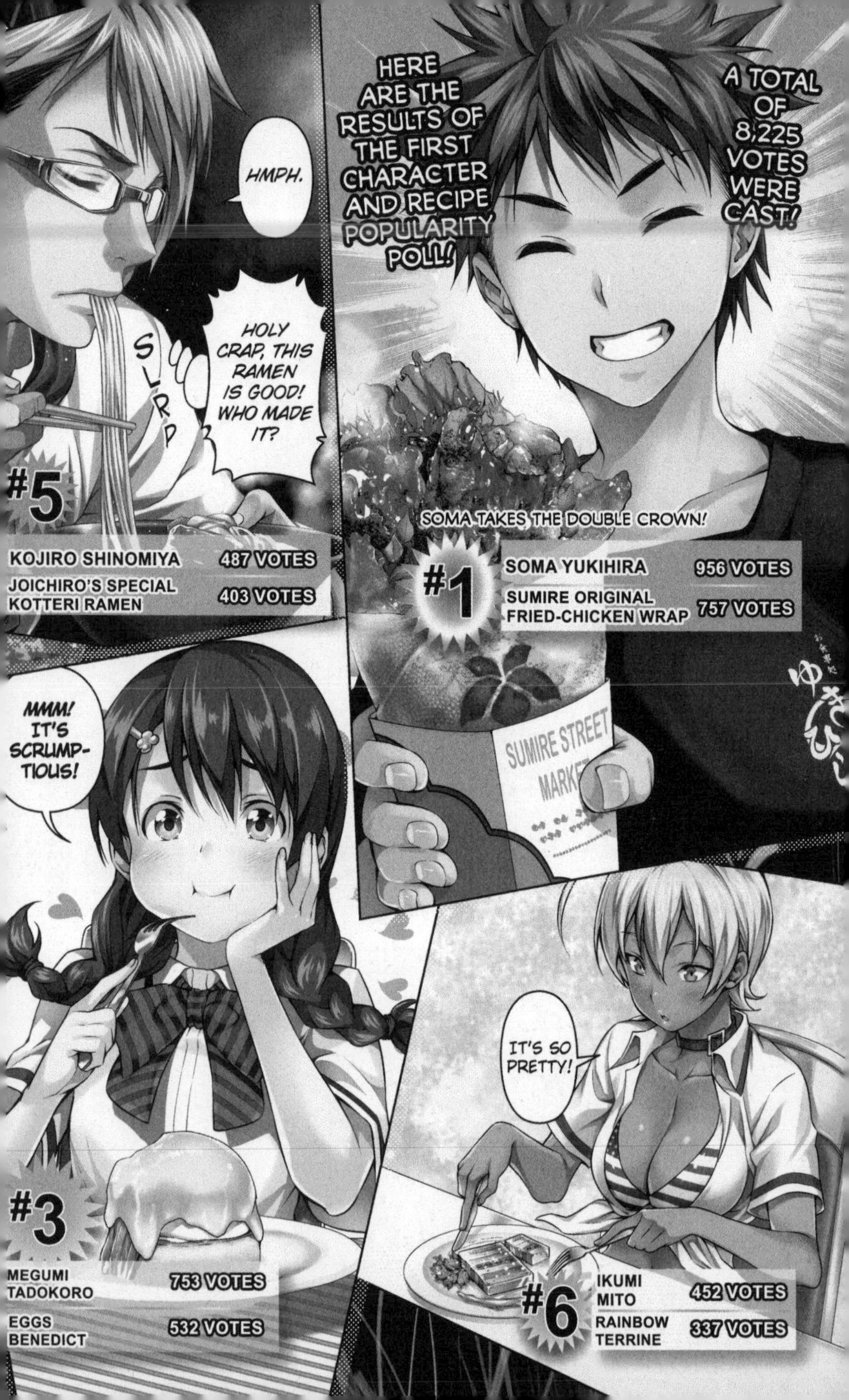
A TOTAL OF 8,225 VOTES WERE CAST!
HERE ARE THE RESULTS OF THE FIRST CHARACTER AND RECIPE POPULARITY POLL!
SOMA TAKES THE DOUBLE CROWN!
#1
SOMA YUKIHIRA 956 VOTES
SUMIRE ORIGINAL FRIED-CHICKEN WRAP 757 VOTES
SUMIRE STREET
HMPH.
HOLY CRAP, THIS RAMEN IS GOOD! WHO MADE IT?
SLRP
#5
KOJIRO SHINOMIYA 487 VOTES
JOICHIRO'S SPECIAL KOTTERI RAMEN 403 VOTES
MMM! IT'S SCRUMP-TIOUS!
#3
MEGUMI TADOKORO 753 VOTES
EGGS BENEDICT 532 VOTES
IT'S SO PRETTY!
#6
IKUMI MITO 452 VOTES
RAINBOW TERRINE 337 VOTES

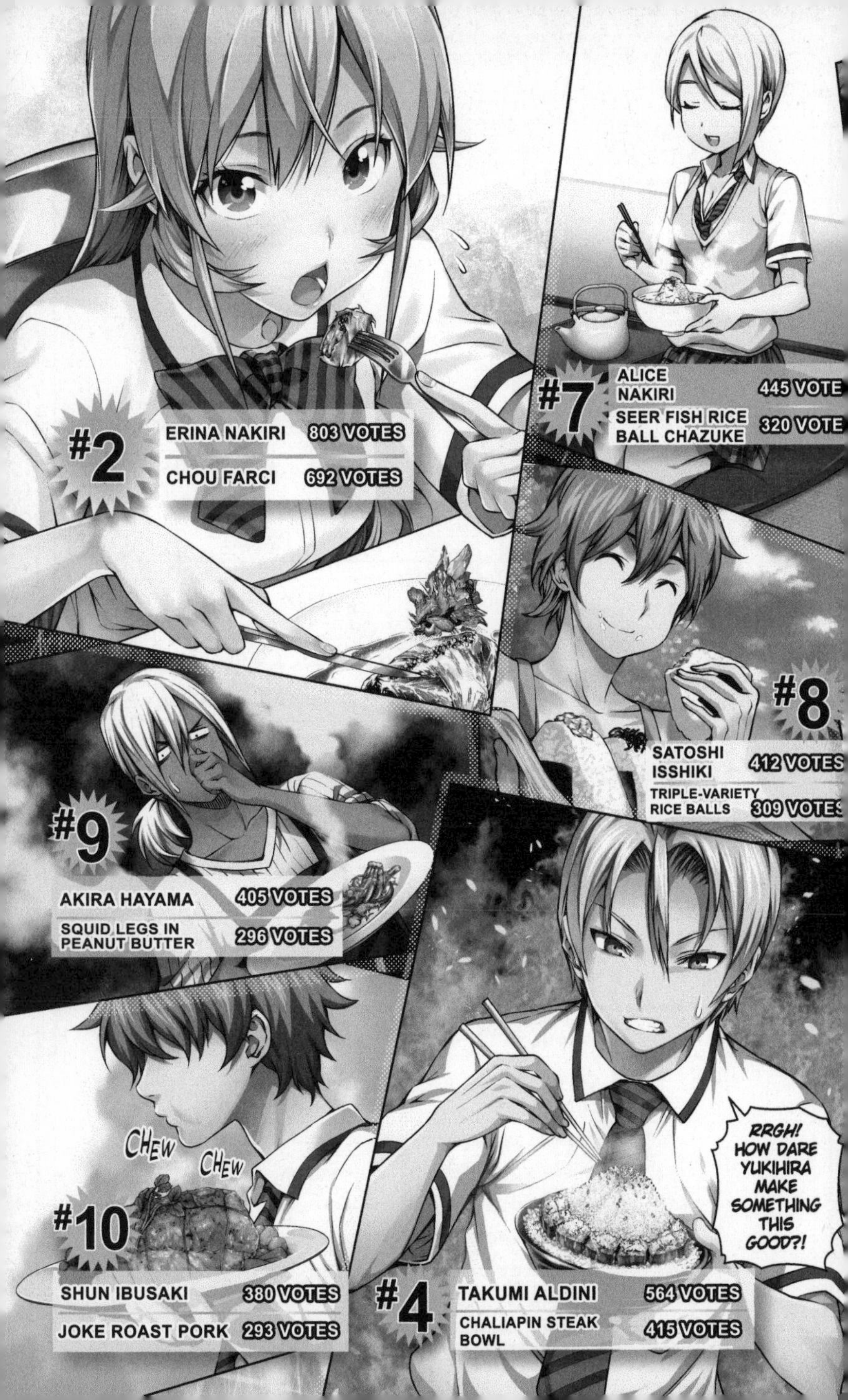
#7
ALICE NAKIRI
445 VOTE
SEER FISH RICE BALL CHAZUKE
320 VOTE
#2
ERINA NAKIRI
803 VOTES
CHOU FARCI
692 VOTES
#8
SATOSHI ISSHIKI
412 VOTES
TRIPLE-VARIETY RICE BALLS
309 VOTES
#9
AKIRA HAYAMA
405 VOTES
SQUID LEGS IN PEANUT BUTTER
296 VOTES
RRGH! HOW DARE YUKIHIRA MAKE SOMETHING THIS GOOD?!
#4
TAKUMI ALDINI
564 VOTES
CHALIAPIN STEAK BOWL
415 VOTES
CHEW
CHEW
#10
SHUN IBUSAKI
380 VOTES
JOKE ROAST PORK
293 VOTES

**#11** HINAKO INUI
SPICY ROAST DUCK ~WITH GREEN SALSA~

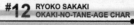

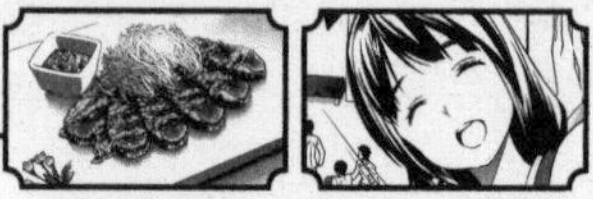

**#12** RYOKO SAKAKI
OKAKI-NO-TANE-AGE CHAR

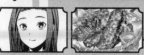

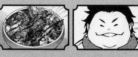

**#13** ISAMI ALDINI
INSALATA FRITTATA

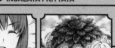

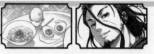

**#14** HISAKO ARATO
A5 WAGYU RÔTI BOWL

**#15** JOICHIRO YUKIHIRA
THREE-FACES-OF-AN-EGG BREAKFAST

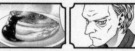

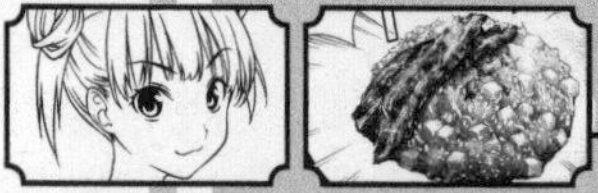

**#16** YUKI YOSHINO
APPLE RISOTTO

**#17** ROLAND CHAPELLE
SOUFFLÉ OMELET

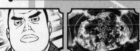

**#18** KIYOSHI GODABAYASHI
EGGS OVER RICE (FROM THE ONE SHOT)

**#19** MAYUMI KURASE
RAVIOLI LANGOUSTINE

**#20** URARA KAWASHIMA
BITE-SIZED BREAKFAST STEW

| | <CHARACTER> | <DISH> |
|---|---|---|
| #21 | FUYUMI MIZUHARA | YUKIHIRA ORIGINAL MISHMASH MACKBURGER SPECIAL |
| #22 | GIN DOJIMA | FRIED CHICKEN |
| #23 | ZENJI MARUI | KOZHI VARUTHA CHICKEN CURRY |
| #24 | JUN SHIOMI | PEPPER-GRILLED SEER FISH WITH SPRING CABBAGE PUREE |
| #25 | MIYOKO HOJO | BOEUF BOURGUIGNON |
| #26 | JOICHIRO SAIBA (TEEN) | MOZUYA SPECIALTY FRIED CHICKEN |
| #27 | KANICHI KONISHI | NINE-VEGETABLE TERRINE |
| #28 | FUMIO DAIMIDO (TEEN) | FISH-HEAD CURRY |
| #29 | SENZAEMON NAKIRI | PETITE LOCO MOCO BOWL |
| #30 | YAEKO MINEGASAKI | GOAN FISH CURRY |

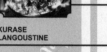

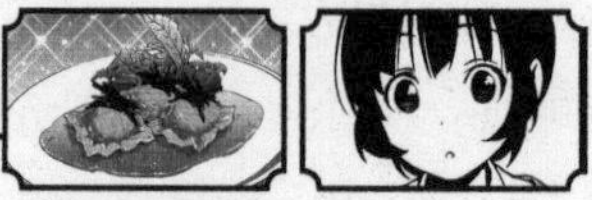

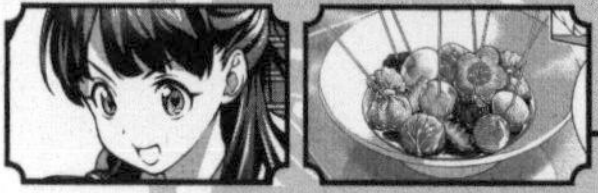

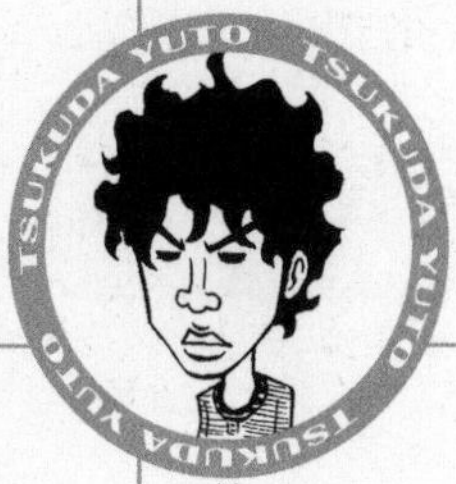
TSUKUDA YUTO
TSUKUDA YUTO
TSUKUDA YUTO
TSUKUDA YUTO

## THOUGHTS ON THE FIRST CHARACTER AND RECIPE POPULARITY POLL

>>> Honestly, going into the poll I figured Soma would get the lion's share of the votes. I didn't expect them to be as well spread out as they were. The top ten, though... Yeah, I pretty much saw those coming. And there is something funny about Hinako coming in at eleventh, just barely missing the top ten.

Personally, the biggest surprise for me was Hayama in ninth. He had only just been introduced when the vote was conducted, but he still made it into the top ten. (Though the results announcement made that the worst spot to be in... Sorry, Hayama.)

Thank you very much to everyone who voted!

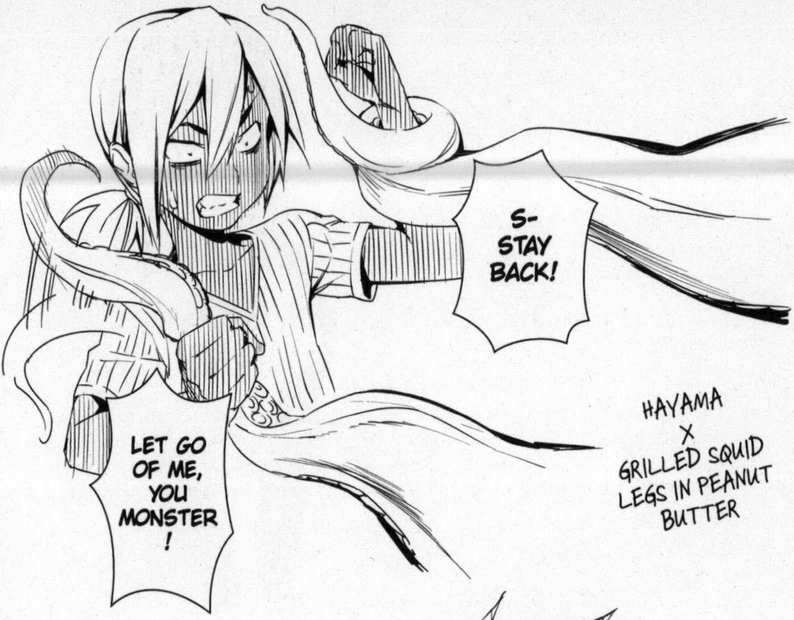
S-STAY BACK!
LET GO OF ME, YOU MONSTER!
HAYAMA
X
GRILLED SQUID LEGS IN PEANUT BUTTER

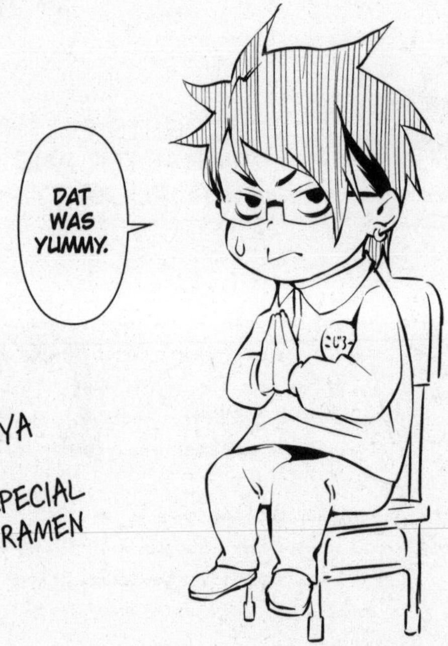
DAT WAS YUMMY.
SHINOMIYA
X
JOICHIRO SPECIAL KOTTERI RAMEN

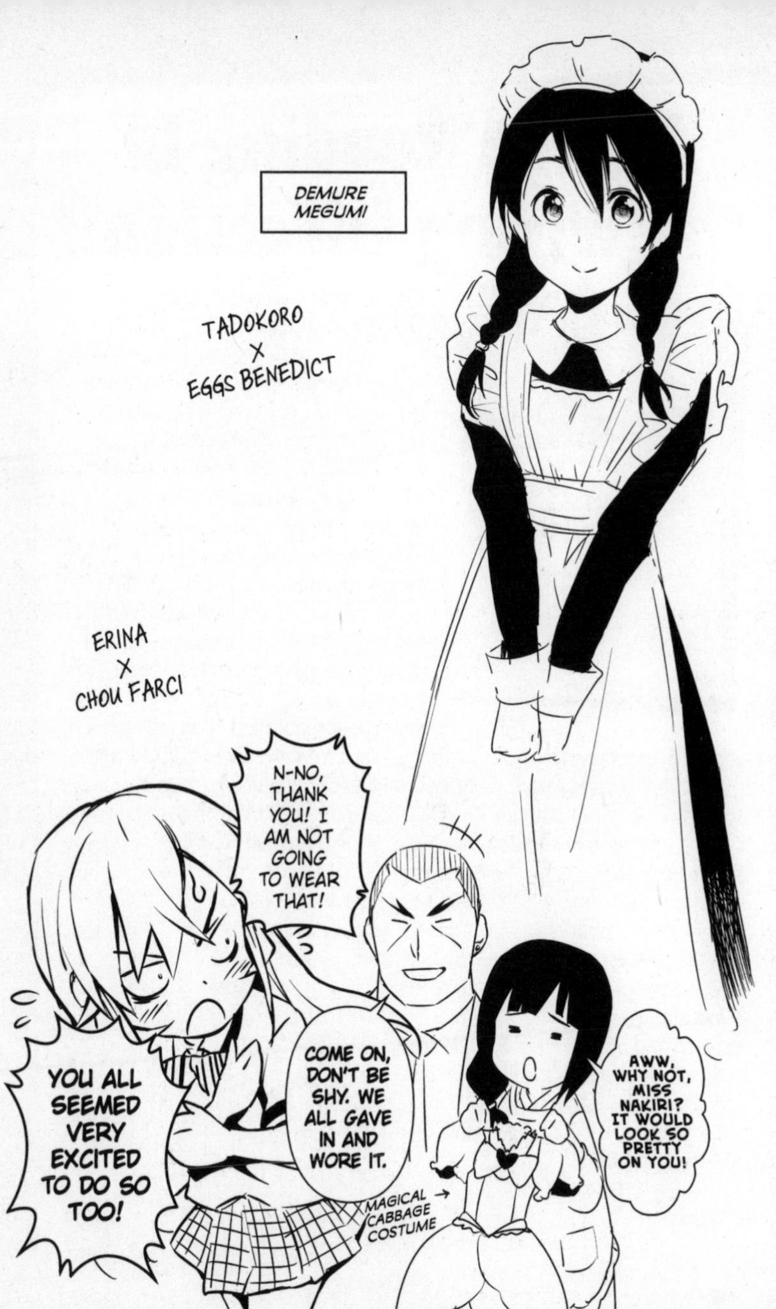
DEMURE MEGUMI
TADOKORO X EGGS BENEDICT
ERINA X CHOU FARCI
N-NO, THANK YOU! I AM NOT GOING TO WEAR THAT!
AWW, WHY NOT, MISS NAKIRI? IT WOULD LOOK SO PRETTY ON YOU!
COME ON, DON'T BE SHY. WE ALL GAVE IN AND WORE IT.
YOU ALL SEEMED VERY EXCITED TO DO SO TOO!
MAGICAL CABBAGE COSTUME →

# You're Reading in the Wrong Direction!!

1
3
2
2
1
3
5
6
4


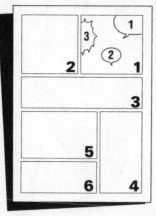

**W**hoops! Guess what? You're starting at the wrong end of the comic!

...It's true! In keeping with the original Japanese format, **Food Wars!** is meant to be read from right to left, starting in the upper-right corner.

Unlike English, which is read from left to right, Japanese is read from right to left, meaning that action, sound effects and word-balloon order are completely reversed... something which can make readers unfamiliar with Japanese feel pretty backwards themselves. For this reason, manga or Japanese comics published in the U.S. in English have sometimes been published "flopped"—that is, printed in exact reverse order, as though seen from the other side of a mirror.

By flopping pages, U.S. publishers can avoid confusing readers, but the compromise is not without its downside. For one thing, a character in a flopped manga series who once wore in the original Japanese version a T-shirt emblazoned with "M A Y" (as in "the merry month of") now wears one which reads "Y A M"! Additionally, many manga creators in Japan are themselves unhappy with the process, as some feel the mirror-imaging of their art skews their original intentions.

We are proud to bring you Yuto Tsukuda and Shun Saeki's **Food Wars!** in the original unflopped format.

For now, though, turn to the other side of the book and let the adventure begin...!

—Editor

MM, SUCH DELICIOUS TEA, AS ALWAYS.
WHAT A GOOD GIRL YOU ARE.
I-I DON'T DESERVE SUCH PRAISE, MISTRESS. YOU HONOR ME!